The Food Lover's Guide to Paris

Publication Date: Updated in 1988

Price $ 18.95

In giving this book mention in your
column, would you kindly refer to
it as being
published in Canada by

THOMAS ALLEN & SON LIMITED
A Copy of your review
would be appreciated.

SECOND EDITION

The Food Lover's Guide to Paris

PATRICIA WELLS

Assisted by SUSAN HERRMANN LOOMIS
Photographs by PETER TURNLEY
Front Cover Photographs by ROBERT FRESON

Workman Publishing, New York

To Walter, with gratitude
for his unwavering love,
trust, and support

Copyright © 1984, 1988 by Patricia Wells
Photographs copyright © 1984, 1988 by Peter Turnley
Front cover photographs © 1988 by Robert Freson

Library of Congress Cataloging-in-Publication Data
Wells, Patricia.   The food lover's guide to Paris.
Includes index.   1. Restaurants, lunch rooms, etc.—France—Paris—Guide-books.
2. Grocery trade—France—Paris—Guide-books.
3. Cookery, French.
4. Hotels, taverns, etc.—France—Paris—Guide-books.
5. Paris (France)—Description—1975–   —Guide-books.
I. Loomis, Susan Herrmann. II. Title.
TX910.F8W383 1988   647'.9544   87-40645   ISBN 0-89480-575-4

Book design: Susan Aronson Stirling
Front cover photographs: Robert Freson
Book photographs: Peter Turnley

Workman Publishing Company, Inc.
708 Broadway
New York, NY 10003

Manufactured in the United States of America
Second edition first printing, May 1988
10   9   8   7   6   5   4   3   2   1

Acknowledgments

Thanks to the generosity, enthusiasm, and encouragement of so many fine people, much of the work on this book was transformed into sheer pleasure. I am deeply grateful to Susan Herrmann Loomis, whose friendship and fidelity, energy and inspiration sustained me throughout; to Jane Sigal, who in the midst of chaos always managed to hold the office together; to Nihal Goonesekera, who kept my world scrubbed and polished as I drowned in a sea of clips and files.

I was touched by the generosity of the French chefs, bakers, restaurateurs, and shopkeepers who gave so freely of their time and expertise, and shared their recipes. Special thanks to Jean-Claude Vrinat of Taillevent, Joël Robuchon of Jamin, and bakers Bernard Ganachaud, Lionel and Max Poilâne, and Jean-Luc Poujauran.

None of this would have been possible without the remarkable confidence of Peter Workman and the expert attention of my editor, Suzanne Rafer, who believed in both me and the book when others remained doubtful. Thanks also go to Kathie Ness, Kim Honig, and Amy Gateff for their careful checking of information, and to Paul Hanson, Susan Aronson Stirling, and Barbara Scott-Goodman for the beautiful design of the book.

Throughout my career, dozens of friends and colleagues have advised, assisted, steered me in the proper direction, and I am delighted to acknowledge them here. Special thanks to all those at the *New York Times,* particularly Craig Claiborne, Arthur Gelb, Annette Grant, and Mike Leahy, who allowed me to combine my love for journalism with my passion for food; to Sam Abt and Vicky Elliott at the *International Herald Tribune,* for their careful and diligent editing of my restaurant reviews; to Berna Huebner and Vivian Cruise, for their companionship and healthy appetites.

I want to offer special thanks to our dearest friends, Rita and Yale Kramer and Lydie and Wayne Marshall, with whom we have shared so many fine feasts on both sides of the ocean, for their encouragement and special friendship. Finally, I thank my parents, Vera and Joseph Kleiber, who instilled in me without fuss or fanfare a natural love and respect for the world's gastronomic bounties.

Introduction to the New Edition

There are so many reasons to love Paris, one rarely stops to count. Certainly, one of the city's greatest assets is its history— a romantic, nostalgic, pull-at-the-heartstrings past that jumps out at you from nearly every corner bistro, every brightly lit café, every Belle Epoque *boulangerie.*

Over the past four years (the time between publication of the first and second editions of this book), the city has changed enormously, and not always in a way that flatters the past we love so well.

Bigger supermarkets filled with frozen food cases and pre-packaged vegetables, diet cuisine, and pop-in-the-microwave pack-aged goods are now the norm. Barely a week goes by that a corner café is not transformed into a fast-food eatery. *Baguettes* seem to get flabbier by the day, and sometimes I honestly worry that bland, flavorless cheeses are going to overtake the well-aged, aromatic versions of the past.

Despite these concerns I don't know that I've ever loved Paris more, or felt more positive or hopeful for its future. Precisely, it is Paris's rich history that allows it to confidently balance past and present, granting its residents and visitors the very same privilege.

In any culture, the search for quality must be just that, a search. So we must accept the reality that impersonalized restau-rant chains, microwave carry-outs, and prewashed, plastic-wrapped lettuce will live side-by-side with 1930s bistros serving up the finest French home cooking; with *boulangeries* selling unforgettably won-derful hand-formed *baguettes* made with stone-ground flour; with wine shops offering more than 350 independently produced wines, each selected with passion and care; and with chefs who take the time to bake their own bread, prepare their own chocolates, and even grow fresh herbs in pocket gardens perched on the city's rooftops.

Day in and day out, as I chat with bakers and chefs, candy-makers and cheese agers, I am constantly uplifted by their single-minded dedication to their craft. They are businessmen, yes, but the only greed I see in their eyes is a greed for perfection.

On the practical side, as I revisited and reevaluated each address in the first edition, I found many surprises. Except in cases where a restaurant or shop had changed owners or focus, almost all establishments were as good as, if not better than, I remembered them.

Details I had overlooked, or simply failed to note, added a new dimension of pleasure. Likewise, the fact that so many establishments had changed not at all only nourished my determination to do everything I could to make them better known to the public.

I felt I had combed the depth and breadth of gastronomic Paris in researching the first edition, never imagining how many authentic and superbly Parisian addresses I had left unturned. Today I know there are many yet to be discovered, and in this second edition I share dozens of new finds.

I have to admit my own surprise at how long it took me to really fall in love with—and give due respect to—the tiny no-name bistros one finds sprinkled all over Paris. I expect that the early part of the decade will go down as a period of discovery, of refinement of *nouvelle cuisine,* a time when the young super-chefs such as Joël Robuchon, Bernard Pacaud, Guy Savoy, and Alain Dutournier established their place in French cuisine. The end of the decade will no doubt be remembered as a time when diners sought out an equilibrium, looking for a balance between the special-occasion, refined, elegant dining experiences and the inexpensive, everyday bistro affairs.

Because of the changing times, and in acknowledgment of ever-shifting foreign exchange rates, I have made a serious effort to add as many low-priced restaurants as I could find, in hopes that everyone's experience in Paris could be as satisfying to the pocketbook as to the palate.

Likewise, I hope that readers, new and old, will discover within a wealth of new gastronomic pleasures, ranging from crusty country breads to sparkling new cheese shops, new adventures in wine as well as unforgettable dining experiences.

Paris, 1988

A Taste for Paris

From the moment I set foot in France one chilly, gray January morning in 1973, I knew that Paris was a city I would love the rest of my life. More than ten years later, after spending four of those years in this gentle city, each day I am moved by Paris's elegance and beauty, its coquettish appeal. The qualify of life here is better than in any other place I know, and eating well has much to do with it.

This is the book I came to Paris to write. Equal only to my passion for food is my love for reporting. I have always thought that one of the most enjoyable aspects of journalism is that you get to know people on their own turf, and you get to poke around, asking the questions that any curious person wants answers to. In researching this book, I—along with Susan Herrmann Loomis as assistant and companion—walked just about every street in Paris in search of the gastronomic best the city has to offer, talking, chatting, interviewing, meeting with the city's men and women who are responsible for all things great and edible. We set out to find the crispest *baguette,* the thickest cup of steaming hot chocolate; to spot the most romantic site for a warm morning *croissant* or a sun-kissed summer lunch; to track down the trustiest cheese or chocolate shop; to uncover the happiest place to sip wine on a brisk winter's day. We quickly gave up counting the number of times we got lost or rained out as we checked off addresses and discovered back streets and sleepy neighborhoods. We toured the markets and tea salons, sparred with butchers, laughed with the owners of a favorite bistro, and shared the incomparable aroma of a great loaf of bread as it came crackling from the oven. We rose eagerly at dawn to catch a pastry chef as he pulled the first batch of steaming *croissants* from his wood-fired oven; climbed down rickety ladders into warm and cozy baking cellars to discuss the state of the French *baguette* with a skilled baker; shivered as we toured aromatic, humid, spotless rooms stacked with aging Brie and Camembert, Vacherin and Roquefort. Each day we lunched and dined, sometimes at modest neighborhood bistros, sometimes in fine restaurants. We gathered recipes from pastry chefs, cooks, bakers, and tea shop owners, and tested, tested, tested until my apartment took on the same irresistible mixture of aromas as the food streets and shops of Paris. Throughout, it was an exhilarating labor of love, one from which I hope you will profit, the joy of which I hope you will share.

This is a personal guide, and whenever I had to decide whether to include or delete a shop, a restaurant, a market, I asked myself one question: Would I want to go back there again? If the answer was no, the address was tossed into the ever-growing reject file.

In choosing restaurants, I have tried to be comprehensive but selective. I have tried as best I know how to tell you exactly what I think you will want to know about a restaurant: why you should go, where it is, how to get there, what you'll find when you arrive, and what it will cost. I intentionally did not rate restaurants, for I find personal restaurant ratings clumsy, arbitrary, and generally unreliable. Besides, they make a burdensome science out of what should, essentially, be joyful discovery.

No doubt, some places you will love less than I. Some you will love more. I hope this book will stimulate every reader to explore, look around, and ask questions, and will help everyone to understand just a bit more clearly the history, daily customs, and rich texture of Paris, the great gastronomic capital of the world.

HOW TO USE THIS BOOK

Alphabetizing

Within each chapter (with the exception of the chapter on markets), establishments are grouped by the neighborhoods in which they are located, then listed in alphabetical order. Following French style, any articles such as *au, la,* or *le* and words such as *bistro, brasserie, café,* or *chez* that appear before the proper name of the establishment are ignored in the alphabetizing. For example, Chez Pauline, Le Petit Marguery, and Au Pied de Cochon are all listed under the letter *P.* Likewise, when the name of a restaurant is also the full name of a person, such as Jacqueline Fénix, Michel Rostang, or Guy Savoy, the last name (Fénix, Rostang, Savoy) is used for purposes of alphabetizing.

What's an arrondissement?

While many major cities are divided into variously named quarters for easy identification and organization, Paris is divided into twenty *arrondissements.* The *arrondissements* are arranged numerically in a spiral, beginning in the center of the city on the Right Bank (with the 1st *arrondissement* at the Louvre and Les Halles) and moving clockwise, making two complete spirals until reaching the central eastern edge of the city (at the 20th *arrondissement,* at Père Lachaise cemetery).

In organizing the book, we have listed establishments by *arrondissement,* also noting the popular quarters—the Madeleine, Montmartre, Invalides—in which they are located. Because of the spiral arrangement, *arrondissements* that adjoin one another—such as the 3rd, 4th, and 11th at the Marais and the Bastille—are generally listed together, since they overlap within a specific neighborhood, even though *arrondissement* numbers are not consecutive. For convenience, *arrondissements* may be grouped together differently from one chapter to another.

Listings

Each listing presented in *The Food Lover's Guide to Paris* includes the following information: the name of the establishment; its address; its phone number (in parentheses); the closest Métro stop; when it is open and closed.

If applicable, any or all of the following information is also included: whether the establishment is air-conditioned; whether it has a terrace, outdoor dining, or private dining facilities; what the specialties include; and what you can expect to spend.

Abbreviations

The following abbreviations are used for credit cards in the listings:
AE: American Express
DC: Diners Club
EC: Eurocard or MasterCard
V: Visa or Carte Bleue

The following abbreviations are used in the recipes to indicate weights and measures:
cm: centimeter   ml: milliliter
g: gram   kg: kilogram

Contents

Marchés
MARKETS *166*

Pâtisseries
PASTRY SHOPS *181*

Boulangeries
BAKERIES   *199*

Fromageries
CHEESE SHOPS   *223*

Charcuteries

PREPARED FOODS TO GO   242

Chocolateries

CHOCOLATE SHOPS   255

Pour la Maison

KITCHEN AND TABLEWARE SHOPS   *301*

Recipe Contents

Cafés
CAFES

Salons de Thé
TEA SALONS

Pâtisseries
PASTRY SHOPS

Boulangeries
BAKERIES

Fromageries
CHEESE SHOPS

Chocolateries
CHOCOLATE SHOPS

Spécialités Gastronomiques
SPECIALTY SHOPS

French/English
FOOD GLOSSARY

The Food Lover's Guide to Paris

Restaurants
RESTAURANTS

Studying the menu in elegant restaurant surroundings.

I am constantly being asked to name my favorite Paris restaurant. For me, that is akin to trying to name my best friend, favorite piece of music, film, or classic novel. The answer depends on the hour, the season, my mood, the company.

This is a personal guide representing a cross section of Paris restaurants, including only those I enjoy returning to, those I recommend to others. I hope they will serve simply as a starting point, enabling you to begin exploring and sorting out until you discover the kind of restaurants you like. You should not have a bad meal at any listed here. But this doesn't mean you can't.

I dine out in Paris four or five times each week. I always make a reservation and always arrive hungry, for that's one of the best compliments one can pay a chef. I dine anonymously and so am known at few of these restaurants. What do I look for? Final judgment rests on the quality of ingredients, the chef's creativity, and overall service. In menus, I look for a healthy balance of dishes. In wine lists, value and variety are essential. A good restaurant is like good theater: One leaves in a good frame of mind, physically and psychologically satisfied, with a feeling that both the time and the money have been well spent.

Likewise, your restaurants and meals should be chosen according to your own mood and appetite, the time of year, and of course, the time of day.

WHERE AM I, ANYWAY?

An American traveler once related this story: She was stopped on a street in Paris by another American visitor, who asked, in a state of sheer frustration, "What I don't understand here is with all these restaurants, how do you tell which ones are French? You know, the ones that serve soufflés." Slightly less complicated, but equally frustrating for visitors, are the distinctions among bistro, brasserie, and restaurant. Although the lines between bistro and restaurant are often blurred, here are a few definitions that should clear the matter.

Bistro

A bistro is a rather small restaurant, traditionally a mom-and-pop establishment with mom at the cash register and pop at the stove. Bistro menus are usually handwritten or mimeographed, and dishes are limited to a small selection of traditional, home-style dishes. Wine is generally offered by the carafe, while wines available by the bottle are listed on the single-page menu. Bistro decor is usually simple, not fancy (though Paris's Belle Epoque bistros have some of the city's most beautiful interiors), often with a long zinc bar, tile floors, paper tablecloths, and sturdy, serviceable tableware. At some of the most modest establishments, diners may share long tables.

Brasserie

Brasserie is French for brewery, and almost all of Paris's large and lively brasseries have an Alsatian connection: That means lots of beer, Alsatian white wines such as Riesling and Gewürztraminer, and usually *choucroute,* that hearty blend of sauerkraut and assorted sausages. Brasseries tend to be brightly lit and full of the sounds of good times, fine places for going with a large group. Generally, snacks or full meals are available whenever the restaurant is open. Brasseries tend to keep late hours, and while a reservation is recommended, one can usually get a table without one.

Restaurants

Beyond bistros and brasseries, Paris offers numerous sorts of full-fledged restaurants, some offering elegant and classic cuisine, some specializing in creative, inventive, modern cooking. As well, there are restaurants that specialize in fish or grilled meats, in the cooking of specific regions of France. Classifications for all restaurants listed in the guide appear on page 336.

Reservations

Almost without exception, reservations are necessary. For the grand restaurants, such as Taillevent, reserve weeks to months in advance. For others, reservations can be made several days ahead for popular weekend dinners, though for a weekday lunch, reserving the same day is often sufficient. If you are unable to keep a reservation, call to cancel. Many restaurants now require that advance reservations be confirmed by telephone the day you plan to dine there. Another good reason for reserving: Restaurants freely, and without warning, change opening and closing times and vacation plans, particularly during summer months and holiday periods. So it is always safest to call to make sure the restaurant will be open when you plan to visit.

Dining Hours

Set aside plenty of time for a Paris restaurant meal. In general, expect to spend anywhere from one and a half to three hours at table for a substantial lunch or dinner. If you want to be in and out within thirty minutes to an hour, visit a café, tea salon, wine bar, or brasserie, but don't attempt to rush through a meal at a serious restaurant. Currently, most Parisians begin lunch at 12:30 or 1 P.M. (although one can begin at noon), and most dine starting at 8:30 or 9 P.M. (although some restaurants will accept reservations for any time after 7:30 P.M.). Despite the later hours, most kitchens close early, so a 2 P.M. lunch or 10 P.M. dinner reservation would be stretching it. On the other hand, the majority of cafés and brasseries serve at almost any hour. A few restaurants continue taking orders until 11 P.M. or later, and a list of those can be found in the Ready Reference beginning on page 336.

Prices

The price range of restaurants listed here goes from

low to high. I have made no attempt to include restaurants serving mediocre food simply because they are inexpensive. Bargains can be found everywhere, and there are always ways to cut costs, even in the most expensive restaurants. Forego the before-dinner drink, after-dinner Cognac or cigar, and if you smoke, buy cigarettes at a neighborhood *tabac,* where they will be cheaper than in the restaurant. Share dishes, if you like. You are not obliged to order either cheese or dessert, and if they do not suit your budget or appetite, forget them. You can often cut costs by ordering from a fixed-price menu (though it is not always cheaper than ordering *à la carte*), or by opting for a carafe of wine or an inexpensive house wine.

In all cases, the price noted with each restaurant listing represents an average meal for one person, including a first course, main course, cheese or dessert, and half a bottle of moderately priced wine, as well as the service charge. Generally, a good inexpensive meal can be had for 150 francs, a good moderately priced meal for 200 francs, while a luxury meal, in a higher class of restaurant with more expensive wines, will range from 400 up to 600 francs. Almost without exception, prices are the same for lunch and dinner.

Advice on Paying the Bill and Tipping

No subject is more confusing to visitors than French restaurant bills. You need remember only one fact: You are never required to pay more than the final total on the bill. Service, which ranges from twelve to fifteen percent, depending upon the class of the restaurant, must now be included in the price of individual dishes, and is part of the final bill. Etiquette does not require you to pay more than the total. If you have particularly enjoyed the meal, if you feel that the *maître d'hôtel* or *sommelier* has offered exceptional service, if you are in a particularly generous mood, then you might leave anywhere from a few francs to five percent of the total bill as an additional tip.

Credit Cards

The majority of Paris restaurants accept credit cards, and almost all will accept traveler's checks in French francs. Although every attempt has been

made to ensure the accuracy of credit card information in this guide, policies change rapidly. When
reserving, it is a good idea to confirm credit card
information. If you are sharing the bill with another
person or couple and you both wish to pay by credit
card, most restaurants will oblige by dividing the
bill between the two credit cards. Out of kindness
to the waiters and *sommelier,* any tips (beyond the
obligatory twelve to fifteen percent service charge)
should be left in cash.

A Private Room

Many restaurants, including such establishments as
Taillevent, Jamin, and Le Grand Véfour, offer private dining rooms for anywhere from eight to
several hundred people. Some rooms, such as those
at Taillevent, are particularly elegant and well appointed. Others may be drab, uncomfortable, and
less appealing than the restaurant's main dining
room, so see the room before making plans.

There are advantages and disadvantages in
reserving a private room. One advantage is privacy,
and it makes it easier to organize a special feast,
discussing and preparing beforehand the complete
menu, including wines. The main disadvantage is
that you must plan several weeks ahead and in most
cases will need a French-speaking person to make
arrangements. Also keep in mind that since your
group will be set apart from the main dining room,
you will miss much of the "theater" and ambience
that goes with the dining experience. There is no
extra charge for the private rooms, and in many
cases the total bill will be less expensive than if the
group chose from the regular menu. Where private
rooms are available, such facilities are noted with
each restaurant description, and a separate listing
can be found in the Ready Reference beginning on
page 336.

WHAT TO EXPECT AT THE TABLE

Suggestions on Ordering

There are four simple things to keep in mind when
ordering in a Paris restaurant. First, think about
what foods are likely to be fresh and in season.
Thank goodness the French are still fanatical about

freshness, and about eating only what is naturally in season. When dining out in Paris, I often go on seasonal "binges," eating asparagus, melon, scallops, oysters, or game day after day when they are at their peak. If you see melon on the menu in January, or scallops during July, beware.

Second, take the time to learn about the restaurant's specialties. Every restaurant has at least one or two dishes of which it is particularly proud, and the majority of restaurants either offer a *plat du jour* or underline or boldface their specialties. These dishes, assuming they are to your liking, will usually be a good buy, and generally fresh. Note that the fish is usually freshest on Fridays (when the demand is greatest) and least fresh on Mondays, when the wholesale market is closed.

Third, stick to your guns and order the kind of food you really like to eat. This is a caveat to those diners who will blindly accept a critic's or a waiter's suggestion, then all too late realize that they hate tripe, or duck, or whatever it was that was recommended.

Finally, today many restaurants offer a tasting menu, or *menu dégustation,* which allows diners to sample small portions of from four to eight different dishes. I am generally opposed to such menus, for in the end they are rarely good buys and inevitably provide more food than it is humanly (and healthily) possible to eat. Because a tasting menu offers so many different dishes, it is difficult, if not impossible, to take with you a memorable impression of the meal or the restaurant. While the *menu dégustation* is often easier on the kitchen, you just may get the feeling that the dishes you are eating came off of an assembly line.

Butter

Most, but not all, restaurants offer butter at the table. If you don't see butter, just ask for it. Only at the smallest cafés will a supplement be charged. Since the French do not ordinarily butter their bread, restaurants do not systematically offer it, unless you order a dish that generally calls for buttered bread—*charcuterie,* oysters served with rye bread, sardines, or radishes, or the cheese course. Almost all French butter is unsalted.

Coffee

The French have very specific coffee-drinking habits. Many Frenchmen begin their day with a *café au lait*—usually lots of hot milk with a little bit of coffee. During the rest of the day they drink either black coffee or *café crème* (coffee with steamed milk). But in restaurants, the coffee taken after meals is always black coffee, never coffee with added milk. Some restaurants will provide cream or milk if requested, some will not. In France coffee is always taken at the very end of the meal, almost served as a course of its own. In finer restaurants, chocolates and/or *petits fours* might also be served.

Fish, Meat, and Poultry

Almost all fish, meat, and poultry taste better when cooked on the bone. If you have problems boning fish, ask if the dish you are ordering is boned *(sans arêtes)*, and if not, ask the waiter to debone it before serving *(enlevez les arêtes)*. The French prefer their meat and some poultry (particularly duck) cooked quite rare. But if rare meat or poultry really bothers you, be insistent, and ask for it *bien cuit* (well done). Be prepared for the waiter to wince. (For rare meat, order it *saignant*; for medium, *à point.)*

Salt and Pepper

Some chefs are insulted if diners alter their creations with additional seasonings, and so do not offer salt and pepper at the table. If you don't see salt or pepper, just ask for it. But do be sure to taste the food before reaching for the mill or shaker.

Water

I am always shocked when, in this day and age, people ask "Is it safe to drink the water in Paris?" Of course it is. Perhaps visitors assume that because the French are so passionate about bottled water—a table of eight diners might include four different preferred brands of mineral water—that tap water is unsafe. Either tap water (ask for *une carafe d'eau)* or mineral water (*plate* is flat bottled water, *gazeuse* is bubbly mineral water) may be ordered with all meals. If ordering Perrier brand mineral water, don't be surprised if only small bottles are available. The French consider Perrier too gaseous to drink with meals, so most restaurants stock only small bottles, for drinking as an *apéritif* or with mixed drinks.

Wines and Liquor

This is one area where I firmly advise you to follow the rule "When in Paris, do as the Parisians do." Most Frenchmen do not drink hard liquor before meals and few restaurants are equipped with a full bar. If you are accustomed to drinking hard liquor before meals, try to change your habits during a Paris visit. The liquor will numb your palate for the pleasures to follow, and requests for a martini or whiskey before a meal will not put you in good stead with the waiter or the management. Almost all restaurants offer a house cocktail—most often a Kir, a blend of either white wine or Champagne with *crème de Cassis* (black currant liqueur). I personally dislike most of these concoctions (which can be expensive and run up the bill) and always ask for the wine list when requesting the menu. Then, I usually order as an *apéritif* a white wine that will be drunk with the meal, or at least with the first course.

Selecting Wines

I have learned almost all I know about wines by tasting, tasting, tasting in restaurants: I study wine lists, keep track of average prices and favorite food and wine combinations, and am always eager to sample a wine that's new or unfamiliar to me.

Although I have found some *sommeliers,* or wine stewards, to be outrageously sexist (I was once refused even a simple glance at a wine list, and a few *sommeliers* still bristle when I insist on ordering the wine), generally I haven't found them to be unfair or unwilling to help when I sought information or assistance. If you don't know a lot about wine, ask the *sommelier's* advice. Give him a rough idea of your tastes and the price you would like to pay. This assumes, of course, that you share a common language. If you do not, ask simply whether there is a *vin de la maison* (house wine).

If you are knowledgeable about wine, you will want to study the wine list. Don't allow yourself to be pressured or bullied into making a quick decision (this isn't always easy), and if pressed, simply explain that you are fascinated by the restaurant's wonderful selection and would like a few minutes to examine and fully appreciate the list of offerings.

Prices for the same wines vary drastically from

restaurant to restaurant: some have large, long-standing wine cellars, others are just getting started. I love wine, consider it an essential part of any good meal, and probably tend to spend slightly more than the average diner on a good bottle. When dining in a bistro or brasserie, I often order the house wine, either by the carafe or by the bottle. When ordering from a wine list, I follow one simple rule: I rarely pay more than 200 to 250 francs for a bottle of wine. In Paris restaurants, the general rule of thumb is that one-third of the final bill should be for wine. That is, if you are paying, say, 400 francs for a meal for two, about 135 francs of that will be spent on wine.

The staff of Julien (see entry, page 78).

PALAIS-ROYAL, LES HALLES, OPERA, BOURSE
1st and 2nd arrondissements

CARRE DES FEUILLANTS
(Alain Dutournier)
14 Rue de Castiglione,
  Paris 1.
(42.86.82.82).
Métro: Tuileries.
Last orders taken at 2:30 P.M.
  and 10:30 P.M.
Closed Saturday lunch and
  Sunday.
Credit cards: AE, V.
Private dining room for 12.
Air-conditioned.
English spoken.
230-franc lunch menu. A la
  carte, 500 francs.

SPECIALTIES:
*Seasonal: ravioles de homard
(lobster ravioli), June to
November: agneau de Paulliac
rôti (roast southwestern lamb),
January to April: râble de lièvre
(saddle of wild hare), mid-October
to mid-December.*

Even years ago, you only had to take one look at the energetic and enthusiastic Alain Dutournier to know that one day he'd be itching to expand beyond the walls of Au Trou Gascon, his small and wildly popular Paris restaurant devoted to the cooking of his native southwest. The litany of foie gras, fatted duck breast, and *cassoulet* seemed to be confining him over in the out-of-the-way 12th *arrondissement,* and he wanted to show the world what he could do with so many of the lesser-known regional specialties. His wife, Nicole, stayed behind to take care of business at the still-thriving Au Trou Gascon when Dutournier packed up his casseroles and moved to a fashionable address off the Place Vendôme. The bright, big, splashy new quarters, decorated with Venetian chandeliers, superrealistic still-life paintings, and *trompe-l'oeil* wood paneling, actually seem just right for Dutournier's frenetic style of cooking. His menus change often and revolve with the seasons. Some of the best dishes include a terrine of rare-roasted wild duck blended with chunks of mellow chestnuts; a carpaccio of scallops on a bed of lentils sprinkled with caviar; a steaming casserole of monkfish, sausage, and lentils. No one dare leave without sampling Dutournier's rich and dreamy *crème brûlée* (sometimes he flavors it with a puckery dose of rhubarb) or his supremely satisfying warm chocolate soufflé. When it comes to choosing wine, I eagerly put myself in the hands of one of Paris's most charming and knowledgeable *sommeliers,* Jean-Guy Loustau. A word of warning: As talented as Dutournier is, the food is not consistent, and he has definite on and off days. Also, I've received numerous complaints from diners who felt they had been rushed through their meal.

AU COCHON D'OR DES HALLES

31 Rue du Jour, Paris 1.
(42.36.38.31 and
    42.36.33.14).
Métro: Les Halles.
Last orders taken at 2:30 P.M.
    and 10:30 P.M.
Closed Saturday lunch and
    Sunday.
Credit cards: AE, DC, V.
Private dining room for 18.
Air-conditioned.
English spoken.
250 francs.

SPECIALTIES:

Bistro: fricassée d'escargots aux girolles (sauté of snails and wild mushrooms), moelle pochée à la croque au sel (poached bone marrow served with coarse salt), grilled meats, andouillettes (chitterling sausages), Beaujolais.

This is one of Les Halles' fine old-time establishments, now under the direction of Robert Viart, who once served as the *maître d'hôtel.* He's a friendly, chatty fellow who assists the amiable Swiss-born waitress in the small forty-seat bistro. Go when you're really hungry, and be prepared to sample a little bit of everything from the classic bistro menu. For starters, there's a fine *salade frisée aux lardons* (curly endive and bacon salad) topped with a perfectly poached egg; a formidable serving of bone marrow for spreading on toast and sprinkling with chives and coarse salt; and a classic *jambon persillé* (parsleyed ham) accompanied by properly tart cornichons. I have rarely sampled better roast lamb chops (*carré d'agneau rôti à l'estragon*) or grilled veal kidneys, and beef eaters will certainly want to try either the *côte de boeuf* with bone marrow sauce or the special beef of the day, accompanied by a lovely shallot butter. A fine wine choice here is a good-buy Bordeaux, a Haut Médoc: Château Ramage la Batisse.

L'EPI D'OR

25 Rue Jean-Jacques
    Rousseau, Paris 1.
(42.36.38.12).
Métro: Les Halles.
Last orders taken at 2 P.M.
    and 1:30 A.M.
Closed Saturday lunch,
    Sunday, and mid-July to
    mid-August.
Credit card: V.
English spoken.
90-franc menu. A la carte,
    150 francs.

SPECIALTIES:

Bistro: jambonneau géant (salt-cured ham shank for two), petit salé aux lentilles (salt-cured pork with lentils), rognon de veau à la moutarde (veal kidneys with mustard sauce).

Close your eyes and return to sometime around 1954, when the Paris dining scene seemed to revolve around those old bistro classics and waiters bustled about serving food that was never astonishing but always quite pleasing. L'Epi d'Or is that sort of unobtrusive bistro, with a cozy decor that offers a welcoming solace from the sometimes cruel world outside. It's the kind of place I love to go on a cold winter's night, forgetting the cares of the modern world to settle into generous portions of curly endive salad, rabbit with mustard sauce, and rations of rough red wine.

Paris bistro conviviality.

**LA FERMETTE DU SUD-
OUEST**
31 Rue Coquillière, Paris 1.
(42.36.73.55).
Métro: Les Halles.
Last orders taken at 2 P.M.
and 10 P.M.
Closed Sunday.
Credit card: V.
Private dining room for 20.
110-franc menu. A la carte,
200 francs.

SPECIALTIES:
*Southwestern: charcuterie, foie
gras, gibiers et champignons en
saison (game and mushrooms in
season), boudin maison (homemade
blood sausage), confit (preserved
duck or goose), cassoulet (here,
casserole of white beans, preserved
goose, and homemade pork
sausage).*

CHEZ GEORGES
1 Rue du Mail, Paris 2.
(42.60.07.11).
Métro: Sentier.
Last orders taken at 2:30 P.M.
and 9:30 P.M.
Closed Sunday and holidays.
Credit cards: AE, V.
Air-conditioned.
English spoken.
230 francs.

SPECIALTIES:
*Bistro: sole au Pouilly, ris de veau
aux morilles (sweetbreads with
morels), pavé du Mail (thick slice
of boned beef in mustard sauce),
steak de canard aux cèpes (pan-
fried duck breast with meaty wild
mushrooms).*

This country *auberge* set right in the center of the city is a great buy, and on top of that you're offered the personality and the talent of Christian Naulet, a butcher turned restaurateur. With his booming voice and handlebar mustache, Naulet fits the image of the aggressive, temperamental *bistrotier,* but beneath the bluster there's a dedicated cook, a proud butcher's son who's a southwestern native. In a city that can at times appear coldly impersonal, Naulet offers a fine human touch as he wanders from table to table, taking orders for his superb homemade blood sausage *(boudin noir),* personally spooning out the first helping of his copious *cassoulet,* pouring the first sip of his nicely chosen Madiran wine.

Chez Georges is one of that dying breed of old-time bistros where the food may never be great but is good enough to keep the place filled day and night. The handwritten menu changes little from day to day, but one can always go assured of finding giant and generous bowls of silvery Baltic herring, *foie de veau* (calf's liver), *steak de canard,* kidneys and sweetbreads, and generally, hot and crunchy fries. The restaurant is small and alleylike, with rows of banquettes and giant arched mirrors, and a cadre of aging waitresses in black dresses protected by frilly white aprons. At lunchtime, men come from the nearby Bourse, while on weeknights and Saturdays bourgeois French couples gather for their grilled *pavé du Mail.* There's a nice fruity Brouilly served from little pewter-colored pitchers, as well as an impressive assortment of Burgundies and Bordeaux. The *steak de canard* is generally good—beefy, rosy red, and often accompanied by garlicky *cèpes,* fresh and perfectly sautéed wild mushrooms. Desserts tend to be traditional and banal.

LE GLOBE D'OR
158 Rue Saint-Honoré,
     Paris 1.
(42.60.23.37).
Métro: Louvre.
Last orders taken at 2:30 P.M.
     and 10:30 P.M.
Closed Saturday, Sunday and
     August.
Credit cards: AE, V.
200 to 250 francs.

SPECIALTIES:
Southwestern: cassoulet (here,
casserole of white beans, mutton,
and tomatoes) Thursdays only,
jambon de pays grillé à l'échalote
(grilled country ham salad with
shallots), confit de canard
(preserved duck), game and wild
mushrooms in season. Wines:
Cahors, Madiran, Pecharmant,
Sauternes.

Le Globe d'Or's owner-chef, Gerard Constiaux, is a native of Agen, where his food-loving family instilled in him a fondness for the local hams, the tiny and flavorful *échalote grise* (the prized French shallot, admired for its role as an aromatic garnish), and aged goat cheese enveloped in its traditional sycamore-leaf wrapping. The chef is a passionate man, and his love for food is readily transferred from kitchen to table. What he loves best are the warm, rustic dishes that remind him of home, dishes such as the wonderfully simple, full-flavored *jambon de pays grillé à l'échalote.* Constiaux marinates sliced shallots in oil for several hours to soften and sweeten them. Then he grills slices of ham lightly on both sides, and seasons them with the marinated shallots and a sprinkling of red wine vinegar. The dish is covered and set to steep for several minutes, then showered with minced chives. Add to it a green salad, a glass of the house Madiran, and you're in heaven. There are some dishes, though, that are deemed too rustic for polite Parisian company. "At home, in the autumn," says Constiaux, "we like to rub toast with garlic, dip the bread in oil, and eat this with freshly picked white chasselas grapes." He would love to serve the dish, but can't imagine sending proper businessmen back into the world reeking of garlic. However, diners with a bent for the rustic will love his *tomates farcies* (tomatoes stuffed with well-seasoned ground meat and topped with the marvelous local ham); his light *confit de porc,* smothered with shallots and served with a fine side dish of pan-fried potatoes; the fabulous *petit salé de canard* (duck marinated for three days in an herb-rich salt solution, then cooked until moist and tender); and the cold sliced duck *confit,* served with potatoes and tomatoes. A special salute to the chef: Although the dishes are meaty, they are neither fatty nor heavy. For dessert, try the extraordinary traditional *pastis,* paper-thin layers of pastry laced with apples and Armagnac, or the *riz au lait,* a cinnamon-rich, soup-like dessert of rice in sweetened milk.

The chef has an extensive collection of postcards, the best of which he has enlarged and framed to decorate his cozy restaurant. Also note the antique plum-drying rack that hangs above the bar. Miniature versions of the harp-shaped wooden racks are used to serve their fresh Cabécou goat cheese, served with moist walnut bread. Chef Constiaux continues the house tradition, serving up *cassoulet* each Thursday. Here it's the Castelnaudary version with tomatoes and mutton—a variation, I must admit, I find marred by an excess of tomatoes.

LE GRAND VEFOUR
17 Rue de Beaujolais,
   Paris 1.
(42.96.56.27).
Métro: Bourse.
Last orders taken at 2 P.M.
   and 10 P.M.
Closed Saturday lunch,
   Sunday, and August.
Credit cards: AE, DC, V.
Private dining room for 8 to
   30.
Air-conditioned.
English spoken.
250-franc menu, at lunch
   only. A la carte, 600
   francs.

SPECIALTIES:
Seasonal: terrine de foies de volailles au thym (chicken liver terrine with thyme); aspic de navarin d'agneau à la tomate fraîche (lamb stew in aspic with fresh tomatoes); rôti d'agneau de Pauillac au jus, cassolette de haricots (roast Pauillac lamb with white bean casserole); joue de boeuf aux choux (beef cheeks on a bed of cabbage); rognons et ris de veau aux champignons (veal kidneys and sweetbreads with wild mushrooms); dessert soufflés.

The dining room at Le Grand Véfour (above).

Le Grand Véfour typifies the lively gaiety of the old Paris world of writers, artists, politicians, and historians. Here in an elegant red, white, and black 1760s café, Napoleon is said to have dined with Josephine. Later diners included Victor Hugo, Colette, and Jean Cocteau, whose drawing still graces the menu cover of one of Paris's most charming restaurants. (Among the sixteen tables, there are several with brass plaques commemorating many of the famous who've dined here, and these tables can be requested when making reservations.) Go when there's an occasion to celebrate a special event—dress fit to kill and imagine the year is 1900. This is a romantic spot for lunch on a sunny summer afternoon, when you can dine looking out onto the bright pink rose garden of the Palais-Royal.

The food and the service have improved here immensely. On our last visit, we feasted on chef Jean-Claude Lhonneur's fabulous *joue de boeuf aux choux,* a delicate, tender, full-flavored wintery dish; the roast Pauillac lamb with white beans; a beautifully seasoned rabbit sausage on a bed of greens; and a stunning marriage of wild *girolle* mushrooms, kidneys, and sweetbreads. The rich chocolate soufflé is a dream, as is the individual apple tart. The wine list is extensive, but be prepared to take a deep breath when you see the prices.

LESCURE
7 Rue de Mondovi, Paris 1.
(42.60.18.91).
Métro: Concorde.
Last orders taken at 2 P.M.
 and 10 P.M.
Closed Saturday dinner,
 Sunday, July, and two
 weeks at Christmas.
Credit card: V.
Sidewalk dining.
Private dining room for 12.
English spoken.
75-franc menu. A la carte,
 about 130 francs.

SPECIALTIES:
*Bistro: terrine de foies de volaille
(chicken liver terrine);
maquereaux au vin blanc
(mackerel in white wine); raie au
beurre noisette (ray fish in
hazelnut butter); poulet au riz
(chicken in tomato sauce with
rice); poule au pot (boiled stuffed
chicken).*

A great address to know when visiting the Louvre or shopping along Rue Saint-Honoré, when you're in the mood for a quick inexpensive meal. In good weather, tables pour out onto the sidewalk (it would be an exaggeration to call it a terrace), while inside diners sit elbow-to-elbow beneath rafters dangling with strings of garlic and country sausages. This is simple French home cooking, nothing fancy but generally satisfying: I've enjoyed the *poulet au riz,* the *poule au pot,* and the *travers de porc demi-sel* (meaty salt-cured spareribs on a bed of cabbage). Many ingredients could be fresher here, but the price is right. Service is swift, and it comes with a smile.

*An after dinner discussion at
Chez Georges (see entry, page 13).*

LOUIS XIV
1 bis Place des Victoires,
    Paris 1.
(40.26.20.81).
Métro: Bourse.
Last orders taken at 2:30 P.M.
    and 10 P.M.
Closed Saturday, Sunday, and
    August.
Credit card: V.
Sidewalk terrace.
Private dining room for 10.
English spoken.
150-franc menu. A la carte,
    220 francs.

SPECIALTIES:

Lyonnais bistro: filets de hareng pommes à l'huile (salad of cured herring and potatoes bathed in oil), pissenlits au lard (salad of dandelion greens and bacon), la mâche betterave (salad of lamb's lettuce and beets), lapin à la moutarde (rabbit with mustard sauce), canard rôti aux olives (roast duck with olives), entrecôte grillée à la moelle (grilled beef rib steak with bone marrow). Beaujolais by the carafe.

A classic bistro, where the food is never great but the service and atmosphere are gay and friendly, and everyone seems to be having a wonderful time. At lunch, the much-prized sidewalk tables overlooking the Place des Victoires are filled with the chic fashion crowd from the boutiques on the square, and at night couples wander in from every part of town to enjoy the city views and often spectacular sunsets. This is the place to drink Beaujolais by the carafe and eat *lapin à la moutarde,* but fish eaters will want to order the fine grilled turbot, classic *sole meunière* (sole sautéed in butter), or a popular daily spring and summer special, salmon with sorrel. Unfortunately, their famous *friture d'éperlans*—fried smelt—can be disastrous. On one occasion, the tiny fish were far from fresh and the oil in which they were fried had seen better days. For those who never get enough butter in French restaurants, this is the place to go: The waiter moves a giant three-pound block from table to table, and everyone helps himself. If it happens to rain, the best table is upstairs, just in front of the arched windows that overlook the square.

AUX LYONNAIS
32 Rue Saint-Marc,
    Paris 2.
(42.96.65.04).
Métro: Bourse.
Last orders taken at 2 P.M.
    and 9:30 P.M.
Closed Saturday lunch and
    Sunday.
Credit Cards: AE, DC, V.
57-franc menu. A la carte,
    125 to 175 francs.

SPECIALTIES:

Bistro: Poule gros sel avec ses légumes (chicken poached with vegetables), lapin aux échalotes (rabbit with shallots), tarte Tatin (upside down apple tart).

One of the long-time Bourse standbys is Aux Lyonnais, once considered among the very top bistros in Paris. It doesn't rate nearly that high today, but for simple perfection, there are few spots to equal it. As one friend exclaimed, "Everything's so clean here, it looks as though it's been washed seven times!"

Aux Lyonnais is a bright, lively place at lunchtime, when office workers pour in, and the noise level reaches a fine, musical high. The food is very basic, but very good bistro fare including a *salade frisée aux lardons* that is topped with a perfectly poached egg and is copious enough for two eager eaters, and crispy baguettes that taste as though they popped out of the oven only seconds before.

Equally appealing are the *petits pâtés chauds* (tiny well-seasoned sausage patties, wrapped in caul fat), and a *confit de poularde,* a dish that's a real revelation: We cook duck and goose and even turkey in fat to flavor as well as preserve them, so why not a good farm hen as well? With it all, sample the fine assortment of Beaujolais from Pierre Ferraud.

You can end the meal here with a giant floating island served out of a hot fudge sundae dish— or a fine *tarte Tatin*, smothered in rich *crème fraîche*.

POMMES PONT NEUF

At the end of the 19th century, merchants with deep-fat fryers on rolling carts lined the Pont-Neuf bridge. They cut potatoes into slender sticks, fried them, and bundled them into paper cones. The French food writer Curnonsky exclaimed: "Fried potatoes are one of the most spiritual creations of the Parisian genius." But potatoes were not always so well loved: In 1787 Antoine Parmentier introduced the potato to France, with great hopes that this curious tuber would become so popular they would call it a *parmentier*. To promote the potato, he offered a dinner for 100 at the Hôtel des Invalides. The menu included potato soup, potato salad, potato fritters, a brioche made with potato flour, and to end the meal, potato liqueur.

CHEZ PAULINE
5 Rue Villedo, Paris 1.
(42.96.20.70 and
   42.61.79.01).
Métro: Pyramides.
Last orders taken at 2:30 P.M.
   and 10:30 P.M.
Closed Saturday dinner,
   Sunday, July, and
   Christmas week.
Credit cards: EC, V.
Private dining room for 16.
Air-conditioned.
English spoken.
280 to 330 francs.

SPECIALTIES:
Updated luxury bistro: salade tiède de tête de veau et de pommes de terre (warm salad of headcheese and potatoes), jambon persillé comme en Bourgogne (Burgundian parsleyed ham).

Chef-owner André Genin continues to follow a steady, even course here, offering a menu that nicely balances classic bistro dishes with personal inspirations of the moment. Dishes I've most enjoyed recently include the moist and flavorful pigeon baked in a salt crust; his fine roast wild duck; and all of his fresh fish preparations, including the salmon braised with olive oil and basil. On the last visit, I found the famous rice pudding overwhelmingly sweet. There's a good wine list, including Duboeuf Beaujolais, a few well-priced Rhône wines, and a fine selection of *eaux-de-vie*, Cognacs, and Armagnacs.

PHARAMOND
24 Rue de la Grande-
    Truanderie, Paris 1.
(42.33.06.72).
Métro: Les Halles.
Last orders taken at 2:15 P.M.
    and 10 P.M.
Closed Sunday, Monday
    lunch, and July.
Credit cards: AE, DC, V.
Small sidewalk terrace.
Private dining room for 18.
English spoken.
160 to 200 francs.

SPECIALTIES:
Norman: tripes à la mode de
Caen (beef tripe and vegetables
cooked in cider and apple brandy),
coquilles Saint-Jacques au cidre
(scallops cooked in cider), crêpes
normandes (varied filled dessert
crêpes). Cider.

Pharamond—also known as A la Petite Normande—is one of those old-time tried and true, beautiful Parisian restaurants that seem to age very well indeed. Traditional, graceful, and spotless, this high-class bistro is almost an anachronism in a neighborhood overrun with fast-food eateries and trendy boutiques.

Pharamond's Belle Epoque interior is among the most beautiful in Paris, with stunning pastel tiles, grand mirrors, cozy banquettes, and crisp white damask linens. Even the waiters seem to have come out of the past, professionals who know how to keep their distance, yet manage to dish out a healthy dose of personal service and charm at the same time.

The food here has remained first-rate as well. Although I have to confess that *tripes à la mode de Caen* (tripe cooked in apple cider and served in old-fashioned brass braziers) is not one of my favorite dishes, this is the place to sample it if you are so inclined. My tastes lean toward the other wintery specialties they do so well, including a warming first course of well-seasoned pork sausage accompanied by sliced warm potatoes bathed in vinaigrette, or their famous *coquilles Saint-Jacques au cidre,* a Norman-inspired dish that's on the menu well into springtime. If the *poule faisan* is on the menu when you go, try it. I will never quite understand why simple roast fowl is so difficult to find anywhere in France. Our order of tender female pheasant—roasted for two—was perfectly moist, delicate, and flavorful, served with healthy helpings of crisp *pommes soufflées,* little inflated pillows of twice-fried potatoes. Other worthy main courses include the *noisettes d'agneau* and fine tender *filet de veau.* Dessert offerings include a superb *tarte Tatin* served with generous portions of *crème fraîche.*

AU PIED DE COCHON
6 Rue Coquillière, Paris 1.
(42.36.11.75).
Métro: Les Halles.
Open daily, 24 hours a day.
Credit cards: AE, DC, V.
Sidewalk terrace.
Private dining room for 30
  to 50.
Air-conditioned.
English spoken.
180 francs.

SPECIALTIES:
Brasserie: plateau de fruits de mer
(fresh shellfish platter), soupe à
l'oignon (onion soup), pied de
cochon grillé (grilled pig's foot),
grilled meats. Good selection of
Beaujolais.

Au Pied de Cochon is one spot that has been newly revived in a charmingly hokey sort of way. While a few years back this all-night Les Halles institution had all but been turned over to tourists in search of a midnight bowl of onion soup, the new Pied de Cochon draws a varied French crowd, a mix of Parisians and those in from the provinces, as well as foreign tourists. The food here has changed little: There's a filling and fairly fresh seafood platter with some of the nuttiest, almond-like raw clams I've sampled in ages; the famed and delicious *andouillette;* and the whole assortment of Georges Duboeuf Beaujolais (including the oddball white) to lighten up the evening. The new decor is properly glitzy, gay, and bright, and there is such an overkill of murals, chandeliers, and marble that somehow more becomes less, and it's quite all right. Right enough, at least, to bring back a bright local crowd and return this part of Les Halles to the neighborhood Parisians. The onion soup, by the way, is not the best in the world, but it's good enough to satisfy a craving and cure nostalgic longings for a Paris of days past. Do not feel slighted if you're sent to dining rooms on the upper levels: Service here is relatively democratic.

Au Pied de Cochon.

MAQUEREAUX AU CIDRE PIERRE TRAITEUR
PIERRE TRAITEUR'S MACKEREL IN CIDER

Marinated or lightly cooked mackerel is popular bistro fare, appearing on dozens and dozens of Paris menus in many different variations. It is the sort of dish that can be delicious or disastrous, depending on the freshness of the fish and the quality of vinegar used. At its best, it is a light and satisfying, full-flavored first course. The finest version I've ever tasted was at Pierre Traiteur (see entry, following page). Here, mackerel and apples come together, combining the meaty flavor of the bright and silvery fish with the apple's mild fruitiness. In preparing the dish, they use French cider, which tends to be much milder and less acidic than American cider. A good fresh apple juice could be substituted.

2 large onions, finely
    chopped
2 pounds (1 kg)
    mackerel, cleaned,
    with heads removed
1 teaspoon salt
Freshly ground black
    pepper to taste
2 firm cooking apples,
    peeled, cut in half,
    and cored
1 quart (1 liter) French
    cider, or substitute
    pure apple juice
1 cup (250 ml) cider
    vinegar
3 tablespoons chopped
    fresh chives

1. In a large, heavy-bottomed skillet that has a cover, evenly spread the chopped onions. Generously season the insides of the mackerel with the salt and pepper and place the fish on top of the onions. Top with the apple halves.

2. Add the cider or apple juice and the vinegar, cover, and bring to a boil over high heat. Reduce the heat to medium and simmer, covered, for 10 minutes. Remove the skillet from the heat, gently lift the mackerel with a slotted spatula, and set the fish aside to cool. Reserve the cooking liquid, apples, and onions. (The dish can be prepared several hours ahead up to this point.)

3. To serve the mackerel, remove the fillets from each fish, being careful to keep them intact. Remove as many bones as possible. Arrange the fillets on a serving platter. Cut the apple halves into very thin slices and arrange on top of the mackerel. Moisten with the cooled cooking liquid and onions. Sprinkle with fresh chives and serve at room temperature.

Yield: 4 to 6 servings.

PIERRE TRAITEUR
10 Rue de Richelieu, Paris 1.
(42.96.09.17 and
   42.96.27.17).
Métro: Palais-Royal.
Last orders taken at 2:30 P.M.
   and 10:15 P.M.
Closed Saturday, Sunday, and
   August.
Credit cards: AE, DC, V.
English spoken.
250 to 300 francs.

SPECIALTIES:
Bistro: jambon persillé (parsleyed ham), maquereaux frais au cidre (mackerel in cider), jésu de Morteau poché au Beaujolais (pork sausage poached in Beaujolais), boeuf ficelle à la ménagère (boiled beef), tarte Tatin. Game, wild mushrooms, and fresh foie gras in season. Wines: Chinon, Cahors, Beaujolais.

A classic and wonderful neighborhood spot, situated right behind the Comédie Française. This welcoming little restaurant is filled with regulars day and night, Frenchmen who come by themselves or with large groups to enjoy the hearty bistro fare. Ingredients here are first-rate, and care is taken in preparation. Best bets are the first course *maquereaux au cidre*, silvery little mackerel cooked in cider and cider vinegar and garnished with apples (see recipe, page 21); the fresh terrine of foie gras; perfectly cooked veal kidneys served with superb *gratin dauphinois* (see recipe below), and a simple but delicious pan-fried *côte de boeuf* (rib of beef).

GRATIN DAUPHINOIS PIERRE TRAITEUR
PIERRE TRAITEUR'S POTATO GRATIN

Is there a French potato dish more classic, and welcoming, than gratin dauphinois? This delicious version is bathed in cream and Gruyère cheese with just a hint of garlic. Traditionally, the potatoes are cut very thin, the thickness of a 5-franc piece—about one-sixteenth of an inch. Use starchy Idaho russets, and be sure not to wash them after they've been sliced or you won't have the wonderful cheese flavor that develops as the potatoes cook.

1 clove garlic, peeled
2 pounds (1 kg)
   potatoes, peeled and
   sliced very thin
1 cup (100 g) grated
   Gruyère cheese
2 cups (500 ml) milk
½ cup (125 ml) *crème fraîche* (see recipe, page 237) or heavy cream, preferably not ultrapasteurized
1 teaspoon salt
Freshly ground black
   pepper to taste

1. Preheat the oven to 375°F (190°C).

2. Rub the inside of an oval porcelain gratin dish (about 14 x 9 x 2 inches or 35.5 x 23 x 5 cm) with garlic.

3. In a large mixing bowl combine the potatoes, ¾ cup (75 g) of the cheese, the milk, *crème fraîche* or cream, salt, and pepper. Mix well, then spoon the potatoes into the baking dish, pouring the liquid over the slices. Sprinkle with the remaining cheese and bake until the top is crisp and golden, about 1 hour.

Yield: 4 to 6 servings.

MARMELADE DE LAPIN AU ROMARIN PILE OU FACE
PILE OU FACE'S RABBIT WITH ROSEMARY

Four and a half cups of rosemary? Yes. This is a remarkably delicious and simple dish to prepare, and a favorite of diners at Pile ou Face (see entry, following page). I sampled it the first time I lunched at Pile ou Face (French for "heads or tails"), and now it's become a favorite at home, made with either rabbit or chicken and served with rice or fresh homemade pasta. The dish can easily be prepared ahead of time, then reheated.

1 fresh rabbit or chicken, 2 ½ to 3 pounds (1.25 to 1.5 kg), cut into serving pieces

1 cup (250 ml) dry white wine

1 quart (1 liter) water

1 onion, halved

2 carrots, sliced into rounds

2 bay leaves

1 teaspoon dried thyme

Salt and freshly ground black pepper to taste

4 ½ cups (100 g) fresh rosemary on the stem, or 1 cup (40 g) dried

1 cup (250 ml) *crème fraîche* (see recipe, page 238) or heavy cream, preferably not ultrapasteurized

½ teaspoon whole black peppercorns

1. In a large skillet combine the rabbit (or chicken), wine, water, onion, carrots, bay leaves, thyme, salt and pepper, and 4 cups (90 g) of fresh rosemary. If you are using dried rosemary, add the entire amount. Cover and simmer for 45 minutes.

2. Remove the rabbit pieces and set them aside to cool. Strain the liquid into a medium-size saucepan, discarding the vegetables and herbs, and, over high heat, reduce to 2 cups (500 ml).

3. Meanwhile, remove the rabbit meat from the bones, cutting the meat into bite-size chunks. (The dish may be prepared several hours ahead to this stage.)

4. Stem the remaining ½ cup of rosemary, if using fresh.

5. In a large skillet combine the reduced stock with the *crème fraîche* or heavy cream and peppercorns and heat through. Add the stemmed rosemary and the rabbit pieces.

6. Cook over medium heat until the flavors have blended and the meat is thoroughly heated. Adjust seasoning, if necessary. Serve hot, with rice or fresh pasta.

Yield: 4 servings.

PILE OU FACE

52 bis Rue Notre-Dame-des-
  Victoires, Paris 2.
(42.33.64.33).
Métro: Bourse.
Last orders taken at 2 P.M.
  and 10 P.M.
Closed Saturday, Sunday, and
  August.
Credit card: V.
Small sidewalk terrace.
Private dining room for 8 to
  12.
Air-conditioned (first floor
  only).
Some English spoken.
A la carte, about 285 francs.

S P E C I A L T I E S :
*Seasonal: ravioles d'escargots aux
herbes (snail ravioli with herbs),
marmelade de lapin au romarin
(rabbit with rosemary), pain
maison* (homemade bread),
*crème brûlée au miel d'acacia
(carmelized cream dessert
sweetened with acacia honey).
More than 30 wines priced under
100 francs.*

Pile ou Face—"heads or tails"—remains one of
my favorite little restaurants in Paris. I say
"little" because of its diminutive size and the
modesty of its attentive owners, but in truth it is a
grand place in the quality and quantity of food and
service. Chef Claude Udron and his partners, Alain
Dumerque and Philippe Marquet, are among the
most passionate of men, working day and night to
perfect their little jewel. They do just about everything here but make their own wine: Chef Claude's
bread is a crispy, fresh delight, and his homemade
chocolate confections outshine most of the finest
chocolate shops in town. Several years ago they
transformed a corner café into a cozy spot decorated like a warm front parlor. The menu here is
modern, imaginative, and ever-changing. A few star
attractions include the ravioli filled with herbs and
earthy snails; the now-classic rabbit with rosemary
(see recipe, page 23); fresh pasta with salmon and
olives; and the burnt cream, or *crème brûlée,* with
delicate acacia honey.

RITZ-ESPADON

15 Place Vendôme, Paris 1.
(42.60.38.30).
Métro: Opéra.
Last orders taken at 4 P.M.
  and 11:30 P.M.
Open daily.
Credit cards: AE, DC, EC, V.
Terrace dining.
Private dining rooms for 20
  to 150.
Air-conditioned.
English spoken.
550 to 600 francs.

S P E C I A L T I E S :
*Grilled and roasted fish and
meats: noisettes de chevreuil grand
veneur (filet of venison, hunter's
style), during game season; omble
chevalier du lac Pavin (fresh lake
fish), November and December
only; crêpes flambées Coco Chanel
(warm, flaming dessert crêpes).*

Some sunny summer afternoon when you want to
feel special, get all dressed up and reserve an
outdoor table on the lovely pink and green, flower-
filled terrace at the Ritz-Espadon. Service here is
attentive and professional and the crowd always
interesting (eavesdropping is permitted). The food
is not spectacular, but if you order simple grilled
dishes, you shouldn't be disappointed. Best bets are
the grilled *bar,* a sea bass which arrives accompanied by flaming, aromatic stalks of dried fennel,
and the grilled turbot with mustard sauce. The Ritz
offers nice, elegant touches one rarely finds these
days: If you go during asparagus season in the
spring, you'll be served tiny individual silver asparagus tongs to assist in your enjoyment. (See facing
page for chef Guy Legay's flavorful recipe for a
gratin of fennel, zucchini, and fresh tomatoes.)

GRATIN DE FENOUIL, COURGETTES, ET TOMATES FRAICHES
GRATIN OF FENNEL, ZUCCHINI, AND FRESH TOMATOES

A simple and appealing vegetable gratin, this combination of fennel, zucchini, and tomatoes can be served as a main luncheon course or as a side dish to accompany grilled fish, fowl, or meat. The recipe comes from chef Guy Legay of the Ritz-Espadon (see entry, facing page), where it is served with grilled sea bass, which arrives surrounded by flaming, aromatic stalks of dried fennel. The long, slow cooking of the fennel in this gratin gives it a particularly elegant flavor. The fennel and zucchini portion of the gratin can be made several hours ahead, then thoroughly heated just before serving. Make the tomato sauce at the last minute, to really profit from its freshness.

3 to 4 medium-size bulbs fennel, about 2 pounds (1 kg), trimmed and finely chopped
1 large onion, finely chopped
3 tablespoons olive oil
Salt and freshly ground black pepper to taste
2 medium-size zucchini, about 1 pound (500 g), thinly sliced
2 pounds (1 kg) tomatoes, peeled, cored, seeded, and finely chopped

1. In a large skillet combine the fennel, onion, and 1 tablespoon olive oil. Season with salt and freshly ground black pepper and cook, uncovered, over very low heat for 1 hour, stirring frequently.

2. In another large skillet heat 1 tablespoon olive oil over high heat. Add the zucchini and sauté until just cooked through, 3 to 4 minutes. Remove the zucchini and drain on paper towels.

3. In the skillet in which you cooked the zucchini, heat the remaining 1 tablespoon oil, add the tomatoes, and cook over medium-high heat until the pieces cook down and the sauce is quite thick, about 15 minutes. Season to taste with salt and pepper.

4. Preheat the broiler.

5. Spoon the fennel and onion mixture into an oval gratin dish (about 7 x 12 inches, or 18 x 30½ cm), and decoratively arrange the zucchini slices on top of the fennel. Season lightly with salt and pepper and place under a broiler until the zucchini is golden on top, 2 to 3 minutes. Remove and mound the tomato sauce in the center of the gratin. Serve immediately.

Yield: 4 to 6 servings.

LE RUBAN BLEU
29 Rue d'Argenteuil, Paris 1.
(42.61.47.53).
Métro: Pyramides.
Open for lunch only; last
  orders taken at 2:15 P.M.
Closed Saturday, Sunday, and
  August.
Credit card: V.
220 to 250 francs.

S P E C I A L T I E S :
*Bistro: Saint-Jacques tièdes sur
feuilles de mâche (warm scallops
on a bed of lamb's lettuce), crottin
chaud du Berry sur toast (warm
grilled goat's cheese on toast), sole
meunière sur fondue de poireaux
(pan-fried fish on a bed of leeks),
confit de canard pommes sautées
(preserved duck with sautéed
potatoes). Wines: Sancerre,
Saumur, Champigny.*

Everything about Le Ruban Bleu is neat, tidy, and welcoming—from the very simple, no-nonsense menu to the bright blue plaster ribbon (*ruban bleu*) that floats along the crisp white walls. The friendly patron, Roger Simon, recently took over this 1940s bistro, originally decorated by a man with a passion for ships. The restaurant was named in honor of the famed *Normandie*, which won a blue ribbon for making the fastest trip across the Atlantic. Specialties include a fine *salade frisée*, a curly endive salad with hot sautéed chicken livers; roast rack of lamb; *confit de canard*; and an American-style T-bone steak, served with marrow. And with each cup of coffee, they offer a little cube of delicious Lindt chocolate.

LA TABLE DE JEANNETTE
12-14 Rue Duphot, Paris 1.
(42.60.05.64 and
  42.60.05.76).
Métro: Madeleine.
Last orders taken at 2 P.M.
  and 10 P.M.
Closed Saturday and Sunday.
Credit cards: AE, DC, V.
Small terrace, summer
  evenings only.
Private dining room for 25
  to 60.
Air-conditioned.
English spoken.
275 francs.

S P E C I A L T I E S :
*Seasonal: salade de foie gras
chaud aux pignons de pin et
vinaigre de framboise (salad of
foie gras and pine nuts in
raspberry vinegar), paupiettes de
sole aux langoustines (filet of sole,
rolled and filled with
langoustines), jambonneau de
canard farci au crabe (leg of duck
stuffed with crabmeat).*

Hidden inside a little courtyard not far from the Concorde and the Place de la Madeleine, this elegant, pleasant restaurant is the place to go on a cold wintry day, when the huge stone fireplace and soft classical music offer diners warmth and a touch of the country. The decor is simple and refreshing, service is friendly and attentive, the hearty southwestern French cuisine served in copious portions worthy of a serious gourmand. Innovative dishes at La Table de Jeannette—transformed a few years ago from an old neighborhood bar—include a salad that cleverly combines steaming hot sliced turnips with fresh foie gras; superb *confit d'oie* (preserved goose) served with delicious *pommes à la sarladaise*, a garlicky potato gratin; and *lapin aux aromates*, rabbit with an herb and mustard sauce. At times the food is oversalted, the fish items are not always fresh, and the desserts are not particularly exciting. But do go when you're in the mood for a southwestern meal and a warming fire, and you shouldn't be disappointed. The red house Graves, Château de l'Etoile, is pleasant and reasonably priced.

LA TOUR DE MONTLHERY

5 Rue des Prouvaires,
   Paris 1.
(42.36.21.82).
Métro: Louvre.
Open 24 hours a day. Closed
   Saturday, Sunday, and
   mid-July through mid-
   August.
Credit card: V.
English spoken.
180 to 200 francs.

SPECIALTIES:

*Bistro: salade frisée aux croutons
ailés (curly endive salad with
garlic croutons); haricot de mouton
(mutton and white beans); pied de
porc pané (breaded pig's foot);
profiteroles (choux pastry with ice
cream and chocolate sauce);
Brouilly (Beaujolais). Pot-au-feu
(boiled beef with vegetables) on
Thursday.*

If I had not been in the city in a long, long time and wanted an instant hit of old Paris, I'd go straight from the airport to La Tour de Montlhéry, a modest, bustling, elbow-to-elbow bistro in the heart of old Les Halles. With walls chockablock full of artwork, hams and sausages dangling from the beams, and waiters who gently tease every female in sight, this long, narrow bistro is right out of an old-time French film. Lots of hugging and hand-shaking go on here, for most of the crowd is made up of regulars, but that doesn't mean that strangers are met with cold, dark stares. Much of the food is remarkably good and fresh, particularly the state-of-the-art curly endive salad (tossed with Poilâne country bread deliciously laden with garlic) and the soul-satisfying mutton with white beans, served in gigantic portions out of huge white porcelain gratin dishes. The house Brouilly goes down very well, and waiters serve up endless baskets of fresh Poilâne bread. If I were a cartoonist, I'd come here just to sketch the clientele—mostly beefy, happy, hearty men who've lived a fine gastronomic life indeed.

VAUDEVILLE

29 Rue Vivienne, Paris 2.
(42.33.39.31).
Métro: Bourse.
Last orders taken at 3:30 P.M.
   and 1:30 A.M.
Open daily.
Credit card: V.
Sidewalk terrace.
Air-conditioned.
English spoken.
100 to 240 francs.

SPECIALTIES:

*Brasserie: banc d'huîtres et de
fruits de mer toute l'année (fresh
oysters and shellfish, year-round);
foie gras frais, gelée au Riesling
(fresh foie gras in a Riesling
gelatin); poissons du marché (fish
according to the market); grillades
(grilled meats).*

A lively 1925 brasserie full of mirrors and marble and the sounds of great times. Go with a large group, order up carafes of the house Riesling, and feast on oysters, scallops, mussels, or sole. Meatier specialties, such as pork knuckle with lentils, calf's liver, and a duck and white bean *cassoulet*, are also part of the huge brasserie menu that changes from day to day. In warm weather, opt for a table on the sidewalk terrace, facing the imposing Bourse, or stock exchange.

CHEZ LA VIEILLE
37 Rue de l'Arbre-Sec,
 Paris 1.
(42.60.15.78).
Métro: Pont-Neuf.
Open for lunch only. Closed
 Saturday, Sunday, and
 August.
Credit card: AE.
Private dining room for 15.
260 francs.

SPECIALTIES:
*Bistro: terrine de foies de volaille
(chicken liver terrine), navarin
d'agneau (lamb stew with spring
vegetables), petit salé aux lentilles
(salted pork with lentils), harengs
pommes à l'huile (salad of herring
and potatoes bathed in oil), pot-
au-feu (beef with vegetables),
gâteau au chocolat (chocolate
cake).*

Adrienne Biasin has been serving up her famous pot-au-feu for several decades, and if you can secure a lunchtime table (reservations seem to be dispensed with a great deal of subjectivity), it's worth the journey. Everything here is served up family-style, with a menu that's delivered brusquely and orally by the all-female, matronly staff. A typical lunch will begin with a procession of hearty, homey appetizers: an excellent *museau de boeuf* (beef headcheese), a well-seasoned pork liver pâté, and hot sautéed chicken livers. The *pot-au-feu* is copious and filling, and includes moist, flavorful chunks of beef, carrots, nicely cooked leeks, and turnips. There is more quantity than quality in the dessert assortment, which on a given day will include traditional sweets such as chocolate mousse, floating island, and chocolate cake.

REPUBLIQUE, BASTILLE, LES HALLES, ILE SAINT-LOUIS

3rd, 4th, and 11th arrondissements

**AMBASSADE
  D'AUVERGNE**
22 Rue du Grenier-Saint-
 Lazare, Paris 3.
(42.72.31.22).
Métro: Rambuteau.
Last orders taken at 2:30 P.M.
 and midnight.
Open daily.
Credit cards: EC, V.
Private dining rooms for 10
 to 35.
Air-conditioned.
English spoken.
200 francs.

I consider Ambassade d'Auvergne the best and most authentic Paris restaurant devoted to a single regional cuisine, that of the rugged Auvergne region of south central France. Those who know the restaurant from days past will probably not even notice the recent sprucing up, such as the new stucco walls, a more elegant staircase, a lightening of what was a rather heavy country decor. Ambassade d'Auvergne remains, as ever, one of the city's better buys, with a hearty but not heavy assortment of very satisfying, gratifying Auvergnat fare. This is the land of plenty—plenty of sausage and cabbage, *boudin* blood sausage, mashed potatoes with garlic, delicious green lentils, and crusty peasant bread. Best bets remain the first course *émincé de choux verts aux lardons chauds* (very finely shredded cabbage doused with warm red vinegar and tossed with meaty chunks of bacon; see recipe, facing page), the *saucisse d'Auvergne aux lentilles du Puy* (well-seasoned pork sausage served in a veritable lake of green

SPECIALTIES:
Auvergnat, including daily
specialties: Monday, pot-au-feu
(beef with vegetables); Tuesday,
daube de canard (duck stew);
Wednesday, potée (stew of five
meats and five vegetables);
Thursday, cassoulet aux lentilles
du Puy (stew of lamb, duck,
sausage, and lentils); Friday,
estofinado (codfish casserole);
Saturday, chou farci (stuffed
cabbage; see recipe, following
page). Regional wines:
Chateaugay, Chanturgue, Saint-
Pourçain.

lentils), and anything they serve with the local *aligot*, a soothing blend of potatoes and chunks of garlic whisked and enriched with fresh curds of Cantal cheese. Two local wines worth noting: the Madiran from Château Peyros, and the Côtes d'Auvergne Chanturge. The last time I dined here, a most delightful discovery was their superb chocolate mousse, an ideal version of what that dessert should be and rarely is: rich, thick, airy, and distinctly, darkly chocolate.

EMINCE DE CHOUX VERTS AUX LARDONS CHAUDS
HOT CABBAGE AND BACON SALAD

This is such a simple and delicious dish, I'm surprised more Paris restaurants don't offer it. The salad is generally on the menu at Ambassade d'Auvergne, a solid restaurant with hearty fare (see entry, above). There it's served as a first course, but at home I make the salad often as part of a light meal that might also include a cheese tray, fresh homemade bread, and a favorite red wine from Provence. Do use the best-quality slab bacon or side pork and red wine vinegar you can find. I like to add lots and lots of coarsely ground black pepper.

½ medium-size
  cabbage
Salt and freshly ground
  black pepper to taste
6 ounces (185 g) slab
  bacon or side pork,
  rind removed, cut
  into bite-sized cubes
½ cup (125 ml) best-
  quality red wine
  vinegar

1. Cut the cabbage by hand into thin (⅛-inch; 4-mm) slivers. Do not use a food processor or the cabbage is likely to be too fine and will release too much liquid. Place in a large salad bowl and sprinkle lightly with salt and pepper.

2. In a large skillet, cook the bacon over medium-high heat, stirring frequently. Cook until very crisp. Leaving the bacon and the rendered fat in the pan, deglaze it with the red wine vinegar, stirring constantly. There will be a lot of smoke, but don't be concerned.

3. Add the cabbage, stir, then reduce the heat to low. Cover the pan to allow the cabbage to sweat a bit, and to allow the flavors to blend. Let sit for about 5 minutes, stir, then taste for seasoning. The cabbage should be just slightly wilted, but still crisp. Serve immediately.

Yield: 4 to 6 servings.

CHOU FARCI AMBASSADE D'AUVERGNE
AMBASSADE D'AUVERGNE'S STUFFED CABBAGE

This is a "Sunday-night supper" dish; it's easy to make and popular with those who love hearty one-dish meals. I also find it fun to make. The Ambassade d'Auvergne (see entry, page 28) features the cuisine of the Auvergne region in central France, where cabbage, sausage, and smoked bacon are daily fare. The restaurant's version is stuffed with well-seasoned pork sausage, prunes, and Swiss chard, the popular green and white ribbed vegetable known in France as blette. *Chopped fresh spinach can be substituted, but when I could find neither Swiss chard nor spinach in the market, I made the dish anyway, and it was a big hit. Be sure to cook the bacon just before serving, so it offers a crispy contrast in color and texture. Bring the whole cabbage to the table on a platter, and slice it in front of the family or guests, for it forms a pretty mosaic pattern.*

Stuffing:
6 ounces (185 g) fresh
  Swiss chard or
  spinach, rinsed,
  dried, and coarsely
  chopped
1 large bunch parsley,
  minced
1 large onion, minced
1 clove garlic, minced
10 ounces (310 g) pork
  sausage meat
1 egg
1 slice white bread,
  soaked in 2
  tablespoons milk
Salt and freshly ground
  black pepper

1 cabbage
Salt and freshly ground
  black pepper to taste
6 ounces (185 g)
  prunes, pitted
1 cup (250 ml) dry
  white wine
1 quart (1 liter) meat or
  poultry stock
6 ounces (185 g) slab
  bacon, rind
  removed, cut into
  bite-sized pieces

1. Preheat the oven to 475°F (245°C).

2. In a large bowl, combine the stuffing ingredients and mix until well blended. Season to taste.

3. Bring a large pot of water to boil. Separate the leaves of the cabbage and blanch them in the boiling water for 5 minutes. Rinse under cold water until cool, then drain.

4. Lay a dampened 24 x 24-inch (60 x 60-cm) piece of cheesecloth on a work surface. "Reconstruct" the cabbage, beginning with the largest leaves, arranging the leaves so the outer side, where the rib is most prominent, is on the inside. Season each layer with salt and pepper. Continue until all the leaves have been used.

5. Form the stuffing into a ball, pushing 4 pitted prunes into the center. Place the ball of stuffing in the center of the cabbage and bring the leaves up to envelop the stuffing. Bring the cheesecloth up around the rounded cabbage and tie securely. Place the cabbage in a deep baking dish. Add the remaining prunes and the wine, season to taste, and cover with the stock.

6. Bake for 1½ to 2 hours. Just before serving, sauté the slab bacon in a small skillet until very crisp. Unwrap the cabbage and place on a serving platter. Garnish with the prunes and grilled bacon. Cut into wedge-shaped pieces and serve immediately.

Yield: 4 to 6 servings.

L'AMBROISIE

9 Place des Vosges, Paris 4.
(42.78.51.45 and
42.78.50.99).
Métros: Saint-Paul or
Chemin-Vert.
Last orders taken at 2:15 P.M.
and 10:15 P.M.
Closed Sunday, Monday
lunch, three weeks in
August, and one week in
February.
Credit cards: AE, V.
Private dining room for 12
to 14.
Air-conditioned.
English spoken.
255-franc lunch menu, 450-
franc tasting menu. A la
carte, 550 francs.

SPECIALTIES:
*Seasonal: feuilleté de truffes (fresh
truffles in puff pastry), mid-
December to mid-March; dariole
de foie gras aux morilles (terrine of
foie gras and morel mushrooms),
mid-March to mid-May; bar à
l'huile parfumée (striped bass in
seasoned oil).*

Throughout his career, chef Bernard Pacaud has lived by three commonsense rules: Keep the restaurant small, keep the menu simple, make sure the food is fresh. These rules managed to make his nine-table Left Bank restaurant one of the most popular in Paris. After a three-year search for better quarters, Bernard and his wife, Danièle, reopened in December 1986, transforming an old silver-smith's shop under the romantic arcades of the Place des Vosges. While the old L'Ambroisie was a cool, contemporary study in gray, black, and white, the new establishment glows with an antique, upper-class French charm. The food, thank good-ness, has changed little: Diners can still be assured of finding his ethereal, smooth red pepper mousse set in a pool of fresh tomato *coulis* (see recipe, page 33); his ray fish set on a bed of wilted but still crunchy white cabbage, and showered with slivered raw scallions; and feather-light puff pastry desserts with seasonal variations. Some new creations not to miss: warm oysters bathed in a briny butter sauce and sprinkled with matchsticks of crisp, tender vegetables; plump and juicy Breton scallops served with a spare, saffron-flecked butter sauce; huge chunks of rare and gamey wild duck pressed, with foie gras, into a vibrantly flavored terrine; and fresh *langoustines,* broiled quickly and bathed in a touch of tarragon butter.

L'AMI LOUIS

32 Rue du Vertbois, Paris 3.
(48.87.77.48).
Métro: Temple.
Last orders taken at 2 P.M.
and 10 P.M.
Closed Monday, Tuesday,
and August.
Credit cards: AE, DC, V.
450 to 600 francs.

SPECIALTIES:
*Bistro: foie gras; roast chicken;
frog's legs; coquilles Saint-Jacques
(scallops sautéed with garlic and
tomatoes), from October to April
only; gibier (game), from October
to February.*

The great Antoine Magnin is gone, after giving more than five decades of his life to one of Paris's favored bistros. New owners promise to change nothing but the light bulbs, and only time will tell if L'Ami Louis will continue to attract its varied clientele, a mix of savvy working-class locals and international elite. This dilapidated bistro re-mains one of my favorite eating spots in all of Paris, the place to come with an appetite as well as good friends. I have to admit that over the years, the quality of the cuisine has not remained at the highest of levels (the foie gras, for instance, seems to have its ups and downs), but I am never disap-pointed by the superb roast chicken (note that you have to be two!), the *pommes allumettes* (tiny shoe-string potatoes), the thick potato cake showered

L'Ami Louis.

with garlic and parsley, or the seasonal *coquilles Saint-Jacques,* reeking of garlic and brightened by a tiny *tomate à la provençale,* all treasures that cause eyes to open wide as they come sizzling from the cramped, copper-filled kitchen.

Whoever it was that said snails are simply a vehicle for butter and garlic never tasted the snails at L'Ami Louis. Here you'll find some of the biggest, most flavorful *escargots* in Paris. The snails are earthy, not rubbery, and they're allowed to hold their own, not being camouflaged by an overdose of garlic, parsley, and butter. The chefs here excel at roasting, and fall or winter is the time to come for the simple roast pheasant, partridge, or wild duck, all cooked in an ancient wood-fired oven. Best forgotten are the thin and greasy *côtes de mouton,* or mutton chops; the tasteless *baguettes;* and dessert, which you won't have room for anyway. So order up a bottle of their Fleurie, and enjoy.

ASTIER
44 Rue Jean-Pierre
  Timbaud, Paris 11.
(43.57.16.35).
Métro: Parmetier or
  République.
Last orders taken at 1:30 P.M.
  and 9 P.M.
Closed Saturday, Sunday, and
  August.
Credit card: V.
Some English spoken.
Universal 98-franc menu.
  About 125 francs per
  person, including wine.

Michel Picquart's restaurant is filled with charm, vitality, and what the French call *qualité-prix.* In other words, it's a bargain. Situated on a dreary side street off the Place de la République, this 1930s-style bistro is filled day and night with neighborhood regulars. People come in pairs, in groups, in families, to feast on chef Picquart's bargain 98-franc menu, which includes a remarkable cheese tray and better-than-average desserts. For starters try the generous *salade de gésiers,* a mound of greens mingled with soft, chewy preserved duck gizzards; or a platter of the freshest, tiny fried sole, simply garnished with a wedge of

SPECIALTIES:

Bistro: terrine de foies de volaille (chicken liver terrine), filets de harengs pommes à l'huile (salad of cured herring and potatoes bathed in oil), lapin à la moutarde (rabbit with mustard sauce). Chinon by the carafe.

lemon. But my favorite dish of all is his state-of-the-art *lapin à la moutarde,* featuring incredibly moist rabbit bathed in a rich and creamy sauce with just the right dose of mustard. Desserts here include a rich bitter-chocolate cake and pears in red wine, a dish marred only by an excess of sugar in the wine-infused syrup.

MOUSSE DE POIVRONS DOUX AU COULIS DE TOMATES
RED PEPPER PUREE WITH FRESH TOMATO SAUCE

This is one of the specialties at L'Ambroisie (see entry, page 31). Chef Bernard Pacaud created the sublime red pepper mousse when he worked at Paris's Vivarois restaurant, then added the dish to his small but imaginative menu when he opened L'Ambroisie in 1981. There are no tricks to this recipe; just be certain that the red peppers are cooked to a thick paste and that the cream and whipping utensils are very cold.

Mousse:
4 red bell peppers
Pinch of salt
½ cup (125 ml) *crème fraîche* (see recipe, page 237) or heavy cream, preferably not ultra-pasteurized

Tomato Sauce:
4 medium tomatoes
½ teaspoon salt
½ teaspoon sugar
½ teaspoon sherry wine vinegar

1. Preheat the broiler with the rack about 2 inches (5 cm) from the heat, then broil the whole peppers for approximately 10 minutes, turning them as their skins blister and turn black. Remove the peppers from the broiler, and when they are cool enough to handle, peel and seed them.

2. Purée the peppers in a food processor until smooth. For an extra-fine purée, force it through a fine-mesh sieve.

3. In a small saucepan over medium heat, cook the purée with the salt until it is very thick. Transfer to a bowl, cover, and chill.

4. Put a whisk or electric beaters and a mixing bowl in the freezer for at least 1 hour, so they will be very cold and will whip the cream very stiff.

5. Meanwhile, prepare the sauce: Peel, seed, and core the tomatoes and chop them very fine. Season with the salt, sugar, and vinegar, place in a fine stainless-steel strainer that is resting in a bowl, and drain in the refrigerator for at least 1 hour.

6. To assemble the mousse, whip the *crème fraîche* or heavy cream until very stiff, and carefully fold in the cold pepper purée.

7. To serve, place a scoop of the mousse in the center of a plate and surround with the tomato sauce.

Yield: 4 servings.

BENOIT
20 Rue Saint-Martin,
    Paris 4.
(42.72.25.76).
Métro: Châtelet.
Last orders taken at 2 P.M.
    and 10 P.M.
Closed Saturday, Sunday, and
    August.
No credit cards.
Sidewalk terrace.
Private dining room for 18.
Air-conditioned.
English spoken.
280 to 330 francs.

SPECIALTIES:
Bistro: salade de confit de canard
(salad of cabbage and preserved
duck), coquilles Saint-Jacques
maison (sauté of scallops, butter,
and shallots), blanquette de veau
à l'ancienne (sauté of veal, cream,
mushrooms, and onions).
Excellent, well-priced wine list.

Owner Michel Petit continues to run one of the city's best high-class bistros, always making an effort to please and to satisfy. Over the years, Benoit has remained one of my standbys, the place I go to for a superb *boeuf mode* (braised beef with carrots), a very imaginative *soupe de moules* (mussel soup flavored with smoked bacon), fabulous game and wild mushrooms during the winter months, and cool, imaginative mixed salads during the warmer months. Benoit is a fresh, sparkling, plant-filled spot that's equally appealing at lunch and dinner, whether it's a business lunch, dinner for a crowd, or a romantic evening for two. The wine list offers some real bargains: Note their fine house Champagne, the good-buy Saumur-Champigny, and the incomparable Côtes-du-Rhône Château Fonsalette.

BOFINGER
5 Rue de la Bastille, Paris 4.
(42.72.87.82).
Métro: Bastille.
Last orders taken at 3 P.M.
    and 1 A.M.
Open daily.
Credit cards: AE, DC, V.
Sidewalk terrace in summer.
Private dining room for 25.
Air-conditioned (first floor
    only).
English spoken.
100- and 125-franc menus.
    A la carte, 170 to 190
    francs.

SPECIALTIES:
Brasserie: fruits de mer (fresh
shellfish), soupe à l'oignon
gratinée (gratinéed onion soup),
choucroute (sauerkraut, pork, and
sausages). Beer on tap, wines by
the carafe.

One of the prettiest brasseries in Paris, festive and classy, with attentive service and a varied menu. Try the famous *choucroute* (sauerkraut served with *boudin noir,* or blood sausage, spicy pork sausage, and excellent frankfurters) or the always-fresh platter of fish and shellfish. The house Riesling is just fine. Forget most of the other fare, which tends to be overreaching. And don't feel insulted if they send you upstairs. The first-floor dining room is lively, and thoroughly Alsatian in decor.

CROUTES AUX MORILLES MADAME CARTET
MADAME CARTET'S MORELS AND COMTE CHEESE ON GRILLED TOAST

When I first moved to Paris, friends took me to Madame Cartet's minuscule restaurant near the Place de la République (see entry, following page), where I first learned to love the cooking of her native Bourg-en-Bresse, northeast of Lyons. There, wild morel mushrooms were once abundant, and families would serve up hearty portions of fresh mushrooms cooked in cream, then grilled on fresh country bread. I've embellished Madame Cartet's recipe a bit, combining fresh and dried mushrooms and adding a touch of rich cow's-milk cheese from the Jura, an authentic, well-aged Comté. This recipe can serve as a main course luncheon dish, or as an introduction to a wintertime dinner. Serve it with a fruity red wine.

1 ounce (30 g) dried
   morels
3 ounces (90 g) fresh
   mushrooms, washed
   and thinly sliced
½ cup (125 ml) *crème
   fraîche* (see page 237)
   or sour cream
8 slices whole-wheat
   bread
4 ounces (125 g)
   Comté, or Gruyère,
   finely grated
Salt and freshly ground
   black pepper to taste
Small handful of fresh
   chives, minced

1. Combine the morels with 2 cups (500 ml) of water in a medium-size saucepan. Bring to a boil over high heat, then allow to cook away vigorously, uncovered, until the liquid is reduced by half. This should take about 20 minutes. Strain the liquid through dampened cheesecloth. Rinse the morels, return them to the strained liquid, and reserve.

2. Preheat the broiler.

3. Combine the morels and their liquid, the fresh mushrooms, and the *crème fraîche* in a medium-size saucepan, and cook over medium heat until about half the liquid has been absorbed. The mixture should be fairly thick and creamy, and not too dry.

4. Toast the bread on both sides under the broiler.

5. Add the cheese to the mushroom mixture and cook, stirring constantly, just until the cheese has melted and is incorporated into the mixture. Season with salt and pepper.

6. Spread a generous portion of the mushroom and cheese mixture onto each piece of toast, sprinkle liberally with chives, and broil just until hot and bubbling. Serve immediately.

Yield: 8 servings.

CARTET
62 Rue de Malte, Paris 11.
(48.05.17.65).
Métro: République.
Last orders taken at 1:30 P.M.
    and 9 P.M.
Closed Saturday, Sunday, and
    August.
No credit cards.
English menu.
250 francs.

SPECIALTIES:
Lyonnais bistro: choix de
charcuteries maison (choice of
homemade charcuterie, including
parsleyed ham, headcheese, and
chicken liver terrine), soufflé de
tourteaux (crabmeat soufflé), boeuf
à la ficelle (boiled beef and
vegetables), saucisson chaud de
Lyon (warm pork sausage from
Lyon). White Savoie wines.

Madame Cartet no longer holds court here, urging, coaxing the handful of diners who, since 1932, have filled her minuscule six-table restaurant. But her replacement, the unflappable Marie-Thérèse, and her husband, Raymond Nouaille, have tried to keep things as they were. They've succeeded about as well as anyone might: The decor is still 1930s, with green plastic banquettes full of cigarette holes and wooden walls covered with mirrors and dime-store paintings. People still flock here for *la grande bouffe,* filling up on dishes that don't stop coming until you waddle out the door. Sample the *brandade de morue,* a silken purée of salt cod, garlic, and olive oil, smooth as mashed potatoes and even more filling, and the *gigot d'agneaux aux herbes de Provence,* a pink, soft, and fragrant leg of lamb accompanied by a casserole of tiny dried *flageolets.* The *salade au lard* is a classic: crispy *frisée* (curly endive) with copious chunks of bacon and a perfectly pungent vinegary dressing. The *pâté de campagne* is simple and honest, the *terrine aux herbes de Provence* is one of the best I've ever tasted, and the *saucisson chaud de Lyon* is pure pork and large enough to feed an army. I'm not a fan of the famous *soufflé de tourteau,* a crabmeat soufflé that is often limp, deflated, and bitter. The bread is dreadful and the desserts—with the exception of the superb lemon tart—are more copious than satisfying. But I go anyway, and I eat.

CHARDENOUX
1 Rue Jules-Vallès, Paris 11.
(43.71.49.52).
Métro: Charonne.
Last orders taken at 2:30 P.M.
    and 11 P.M.
Closed Saturday lunch,
    Sunday, and August.
Credit cards: AE, V.
Sidewalk terrace.
Private dining room for 20.
English spoken.
120-franc menu, lunch only.
    A la carte, 180.

Although this beautiful 1900s neighborhood bistro has seen numerous changes over the years, it seems best suited to its current role, that of a traditional Parisian bistro. Behind the etched glass windows, beyond the undulating zinc bar, beneath the Belle Epoque lamps, guests feast on lusty, well-conceived bistro fare. The menu is small but varied, allowing for plenty of choice. Best dishes sampled during our last visit included the classic salad of Roquefort, walnuts, and Belgian endive; a well-seasoned *boudin* blood sausage surrounded by generous portions of sautéed apples and crusty potato gratin, and a beautiful serving of salmon, cooked quickly, skin side only, and surrounded by spinach and a fine watercress purée.

SPECIALTIES:
Bistro: salade roquefort, noix et
endives (Belgian endive,
Roquefort, and walnut salad);
boudin noir aux deux pommes
(blood sausage with sautéed apples
and potatoes); confit de canard,
pommes Anna (preserved duck
with golden potato cake); saumon
à l'unilatéral (salmon fillet
sautéed on one side).

Desserts are rich and plentiful, and include a soul-satisfying *cerises à la savoyarde* (rich vanilla ice cream surrounded by warmed sweet cherries) and a marvelous caramel ice cream with caramel sauce, sure to win the hearts of any caramel-lover. Service is a bit casual, but swift and friendly, and their well-priced luncheon menu—which allows diners a large choice of items from the regular menu—is an idea other restaurateurs should follow. The wine list is short (and almost totally illegible) but offers some decent buys, including Alphonse Mellot's white and red Sancerre; the always agreeable Loire Valley red, Saumur Champigny, Roches Neuves; and numerous vintages of the solid, crimson-hued Cahors, Château de Haute Serre.

LA GALOCHE
D'AURILLAC
41 Rue de Lappe, Paris 11.
(47.00.77.15).
Métro: Ledru-Rollin.
Last orders taken at 2:30 P.M.
and 10:30 P.M.
Closed Sunday, Monday, and
the last week in July
through the first week in
September.
No credit cards.
Wine, *charcuterie,* and
cheese may be purchased
to take home.
150 to 300 francs.

SPECIALTIES:
Auvergnat: charcuterie, pounti,
dried-bean salads, confits
(preserved meats), viandes rouges
(red meat), potée du Cantal (pork,
cabbage, and white bean stew),
Auvergnat cheeses.

As the neighborhood becomes more and more trendy, the Rue de Lappe has lost some of its funky charm, but this Auvergnat hangout remains as authentic as ever. All the earthy peasant dishes of south central France find their way to the table here, including the rustic *pounti* (a meat loaf that blends meats, Swiss chard, eggs, and prunes), the hearty *potée,* and the marvelous huge country loaves, shipped in direct several times a week.

A good meal always deserves a bit
of concentration.

BRASSERIE DE L'ILE SAINT-LOUIS

55 Quai de Bourbon,
Paris 4.
(43.54.02.59).
Métro: Pont-Marie.
Continuous service, noon to
1 A.M.
Closed Wednesday,
Thursday lunch,
February school
vacation, and August.
No credit cards.
English spoken.
80 to 130 francs.

SPECIALTIES:
*Alsatian brasserie: choucroute
(sauerkraut, pork, and sausages),
jarret de porc aux lentilles (pork
knuckle with lentils), omelettes,
munster au cumin (Alsatian
munster cheese with cumin seeds),
Berthillon sorbet.*

This lively, always crowded brasserie serves as the neighborhood gathering spot for all of Ile Saint-Louis. Go with the entire family on a Sunday afternoon after visiting Notre-Dame, sit down at one of the long communal tables, and order the sauerkraut and sausages, a mug of beer, and a slice of Alsatian Munster. You won't dine like a king, but you won't spend a fortune, either.

CHEZ JENNY

39 Boulevard du Temple,
Paris 3.
(42.74.75.75).
Métro: République.
Continuous service,
11:30 A.M. to 1 A.M.
Open daily.
Credit cards: DC, V.
Sidewalk terrace in summer.
Private dining room for 12
to 20.
English spoken.
84-franc menu. A la carte,
100 to 180 francs.

SPECIALTIES:
*Alsatian, brasserie: fruits de mer
toute l'année (fresh shellfish year-
round), choucroute (sauerkraut,
pork, and sausages), presskopf
(Alsatian headcheese), leberwurst
(pork liver sausage), grillades au
feu de bois (meats grilled over an
open fire). Alsatian wines.*

This huge Alsatian brasserie just off Place de la République may not serve the best *choucroute* in town, but it is certainly in the running for first place. From the outside, Chez Jenny looks like any ordinary brasserie, but step inside the gigantic wood-paneled dining room and you'll instantly be transported to Alsace, land of chilled white Riesling, pork, and *choucroute*. Matronly waitresses dressed in regional costumes serve the hearty fare off of giant copper platters, and they're swift, open, and friendly. Perhaps best of all, you can dine well here for less than 100 francs a person, selecting the copious *choucroute paysanne* (which includes grilled expertly cured slab bacon, well-seasoned bratwurst, frankfurters, and fresh *palette* of pork; see recipe, facing page), washed down with a dependable house Riesling. Other specialties, all moderately priced, include grilled saddle of lamb, *coq au vin*, and a hefty *jarret de porc*, or pork knuckle, garnished with sauerkraut. Forget about the waterlogged, tasteless *choucroute aux trois boudins de poisson*, a bizarre trio of fish sausages served with sauerkraut.

CHOUCROUTE CHEZ JENNY
CHEZ JENNY'S SAUERKRAUT, SAUSAGES, AND BACON

I've yet to find better choucroute *in Paris than the variation served at Chez Jenny, a giant Alsatian brasserie (see entry, facing page). Here the hearty platters of sauerkraut, sausages, bacon, and potatoes arrive in perfect order: The sauerkraut is ultimately digestible (not too bland, acidic, fatty, or greasy), and it is neither dried out from overcooking nor swimming in watery juices, as is too often the case. The sausages are first-rate, and fresh, and the crisply grilled slab bacon is a wonderful touch. You know the platter is at its best when it complements, as well as compliments, chilled Alsatian Riesling. Here is a home version of Chez Jenny's house specialty.*

3 pounds (1 kg, 500 g)
sauerkraut,
preferably fresh bulk
sauerkraut, not
canned

3 tablespoons lard or
goose or chicken fat

2 onions, coarsely
chopped

2 cups (500 ml)
Riesling wine

1 cup (250 ml) fresh
chicken stock or
water

2 pounds (1 kg) pork
chops

Freshly ground black
pepper to taste

2 cloves

6 juniper berries

2 bay leaves

2 cloves garlic

6 knackwurst

6 fresh German
frankfurters

1 pound (500 g)
smoked pork sausage
such as Polish
kielbasa

2 pounds (1 kg) new
potatoes

1 pound (500 g) slab
bacon, cut into large
chunks

1. Preheat the oven to 350°F (175°C).

2. Rinse the sauerkraut in a colander under cold running water. If it is very acidic or very salty, repeat several times. Drain well.

3. In a large casserole over low heat, melt the fat and add the onions. Sauté until the onions are wilted, then add the wine and stock or water.

4. Add the pork chops. Cover with the sauerkraut. Add the pepper, cloves, juniper berries, bay leaves, and garlic. Cover, and bake in the oven for 1 to 1½ hours.

5. In separate saucepans cook each variety of sausage in gently simmering water for about 20 minutes. Do not allow the water to boil or the sausages will burst. Drain all the sausages, slice the kielbasa, and keep all warm until serving time.

6. Meanwhile, steam or boil the potatoes. Allow them to cool just enough to handle, then peel. Keep warm.

7. Just before serving, grill the slab bacon until very crisp.

8. To serve, drain the sauerkraut (removing the herbs and spices) and mound it in the center of a large heated platter. Surround the sauerkraut with the pork chops, the sausages, including the sliced kielbasa, the potatoes, and the grilled bacon. Serve with several kinds of mustard and plenty of chilled white Riesling wine.

Yield: 8 to 10 servings.

CHEZ PHILIPPE
(Auberge Pyrénées-
    Cevennes)
106 Rue de la Folie-
    Méricourt, Paris 11.
(43.57.33.78).
Métro: République.
Last orders taken at 2:30 P.M.
    and 10 P.M.
Closed Saturday, Sunday, and
    August.
No credit cards.
Air-conditioned.
English spoken.
230 francs.

SPECIALTIES:
Burgundian, bistro: foie gras de
canard au naturel (duck foie
gras), cassoulet d'oie toulousain
(stew of beans and preserved
goose), entrecôte poêlée à la moelle
(pan-fried steak with bone
marrow).

Auberge Pyrénées-Cévennes, or more simply, Chez Philippe, is so unpretentious from the outside that one is tempted to go no farther than the front door. But give it a chance. Inside you'll find a quiet, private Parisian world, filled with French journalists, businessmen, and neighborhood regulars. It's a world where people come to eat well and eat a lot.

The stone walls, shining beamed ceilings, red tile floors, and crisp white linens all make for cozy surroundings, and the menu includes both the hearty Gascon food of the southwest and the more spicy, peppered foods of the Basque region of the Pyrénées, bordering Spain. Order *crudités* (raw vegetables), and the outgoing Burgundian owner, Philippe Serbource, will frown, saying "that sounds awfully sad," then bring along a gigantic salad of carrots, tomatoes, lettuce, and cucumbers in a big white terrine. What he really wants you to order—and swoon over—is the rich and silky foie gras (they make it fresh every day), the *cochonnailles du pays,* huge baskets of country sausages (eat as much as you like), and the *cassoulet d'oie toulousain,* an authentic combination of sausage, goose, pork, and white beans. Equally good are the fresh grilled *rougets,* or mullet, served with anchovy butter. Mr. Serbource does all the marketing and selects the wines himself: There's a small but good selection of wines representing all the major regions of France.

A SOUSCEYRAC
35 Rue Faidherbe, Paris 11.
(43.71.65.30).
Métro: Faidherbe-Chaligny.
Last orders taken at 2 P.M.
    and 10 P.M.
Closed Saturday, Sunday, and
    August.
Credit cards: AE, V.
Terrace dining.
Air-conditioned.
English spoken.
250 to 300 francs.

If you're looking for a real, honest, neighborhood restaurant full of faithful Parisian diners, this is it. Situated in the out-of-the-way 11th *arrondissement,* the home of cabinetmakers and artisans, A Sousceyrac is a typical, traditional bistro where the chef-owner—Gabriel Asfaux—tends to the marketing and wine buying, and keeps careful tabs on the dining room to be sure everyone's satisfied. The old-fashioned mimeographed menu tips you off right away: You're in the land of plenty. Plenty of fresh *foie gras,* plenty of sturdy pistachio-studded *saucisson chaud.* If you love game, do come on a Friday night in the fall to sample their famous *lièvre à la royale,* a mahogany-hued wild hare stew that is long on execution and, when properly prepared, a

SPECIALTIES:
*Bistro: foie gras; saucisson chaud
pistaché sauce crème et morilles
(warm pistachio-studded pork
sausage in a sauce of cream and
wild morel mushrooms); lièvre à
la royale (wild hare stew), served
Fridays only, October 8 to mid-
December.*

unique gastronomic experience. The hare is marinated for at least ten hours in a heady blend of red wine, shallots, onions, carrots, cinnamon, and herbs, stewed for hours, and finally compacted into a coarse, chunky, pâté-like roll filled with both *foie gras* and truffles. All this makes for a dark, dense, and gamey dish that, one must admit, is not to everyone's taste. The small wine list offers some exceptional buys.

LA TCHAIKA
7 Rue de Lappe, Paris 11.
(47.00.73.61).
Métro: Bastille.
Last orders taken at 2:30 P.M.
and 10:30 P.M.
Closed Saturday lunch,
Sunday, and mid-July to
mid-August.
Credit card: V.
English spoken.
Pastries may be purchased
to take home.
150 francs.

SPECIALTIES:
*Russian: vodka, borscht (beet and
cabbage soup), zakouskis (Russian
appetizers), gâteau au chocolat
(chocolate cake).*

This is the offspring of the Tchaïka on Rue de l'Eperon (see page 56), the tea salon that grew into a pleasant, cozy restaurant. Both restaurants offer the very same fare, including superb platters of assorted herring, a rich and soothing borscht (see recipe, page 57), as well as one of the best chocolate cakes (see recipe, page 90) in the city. Also try their light cheesecake, better known as *vatrouchka*. I prefer the atmosphere on Rue de l'Eperon—it's warmer and calmer—but this is a nice place to know about if you're looking for an inexpensive meal near the Bastille.

LE TRUMILOU
84 Quai de l'Hôtel-de-Ville,
Paris 4.
(42.77.63.98).
Métros: Hôtel-de-Ville or
Pont-Marie.
Last orders taken at 2:45 P.M.
and 10:45 P.M.
Closed Monday and
Christmas Eve.
Credit card: V.
Some English spoken.
50-, 65-, and 120-franc
menus. A la carte, about
150 francs.

SPECIALTIES:
*Salade frisée aux lardons (curly
endive salad with bacon), gigot
aux haricots (leg of lamb with
white beans), moules marinière
(steamed mussels).*

You can't get much cheaper, or more authentic, than this. Throw in a window table with a view of the Seine and Notre-Dame, and you're in business. Don't come to Le Trumilou if you're expecting crisp linens, polished silver, sophisticated decor, or frills, but you're likely to walk out the door with a satisfied palate and a pocket full of change. Our last lunch here included a fine *poulet à la provençale* (a huge portion of chicken bathed in tomato sauce), generous helpings of mussels, a curly endive salad that came to the table topped with still-sizzling bacon, and enough lamb with white beans to feed an army, in any language!

> "*Lunch as though you shall not eat dinner, dine as though you have not eaten lunch.*"—Code Gourmand, 1827

OYSTERS

He was, indeed, a brave man who first ate an oyster. But from the moment that intrepid gentleman slid it down his throat, this pale, glistening, meaty shellfish was destined for stardom, and one can be certain that Frenchmen eagerly shouldered their gastronomic responsibilities.

Up until the 1850s oysters were so plentiful in Paris they were considered poor man's food, even though the journey from the Brittany shores to Paris was never a simple one. Oysters traveled in wooden carts laden with ice, and as it melted it was regularly replenished at ice houses set along the route.

During the 18th century, oyster criers filled the streets of Paris, carrying wicker hampers on their backs filled with their inexpensive fare. Although the colorful hawkers are gone, today France remains a major oyster producer—cultivating some 1,400 tons of precious shallow, round, flat-shelled Belon-style *plates* oysters and more than 81,000 tons of deep, elongated, crinkle-shelled *creuses* oysters. From Cherbourg in the north to Toulon along the Mediterranean, French fishermen in high rubber boots and thick blue jerseys carry out their battle with nature. Each oyster is nursed from infancy to maturity, a labor of three to four years.

Baby oyster larvae begin life floating in the sea with plankton, searching about for something to grip onto. Their survival rate is low: Out of a batch of 100,000 larvae, only a dozen survive.

Six to seven months later the larvae have grown to spats—now about the size of a fingernail—and are detached and moved along to another *parc* (oyster bed) where they remain from 1 to 2½ years.

Then, the flat-shelled *plates* are often dispatched to river estuaries, where the shallow, warmish blend of salt and fresh water helps them develop their distinctly sweet, creamy flavor.

The more common, crinkle-shelled *creuses*—which grow twice as fast as the *plates*—might be transferred several times before they swing into their final stage of development. They spend the last few months of their lives in swampy, shallow, slightly alkaline fattening beds known as *claires*, where they pick up their unusual green tinge by feasting on certain flourishing microscopic blue algae. The longer the oysters remain in the fattening beds, the greener, more richly flavored, and more valuable they become.

Just before oysters are ready for the market, they spend a few days being purified in reservoirs. There they are dipped in and out of water so they learn to keep their shells shut. As long as the oyster remains chilled and the shell stays closed during transport, the oyster can survive on its own store of saline solution. Once out of the water, it will easily stay alive for eight days in winter, two days in warmer summer months.

Oysters are generally available in a number of sizes. The larger are more expensive, though not necessarily better. They are best eaten raw, on the half shell from a bed of crushed ice, without lemon or vinegar. They need no further embellishment than a glass of Muscadet or Sancerre and a slice of buttered rye bread.

Plates: The two most popular types of flat French oyster are the prized *Belon*, a small, elegant oyster that is slightly salty, faintly oily, with a hint of hazelnut; and the fringy, green tinged *Marennes. Plates* are calibrated according to their weight; the smallest, and least expensive, no. 5, offers about 1 ounce (30 grams) of meat, while the largest, and most expensive, no. 0000, called the *pied de cheval*, or horse's hoof, about 3 ounces (100 grams).

Creuses: France's most common oyster—deep, elongated and crinkle-shelled. The *creuse* is sometimes called the *Portugaise*, even though this variety of oyster was essentially replaced by the *Japonaise* after the Portuguese oyster was struck by a gill disease in 1967.

The three common subcategories of *creuse* relate to the method of final aging, or fattening. The smallest are the *huîtres de parc*; the medium-size is known as *fines de claires*, oysters that have spent about two months aging in the fattening beds or *claires*, with forty to fifty oysters to the square meter; and the *spéciales*, the largest, aged in fattening beds for up to six months, just three to five oysters to the square meter.

Creuses are calibrated according to weight, from the smallest, and least expensive, *petite*, which weighs a bit over 1 ounce (50 grams), to the largest, and most expensive *très grosse*, about 3 ounces (100 grams).

LATIN QUARTER, LUXEMBOURG, SEVRES-BABYLONE

5th and 6th arrondissements

ALLARD
41 Rue Saint-André-des-
Arts, Paris 6.
(43.26.48.23).
Métros: Saint-Michel or
Odéon.
Last orders taken at 1:45 P.M.
and 9:45 P.M.
Closed Saturday, Sunday,
August, and Christmas
week.
Credit cards: AE, DC, EC, V.
Air-conditioned.
English spoken.
280 to 300 francs.

SPECIALTIES:
*Bistro: plats du jour (changing
daily specials), terrine maison
(homemade pork terrine), gibier
(wild game) from September to
January, coquilles Saint-Jacques
(scallops) from October to May,
canard aux olives (duck with
olives) in May and June, cèpes
(wild mushrooms) in September.*

S aying something negative about the popular Left
Bank Allard is akin to attacking motherhood
and world peace. This landmark Parisian bistro was
sold several years ago, although Fernande Allard
still comes by from time to time to help out the
current owner, Bernard Bouchard. The classic bistro menu promises all the traditional specialties,
and the two little dining rooms appear as homey as
ever. In essence, nothing has changed. Or has it?
Our last meal offered some nice familiar notes, but
certainly no real symphony. The rubbery *jambon
persillé* (parsleyed ham) lacked flavor and character,
the lukewarm *petit salé aux haricots rouges* (salt-cured
pork with kidney beans) seemed tired and bland,
and the chocolate cake with *crème anglaise* turned
out to be simply indigestible. And barely a word of
French could be heard in the room. The evening
was saved by a copious salad of dandelion greens, a
serviceable platter of lamb with white beans, and
the plump, sizzling *escargots,* which were just as one
remembers. Service, though hurried, arrived with a
smile, and I left with the feeling that I'd remain a
faithful, if somewhat doubtful, regular.

BRASSERIE BALZAR
49 Rue des Ecoles, Paris 5.
(43.54.13.67).
Métro: Cardinal-Lemoine.
Continuous service noon to
12:30 A.M. Open daily.
Closed August and
Christmas week.
Credit card: V.
English spoken.
180 francs.

SPECIALTIES:
*Brasserie: choucroute (sauerkraut
and sausages), pied de porc pané
(breaded pig's foot), foie de veau
(calf's liver).*

B right lights, a great mix of people, rapid service, and a place that serves non-stop, from
noon to on past midnight—who could ask for
more? Add the Left Bank location and you've got it
made. Brasserie Balzar, which is really more bistro-
size, is a fine, democratic spot to try out any time of
day, when you find yourself craving a platter of
choucroute, a dozen briny oysters, a fine roast
chicken, or a platter of *frites.* The fish offerings are
less appealing (the *raie au beurre noir,* or ray fish in
black butter, arrived drowning in butter), and desserts are nothing special. With the meal, sample the
Saumur-Champigny, a well-priced Loire Valley red.
At night they add the traditional gratinéed onion
soup, one of the better versions in town.

LAPIN A LA MOUTARDE
RABBIT WITH MUSTARD

Rabbit with mustard sauce is a classic bistro dish, and a year-round favorite. Traditionally, lapin à la moutarde *is served with rice, but I love it with fresh homemade pasta, which absorbs the wonderfully delicious sauce. Do use top-quality French whole-grain mustard; fresh, not frozen, rabbit; and a solid, full-bodied white wine. An Alsatian Riesling is an excellent wine for this dish, but I've also prepared it with Gewürztraminer, as well as with a white Hermitage. You can also experiment by adding various herbs to the sauce just before serving: Fresh rosemary, summer savory, or thyme would be lovely. If you can't find fresh rabbit, chicken makes an excellent substitute.*

⅓ cup (80 ml) peanut oil
1 tablespoon (½ oz; 15 g) unsalted butter
1 fresh rabbit (or chicken), 2½ to 3 pounds (1.25 to 1.5 kg), cut into serving pieces
½ cup (125 ml) whole-grain mustard
3 cups (750 ml) dry white wine
1 cup (250 ml) *crème fraîche* (see recipe, page 237) or sour cream
Salt to taste
1 small handful minced fresh parsley

1. Preheat the oven to 350°F (175°C).

2. In a Dutch oven or large ovenproof skillet, heat the oil and butter over medium-high heat. When hot, quickly brown the rabbit. Do not crowd the pan, and turn the pieces, making sure that each is thoroughly browned. Discard the excess oil.

3. Brush the rabbit pieces evenly with mustard, reserving 3 tablespoons for the sauce. Place the rabbit in the oven, covered, and bake for 20 minutes. Pour the wine over the rabbit, making sure all pieces are moistened, and continue cooking, covered, another 25 minutes.

4. Remove from the oven, and reserving the cooking liquid, place the rabbit pieces on an ovenproof dish. Lower the oven heat to 200°F (90°C). Cover the rabbit with foil and keep warm in the very low oven.

5. Prepare the sauce: Over high heat reduce the reserved cooking liquid by half. This should take 8 to 10 minutes. Whisk in the *crème fraîche* or sour cream, the reserved mustard, and salt. Reduce the heat and continue cooking for 3 to 4 minutes.

6. To serve, arrange the rabbit pieces on a platter, and cover with the sauce. (Or fill a platter with fresh cooked pasta, toss with the sauce, and arrange the rabbit pieces on top of the pasta.) Sprinkle with the minced parsley.

Yield: 4 to 6 servings.

LA BONNE TABLE
DES FES

5 Rue Sainte-Beuve, Paris 6.
(45.48.07.22).
Métro: Vavin.
Open for dinner only; last
   orders taken at 12:15 A.M.
Closed Sunday, Monday, and
   August.
Credit card: V.
130 francs.

SPECIALTIES:
*Moroccan: couscous, pastilla des
fés (savory pigeon pastry), tajine
de mouton (mutton stew).*

Paris has scores of cafés and restaurants serving North African couscous, and this is one of the best. Open for dinner only, the brilliantly decorated Moroccan-style dining room doesn't really get going until 10:30 or so, when the *patron* races around taking orders, flirting with the customers, and generally inspiring a good time. Go with a group so you can sample a variety of dishes, including the spicy lamb sausage known as *merguez* and the heavenly *tajines,* or stews, one of mutton and pickled lemons, and another of chicken and plump prunes. Everything comes with unlimited servings of couscous, offered from a platter piled high with the fine, delicate, and tender grains of hand-rolled semolina that have been steamed over a savory broth. With the couscous comes the delicious broth, containing chick-peas and raisins, and with it, as much fiery *harissa* pepper sauce as your palate will tolerate. Formerly known as Aissa Fils, this popular restaurant is always crowded, lively, and noisy, as everyone gets happy on the heady Moroccan red wine.

LE CAMELEON

6 Rue de Chevreuse, Paris 6.
(43.20.63.43).
Métro: Vavin.
Last orders taken at 2 P.M.
   and 10:45 P.M.
Closed Sunday, Monday, and
   August.
No credit cards.
150 francs.

SPECIALTIES:
*Bistro: courgettes marinées au
citron (zucchini marinated in
lemon), tendron de veau aux pâtes
fraîches (veal stew with fresh
pasta), haddock à la ciboulette
(smoked haddock with chives),
mousse au chocolat blanc (white
chocolate mousse), soufflé glacé au
thé (tea-flavored frozen soufflé).*

This funky neighborhood bistro, just steps from the heart of Montparnasse, is one of my favorite finds of recent years. Although the menu includes the litany of standard bistro fare—steak, fries, and apple pie—it also offers many imaginative, surprising specialties. The food sparkles with freshness, and there's a wealth of salads, a concept I adore. There's a warm *salade de queue de boeuf,* a giant mound of perfectly moist, well-seasoned shredded oxtail set on a bed of curly endive and radicchio; as well as mixed salads topped with *lardons* and a poached egg, meltingly tender *gésiers,* or duck gizzards, or gently grilled *crottins,* or goat cheese. My favorite main course here is the *morue à la provençale,* a warm blend of salt cod and tomatoes, served with a super-garlicky *aïoli* and tender boiled tomatoes. And don't leave without trying their classic *tendrons de veau,* strips of tender veal served with fresh pasta. You don't come to Le Caméléon for the decor: The floral-patterned wallpaper with its deadening black background could give you a headache, and not a lot of thought seems to have gone into the rest of the decor, mostly castoffs from grandmother's attic. But to reject the restaurant on this basis would be to miss the point altogether. Madame Faucher is a warm, gentle hostess, and her husband, Raymond, seems to have it all under control in the kitchen. This is a place one could return to time and again, with an assurance of satisfaction.

AUX CHARPENTIERS
10 Rue Mabillon, Paris 6.
(43.26.30.05).
Métro: Mabillon.
Last orders taken at 3 P.M.
    and 11:30 P.M.
Closed Sunday, holidays, and
    Christmas week.
Credit cards: AE, DC, V.
Sidewalk terrace.
English spoken.
130 to 150 francs.

SPECIALTIES:
Bistro: plats du jour (changing daily specials), boeuf à la ficelle (boiled beef and vegetables), caneton rôti sauce olives et porto (roast duck in a sauce of olives and port wine).

An authentic bistro serving solid, uncomplicated food at reasonable prices. The restaurant takes its name and decor from the *compagnons charpentiers*—master carpenters and cabinetmakers whose organization stemmed from the medieval guilds. The museum that housed their work used to be next door and this was their hangout. The carpenters and the museum are gone, leaving a simple, friendly place to eat right across from the Saint-Germain market. Try the roast duck with olives, the stuffed cabbage, the pork with lentils, the fine roast chicken, and the delicious rabbit with mustard. If it is still on the wine list, be sure to sample the outstanding red from Provence, Domaine de Trévallon.

DODIN BOUFFANT
25 Rue Frédéric-Sauton,
    Paris 5.
(43.25.25.14).
Métro: Maubert-Mutualité.
Last orders taken at 2 P.M.
    and midnight.
Closed Sunday, August, and
    Christmas week.
Credit cards: DC, V.
Sidewalk terrace.
Air-conditioned.
English spoken.
155-franc menu, lunch only.
    A la carte, 300 francs.

SPECIALTIES:
Seasonal, fish: fruits de mer (fresh seafood platter), saumon fumé (house smoked salmon), fricassée de morue à la provençale (salt cod, onions, tomatoes, zucchini, and potatoes with fresh basil and parsley).

One could list numerous reasons to visit Dodin Bouffant: imaginative ways with fish, bargain prices on food and wine, and convenient late hours. The service is not always attentive (much of the time you feel as though they don't care that you are there), and the decor is definitely on the blah side. But keep fine, fresh fish in mind, and you should have a satisfying experience. For a lovely meal here, start with either the herring or the salmon, both of which are smoked for just a few hours each morning over shavings of *hêtre,* or beechwood. As chef Philippe Valin explains, this is not a smoke cure, but a smoke flavoring, so the fish remains moist and fresh-tasting, with just the subtlest smoke essence. Everything is made in house, including the delicious fresh noodles, which appear alongside numerous daily specials. The best dishes sampled on our last visit included the *bar à ligne au fenouil* (steamed bass set on a delicious Provençal-inspired bed of fennel, *crème fraîche,* tomatoes, basil, and chervil) and the ever-wonderful *fricassée de morue à la provençale* (see facing page). With the meal, sample Léon Beyer's Riesling, *cuvée des Ecaillers.*

LA GUEUZE
19 Rue Soufflot, Paris 5.
(43.54.63.00).
Métro: Luxembourg.
Continuous service, noon to 2 A.M.
Closed Sunday.
Credit card: V.
English spoken.
Beer may be purchased to take home.
A la carte, 100 francs.

SPECIALTIES:
Flemish: carbonnade flamande (beef stew with beer), lapin à la Gueuze (rabbit stew), waterzooï (poached chicken and vegetables with a béchamel sauce); 150 beers, 12 on tap.

For years I've called this the *"moules-frites* café," for it's *the* spot we like to gather with friends on a sunny Saturday afternoon to down giant bowls of steamed mussels, platters of sizzling fries, and plenty of hearty Belgian beer. This nondescript café, situated near the Luxembourg Gardens and down the street from the Panthéon, is a haven for beer lovers. Try the foamy Chimay, with its sweet apple aroma and strong herbal flavor; the distinctive Kriek Lambic, with its faint taste of cherries; and the deep reddish brown Abbey de Leffe Bière Luxe, with the aroma of pure barley malt and a 6.5 percent alcohol content that encourages you to stop after a single glass!

LA LOZERE
4 Rue Hautefeuille, Paris 6.
(43.54.26.64).
Métro: Saint-Michel.
Last orders taken at 2 P.M. and 10:30 P.M.
Closed Sunday, Monday, the last three weeks in August, and Christmas week.
No credit cards.
70- (lunch only), 86-, and 104-franc menus. A la carte, 150 francs.

SPECIALTIES:
Auvergnat: aligot (mashed potatoes with garlic and fresh curds of Cantal cheese), served Thursday only; saucisse d'herbes (herb-seasoned pork sausage); omelets; country hams; country bread.

La Lozère, half restaurant, half tourist office, represents the hearty cuisine of the Lozère region in central France. The decor is simple and rustic, and diners sit elbow-to-elbow at the five bare wooden tables, slicing their own bread from hefty loaves of *pain de campagne* that are brought straight from the region three times a week. (You can buy the same bread at the Produits d'Auvergne market at 32 Rue de Buci. It arrives there fresh on Tuesday, Thursday, and Saturday.) The clientele is a mix of young workers looking for a bargain and well-fed, old-time Parisians who bring their newspapers or invite their wives to feast on omelets, salty country cured ham *(jambon cru),* and filling meaty *plats du jour.* There is always soup, salad, and good regional cheese, such as the nutty, smooth-textured Cantal and the sharp, farm-ripened Bleu d'Auvergne. Good bets here are the *salade aux lardons et au Cantal* (wilted greens tossed with chunks of crispy bacon and Cantal; see page 50) and the daily specials. Note that *aligot,* Thursday's specialty, is popular with La Lozère patrons, so be sure to book a table at least a day ahead.

FRICASSEE DE MORUE A LA PROVENCALE DODIN BOUFFANT
DODIN BOUFFANT'S FRICASSEE OF SALT COD, TOMATOES, POTATOES, AND ONIONS

This is a vibrant, summer sort of dish from Dodin Bouffant (see entry, page 47) that virtually delivers the sun and the sea to the table. I love the abundance of fresh vegetables, the play of lively flavors, the crunch of the zucchini, and the soft soothing quality of the salt cod. Be sure to prepare this in a large quick-reacting skillet that will maintain high heat and let things really sauté, not get soggy. I like to use an old-fashioned thin black metal frying pan. With this dish, try a chilled rosé de Provence.

1 pound (500 g) salt cod
2 tablespoons extra-virgin olive oil
½ pound (250 g) onions, peeled and cut lengthwise into thin strips
½ pound (about 2 medium; 250 g) potatoes, peeled and thinly sliced
½ teaspoon fresh thyme, or ¼ teaspoon dried
½ pound (250 g) zucchini, cut into thin rounds
½ pound (about 3 medium; 250 g) tomatoes, cored, peeled, seeded, and coarsely chopped
1 tablespoon best-quality sherry wine vinegar
Small bunch fresh parsley leaves, minced

1. One day before preparing the *fricassée,* soak the salt cod in plenty of cold water, changing the water at least three or four times during the soaking period.

2. Cook the cod: Drain the cod and cover it with fresh water. Bring just to a simmer and immediately remove the pan from the heat. Cover, and let stand for 15 minutes. Drain, scrape off the fatty skin, and remove any bones. Cut or tear into bite-size pieces and set aside. The cod is now ready to use.

3. Heat the oil in a large skillet over medium-high heat. Add the onions and cook, stirring constantly, until soft, just 3 to 4 minutes. Add the potatoes and thyme and continue to sauté, keeping the vegetables in constant motion. Cook just until the potatoes begin to soften but are still crunchy. Add the zucchini and toss for about 2 more minutes, then the salt cod, tomatoes, and vinegar for an additional 2 minutes.

4. Serve immediately, showered with parsley. The dish is also delicious cold, and can be refrigerated for up to one day.

Yield: 4 to 6 servings.

SALADE AUX LARDONS ET AU CANTAL LA LOZERE
LA LOZERE'S WARM ENDIVE, BACON, AND CHEESE SALAD

I love this wonderfully hearty and tangy warm winter salad. It makes for a perfect Saturday lunch, especially when served with freshly grilled country bread and a glass of Beaujolais. The rich and rustic flavor of the Cantal cheese marries beautifully with the earthy bacon and the slightly bitter endive, or frisée. I sampled this dish the first time I lunched at the tiny Left Bank restaurant/tourist office La Lozère (see entry, page 48), where it's a standard first course, served with their substantial country rye bread.

Vinaigrette:
2 cloves garlic, finely minced
¼ cup (60 ml) best-quality red wine vinegar
Salt to taste
½ cup (125 ml) extra-virgin olive oil

1 head curly endive, rinsed and dried
5 ounces (150 grams) Cantal cheese, cut into bite-size cubes (or substitute an aged farmhouse Cheddar)
Freshly ground black pepper to taste
7 ounces (200 grams) slab bacon, cut into bite-size cubes

1. Prepare the vinaigrette: Combine the garlic, vinegar, and salt in a small bowl. Slowly add the oil, and stir until well blended.

2. Tear the leaves of endive into bite-size pieces. Combine the endive and cheese in a large salad bowl, toss, and sprinkle with a generous amount of freshly ground black pepper.

3. Place the bacon in a large skillet. Adding no additional fat, cook, stirring frequently, over medium-high heat until crisp. Slowly deglaze the pan with the vinaigrette, stirring until the bacon is well coated. Pour the bacon and warm vinaigrette over the greens, and toss well. Season with additional pepper and salt, if necessary, and serve immediately with plenty of grilled country bread.

Yield: 4 servings.

CHEZ MAITRE PAUL
12 Rue Monsieur-le-Prince,
  Paris 6.
(43.54.74.59).
Métros: Odéon or
  Luxembourg.
Last orders taken at 2:30 P.M.
  and 10:30 P.M.
Closed Sunday, Monday, and
  August.
Credit cards: AE, DC, V.
Private dining room for 25.
155-franc menu, including
  wine. A la carte, 150 to
  200 francs.

SPECIALTIES:
*Bistro, from the Jura and the
Franche-Comté: saucisse de
Montbéliard chaude à l'huile
(warm pork sausage bathed in
potatoes, vinegar, and oil), poulet
au vin jaune (chicken in white
wine), foie de veau au vin de
paille (calf's liver in white wine).
White wines of the Jura.*

Tiny, tidy, and friendly, Chez Maître Paul is a refreshing family-run restaurant offering the rustic cuisine of the Jura/Franche-Comté region of eastern France. There are just seven little tables in the cottagelike main floor dining room, from which diners can watch the activity in the small corner kitchen. Start with the absolutely delicious smoked garlic sausage, served warm with potatoes bathed in vinegar and parsley. Then move on to the *coq au vin jaune* (this version with tomatoes, meaty mushrooms, and white wine is better than the one with cream), a light and pleasant dish that's prepared with the regional white Arbois wine and is definitely worth sampling. The *baguettes* are delicious, desserts forgettable, and the choice of regional wines appealing.

A staff luncheon at Chez Maître Paul.

MOISSONNIER
28 Rue des Fossés-Saint-
  Bernard, Paris 5.
(43.29.87.65).
Métros: Jussieu or Cardinal-
  Lemoine.
Last orders taken at 2:30 P.M.
  and 10 P.M.
Closed Sunday dinner,
  Monday, and August.
No credit cards.
English spoken.
180 to 200 francs.

SPECIALTIES:
*Bistro, from Lyon and the
Franche-Comté. Red and white
wines of the Jura.*

Solid, substantial, and old-fashioned, Moissonnier is the sort of homey place where giant *saladiers*—glass salad bowls—laden with assorted *charcuterie* seem to appear out of nowhere. Portions are copious, copious, copious, and service could not be friendlier. Ask them to cook the roast lamb chops any other way than *rosé,* and the matronly waitress explains, "This is fragile lamb, not old mutton, and if we overcook it, we ruin it." A gentle way of suggesting things be done their way. The menu is large, offering starters of terrines, salads with bacon or cheese, Lyonnais sausages, and mackerel marinated in white wine. Popular main courses include roast kidneys, *boudin noir* (blood sausage), duck with turnips, and the superb roast rack of lamb. A single complaint: The food generally lacks seasoning. Cheese lovers should make room for the fine assortment of regional cheeses, including the nutty Swiss Tête de Moine, creamy Vacherin, and hearty Comté. This is a popular gathering spot for winemakers and wine merchants; thus the wine list offers some fine choices, ranging from inexpensive Beaujolais to well-priced Burgundies and Bordeaux.

An informal formality—attentive tableside service.

PERRAUDIN
157 Rue Saint-Jacques,
    Paris 5.
(46.33.15.75).
Métro: Luxembourg.
Last orders taken at 2 P.M.
    and 10 P.M.
Closed Saturday, Sunday, and
    August.
No credit cards.
100 francs.

SPECIALTIES:
*Bistro: potage de légumes
(vegetable soup); petit salé aux
lentilles (salt pork with lentils);
sauté d'agneau aux flageolets
(sautéed lamb with white beans).*

Perraudin, with its red and white damask tablecloths, worn Art Deco tile floors, lace-curtained windows, and motherly waitresses, is an authentic student bistro, where students and non-students come alone or in groups to fill up on the cheap, hearty, no-frills fare. The soup here is honest, the *plats du jours* homey, and I doubt that anyone has ever left with an empty stomach. I love the *estouffade de boeuf* (a well-seasoned beef stew, marinated in wine and topped with a few complementary olives), the fine potato gratin served with thick slices of lamb, and the filling lentils and salted pork. The apple *tarte Tatin* is okay (with that decayed sort of crust you find in so many cheap bistro desserts), and this is one of the last spots in Paris you'll find the old-fashioned filtered coffee, served in tiny individual metal filters set atop your coffee cup.

THAT PARISIAN PALLOR

"City dwellers of long standing and newly arrived rustics were widely different in appearance and manners. The former were large and plump, pink and white, their complexion unspoilt by work in the fields, and their physical ideal was the round-bellied bulk of the self-made bourgeois, accustomed to good food and unwearied by manual labor. The *patronnes* of inns and brothels were always fresh and pale, real Parisians who neither knew nor liked the sun, which scarcely penetrated the narrow streets of the old *quartiers*."

—From *The People of Paris, An Essay in Popular Culture in the 18th Century,* by Daniel Roche

LE PETIT ZINC
25 Rue de Buci, Paris 6.
(43.54.79.34).
Metro: Saint-Germain-des-Prés.
Open daily until 3 A.M. Last orders taken at 3 P.M. and 2:30 A.M.
Credit cards: AE, DC, V.
129-franc menu, including wine. A la carte, 180 francs.

SPECIALTIES:
Bistro: moules farcies (stuffed mussels), gigot aux flageolets (leg of lamb with white beans), tarte fine aux pommes chaudes (thin-crusted, warm apple tart).

Le Petit Zinc is a favorite Left Bank bistro, a late night spot where you can feast on platters of shellfish until 3 in the morning. The crowd here is varied, waiters are harried but thoroughly professional, and the *qualité-prix* scale is one of the best in town. Best bets include the *moules farcies*, a dozen gigantic Spanish mussels filled with a piquant blend of garlic, oil, and bread crumbs; and the *filet de rouget basquaise*, a brightly-colored main course that blends sautéed onions, tomatoes, red peppers, and zucchini with the tiniest, freshest grilled red mullet fillets (see recipe, following page). Along with a half-bottle of Bandol rosé, one shouldn't pay more than 185 francs for a satisfying meal.

An every day affair.

POISSONS GRILLES A LA BASQUAISE LE PETIT ZINC
LE PETIT ZINC'S GRILLED FISH WITH TOMATOES, ONIONS, RED PEPPERS, AND ZUCCHINI

I first sampled this dish at Le Petit Zinc (see entry, page 53) one hot Saturday night in August, and it took me back to the red, white, and green countryside of the Pays Basque. The presentation was such a revelation—really much like ratatouille without the eggplant, with all the ingredients presented separately—that the next day I prepared it for Sunday lunch, using fresh rouget, (red mullet) from a neighborhood market. This soothing blend of crispy vegetables has become a popular dish with friends, who also enjoy it as a vegetarian main course, served either warm or cold. Don't let the idea of cooking each vegetable separately throw you off. Once you've sampled the dish, you won't do it any other way. Any good fresh fish fillets may be used.

2 pounds (about 10 medium; 1 kg) tomatoes, cored, peeled, seeded, and coarsely chopped
⅛ teaspoon red pepper flakes (optional)
Salt to taste
About ½ cup (125 ml) extra-virgin olive oil
1 pound (500 g) onions, peeled and cut in half lengthwise, then cut into matchstick slices
1 teaspoon fresh thyme or ½ teaspoon dried
Freshly ground black pepper to taste
3 large red peppers, cut lengthwise into matchstick slices
1 pound (500 g) zucchini, cut into matchstick slices
8 small fish fillets (about 4 ounces; 125 g each) such as brill or cod

1. Prepare the tomatoes: Place the tomatoes in a large nonstick pan over medium-high heat and cook, uncovered, stirring occasionally, until almost all the liquid has evaporated, about 15 minutes. Add the red pepper flakes and salt to taste. Transfer to a bowl and cover.

2. Prepare the onions: Heat 2 tablespoons of the oil in a large skillet over medium heat, and add the onions. Toss to coat thoroughly, add the thyme, and cook, uncovered, until soft but still crisp, about 8 to 10 minutes. Add salt and black pepper to taste, transfer to a bowl and cover.

3. Prepare the peppers: Heat 2 tablespoons of the oil in a large skillet over medium-high heat, and add the peppers. Toss to coat thoroughly and cook, uncovered, until soft but still crunchy, about 10 minutes. Add salt and black pepper to taste, transfer to a bowl and cover.

4. Prepare the zucchini: Heat 2 tablespoons of the oil in a large skillet over medium-high heat, and add the zucchini. Toss to coat thoroughly and cook, uncovered, until soft but still crunchy, about 4 minutes. Add salt and black pepper to taste, transfer to a bowl and cover.

5. Evenly divide the vegetables among four warmed dinner plates. Cover and keep warm.

6. Brush the fish with the remaining oil, then season with salt and pepper. Heat a ribbed grill pan over medium-high heat and grill the fillets just until opaque, about 2 minutes on each side.

7. Arrange the fillets in spokelike fashion over the vegetables, and serve immediately.

Yield: 4 servings.

Stop in at Polidor for Art Deco atmosphere and delicious home cooking.

POLIDOR
41 Rue Monsieur-le-Prince,
   Paris 6.
(43.26.95.34).
Métros: Odéon or
   Luxembourg.
Last orders taken at 2:30 P.M.
   and 10 P.M.
Closed Sunday, Monday, and
   August.
No credit cards, no
   reservations.
Private dining room for 35.
English menu-translation,
   English spoken.
80 to 100 francs.

S P E C I A L T I E S :
Bistro, cuisine familiale
traditionnelle (traditional home
cooking): escargots (snails), sauté
d'agneau aux flageolets (sauté of
lamb with white beans),
pintadeau aux lardons et aux
choux (guinea fowl with bacon
and cabbage), mousse au chocolat
(chocolate mousse).

With its Art Deco light fixtures and fresh home cooking, Polidor is a lively old bistro that's aged with grace and charm. A meal here should not cost any more than 100 francs a person, and those on a tight budget can get by for even less.

Order the piping-hot garlicky and buttery snails and the waitress breaks into a wide grin of approval and tells you that they are *fait maison*—not plucked from a plastic freezer bag—so you'll have to wait a few minutes. Here, a few minutes means two, maybe three.

Regulars—well-dressed businessmen who come alone and doodle on the paper tablecloths—don't even bother with the menu. They just wait for the waitress to tell them what's good that day.

There is steak and fries, pumpkin soup, and a generous serving of well-spiced marinated *champignons à la grecque.* Do try the moist and succulent *pintadeau* served with fresh curly green cabbage, or the saddle of lamb with deliciously warming white *flageolet* beans. The bread is crisp, the wine selection decent, and the *tarte Tatin* is prepared authentically, with huge chunks of apples, though at times it may be overcaramelized and slightly bitter. If you go at noontime, profit from the location by taking an afternoon walk through the Luxembourg Gardens.

CHEZ RENE

14 Boulevard Saint-
   Germain, Paris 5.
(43.54.30.23).
Métro: Cardinal-Lemoine.
Last orders taken at 2:15 P.M.
   and 10:15 P.M.
Closed Saturday, Sunday, and
   August.
No credit cards.
200 francs.

SPECIALTIES:

*Bistro: plats du jour (changing
daily specials); huîtres (oysters);
coquilles Saint-Jacques (scallops),
December to March; saucisson
chaud (warm poached sausage);
andouillettes au vin blanc
(chitterling sausages cooked in
white wine); boeuf bourguignon
(beef stew); coq au vin (chicken in
red wine); assiette de cochonnailles
(assorted cured sausages, terrines,
and ham).*

A simple, honest bistro with a menu that's as steady as its clientele. The line-up of daily specials has barely changed for three decades, though many of the young, chic diners who populate the large, unadorned dining room have not been around that long. The daily special is inevitably the best dish on the menu—precede it with seasonal *pleurotes provençales,* fresh wild mushrooms bathed in garlic and oil; a simple salad; or a dish of country sausages. Wash it down with the house Beaujolais and enjoy the fresh *baguettes* from André Lerch, the pastry shop right next door. (See page 334 for Chez René's classic recipe for mutton with white beans.)

LA TCHAIKA

9 Rue de L'Eperon, Paris 6.
(43.54.47.02).
Métro: Odéon.
Last orders taken at 2:30 P.M.
   and 10:30 P.M.
Closed Saturday lunch,
   Sunday, and mid-July to
   mid-August.
Credit card: V.
English spoken.
Pastries may be purchased
   to take home.
150 francs.

SPECIALTIES:

*Russian: vodka, nalesniki (sweet
cheese crêpes with cinnamon),
borscht (beet and cabbage soup),
vatrouchka (cheesecake), gâteau
au chocolat (chocolate cake).*

This is the Russian-inspired tea salon that grew up to become a restaurant. But in truth only the hours have changed, for La Tchaïka still offers fine and simple Russian fare, including superb platters of assorted herring, a rich and soothing borscht (see recipe, facing page), and one of the best chocolate cakes in the city (see recipe, page 90). Also try their light cheesecake, better known as *vatrouchka.*

BORSCHT *LA TCHAIKA*
LA TCHAIKA'S BEET AND CABBAGE SOUP

This is a tart, refreshing version of the popular Russian soup, with its blend of cabbage, broth, and beets, enlivened with fresh dill and a touch of vinegar. It's the sort of soup M.F. K. Fisher calls "a little borscht" as opposed to one that's long and complicated to prepare.

The first time I sampled this soup at La Tchaïka (see entry, facing page), I also ordered Cassis, a crisp, cool white Provençal wine, and found the contrast in colors and temperature most refreshing. At home I enjoy it with a chilled Loire Valley white, such as Sancerre or Pouilly Fumé, and crusty rye bread.

In France the soup takes about twenty minutes to prepare, since the beets found in French markets are already cooked. The soup can be made ahead and reheated or served cold. At La Tchaïka, the chef, Maud Seligmann, prepares it with beef broth, but I've found any good meat or poultry stock will do. In a pinch, I've used goose stock and it was delicious. Traditionally, the soup is served with a dollop of crème fraîche *floating in the center of the bowl.*

2 tablespoons (1 oz; 30 g) unsalted butter
½ medium cabbage, very finely sliced
2 quarts (2 liters) warm meat or poultry stock
1 large beet, cooked, peeled, and cut into thin julienne strips
1 small handful fresh dill, finely minced
¼ cup (60 ml) best-quality red wine vinegar
Salt to taste
¼ cup (60 ml) *crème fraîche* (see recipe, page 237) or sour cream (optional)

1. In a large heavy saucepan, melt the butter over low heat. Add the cabbage and cook, stirring, until wilted. Do not let it brown.

2. Add the warm stock, then the beets, and cook until the mixture is very hot, about 15 minutes. Add the dill, vinegar, and salt. Taste, and adjust seasoning if necessary. Serve hot, with *crème fraîche* if desired.

Yield: 4 servings.

LA TOUR D'ARGENT
15 Quai de la Tournelle,
   Paris 5.
(43.54.23.31).
Métro: Maubert-Mutualité.
Last orders taken at 2 P.M.
   and 10:30 P.M.
Closed Monday.
Credit cards: AE, DC, EC, V.
Private dining room for 60.
English spoken.
330-franc menu (lunch
   only). A la carte, 850
   francs.

SPECIALTIES:
Seasonal; canard au sang Tour
d'Argent (duck) year-round.

Paris's best-known restaurant, though far from the best. But go, at least once in your life, for the record. If you reserve at lunchtime, you'll have a better shot at one of the coveted window tables overlooking the Seine and Notre Dame. Over the years, my meals here have varied from thoroughly memorable to downright inedible. Hope that yours falls comfortably somewhere near the top of that range. Prices are high and often out of line, and service can be incredibly condescending.

LET THEM EAT PEAS

"**E**at peas with the rich and cherries with the poor" is an old French saying. The rich were able to afford the best crop of peas, the very earliest. The finest cherries of the season, however, are the last: They are usually the ripest and most flavorful, also the cheapest and most plentiful. During the 17th century, the French became impassioned over the fashionable pea: At court, women would dine with the king, feasting on peas, then return home to eat more before going to bed, even if it meant indigestion. "It is a fashion, a furor," wrote one court chronicler.

CHEZ TOUTOUNE
5 Rue de Pontoise, Paris 5.
(43.26.56.81).
Métro: Maubert-Mutualité.
Last orders taken at 2 P.M.
   and 10:45 P.M.
Closed Sunday, mid-August
   to mid-September, and
   two weeks at Christmas.
Credit card: V.
137-franc menu universal.

SPECIALTIES:
Seasonal, home cooking: harengs
marinés pommes tièdes aux herbes
(marinated herring with sliced
potatoes and herbs), gratin
d'artichauts (artichoke gratin),
tian de morue (salt-cod gratin),
magret de canard aux navets
confits (duck breast with turnips),
soufflé au chocolat (chocolate
soufflé).

One wonders how "Toutoune" (Colette Dejean—blond, petite, and businesslike) does it. Day after day, night after night, Parisians crowd into her tiny, homey restaurant to feast on her fresh, lively, ever-changing repertoire and to take part in one of Paris's best bargain meals. Copious portions of soup, a first course, a main course, and cheese or dessert are served for the inexpensive price of 137 francs. The entire menu is changed nearly every day, following Toutoune's whim, and always offers enough choice so that no one need go away disappointed. A typical meal might include an excellent red pepper mousse or a salad of fresh pasta with shellfish (see recipe, facing page), grilled leg of lamb with delicious French fries, and a fresh red currant tart. The soup course is often a disappointment, and could easily be deleted from the menu. Service can be slow, so order up a bottle of the good house Sancerre and relax.

SALADE DE PATES FRAICHES AUX FRUITS DE MER
FRESH PASTA AND SEAFOOD SALAD

Delicate and satisfying, this colorful salad of fresh pasta, seafood, and herbs is typical of the varied offerings at Chez Toutoune, a little Left Bank bistro (see entry, facing page). The friendly blonde chef, Colette Dejean, serves this dish with several kinds of fresh pasta: She might blend thin, fresh strands of beet, spinach, and white fettuccine together, making for a spectacularly brilliant first course. Strips of roasted red pepper could be added for even more color and flavor.

½ cup (125 ml) dry
   white wine
1 ½ pounds (1 liter)
   mussels
1 ½ pounds (1 liter)
   small clams
10 ounces (310 g) fresh
   fettuccine
¼ cup (60 ml) olive oil
3 tablespoons red wine
   vinegar
1 clove garlic, minced
Salt and freshly ground
   black pepper to taste
1 large handful fresh
   basil leaves, washed
   and dried
1 large handful fresh
   parsley leaves,
   washed and dried

1. Thoroughly scrub the mussels and clams, and rinse with several changes of water. Beard the mussels. (Do not beard the mussels in advance or they will die and spoil.)

2. Place the white wine, mussels, and clams in a 6-quart (6-liter) Dutch oven, and bring to a boil over high heat. Cover and cook for about 5 minutes, or just until the mussels and clams open. Do not overcook. Remove from the heat, strain, and discard the liquid and any mussels and clams that do not open.

3. Cool slightly, and when they are cool enough to handle, remove the mussels and clams from their shells and set aside.

4. Bring a large pot of salted water to a rolling boil. Add the pasta and cook just until tender, but not soft. Drain.

5. In a large salad bowl combine the warm pasta, oil and vinegar, mussels, clams, minced garlic, salt, and pepper. Marinate for about 20 minutes before serving.

6. Just before serving, coarsely chop the basil and parsley and add to the pasta. Toss gently and serve immediately.

Yield: 4 to 6 servings.

FAUBOURG SAINT-GERMAIN, INVALIDES, ECOLE MILITAIRE

7th arrondissement

CHEZ LES ANGES
54 Boulevard La Tour-
   Maubourg, Paris 7.
(47.05.89.86 and
   45.55.69.26).
Métro: La Tour-Maubourg.
Last orders taken at 2:30 P.M.
   and 10:30 P.M.
Closed Sunday dinner.
Credit cards: AE, DC, EC, V.
Private dining rooms for 14
   to 75.
Air-conditioned.
English spoken.
200-franc menu. A la carte,
   350 francs.

SPECIALTIES:
*Gibier (wild game), October
through February; oeufs en
meurette (eggs poached in red
wine); jambon persillé (parsleyed
ham); suprême de turbotin aux
oeufs de saumon (small turbot
with salmon eggs); chariot de
pâtisseries (rolling dessert cart).*

Reserve here for Sunday lunch and join a thoroughly traditional bourgeois crowd—in couples, families, and groups—for a serious afternoon of dining. Both food and service in this large 1950s-style dining room are classic and correct. The menu includes their thinly sliced and perfectly seasoned *jambon persillé,* thick slices of grilled calf's liver, and an eye-opening rolling dessert cart laden with about a dozen pristine, classic fruit tarts.

LE DIVELLEC
107 Rue de l'Université,
   Paris 7.
(45.51.91.96).
Métro: Invalides.
Last orders taken at 2 P.M.
   and 10 P.M.
Closed Sunday, Monday,
   August, and Christmas
   week.
Credit cards: AE, DC, V.
Air-conditioned.
English spoken.
220- and 350-franc menus,
   lunch only. A la carte,
   550 francs.

SPECIALTIES:
*Fish and shellfish: oysters; turbot
sauté, sabayon de ciboulette, pâtes
noires (turbot in chive butter sauce
with black pasta).*

Oysters so huge you can make a meal out of one. Fish so remarkably fresh it makes your teeth squeak. A stunning, shimmering black pasta prepared with the ocean-flavored squid ink. Not to mention a sparkling, contemporary blue and white decor that puts you right in the mood for a trip to the sea. Much of the fish is brought in fresh direct from the coast, where the Le Divellec family ran the famous La Pacha restaurant in La Rochelle. The food here is imaginative and original, but the service is appalling. I've received numerous complaints from readers and have often witnessed outrageous, negligent service: Orders get confused, requests go unfilled, and the waiters remain thoroughly inattentive, even surly. (See facing page for their stunning mint chocolate soufflé.)

SOUFFLE A LA MENTHE ET AU CHOCOLAT AMER LE DIVELLEC
LE DIVELLEC'S MINT SOUFFLE WITH BITTER-CHOCOLATE CREAM

Chocolate is always satisfying, but there is something particularly wonderful about a little hit of chocolate after a meal of fish and shellfish. This heavenly, unusual soufflé is from Le Divellec (see entry, facing page), one of Paris's best and most controversial fish restaurants.

Pastry cream:
1 cup (250 ml) milk
1 cup (250 ml) firmly
  packed, coarsely
  chopped fresh mint
  leaves
2 large egg yolks
½ cup (100 g) sugar
2 tablespoons
  unbleached all-
  purpose flour

Chocolate cream:
1 cup (250 ml) *crème fraîche* (see page 237)
  or heavy cream,
  preferably not ultra-
  pasteurized
6 ounces
  (about 200 g)
  bittersweet
  chocolate, preferably
  Lindt or Tobler
  brand

6 large egg whites, at
  room temperature
½ cup (100 g) sugar
Unsweetened cocoa
  powder, for dusting
  the soufflés
12 fresh mint leaves, for
  garnish

1. Preheat the oven to 400°F (205°C).

2. Prepare the pastry cream: Scald the milk in a large heavy saucepan. Remove from the heat, stir in the mint, cover, and allow to infuse for 15 minutes. Strain the milk, pressing hard to extract as much liquid from the mint as possible. Discard the mint.

3. Use a whisk (or electric beater) to beat the egg yolks with the sugar in a mixing bowl until thick and lemon colored. Gently whisk in the flour. In a large heavy-bottomed saucepan, reheat the milk. Whisk one third of the hot milk into the egg yolk mixture, then pour the egg mixture back into the pan. Bring this mixture to a boil over medium-high heat, stirring constantly, and let boil until thickened, about 2 minutes. Remove from the heat and transfer to a bowl. Cool. (This pastry cream can be made three days in advance, covered, and refrigerated.)

4. Prepare the chocolate cream: Scald the *crème fraîche* in a medium-size saucepan. Remove from the heat and whisk in the chocolate, piece by piece, until it is completely melted and incorporated. Set aside until it is cool and thickened. (This can be made three days in advance, covered, and refrigerated. If it hardens, reheat it gently, beating until spreadable.)

5. Divide the chocolate cream among 4 lightly buttered 6-inch (15-cm) gratin dishes, spreading it evenly.

6. Place the egg whites in a large bowl and beat until very stiff, gradually adding the sugar. Stir one third of the whites into the pastry cream, then gently fold in the remaining whites. Working quickly, divide the mixture among the 4 dishes, spreading it in the shape of a dome over the chocolate cream to cover and seal it.

7. Bake until golden, about 15 minutes. Sift the cocoa powder over the soufflés, and decorate each with mint leaves. Serve immediately.

Yield: 4 servings.

LA FONTAINE DE MARS
129 Rue Saint-Dominique,
    Paris 7.
(47.05.46.44).
Métro: Ecole Militaire.
Last orders taken at 2:30 P.M.
    and 9:30 P.M.
Closed Saturday dinner,
    Sunday, and August.
Credit card: V.
Sidewalk terrace.
Private dining room for 25.
Some English spoken.
60-franc menu (lunch only).
    A la carte, 100 to 120
    francs.

SPECIALTIES:
*Bistro: foie gras frais en gelée
(fresh homemade foie gras),
November to March; salade aux
lardons (chicory salad with
bacon); fricassée de canard (duck
stew).*

*An enclosed terrace provides a
meal with plenty of natural
lighting.*

LA SOLOGNE
8 Rue de Bellechasse,
    Paris 7.
(47.05.98.66).
Métro: Solférino.
Last orders taken at 2 P.M.
    and 10 P.M.
Closed Monday.
Credit cards: AE, DC, V.
Sidewalk terrace.
Private dining room for 24.
English spoken.
140-franc menu. A la carte,
    140 to 180 francs.

SPECIALTIES:
*Solognot: game from October to
February, local river fish the rest
of the year.*

This family bistro, with its almost illegible mimeographed menu, is inexpensive, bright, and airy. The windows overlook the gentle arches leading to the tiny Rue de l'Exposition, service is friendly, the food simple. Good dishes include grilled sardines, thick slabs of country ham, and a rich *mystère* ice cream dessert with chocolate sauce and meringue.

A cozy, countrylike spot in the city, where chef-owner Christian Guillerand and his wife, Jeannine, treat diners as though they're being entertained in a private home. In fall and winter months, the restaurant devotes itself to game, offering crisp-skinned *sauvagine*—young wild duck, grilled simply over an open fire nurtured with grape vines. There's also a nourishing *pot-au-feu de gibiers,* a large, old-fashioned soup plate laden with huge joints of partridge, pheasant, and duck, strips of leek, and chunks of carrot. In the spring and summer, Guillerand turns his attention to local river fish, including *brochet* (pike), *sandre* (pike-perch), and *lotte* (monkfish).

TAN DINH
60 Rue de Verneuil, Paris 7.
(45.44.04.84).
Métro: Rue du Bac.
Last orders taken at 2 P.M.
and 11 P.M.
Closed Sunday and the first
two weeks in August.
No credit cards.
Private dining room for 35.
English spoken. English
menu.
270 francs.

SPECIALTIES:
*Vietnamese: raviolis vietnamiens
à l'oie fumée (steamed Vietnamese
raviolis with smoked goose),
dorade roulée aux poireaux et au
cumin (sea bream with leeks and
cumin), triangles dorés à la
langouste et noix de ginko (spiny
lobster with ginkgo nuts).
Exceptional wine list.*

THOUMIEUX
79 Rue Saint-Dominique,
Paris 7.
(47.05.49.75).
Métro: La Tour-Maubourg.
Last orders taken at 3 P.M.
and 11:30 P.M.
Closed Monday.
Private dining rooms for up
to 120.
English spoken.
46-franc menu. 100 to 150
francs.

SPECIALTIES:
*Southwestern: foie gras, confit
(preserved duck or goose), cassoulet
(casserole of white beans, sausage,
lamb, preserved duck, goose, and
pork).*

Tan Dinh is perhaps the best-known Vietnamese restaurant in Paris, and its popularity is no accident. Conveniently situated in the popular 7th *arrondissement*, not far from the Musée d'Orsay, this little spot directed by the outgoing Vifian family features a very personal style of Oriental cuisine. There's almost no need to recommend dishes, for the convivial Vifians—brothers Robert and Freddy, who take turns at the stove—will lead you through the menu, composing a meal that suits not only the palate of each diner but the size of their appetites as well. The restaurant is justifiably renowned for its wine list (the selection of Bordeaux, especially Pomerols, is extensive), and there is a very drinkable selection of less expensive wines, many priced at around 100 francs a bottle. Dishes I have most enjoyed here include the ravioli filled with snippets of smooth-flavored smoked goose breast; a great pasta dish peppered with spicy shrimp sauce; and a superb assortment of fried spring rolls.

A lively, noisy combination bistro-brasserie not far from the Eiffel Tower, Thoumieux is the sort of place to go with a crowd on nights when you have not too many francs to spare. I love the copious mimeographed menu, the attentive waiters, and the casual crowd that's obviously out to have a good time. I wish that the quality of the food here were better—seasoning is sometimes nonexistent, and freshness is not always a trademark—but on my last visit, I loved the well-seasoned *steak tartare* (they even ask you if you want it *relevé*, or highly seasoned), and the superb grilled sardines. I'd warn against the *salade de betteraves*, with stale unseasoned beets, and the bland lentils in vinaigrette. But really, who can complain about the 46-franc menu, which includes a meaty *pâté*, a choice or fried whiting or grilled *boudin* (blood sausage) with chestnuts and apples, as well as a choice of cheese or dessert?

JULES VERNE
(Eiffel Tower, second level)
Champ-de-Mars, Paris 7.
(45.55.61.44).
Métro: Ecole-Militaire.
Last orders taken at 2 P.M.
    and 10:30 P.M.
Open daily.
Credit cards: AE, DC, EC, V.
Air-conditioned.
English spoken.
220-franc menu, weekday
    lunch only. A la carte,
    600 francs.

SPECIALTIES:
*Seasonal: tarte fine aux huîtres,
courgettes, et lard fumé (thin-
crusted tart with oysters, zucchini,
and bacon); filet de bar aux
champignons et au vin jaune (sea
bass with mushrooms and sherrylike white wine); grouse d'Ecosse
rôtie au chou vert (Scottish grouse
with cabbage).*

One of the most romantic and spectacular res-taurants in all of Paris is the Jules Verne, the high-tech restaurant on the second level of the Eiffel Tower. It goes without saying that the view is a knockout, and the food is far, far better than one would expect from one of Paris's top tourist attrac-tions. Tables are at a premium—you will need to reserve several weeks in advance—but it's definitely the place to choose for a special birthday or anni-versary feast. The cuisine, prepared under the di-rection of chef Louis Grondard, is fresh and uncom-plicated, and although the wine list is expensive, it offers some reasonably priced bottles. The best dishes I've sampled here include the fine house-smoked salmon, the pistachio-studded duck ter-rine, and an expensive but dreamy lobster salad. Service is generally attentive, and the view equally appealing day and night. Reasonably priced wines to sample on the current list include George Duboeuf's white Burgundy, Saint-Véran; Château de Cléray's light white Muscadet; and two notable red Bordeaux, Château Lalande, a dense and rich Saint-Julien, and Château Fourcas-Hosten, a little-known Listrac.

Freshly-opened briny oysters.

MADELEINE, SAINT-LAZARE, CHAMPS-ELYSEES

8th arrondissement

CHEZ ANDRE
12 Rue Marbeuf, Paris 8.
(47.20.59.57).
Métro: Franklin-D.-
    Roosevelt.
Last orders taken at 3:30 P.M.
    and 11:45 P.M.
Closed Tuesday and August.
Credit card: V.
Terrace dining.
Air-conditioned.
English spoken.
200 francs.

SPECIALTIES:
*Bistro: game and scallops in
season; salade de boeuf (warm
salad of beef and potatoes), merlan
frit (fried whiting), sauté de veau
au muscadet (sautéed veal in
Muscadet).*

This is a great address to know when you're looking for a spot to eat off the Champs Elysées. I love it at lunchtime, when chic single women, elderly couples and groups of businessmen sit elbow-to-elbow, sipping their creamy vegetable soup and feasting on platters of *choucroute,* a superb warm salad of beef and potatoes, good sautéed veal stew, and filling platters of smoked haddock with a sauce of butter and lemon. The waitresses are properly motherly, and service is swift and super-attentive. Try the well-priced house Muscadet, or the Château d'Etoile, a white Graves.

ANDROUET
41 Rue d'Amsterdam,
    Paris 8.
(48.74.26.93).
Métro: Liège.
Closed Sunday and holidays.
Credit cards: AE, DC, EC, V.
Private dining room for 26.
200 francs.

SPECIALTIES:
Cheese.

I had planned to delete Androuët from the book altogether, after recent changes in ownership and some rather disappointing meals, but fellow cheese lovers convinced me to leave it in. Androuët is not the homey, cozy, wonderful cheese heaven it was in the past, yet it remains the only spot in Paris where you can truly seek your fill of cheese, waltzing through the entire litany of famous French and Swiss raw-milk cheeses, aged in the cellars beneath the shop. The new butter-yellow decor is bright, but a bit too cute and modern for my taste. And on the last two visits, the cheese, unfortunately, had not been allowed to age, and as a result most varieties were bland, chalky, and anemic—a rejection of all that is pungent, earthy, oozing with character. But this is still the spot to begin—or proceed with—your cheese education, as you march on through the multi-course *dégustation.* As ever, the tasting begins with the high-fat triple-cream cheeses (Lucullus, Grand Vatel, La Butte), moves on to pressed varieties (the Swiss Tête de Moine, Reblochon, Tomme de Savoie), then to the soft Brie and Camembert.

Next come the spiced cheeses and those aged in ash (try the refined Soumaintrain or rustic Feuille de Dreux); a huge assortment of *chèvres* (goat cheeses); the *fromages forts* (Pont l'Evèque and Livarot); and finally the blue varieties, including Roquefort and Fourme d'Ambert. And if you're still hungry on the way out, you can stop and select from the hundred or so offerings in the first-floor cheese boutique. (See also Fromageries.)

ARTOIS
13 Rue d'Artois, Paris 8.
(42.25.01.10).
Métro: Saint-Philippe-du-
    Roule.
Last orders taken at 2 P.M.
    and 9:30 P.M.
Closed Saturday, Sunday, and
    the last two weeks in
    August.
No credit cards.
Private dining room for 12.
200 francs.

SPECIALTIES:
Bistro: céleri rémoulade (celery root in mustard sauce), saucisson chaud pommes à l'huile (warm sausage bathed in oil), boudin grillé (grilled blood sausage), coq au vin (chicken in red wine), game and wild mushrooms in season, crème de marrons Chantilly (cream of chestnuts with sweetened whipped cream).

Honest, generous, authentic—what more can you ask of a modest family bistro? Season after season, Artois continues to hit the spot, satisfying one's need for earthy abundance. A meal might begin with a procession of *charcuterie*—terrines of wild boar, glistening fresh *fromage de tête* (pork headcheese), entire wands of country sausage—served family style, meaning they don't take the dishes away until you give the signal. Other delights include a rosy *gigot* (leg of lamb) served with a side dish of white beans garnished with parsley and a dollop of butter; a fine, mustardy *céleri rémoulade;* and a gamey roast partridge accompanied by golden, crispy fries. During the winter months, wild game hangs outside the front door, as a signal that there are seasonal treats inside. For dessert, sample the creamy, delicious *crème de marrons,* a smooth, pungent chestnut cream served with a thick scoop of whipped, sweetened *crème fraîche* alongside. Service is just fine, and the wine list is

brief but offers a few good buys, including the spicy Cahors Saint Didier; the little-known Bordeaux Château Maucaillou, a well-made Moulis; and the seldom-seen Château Gombaude-Guillot, a fine, rich, unclassified Bordeaux.

LE BOEUF SUR LE TOIT
34 Rue du Colisée, Paris 8.
(43.59.83.80).
Métro: Saint-Philippe-du-Roule.
Continuous service, noon to 2 A.M.
Open daily.
Credit cards: AE, DC, V.
Air-conditioned.
English spoken.
100 to 240 francs.

SPECIALTIES:
Brasserie: banc d'huîtres et de fruits de mer toute l'année (fresh oysters and shellfish, year-round), foie gras frais (fresh foie gras), poissons du marché (fish according to the market), grillades (grilled meats).

When the beautifully renovated Art Deco Boeuf sur le Toit reopened at the end of 1985, some 500 to 700 diners were turned away each and every day. Reservations are a bit easier to come by these days, but the place is always crowded, a testament to the president-director Jean-Paul Bucher (who also directs Paris's Brasserie Flo, Julien, Terminus Nord, Vaudeville, and more recently, the famed La Coupole). The new "Boeuf" is pure 1920s, with towering mirrored walls, posters, spectacular period chandeliers, cozy banquettes, and soaring ferns. The original 1920s brasserie of the same name, which settled at this location in the 1940s, was frequented by Pablo Picasso, Coco Chanel, and Maurice Chevalier. Today, film stars, artists, models, and Parisian businessmen fill the expansive dining room. From the moment you enter—passing mountains of shellfish, glistening oysters, sea urchins, mussels, and clams—you know you're in for a good time. Excellent Riesling by the carafe.

BRISTOL
112 Rue du Faubourg-Saint-Honoré, Paris 8.
(42.66.91.45).
Métro: Saint-Philippe-du-Roule.
Last orders taken at 2:30 P.M. and 10:30 P.M.
Open daily.
Credit cards: AE, DC, V.
Private dining rooms for 12 to 100.
Air-conditioned.
English spoken.
340- and 410-franc menus. A la carte, 500 to 600 francs.

SPECIALTIES:
Seasonal

Of all the grand hotel dining rooms in Paris, it's the food at the Bristol that appeals to me the most. Thanks to the talent and creativity of the Bristol's chef, Emile Tabourdiau, you could easily dine here once a week without repeating a dish. Chef Tabourdiau changes the menu as often as most of us change our minds! His selections remain seasonal, featuring a mix of what the French call *produits nobles* (such as lobster, salmon, caviar, and truffles) with more common fare (such as root vegetables, organ meats, and lentils). Depending upon the time of year, guests dine either in an airy summer room overlooking an immaculate trellised garden or in the interior winter room, decorated with richly colored tapestries and embellished by a frosted glass skylight. No matter the season, a pianist settles in to play favorite tunes on the baby grand set up near the bar.

You may be almost startled by the sheer variety and complexity of many of the dishes here: Tabourdiau boldly arranges an assortment of quickly broiled fish—sole, salmon, and red mullet—on a bed of creamy lentils (see recipe, page 72), a marriage that pleases the eye as well as the palate. He combines raw oysters, salmon, and freshly minced chives in a dish he calls a *tartare*. Brightly colored, brightly flavored, it arrives in a little ramekin with the scent of a sea breeze, accompanied by rye bread canapés layered with horseradish sauce. But for those who prefer something a bit less complex, there is always a black truffle omelet and a tossed green salad, or even a perfectly grilled, unadorned fillet of sole—cooked without salt, if you prefer, for the diet conscious.

CAVIAR KASPIA
17 Place de la Madeleine,
    Paris 8.
(42.65.33.52).
Métro: Madeleine.
Last orders taken at 11 P.M.
Closed Sunday.
Credit cards: AE, DC.
Private dining room for 20.
200 to 250 francs.

SPECIALTIES:
Caviar, salmon, smoked fish.

Elegant but informal, this little restaurant above Caviar Kaspia—a neat shop devoted to a handful of food fantasies—is the perfect spot for a quick lunch in the Madeleine/Opéra neighborhood. Try for one of the window tables overlooking the

A cheerful presentation of l'addition.

church, and settle into the luxurious world of caviar, salmon, and icy vodka. You can make a fine meal out of the fresh, plump blinis served with a few thin slices of tender smoked salmon. Or, if the budget allows, sample 30 grams (about an ounce) of caviar, either Beluga, Sevruga, Oscietra, or pressed caviar, just enough to tease the palate and fill you full of fine food memories for the day.

CHIBERTA
3 Rue Arsène-Houssaye,
Paris 8.
(45.63.77.90 and
45.63.72.44).
Métro: Charles-de-Gaulle/
Etoile.
Last orders taken at 2:30 P.M.
and 10:30 P.M.
Closed Sunday, Monday,
August, and Christmas
week.
Credit cards: AE, DC, V.
Air-conditioned.
English spoken.
450 to 500 francs.

SPECIALTIES:
*Raviolis aux truffles et persil
(raviolis of truffles and parsley),
tartare de homard au fenouil
(lobster terrine with fennel),
ragoût de champignons sauvages
(wild mushroom stew), in season.*

If you are wondering how *nouvelle cuisine* is aging, go to Chiberta for the answer: Very well, thank you. The streamlined Art Deco-style decor, which a decade ago seemed stark and modern, now appears cozy, comfortable, homey. On our last visit, service could not have been more attentive, and non-French-speaking guests were put totally at ease by attentive waiters speaking perfect English. Although I have had my ups and downs with the cooking here—over the years it has ranged from stunning to perfectly boring—the last dinner offered nothing but symphonies of flavors, dashes of excellence, a festive evening of pleasures. The menu varies with the seasons. A late fall visit turned up perfect platters of the freshest sautéed wild mushrooms, raviolis filled with slivers of fragrant black truffles, and the ever-delicious fruit soup flavored with a touch of fresh mint (see recipe, page 71). Bravo for the attentive owner, Louis-Noël Richard, and chef Jean-Michel Bédier.

LUCAS-CARTON
9 Place de la Madeleine,
Paris 8.
(42.65.22.90).
Métro: Madeleine.
Last orders taken at 2:30 P.M.
and 10:30 P.M.
Closed Saturday, Sunday, the
first three weeks of
August, and two weeks at
Christmas.
Credit cards: DC, V.
Private dining room for 14.
English spoken.
500 to 600 francs. 580-franc
tasting menu. A la carte
500 to 600 francs.

For years, as others sang the praises of Alain Senderens, I stood mistrustfully in the wings. I found the chef and his staff too brusque, too haughty, lacking in warmth. Since he moved from the Left Bank to one of Paris's most elegant, historic and romantic dining spots, I've had a minor change of heart. The atmosphere has warmed up slightly, the food is less forced, one can actually smile and laugh just a bit. The new Lucas-Carton is a tasteful blend of old and new: Crisp white ceilings, walls, and linens, and sprays of bright flowers serve as a stunning backdrop for the undulating carved wooden panels, expanses of mirrors, beveled glass room dividers, and spotless windows that look out onto the Place de la Madeleine. Everything's not

> "*An elegant table is the last ray of sunshine to caress an old man.*"—*Louis de Cussy, French gourmand*

Alain Senderens' Lucas-Carton.

SPECIALTIES:
Seasonal: escalope de saumon fumé chaud (warm smoked salmon), foie gras de canard aux choux (warm fatted duck liver with cabbage), canard poché et rôti au miel (duck poached, then roasted, with honey).

perfect here—and in a restaurant of this stature one should find nothing less than perfection—but I've thoroughly enjoyed his inventive house-smoked salmon, served warm with a sprinkling of salmon eggs; lamb in an olive cream sauce, surrounding a gratin of eggplant and lamb; and the marvelous *carpaccio de canard Eventhia,* a mound of tiny roasted potatoes, onions, and thick slices of truffles topped with the thinnest, most delicious, raw duck. Senderens is to be applauded for his fine homemade breads and his exquisite cheese tray, one of the best in all of France. Just hope that someone else is picking up the check!

SOUPE D'ORANGES ET FRAISES A LA MENTHE FRAICHE
ORANGE AND STRAWBERRY SOUP WITH FRESH MINT

A light, refreshing, and beautiful early summer dessert, this lovely blend of candied orange zest, fresh strawberries, and mint is reminiscent of a formal garden party set on a bright green lawn. A recipe from Chiberta (see entry, page 69), the dessert takes a bit of time to prepare, but requires little last-minute attention.

4 navel oranges
6 tablespoons grenadine
    syrup
¼ cup (50 g) sugar
1 pound (500 g)
    strawberries
1 large handful fresh
    mint leaves

1. Carefully remove the zest (the orange portion of the peel) from each orange, being sure not to get any of the white inner peel. Cut the zest into fine (julienne) strips.

2. Fill a small saucepan with water and bring it to a boil. Add the zest, and as soon as the water boils again, remove the zest. Repeat this one more time with a fresh pan of water. Drain zest on paper towels.

3. In a small saucepan over medium heat, combine the grenadine and zest, and cook, stirring constantly, until all the grenadine has evaporated, leaving the zest candylike and bright red. Do not prepare the candied zest more than several hours in advance, as it will lose its crispness.

4. Remove the white pith from the oranges and discard. Divide the oranges into neat sections, being careful to reserve the juice. Set the juice aside and put the orange sections in a bowl. Add 2 tablespoons of the sugar to the sections, mix well, cover with plastic wrap, and refrigerate.

5. Hull and quarter the strawberries, and add them to the reserved orange juice with the remaining sugar. Reserve 8 whole mint leaves and finely chop the rest. Add the chopped mint to the strawberry mixture, cover with plastic wrap, and marinate in the refrigerator for no longer than 15 minutes.

6. To serve: Arrange the orange sections around the edges of very shallow bowls or plates and place the strawberries in the center. Sprinkle with the candied orange zest and the whole mint leaves.

Yield: 4 servings.

PANACHE DE POISSONS AUX LENTILLES VERTES LE BRISTOL
THE BRISTOL'S GRILLED FISH ON A BED OF CREAMY LENTILS

I'm such a lentil fan, I think I'd order them with just about anything except ice cream! I never would have imagined how well fish and lentils go together if I hadn't sampled this version some time back at the elegant restaurant in the Bristol hotel (see entry, page 67). The flavors and textures marry beautifully, and it's the sort of dish that can be prepared with a great variety of fresh fish. For this dish, chef Emile Tabourdiau uses the firm dark green lentils from Le Puy, in the Auvergne. Since these are difficult to find outside of France, I'd suggest the more common brown lentils as a substitute. Just be sure not to overcook them, or they will turn to mush. When presented, the lentils should still hold their shape and should have a fairly firm texture. The choice of fish may vary. At the Bristol they use four different kinds, usually rouget, salmon, langoustines, *and* brill. *I found that three, or even two kinds, are sufficient for variety.*

Lentils:
1 cup (about 6 ounces; 180 g) lentils
1 tablespoon (½ ounce; 15 g) unsalted butter
5 medium shallots, very finely minced
1 medium carrot, very finely minced
Bouquet garni (several sprigs parsley, and thyme, 2 bay leaves)
2 tablespoons white wine
1 quart (1 liter) water
Salt and freshly ground black pepper to taste
⅓ cup (60 ml) *crème fraîche* (see page 237) or heavy cream, preferably not ultra-pasteurized
2 tablespoons minced fresh parsley

Sauce:
Lentil cooking liquid
4 tablespoons (2 ounces; 60 g) unsalted butter, cubed
Salt and freshly ground black pepper to taste

1. Rinse the lentils and sort through them carefully, discarding any pebbles you may find. Melt the butter in a medium-size saucepan over medium-low heat. Add the shallots and carrot and cook, covered, stirring occasionally, until the shallots begin to turn translucent, 3 to 4 minutes. Add the lentils, bouquet garni, wine and water. Bring to a boil, reduce the heat, and simmer 10 minutes. Season with salt and pepper and continue to cook until the lentils are tender, 10 more minutes.

2. Strain the lentil cooking liquid into a small heavy saucepan and set aside. Discard the bouquet garni. Return the drained lentils to the pan in which they were cooked. Just before serving, stir in the cream and cook over medium heat, stirring until the cream is absorbed by the lentils, 2 to 3 minutes. Correct the seasoning, remove from the heat, and stir in the parsley.

3. Prepare the sauce: Boil the lentil cooking liquid until reduced to about ½ cup. Remove from the heat and whisk in the butter. Correct the seasoning and keep warm.

4. Prepare the garnish: Melt the butter in a medium-size skillet over medium-low heat. Add the scallions, radishes, and salt and pepper and cook, stirring, until tender, 8 to 10 minutes. Add the tomatoes and sauté until heated through. Remove from the heat, season to taste with salt and pepper, and keep warm. Just before serving, stir in the basil.

5. Prepare the fish: Brush the fish with the oil, and season with salt and pepper. Heat a ribbed grill pan over the medium-high heat, using no additional oil. Grill the fish, in batches if necessary, just until the flesh turns opaque on both sides, about 2 minutes on each

Garnish:

1 tablespoon (½ ounce;
  15 g) unsalted butter
12 whole scallions, with
  2 inches of green
  stem
16 whole radishes,
  cleaned and trimmed
Salt and freshly ground
  black pepper to taste
12 whole cherry
  tomatoes
1 tablespoon minced
  fresh basil

Fish:

1 tablespoon extra-
  virgin olive oil
Salt and freshly ground
  black pepper to taste
About 10 ounces
  (300 g) fresh salmon
  fillet, skinned and
  boned, cut into 4
  equal portions
About 10 ounces
  (300 g) brill, sole, or
  striped bass fillets,
  skinned and boned,
  cut into 4 equal
  pieces
4 small red mullet
  fillets, or any red-
  skinned fish such as
  snapper, with skin

side, depending upon the thickness of the fish. (The fish may also be grilled under a broiler or on an outdoor grill.)

6. To serve, spread the lentils in the center of four individual warmed dinner plates, leaving a wide border (they should fill a circle of about 5 inches, or 12.5 cm, like a pancake). Spoon sauce around the outer edge of each lentil "pancake." Place the fish on top of the lentils and arrange the garnish around the sauced edge of the lentils.

Yield: 4 generous servings.

LA MAISON DU VALAIS
20 Rue Royale, Paris 8.
(42.60.23.75 and
    42.60.22.72).
Last orders taken at 3 P.M.
    and 11 P.M.
Closed Sunday.
Credit cards: AE, DC, EC, V.
Raclette, 81 francs. A la
    carte, 100 to 150 francs.

SPECIALTIES:
*Raclette (melted Swiss cheese with
potatoes and condiments)*

On those cold, gray, rainy Paris days—of which there are more than most of us care to endure—nothing lifts the spirits and fills the soul like a generous serving of *raclette:* firm, golden cheese that's sliced, then melted to a fragrant, creamy pool, and served with steaming fresh potatoes cooked in their skins. The Maison du Valais, with its cozy first-floor dining room overlooking the glitter of Rue Royale, is my favorite spot in Paris for sampling this Swiss-style specialty. Here the *raclette* is served *à volonté,* which means the refills keep on coming until you put on the breaks. I'd love to know the record for number of helpings, and have to admit that last time I lunched here I lost count (or perhaps, out of embarrassment, didn't count at all). The potatoes are served out of a lovely cone-shaped copper pot, so they stay good and warm, and service is so swift that it's sometimes hard to keep up with the platter after platter of sizzling hot cheese. With the meal they serve a wonderful condiment of onions and mustard, a perfect foil for the rich, warm cheese. If you're particularly hungry that day, begin the meal with an *assiette valaisanne;* a generous platter of thinly sliced country ham (*jambon cru de montagne*) and *viande de grison,* the popular Swiss-style air-dried beef, sliced paper-thin and served with tiny sour *cornichon* pickles. The wine list features some very pleasant Swiss wines, including the light white Swiss Fendant from the Valais region.

Taillevent chef, Claude Deligne.

TAILLEVENT
15 Rue Lamennais, Paris 8.
(45.63.96.01).
Métro: George V.
Last orders taken at 2 P.M.
and 10 P.M.
Closed Saturday, Sunday,
February school holidays,
and the last week in July
to the last week in
August.
No credit cards.
Private dining rooms for 6
to 36.
Air-conditioned.
English spoken.
650 francs.

SPECIALTIES:
Seasonal: millefeuille de homard
aux pointes d'asperges vertes
(lobster with asparagus tips in
puff pastry), suprême de bar au
gros sel (fillet of sea bass with
coarse salt), crépinettes de caneton
aux olives noires (duck and black
olives wrapped in caul fat),
marquis au chocolat et à la
pistache (chocolate cake with
pistachios; see recipe, following
page), soufflé chaud à l'eau-de-vie
de pêche (peach brandy soufflé).
Outstanding wine list.

In a more perfect world, there would be an abundance of men like Jean-Claude Vrinat, the genteel, sophisticated, dedicated owner of Paris's most perfect restaurant. As it is, Vrinat is a one of a kind, and so is the restaurant founded by his father, André, in 1946. Although the polished Monsieur Vrinat is rarely content with himself, he manages, season after season, to improve his already exceptional product. What makes Taillevent so special? Attention to detail, exceptional discipline, a sense of generosity that knows no bounds. Whether you're a wealthy client who dines here frequently or a young couple enjoying a once-in-a-lifetime splurge, you will be treated with style, respect, and honor. Vrinat and the chef, Claude Deligne, have succeeded in an almost impossible task: The cuisine at Taillevent bears no name tag, fits into no single school or style. Rather, it is a perfect distillation of classic and contemporary. On each visit, new surprises appear on the menu—a lively terrine of rabbit, bursting with vibrant flavors; simply roasted salmon, moist with the essence of this rich, regal fish; paper-thin slices of raw scallops with a touch of creamy sauce; the richest vanilla ice cream in the world, sprinkled with sweet cherries.

In short, Taillevent embodies the qualities I look for in a grand restaurant. The well-appointed *hôtel particulier* has the air of a private club, providing wonderful food and great theater, not just glitter and pomp. Service within warm, paneled rooms, decorated with crystal chandeliers and silver goblets filled with fresh flowers, is gracious, discreet, and unselfconscious. A great restaurant is one that provides rich, rewarding, pleasant memories years after that fleeting lunch or romantic dinner.

There may be people who leave Taillevent disappointed—asking "Is that all there is?"—and I can understand why. The food doesn't slap you in the face or make you turn somersaults. It succeeds with quiet refinement, subtlety, an uncompromising dedication to quality. Taillevent offers one of the finest—and most reasonably priced—wine lists in Paris. Take your time examining it, and don't be bashful about asking Mr. Vrinat's educated opinion when organizing the meal.

MARQUISE AU CHOCOLAT TAILLEVENT
TAILLEVENT'S CHOCOLATE CAKE

This is the dessert I order almost every time I dine at Taillevent (see entry, page 75), the finest restaurant in Paris. The cake is rich and classic, rather like a ripened chocolate mousse. A marquise *is easy to make and requires no baking. Taillevent adds its signature by serving it with a rich pistachio sauce, actually a* crème anglaise *flavored with ground pistachio nuts. The sauce is a bit time-consuming, but not difficult. The cake may, of course, be served without a sauce, or with a plain* crème anglaise. *Both the cake and the sauce should be made twenty-four hours before serving.*

9 ounces (280 g)
    bittersweet chocolate
    (preferably Lindt or
    Tobler brand),
    broken into pieces
¾ cup (100 g)
    confectioners' sugar
¾ cup (6 ounces;
    185 g) unsalted
    butter, at room
    temperature
5 eggs, separated
Pinch of salt
Pistachio sauce,
    optional (see recipe)

1. Make the chocolate batter: Place the chocolate in the top of a double boiler, and melt over simmering water. Add these ingredients in the following order, mixing well after each addition: ½ cup (70 g) confectioners' sugar, all the butter, and the egg yolks.

2. In a small mixing bowl, beat the egg whites with a pinch of salt until stiff, then add the remaining sugar and beat another 20 seconds, or until glossy.

3. Remove the chocolate batter from the heat, and add one third of the egg white mixture, folding it in gently but thoroughly. Then gently fold in the remaining whites. Don't overmix, but be sure that the mixture is well blended.

4. Rinse an 8½-inch (22-cm) springform pan with water. Leave the pan wet and fill it with the mixture. Refrigerate for 24 hours. Remove from the refrigerator about 30 minutes before serving. To serve, pour several tablespoons of the pistachio sauce onto a dessert plate. Place a thin slice of the *marquise* in the center of the plate, and serve.

Yield: One 8½-inch (22-cm) cake; 8 to 10 servings.

PATE DE PISTACHE
PISTACHIO PASTE

A generous ½ cup (60 g) shelled raw, unsalted pistachio nuts
⅓ cup (65 g) sugar
White from 1 small egg

1. Preheat the oven to 300°F (150°C).

2. Toast the nuts on a baking sheet in the oven for 5 minutes. Allow them to cool, then, squeezing them between your thumb and forefinger, remove as much skin as possible from the nuts. (If using already roasted, salted nuts, remove as much skin as possible from the shelled nuts, then rinse quickly under boiling water. Drain, then remove as much remaining skin as possible.)

3. Place the nuts in a food processor or nut grinder, and grind the nuts to a paste.

4. In a small bowl mix the nut paste with the sugar, then add the egg white to give it a sticky quality. The pistachio paste will keep in the refrigerator for a week in a tightly sealed container.

Yield: ½ cup (150 g).

SAUCE A LA PISTACHE
PISTACHIO SAUCE

⅓ cup (100 g) pistachio paste (see recipe above)
1 quart (1 liter milk)
8 egg yolks
1 ¼ cups (250 g) sugar

1. Prepare the pistachio paste.

2. In a medium-size saucepan combine the pistachio paste with the milk and bring the mixture to a boil over medium heat. Remove from the heat, cover, and allow it to steep for 5 minutes, then strain through cheesecloth or a fine-mesh sieve into another medium-size saucepan. Set aside.

3. In a medium-size mixing bowl combine the egg yolks and sugar, and beat until thick and light. Whisk in half the warm strained milk, then whisk the mixture back into the remaining milk.

4. Warm the sauce gently over medium heat, stirring constantly, until it thickens. Do not allow the sauce to boil or it will curdle. You can prepare this 24 hours in advance and refrigerate, removing it from the refrigerator 1 hour before using.

Yield: 1 quart (1 liter).

GRANDS BOULEVARDS, PLACE DE CLICHY, GARE DU NORD

9th and 10th arrondissements

CHARLOT, LE ROI DES COQUILLAGES
12 Place de Clichy, Paris 9.
(48.74.49.64).
Métro: Place de Clichy.
Last orders taken at 2:45 P.M.
and 1 A.M.
Open daily.
Credit cards: AE, DC, V.
Air-conditioned.
250 to 350 francs.

SPECIALTIES:
Fish and shellfish.

Whon I want a casual lunch of oysters, mussels, little clams, tiny shrimp, and crab, I go to Charlot, the "King of Shellfish." During the "R" months from September to April, when shellfish is in season, memorable Paris meals are made of a refreshing *plateau de fruits de mer* (a platter of mixed shellfish), served with slices of fresh rye bread, butter, and glasses of chilled, flinty Sancerre. The bright, friendly upstairs dining room overlooks the active Place de Clichy, a lively setting for a long weekend lunch with a group of three or four.

BRASSERIE FLO
7 Cours des Petites-Ecuries,
Paris 10.
(47.70.13.59).
Métro: Château-d'Eau.
Last orders taken at 3 P.M.
and 1:30 A.M.
Open daily.
Credit cards: AE, DC, V.
Air-conditioned.
English spoken.
100 to 230 francs.

SPECIALTIES:
Brasserie: choucroute (sauerkraut,
pork, and sausages), foie gras,
plats du jour (changing daily
specials), fish and grilled meat.

An honest 1900s Alsatian brasserie, with a faithful and flashy Parisian clientele. Flo is frequently too crowded, too noisy, too hectic, but for many regulars, that is part of its charm. Often there is such a crush that they don't take reservations, so just show up, cross your fingers, and plan on a wait. My favorite foods here include the superb *choucroute,* platters of fish and shellfish, and the Granny Smith apple *granité,* served with a healthy dose of Calvados. The standard fare here is accompanied by very drinkable wines by the pitcher.

JULIEN
16 Rue du Faubourg Saint-
Denis, Paris 10.
(47.70.12.06).
Métro: Strasbourg Saint-
Denis.
Last orders taken at 3 P.M.
and 1:30 A.M.
Open daily.
Credit cards: AE, DC, V.
Air-conditioned.
English spoken.
100 to 230 francs.

Despite its rather seedy location, Julien remains one of the city's most chic, most popular nighttime addresses. One look inside this bright, stunning 1890s dining hall and you understand: Who could not love the stained-glass skylights, the mahogany bar, the Art Nouveau mirrors and murals, the noisy brasserie charm? Service can be slow or too rushed, depending on the waiter and the time of day, but the menu offers enough variety to please the most finicky crowd. I generally opt for the restaurant's classics: *saumon en rillettes* (see recipe), their famous Riesling-laced foie gras, or a

SPECIALTIES:

Brasserie: cassoulet d'oie (casserole of goose and white beans), foie gras, homard grillé (grilled lobster), poissons du marché (daily fish specials), plats du jour (changing daily specials), grillades (grilled meats).

warming *cassoulet d'oie*. Dessert lovers should try the *profiteroles au chocolat,* little rounds of *chou* pastry filled with ice cream and served with a steaming hot pitcher of chocolate sauce.

SAUMON EN RILLETTES JULIEN
JULIEN'S SALMON PATE

Julien is one of Paris's prettiest restaurants (see entry, above), and this is one of Julien's most pleasant first courses. The recipe combines smoked and fresh salmon, butter, and Cognac, and it's melt-in-your-mouth delicious, especially served on wedges of toasted homemade rye bread, with a glass of Champagne before a festive meal.

4 ounces (125 g) skinned fresh salmon fillet
½ cup (125 ml) dry white wine
1 tablespoon olive oil
2 tablespoon Cognac
Salt and freshly ground black pepper to taste
4 ounces (125 g) smoked salmon
6 tablespoons (3 ounces; 90 g) unsalted butter
Thin slices of warm toast

1. Cut the fresh salmon into bite-size pieces. In a small saucepan combine the salmon and wine, and bring slowly to a boil over medium heat. Remove from the heat and drain the salmon, discarding the wine.

2. In a small saucepan heat the olive oil and add the salmon. Cook gently over medium heat for about 5 minutes. Do not let it brown. Add the Cognac, salt and pepper. Remove from the heat and set aside.

3. Cut the smoked salmon into bite-size pieces. In a small saucepan over medium heat, sauté the smoked salmon in half the butter until it is heated through, 3 to 5 minutes. Remove from the heat, cool the salmon and the butter, then blend in a food processor, adding the remaining butter.

4. Working by hand, combine the fresh salmon and smoked salmon mixtures with a fork in a small bowl until well blended. Check for seasoning. Transfer the rillettes to a serving dish or bowl, and carefully smooth the top. Refrigerate at least 12 hours before serving.

5. To serve, remove from the refrigerator about 30 minutes before serving. Serve with thin slices of warm toast.

Yield: 4 to 6 servings.

POT-AU-FEU
BEEF SIMMERED WITH VEGETABLES

"Eating pot-au-feu *is an act that gives significance to life," wrote one French critic. A bit precious, to be sure, but few peasant dishes are as healthfully nourishing, fragrant, or satisfying as a superb* pot-au-feu. *In its most classic form, the dish begins with a shallow, steaming bowl of bouillon, ladled from the pot in which the meat, marrow, and vegetables have been slowly simmering. To the bowl one might add garlic-touched croutons, freshly grated Parmesan or Gruyère cheese, a few grains of coarsely ground black pepper. The second course is made up of the meat, vegetables, and accompaniments, a procession of condiments that might include fiery horseradish, three or four varieties of mustard, coarse salt, puckery* cornichons, *and tiny white pickled onions. This recipe is based on the one shared with us by Le Roi du Pot-au-Feu.*

2 pounds (1 kg) short ribs of beef

2 pounds (1 kg) boned beef shank

2 pounds oxtail (1 kg), cut into 2-inch (5-cm) lengths

Coarse (kosher) salt and freshly ground black pepper to taste

6 small onions, each peeled and studded with a clove

4 leeks, cleaned of sand

1 fennel bulb, trimmed,

1. Using household string, tie in two separate bundles the ribs of beef and the boned shank, so they retain their shape and fit compactly into a large stockpot. Place the oxtail on top of the other meat. Cover the meat completely with cold water and cook, uncovered, over medium-high heat. The water should barely simmer, never boil.

2. After about 20 minutes, carefully skim all traces of foam (which is impurities) and grease from the surface of the stock. Careful skimming is necessary to producing a fine *pot-au-feu.*

3. Move the pot halfway off the heat so that the foam rises on one side of the stock only, making it easier to skim. Continue cooking for another 20 minutes.

LE ROI DU POT-AU-FEU
34 Rue Vignon, Paris 9.
(47.42.37.10).
Métro: Madeleine.
Last orders taken at 2:30 P.M. and 9:30 P.M.
Closed Sunday, holidays, and July.
Credit card: V.
Sidewalk terrace.
130 to 150 francs.

SPECIALTIES:
Pot-au-feu.

This funky little bistro off the Place de la Madeleine is great on a chilly fall or winter afternoon, when a nourishing dish of boiled beef, bone marrow, and vegetables is what's needed to warm the soul. The decor here is a bit kitschy but humorous just the same—cartoons paper the walls, an old piano stands beside the zinc bar, and the chatty staff make a *fête* of even the simplest lunch. Here the *pot-au-feu* begins with the traditional bouillon, steaming beef broth ladled from the stockpot in which the meat and vegetables have simmered. Next comes the enormous platter of beef, vegetables, and fresh, fragrant marrow, served with puckery *cornichons,* mustard, and coarse salt. The bistro serves a young Côtes-du-Rhône from Lucien Legrand, one of the city's better wine merchants.

washed, and
quartered
6 whole carrots, peeled
4 cloves garlic, unpeeled
Bouquet garni: 2 bay
leaves, 2 sprigs fresh
parsley, and 1
teaspoon dried
thyme, tied in a
piece of cheesecloth
1 whole apple, washed
Approximately 1½
pounds (750 g) beef
marrow bones, cut
into 2-inch (5-cm)
lengths, and each
length wrapped in
green portion of leek
(to seal in the marrow)
**Garnishes and
condiments:**
Toast rubbed with garlic
Freshly grated
Parmesan cheese
Horseradish
Several mustards
Cornichons

4. Season the liquid lightly with coarse salt (about 1 tablespoon should finely season this dish) and pepper. Add the vegetables, using only the white portions of the leeks; the garlic; the bouquet garni; and the apple, which will help absorb some of the fat. Skim again and cook another 40 minutes. Skim frequently, and after about 30 minutes, test the vegetables to see if they are cooked.

5. Once the vegetables have cooked, transfer them to a heatproof dish and moisten with bouillon. Cover with aluminum foil and keep warm in a low oven.

6. Continue cooking the meat, skimming if necessary, for 1 hour more. About 15 minutes before serving, add the marrow bones, submerging them in the bouillon.

7. To serve the first course, place a slice of toast rubbed with garlic in a warmed soup bowl, cover with bouillon, and sprinkle with freshly grated Parmesan cheese.

8. To serve the second course, remove the twine from the meat and cut it into chunks. Place it on a warmed platter, surrounded by the marrow bones and the vegetables, discarding the bouquet garni and the apple. Serve with the horseradish, a variety of mustards, *cornichons,* coarse salt, and pepper. The dish can easily be reheated.

Yield: 4 to 6 servings.

TERMINUS NORD
23 Rue de Dunkerque,
Paris 10.
(42.85.05.15).
Métro: Gare du Nord.
Continuous service from
11 A.M. to 12:30 A.M.
Open daily.
Credit cards: AE, DC, V.
Sidewalk terrace.
Private dining room for 10.
Air-conditioned.
English spoken.
100 to 230 francs.

SPECIALTIES:
Brasserie: banc d'huîtres et fruits de mer toute l'année (oysters and fresh shellfish, year-round), foie gras, choucroute (sauerkraut, pork, and sausages), plats du jour (changing daily specials).

Terminus Nord is a rambling authentic 1925 brasserie just outside the Gare du Nord train station, but you don't have to wait until a journey brings you to this end of town. The year-round *banc* of fresh oysters and shellfish is enough to lure most diners, along with excellent grilled Mediterranean *rouget* (red mullet), grilled sliced leg of lamb, and inexpensive wines that go down so easily amid the lively old-time atmosphere.

GARE DE LYON, VAUGIRARD, MONTPARNASSE, DENFERT-ROCHEREAU

12th, 13th, 14th, and 15th arrondissements

CHEZ ALBERT
122 Avenue du Maine,
    Paris 14.
(43.20.05.19).
Métro: Gaîté.
Last orders taken at 2:30 P.M.
    and 10:30 P.M.
Closed all day Friday and
    Saturday lunch.
Credit cards: AE, DC, V.
Enclosed terrace.
Air-conditioned.
English spoken.
120-franc menu, lunch only;
    250-franc menu. A la
    carte, 250 to 300 francs.

SPECIALTIES:
Seasonal: foie gras de canard
(duck foie gras), ragoût de homard
aux navets (lobster stew with
turnips), rouget aux olives (red
mullet with olives).

One of the newer, more talented young chefs on the Paris horizon is Stéphane Pruvot, who has taken over the classic Parisian bistro Chez Albert on the Avenue du Maine. Pruvot is a hard-working, ambitious young man with a head on his shoulders, and for the moment at least, he offers a bargain 120-franc menu (not including wine) weekdays at lunchtime.

Chef Pruvot trained with the noted chef Michel Lorain in Joigny, and he seems to have learned well, adopting the concept of saucing fish with very thin but flavorful meat stocks. His menu changes often, but usually includes a series of

The business lunch, a Paris
tradition.

composed salads, such as his *compote de lapereau*, a well-seasoned, chunky rabbit terrine set atop a scissor-cut salad of mixed greens tossed with a fine sherry vinegar dressing; as well as a good selection of fish and meats, including a *salmis*, or stew, of pigeon set on a bed of fresh pasta. For dessert, try the *salade d'agrumes* (perfect slices of grapefruit and orange tossed with delicately candied orange peel), and the *gratin de fruits* (lots of fresh berries topped with just a touch of Champagne-laced sabayon). The rather high-priced wine selection offsets savings here, but there are two excellent whites on the list: a Dagueneau Pouilly Fumé and Michelot Meursault.

L'AQUITAINE
54 Rue de Dantzig, Paris 15.
(48.28.67.38).
Métro: Convention.
Last orders taken at 2:30 P.M. and 11 P.M.
Closed Sunday and Monday.
Credit cards: AE, DC, EC, V.
Terrace dining in summer.
Air-conditioned.
English spoken.
330 francs.

SPECIALTIES:
Updated southwestern and fish: pibales (tiny eels), February and March; alose (shad), April and May; wild mushrooms, August to November; scallops, October to April.

Christiane Massia is one of Paris's most inventive chefs, creatively combining ingredients from her native Aquitaine, along the Atlantic coast just south of Bordeaux. It's a rich area, full of river fish, wild mushrooms, meat from the Chalosse, and fish from the Golfe de Gascogne. Madame Massia weaves all of these delights into a menu that offers innumerable choices—I always seem to want to try everything on this menu, so much appeals. On the last visit, I fell in love with her tiny *lotte*, or monkfish, served with a medley of the freshest wild mushrooms; enjoyed a *fricassée* of the freshest of fish and shellfish; and sampled for the first time in my life *joues de lotte*, the meaty, chewy cheeks from giant monkfish. More standard fare here includes *bar*, or sea bass, in *beurre blanc*, salmon with Champagne sauce, and turbot cooked in sweet Sauternes wine. (The recipe for Madame Massia's *chiffonnade de saumon*—a salad of shredded greens and smoked salmon—appears on page 85.)

I wish I could be as wildly enthusiastic about the service (which can be rude, offensive, or simply nonexistent) and the decor (which I find painfully depressing). I think lunch is a better bet here than dinner, especially in good weather, when you can dine out on the rooftop terrace.

In 1806 the Restaurant Véry, the "dearest restaurant in Paris," opened near the Palais Royal and soon became host to the famous. The painter Fragonard died there while eating an ice cream, and Balzac ate Pantagruelian meals there, usually at the expense of his editor. The restaurant enjoyed a huge success, according to reviews of the day: "Impeccable decor, delicious cuisine."

Lucette Rousseau, organized and passionate.

L'ASSIETTE
181 Rue du Château, Paris 14.
(43.22.64.86).
Métro: Mouton-Duvernet.
Last orders taken at 2:30 P.M. and 10:30 P.M.
Closed Monday, Tuesday, August, and Easter.
Credit cards: AE, V.
English spoken.
250 francs.

SPECIALTIES:
Bistro, home cooking: game and wild mushrooms in season, fish.

Lucette Rousseau, better known as Lulu, personifies the contemporary, independent style of Parisian *bistrotiers*. Hard working, well organized, and passionate about her *métier*, the sharp-talking Lulu has managed in just a few short years to create exactly the style of restaurant she wants. Her spotless, cozy bistro has been carved out of a lovely 1930s *charcuterie*, a space adorned with etched-glass windows and decorative glass ceiling, lightened by butter-yellow walls and a touch of greenery. There's just enough room for 40 or 50 diners, an ideal-size bistro. Eating at Lulu's is never a quiet affair, for decked out in red beret, jeans, and work shirt, she rambles in and out of the kitchen throughout the service, shouting, raving, cracking jokes with friends as well as strangers. In short, not the place to go for a private *tête à tête* or serious business lunch. But for all her craziness, there is real sanity here: The food is clear, full of flavor, and well thought out. Side dishes aren't just there as ornament, but truly complement the main dish. A case in point is her giant, earthy *boudin* blood sausage, grilled to a crisp and accompanied by sautéed potatoes, whole cloves of garlic in their skins, and a slice of tangy apple tart. Her *petit salé de canard*—duck that's been marinated for days in a salt brine infused with herbs and spices, then poached—is beautiful, rosy, and not overly salty. She serves it on a bed of soft, buttery, golden cabbage, a soothing cold-weather dish if there ever was one.

Although the menu leans heavily toward southwestern specialties—in fall and winter there's a good assortment of game, as well as wild cèpe mushrooms with garlic—her menu does not read like a hackneyed litany of foie gras and *confit*. She does wonderful things with fish (note the grilled tuna seasoned with Breton sea salt) and includes a few bistro standbys, such as *boeuf à la ficelle*, or beef tied with a string and poached in broth. L'Assiette's wine list has improved over the years, and includes a robust Cahors, Prieuré de Cénac, from Lulu's native southwest.

CHIFFONNADE DE SAUMON
SALAD OF SHREDDED GREENS AND SMOKED SALMON

This dish is the creation of Christiane Massia, the imaginative chef at L'Aquitaine (see entry, page 83). The dressing can be made a day in advance then refrigerated, but prepare the rest of the ingredients just before serving.

½ cup (125 ml) *crème fraîche* (see recipe, page 237) or sour cream
1 tablespoon lemon juice
¼ teaspoon hot paprika
1 head Boston or butter lettuce, rinsed and dried
4 slices smoked salmon, cut into thin (¼-inch; 7-mm) strips

1. In a small bowl, combine the *crème fraîche* or sour cream, lemon juice, and paprika.

2. Stack the lettuce leaves on top of one another and using a long chef's knife, cut the lettuce into very fine strips, almost as if you were slicing cabbage for cole slaw. Place in a large bowl, add the dressing, and toss until the lettuce is thoroughly coated.

3. Evenly divide the lettuce among four salad plates, and lay several strips of smoked salmon on top of each serving. Serve immediately.

Yield: 4 servings.

LA CAGOUILLE
10-12 Place Constantin-
  Brancusi (across from 23
  Rue de l'Ouest), Paris 14.
(43.22.09.01).
Métro: Gaîté.
Last orders taken at 2 P.M.
  and midnight.
Closed Sunday, Monday, and
  one week at Christmas.
No credit cards.
Sidewalk terrace in summer.
Private dining room for 12.
260 to 300 francs.

SPECIALTIES:
Fish and shellfish.

Paris does not lack for fine seafood restaurants, but the trick is to find fresh, fresh fish at moderate prices. If you love fish as well as you love a bargain, then head straight for my favorite fish bistro of all, La Cagouille. Here, in newly installed quarters not far from the Tour Montparnasse, the passionate, zany, hard working Gérard Allemandou holds forth, offering up a series of changing specialties inspired by his childhood in Cognac country. He scours the Rungis wholesale market in the early morning hours, searching not just for freshness but for value. This is not the place to look for pricey lobster, but few diners will be disappointed by his superb *moules brule doigts* (literally, "burn your fingers"), meaty mussels that are opened on top of the

---

SALADE DE LARDONS DE THON LA CAGOUILLE
LA CAGOUILLE'S SALAD OF TUNA AND CURLY ENDIVE

This wonderfully modern bistro dish is an updated version of the classic frisée aux lardons, or curly endive salad with bacon. I sampled it during one of my frequent visits to the popular fish bistro La Cagouille (see entry, above), where the menu seems to change moment by moment, depending upon what bargains chef Gérard Allemandou has found in the wholesale market that morning. It's a fine main course salad, for serving with a chilled red Chinon or Beaujolais and crusty grilled bread.

1 head curly endive,
  rinsed and dried
1 large bunch chives
4 small white onions,
  shallots, or scallions,
  cut into thin rings
1 thick slice fresh tuna
  (about 1 pound;
  500 g, untrimmed)
Salt and freshly ground
  black pepper to taste
⅓ cup (80 ml) extra-
  virgin olive oil
⅓ cup (80 ml) best-
  quality red wine
  vinegar

1. Tear the leaves of curly endive into bite-size pieces. Combine the endive, chives, and onions in a large shallow salad bowl, and toss.

2. Cut the tuna into 1-inch (2.5-cm) cubes.

3. Place the tuna in a nonstick frying pan, and, over medium-high heat, quickly brown the cubes. They will cook in just a minute or two and should remain rather rare on the inside. Season generously with salt and plenty of freshly ground black pepper.

4. Add the oil to the tuna in the pan and heat until it sizzles. Then very slowly add the red wine vinegar, stirring to coat the tuna with the oil and vinegar.

5. Quickly spoon the tuna, oil, and vinegar on top of the greens, toss thoroughly, and serve immediately.

Yield: 4 servings.

stove and set on flat, thick cast-iron pans, so all you're tasting is pure, sweet, flavorful mussels dripping with their natural juices. Other fine dishes I've sampled here include a satisfying *salade frisée au thon* (cubes of rare tuna tossed with curly endive, shallots, and chives in a tart vinaigrette; see recipe, facing page), tiny pan-fried Saint-Pierre, or John Dory, served with a side dish of sautéed zucchini; piping hot sautéed squid; tiny bass, the size of sardines, simply steamed; grilled turbot, so fine that it competes with the version at Taillevent; and giant *rouget*, or red mullet, grilled to perfection. There's usually a superb platter of goat cheese from Allemandou's native Poitou, and if they're offering it that day, try the *quatre-quarts aux poires*, a moist and fruity pound cake filled with sliced fresh pears. Chef Allemandou offers a wide selection of inexpensive wines, including a superb white, the well-priced Burgundian Aligoté de Bouzeron, from the house of Chanzy. Cognac lovers should note that Allemandou probably knows more about Cognac than any chef in France, and after working one's way through a just portion of his magnificent selection, one can purchase bottles to take home.

LA COUPOLE
102 Boulevard du
  Montparnasse, Paris 14.
(43.20.14.20).
Métro: Vavin.
Continuous service from
  noon to 2 A.M.
La Coupole will reopen in
  early 1989 and be open
  daily.
Credit card: V.
Air-conditioned.
150 francs.

SPECIALTIES:
*Brasserie: oysters, grilled meats,
curry d'agneau (lamb curry).*

The Brasserie magnate Jean-Paul Bucher (whose high quality "Flo" brasseries continue to multiply) has purchased this 100-year-old Left Bank hangout, and promises to keep it "just as it was." Over the years, in all of Paris, there have been few restaurants as democratic as La Coupole. First-timers, foreigners, old-timers, Parisians who have been coming here for decades are greeted with the same professional welcome and open arms. With a brasserie-sized dining room offering traditional fare, La Coupole is the place to take first-time visitors to Paris, for it's the kind of restaurant where people-watching is as much a part of the menu as the famous lamb curry, the giant *côte de boeuf,* or the fillets of herring doused in thick cream. My favorite time to visit La Coupole is Sunday lunch, when families take *grand-mère* out for a weekly feast, and couples old and young carry on their longtime gastronomic rituals, served by tall, lean waiters in white aprons that reach right down to their toes. I love nothing better than settling into a large *plateau de fruits de mer,* downing sea urchins and plump, briny oysters, and washing them down with this season's mellow Muscadet. At night, there is always the famous onion soup *gratinée, merlan frit* (fried whiting), served with generous portions of caper-rich tartar sauce, and enough traditional creamy desserts to send you back to the 1930s. In short, food that's good, that's honest, in an ambience well worth the price of admission.

LE DUC
243 Boulevard Raspail,
  Paris 14.
(43.22.59.59).
Métro: Raspail.
Last orders taken at 2 P.M.
  and 10:30 P.M.
Closed Saturday, Sunday, and
  Monday.
400 to 500 francs.

SPECIALTIES:
Fish and shellfish, including plateau de fruits de mer (fish and seafood platter).

I seem to enjoy Le Duc more and more on each return visit. There's a vivid freshness about the food, and though the casual nature of the dining room hardly matches the price (there's no getting away from it, fish is expensive), this remains one of the better fish restaurants in Paris. On my last visit, I loved the *fricassée de lotte* (a Mediterranean-inspired blend of cubed monkfish, tomatoes, and mushrooms, sautéed with a touch of olive oil and served piping hot) as well as the *dorade au basilic,* porgy flavored with basil and tomatoes. With the meal, sample Le Duc's well-priced house white, Louis Metaireau's Muscadet. Note that at dinnertime this tends to be a late-night spot, so if you arrive at 8:30 you may find yourself in an empty dining room. (See facing page for Le Duc's Salmon with Basil Sauce.)

GERARD ET NICOLE
6 Avenue Jean-Moulin,
  Paris 14.
(45.42.39.56).
Métro: Alésia.
Last orders taken at 2 P.M.
  and 10:30 P.M.
Closed Saturday, Sunday, and
  mid-July to mid-August.
Credit cards: V.
Private dining room for 16.
English spoken.
330-franc tasting menu. A la
  carte, 400 francs.

It is always a rare treat to fall a little bit in love with a restaurant the first time around. It's even better to have that impression reinforced on return visits. Gérard et Nicole, a rustic, homey little dining room tucked away in the Alésia section of the 14th *arrondissement,* it is the kind of place you warm to immediately, one of that dying breed of establishments run by a husband and wife, the type of restaurant that has helped build Paris's culinary reputation. Gérard Faucher and his wife, Nicole, enjoy a pleasantly appointed spot, a charming urban *auberge* decorated with oil paintings, country armoires, and Oriental rugs the couple find on their weekend outings to flea markets around the country. Their personal touch is everywhere, extending into the handkerchief-size kitchen, where

SPECIALTIES:
Seasonal: tartare de saumon cru et fumé à la gelée de soja (chopped raw and smoked salmon in a soy-sauce aspic), tournedos de lotte bardé de jambon fumé, jus de viande (ham-wrapped monkfish with meat stock–based sauce), râble de lapin au basilic et tomate, gratin d'artichauts poivrade (saddle of rabbit with tomato and basil, with a gratin of tiny artichokes).

Gérard continues to turn out modern, imaginative, light French fare. On my last visit, I was lured by his minestrone, a vibrantly flavored blend of scallops and oysters, a soup that offered a beautiful marriage of ocean flavors mixed with a touch of pasta and tiny cubed vegetables in a heavenly broth. Equally appealing is the *tournedos de lotte bardé de jambon fumé*, huge chunks of mild monkfish wrapped in paper-thin slices of very delicately smoked ham. Faucher's cuisine is in fact a sort of a textbook example of how the best of *nouvelle cuisine* has evolved. His food is pretty but not fussy. Portions are substantial but not overwhelming. In all, there's a casual elegance about it, and just the right balance of familiar fare and new surprises, good enough to keep us coming back for more.

SAUMON NATURE SAUCE BASILIC LE DUC
LE DUC'S SALMON WITH BASIL SAUCE

There are many versions of fish cooked on a plate, and this is one of my favorites. It is such a simple, natural, uncomplicated method of steaming fish that I wonder why it isn't more popular. At Le Duc, a Left Bank restaurant devoted to fish (see entry, facing page), this version appears on the menu from time to time. When preparing it, I use two large Pyrex pie plates—so that I can keep track of the salmon steaks as they cook—placed on top of a couscous cooker. At Le Duc, the salmon is served quite rare; it is considered done when the base of the fish turns white. Those who prefer their salmon fully cooked can just continue cooking until the fish is opaque throughout, about 20 minutes.

Sauce:
¼ cup (60 ml) fresh basil leaves, firmly packed
½ cup (125 ml) extra-virgin olive oil
3 medium tomatoes, cored, peeled, seeded, and chopped
Salt and freshly ground black pepper to taste
1 tablespoon (½ ounce; 15 g) unsalted butter
4 salmon steaks, (each weighing about 6 to 8 ounces; 180 to 250 g)

1. Prepare the sauce: Wash and dry the basil leaves and snip into shreds, or a *chiffonnade*, with a scissors. Combine the basil, oil, tomatoes, salt, and pepper in a small bowl. Cover, and set aside to marinate for 1 hour.

2. Place the salmon steaks in a single layer on the bottom of a large buttered pie plate, preferably glass. Invert a second buttered pie plate, also preferably glass, over the first plate. Place the plates on top of a large pot of boiling water and cook to desired doneness. It will take about 10 minutes for rare salmon, 20 minutes for the salmon to be cooked through.

3. To serve, place each steak in the center of a warmed dinner plate, and spoon the basil sauce all over.

Yield: 4 servings.

GATEAU AU CHOCOLAT LA TCHAIKA
LA TCHAIKA'S CHOCOLATE CAKE

All good chocolate cakes are by their very nature "sinful." This one is more sinful than most. It's usually on the pastry tray at La Tchaïka (see entry, page 56), where the young and the old linger, unable to decide between it and vatrouchka, the Russian version of cheesecake.

Cake:

1 pound (500 g)
  bittersweet chocolate
  (preferably Lindt or
  Tobler brand),
  broken into pieces
2 teaspoons vanilla
  extract
6 eggs, separated
¾ cup (100 g)
  confectioners' sugar
1 cup (140 g) almonds,
  ground to a fine
  powder
1 tablespoon cornstarch
¾ cup (6 ounces;
  185 g) unsalted
  butter at room
  temperature
Pinch of salt
1 teaspoon unsalted
  butter, for buttering
  cake pan

Icing:

½ cup (125 ml) *crème
  fraîche* (see recipe,
  page 237)
3 ounces (95 g)
  bittersweet
  chocolate, broken
  into small bits

1. Preheat the oven to 375°F (190°C).

2. Prepare the cake: Place the chocolate and vanilla extract in the top of a double boiler placed over simmering water.

3. In a medium-size bowl beat the egg yokes with the sugar until pale lemon-colored. Add the next ingredients to the egg yolk mixture in the following order, mixing well after each addition: the melted chocolate, ground almonds, cornstarch, and butter. Set aside.

4. In a second bowl, beat the egg whites with the pinch of salt until stiff but not dry.

5. Add one third of the egg white mixture to the chocolate batter and fold in gently but thoroughly. Then gently fold in the remaining whites. Don't overmix, but be sure the mixture is well blended.

6. Butter an 8½-inch (22-cm) springform pan and fill it with the batter. Bake until the top of the cake is firm and springy, 35 to 40 minutes. Cool before unmolding, and when completely cooled, make the icing.

7. Prepare the icing: In a small saucepan, bring the *crème fraîche* to a boil over low heat. Reduce the heat and add the chocolate, bit by bit, stirring until it is all melted. Remove from the heat and let cool. The icing should have the consistency of a thick but spreadable frosting. (If the icing hardens before the cake is frosted, reheat gently until it reaches the proper consistency.) Cover the top and sides of the cake with a thin layer of icing. Let the cake sit for about 30 minutes before serving.

Yield: One 8½-inch (22 cm) cake.

LA MAISON BLANCHE
82 Boulevard Lefebvre,
   Paris 15.
(48.28.38.83).
Métro: Porte de Versailles.
Last orders taken at 2 P.M.
   and 11 P.M.
Closed Saturday lunch,
   Sunday, Monday, first
   week in January, the
   week after Easter, and the
   first two weeks in
   September.
Credit card: V.
Air-conditioned.
English spoken.
195-franc menu, lunch only.
   A la carte, 350 francs.

S P E C I A L T I E S :
Modern: gâteau landais (layered
terrine of foie gras and potatoes),
cabillaud peau d'épices (cod with
spices), croquant de riz (custard
with a base of rice pudding).

When José Lampreia was growing up in southern Portugal, he dreamed of someday living in a big white house. So naturally, when he opened his restaurant in Paris at the age of twenty-eight, he called it La Maison Blanche. Lampreia has wholeheartedly warmed the hearts and palates of Parisians with a restaurant and a style of cuisine that resembles no other. And he has shown the French food world that there is room for new styles, new flavors, new concepts. The slim, dark-eyed chef opened La Maison Blanche with no formal culinary training—just a love for manual work and for cooking, a love that blossomed into a full-fledged passion.

Lampreia's striking, full-flavored cuisine is filled with scents and tastes of the Mediterranean. Sweet figs, Moroccan spices, garlic, ginger, fresh coriander, preserved lemons, and sweet Italian balsamic vinegar play a supporting role here, adding character to a food that is at once boldly flavored, amazingly uncomplicated, and refreshingly imaginative. In nearly every dish one feels the sun, whether it's Morocco, Portugal, the south of France, or Italy. Even his wine list looks to the south, with an extensive well-priced offering from the Rhône valley, Provence, and France's southwest, as well as a complete selection of *eaux-de-vie* from Etienne Brana's estate in the Pays Basque.

Although all the outward signs at La Maison Blanche are modern—shiny wooden floors and Oriental rugs, towering ficus trees, cozy cane chairs, an open, white-tiled kitchen—the atmosphere is warm, welcoming, and familiar. Giant glass jars of preserved fruits sit atop the bar (a collection of recipes from José's grandmother in Albufeira), and the menu includes many classic bistro favorites, such as a traditional *boeuf mode* and a rich, golden *riz au lait.* Yet in his hands, homey, old-fashioned dishes become somehow modern, up-to-date. He turns soothing mashed potatoes into a majestic dish, flavoring the purée with virgin olive oil from Portugal (see recipe). *Riz au lait* becomes a rich, voluptuous cross between Mom's rice pudding and sinful *crème brûlée.* And while his food has a sense of fantasy about it, it is never frivolous. It is pretty, but never precious.

Lampreia uses a minimum of butter, just a touch of oil, and no heavy sauces in his cooking, and although his food is light and highly digestible, one does not feel the least bit deprived. While neither his food nor his restaurant fits a definable mold, one quickly understands that nothing is haphazardly left to chance. The crusty sourdough bread served at La Maison Blanche is among the best in Paris, baked in the turn-of-the-century wood-fired oven at the nearby Moulin de la Vierge bakery. Lampreia loves fish, and loves to cook it, and each morning, come 2 A.M., his fish is personally selected by a trusted merchant at the Rungis

PUREE A L'HUILE D'OLIVE LA MAISON BLANCHE
LA MAISON BLANCHE'S MASHED POTATOES WITH OLIVE OIL

Chef José Lampreia's potato purée has become the passion of everyone who dines at his restaurant, La Maison Blanche (see entry, above). Nearly every diner asks for seconds, sometimes even thirds—requesting a side order even when it's not meant to be part of the main course. I love to prepare this dish at home, for the fragrant aroma of the rich virgin oil wafts through the kitchen as I stir the oil into the elegant purée. It is recipes such as this that make one realize that the fewer the ingredients in a dish, the more important it is that they all be of top quality. Note that this is a dish that must be prepared at the very last moment. Do not use a food processor to prepare the mashed potatoes: their starch will be transformed into a gluey mass. Be sure to have a warm serving bowl and hungry guests standing by!

1½ pounds (750 g) potatoes, preferably long white, round white, or round red boiling potatoes, peeled and quartered
Approximately ⅓ cup (80 ml) extra virgin olive oil
Salt and freshly ground black pepper to taste

1. Place the potatoes in a pan large enough to hold them in a single layer, cover with cold water, and season with salt. Bring to a boil and cook, covered, until the potatoes are cooked through but are not so soft they are falling apart, about 20 minutes. Drain thoroughly.

2. Using a potato masher, a spoon and sieve, or a food mill, purée the potatoes. Return the potatoes to the pan, and over low heat, slowly incorporate the oil, drop by drop, stirring all the while. Use as much oil as necessary to form a fragrant, smooth purée. Season to taste and serve immediately.

Yield: 4 servings.

wholesale food market outside Paris. Twice each week he goes to Rungis himself to select the herbs, vegetables, meats, and spices used at La Maison Blanche. The effort has paid off. La Maison Blanche is generally filled lunch and dinner, so advance reservations are in order.

LE RESTAURANT D'OLYMPE
8 Rue Nicolas-Charlet, Paris 15.
(47.34.86.08).
Métro: Pasteur.
Last orders taken at 2 P.M. and midnight.
Closed Saturday and Sunday lunch, Monday, August, and one week at Christmas.
Credit cards: AE, DC, V.
Air-conditioned.
English spoken.
180-franc menu, lunch only. A la carte, 500 francs.

S P E C I A L T I E S :
Seasonal: terrine de joue de boeuf aux poireaux (layered terrine of beef cheeks and leeks), daurade et saumon crus aux herbes (fresh raw sea bream and salmon with herbs), ravioli de homard (lobster ravioli), lapin rôti au pistou (roast rabbit with pesto sauce).

Dominique Nahmias continues to offer Parisian diners food with a sparkle: imaginative, Mediterranean-inspired fare that's all her own. The all-red Art Deco restaurant looks a little dated now, and the crowds seem to have thinned a bit, yet l'Olympe is worth checking out, if only for the chef's ideas of the moment. Madame Nahmias does lovely things with ravioli, salmon, and *langoustines,* foods that always appeal, and she makes us all fall in love with her pungent, solid rabbit with pesto, a very substantial, sophisticated herb-infused preparation. The wine list shows a good deal of care, and on my last visit, I particularly enjoyed the well-priced Macon-Villages from the house of Faiveley.

Readying the next mouthful.

LE PETIT MARGUERY

9 Boulevard de Port-Royal,
Paris 13.
(43.31.58.59).
Métro: Gobelins.
Last orders taken at 2 P.M.
and 10 P.M.
Closed Sunday, Monday, and
August.
Credit cards: AE, DC, V.
Enclosed terrace dining.
Private dining room for 14.
English spoken.
250 to 300 francs.

SPECIALTIES:

*Seasonal: game, wild mushrooms,
scallops, pibales (tiny eels) in
season; dos de bar rôti aux
lentilles à l'huile d'olive (sea bass
and lentils with olive oil),
pintadeau fermier aux cèpes (farm
guinea hen with wild
mushrooms), civet de marcassin
vieille France aux pâtes fraîches
(wild boar stew with fresh pasta).*

Parisians continue to thrive on old-fashioned bistros where the jovial *patron* races from table to table shaking hands, taking orders, and pouring simple country wines. At Le Petit Marguery—a sort of "underground" bistro that gets little publicity yet manages to attract a solid and fashionable clientele—diners have the benefit of not one but three *patrons,* in the form of the three *frères* Cousin. While brothers Michel and Jacques tend to the stoves, mustachioed young Alain handles the front of the house, a model turn-of-the-century neighborhood bistro, complete with old-fashioned chandeliers, beautiful tile floors, mirrored walls, and a handwritten menu that changes from day to day. The brilliant blue and terra-cotta walls offer a festive air. The fare is both classic and inventive, including a refreshing mixed salad dressed with walnut oil and topped with thin slices of sausage marinated in herbs and olive oil; a festival of game and wild mushrooms in the fall and winter months; and a marvelous *petit salé de canard,* duck that is cured in a salt brine for a full week, then poached and served with butter-infused cabbage. The small wine lists offers some good buys, including the seldom-seen Rhône valley red Cornas, from the house of Delas; and some fine, well-priced, little-known red Bordeaux, including a Moulis, Château Maucaillou, and a *grand bourgeois exceptionnel,* Château Haut-Marbuzet.

Beginning dinner with a toast.

LE TRAIN BLEU
20 Boulevard Diderot, Gare
  de Lyon (one flight up),
  Paris 12.
(43.43.09.06).
Métro: Gare de Lyon.
Last orders taken at 2:30 P.M.
  and 10 P.M.
Open daily.
Credit cards: AE, DC, EC, V.
Private dining room for 30.
English spoken.
200-franc menu. A la carte,
  250 to 300 francs.

SPECIALTIES:
*Lyonnais, including quenelles de
brochet (pike dumplings).*

One of the grandest Belle Epoque decors in all of Paris, Le Train Bleu is a classic that should not be missed. Everything from the starched white linens to the stiff but friendly old waiters, from the sculpted ceilings to the portrait of Sarah Bernhardt, makes this spot quintessentially Parisian. It's the kind of place that's fun to go to alone at odd hours, just to people-watch and enjoy a leisurely meal. The old-fashioned tableside service is friendly and attentive, but remember that you're not here principally for the food. If it happens to be good that day, so much the better. Order the simplest, least complicated dishes, and you should have a pleasant meal. Even you don't have time for a meal, you can enjoy the decor by spending a few minutes at the bar.

AU TROU GASCON
40 Rue Taine, Paris 12.
(43.44.34.26).
Métro: Daumesnil.
Last orders taken at 2 P.M.
  and 10 P.M..
Closed Saturday, Sunday, and
  August.
Credit cards: AE, V.
English spoken.
190-franc menu. A la carte,
  320 to 350 francs.

SPECIALTIES:
*Updated southwestern: cassoulet
maison (casserole of white beans,
homemade sausages, mutton, pork,
duck, and tomatoes); huîtres en
crépinettes (oysters and sausages),
September to February; tourtière
landaise (thin pastry filled with
apples).*

Au Trou Gascon, Alain and Nicole Dutournier's charming southwestern bistro, remains one of my favorite Parisian dining spots. Yes, it's hidden way out at the edge of town. Yes, chef Dutournier has put the restaurant's direction in the hands of his wife, Nicole. Yes, the atmosphere is less lively now that both Dutournier and his knowledgeable *sommelier,* Jean-Guy Loustau, spend their time at the Dutourniers' second Paris restaurant, Carré des Feuillants (see page 11). But don't let that concern you, for the food at Au Trou Gascon is as fine and varied as ever, and service remains swift and attentive. Here one can still sample all of the trustworthy southwestern specialties, from *cassoulet* to foie gras, lamb and white beans to *confit* of duck. But Dutournier and his chef also continue to amuse and excite the palate with carefully conceived modern fare, a fine litany of seasonal dishes with a southwestern accent. For fish lovers there is always a fresh selection (such as salmon roasted with fresh fava beans; or tiny *plie,* or flounder, served with wild cèpe mushrooms), and cheese lovers must sample the exceptional *brebis* sheep's-milk cheese from Dutournier's native Basque country, along with the *Cabécous de Rocamadour,* tiny discs of goat's-milk cheese, some of the best you'll find in France. As ever, the wine list is appealing and fairly priced, with a changing list of *bouteilles du moment,* specially priced wines from Au Trou Gascon's vast cellars.

ARC DE TRIOMPHE, TROCADERO, BOIS DE BOULOGNE, NEUILLY

16th arrondissement and Neuilly-sur-Seine

LA BOUTARDE
4 Rue Boutard, 92200
  Neuilly-sur-Seine.
(47.45.34.55).
Métro: Pont de Neuilly.
Last orders taken at 2:30 P.M.
  and 10:30 P.M.
Closed Saturday lunch and
  Sunday.
Credit cards: DC, V.
Sidewalk terrace.
English spoken.
150 francs.

S P E C I A L T I E S :
Classic and updated bistro:
flamiche aux blancs de poireaux
(leek tart), sauté d'agneau aux
haricots rouges (lamb and kidney
bean stew), pot-au-feu de canard
aux petits légumes (boiled duck
and vegetables), profiteroles (choux
puffs filled with vanilla ice cream
and topped with chocolate sauce).

Throughout the years, La Boutarde has remained one of my favorite little Paris restaurants—lively, always bustling, serving a mix of classic bistro fare with a few (not always successful) modern touches. Set off on a side street in Neuilly, at the western edge of the city, La Boutarde is always impeccably clean, friendly, and filled with well-heeled Neuilly residents and office workers. The tables are covered with red-checkered cloths, and the daily wine specials and *plats du jour* (such as sautéed veal with carrots; or poached duck and vegetable stew) are scribbled on mirrors that line the walls. The classic fare is much more successful than some of the modern creations, so stick with such specials as *céleri rémoulade* and the *sauté d'agneau* and you should have a fine time. Don't miss the delicious *glace au miel, au coulis de framboise,* honey ice cream with raspberry sauce. And do sample the generally good house Chinon, a delicate, fruity Loire Valley red.

JACQUELINE FENIX
42 Avenue Charles-de-
  Gaulle, 92200 Neuilly-
  sur-Seine.
(46.24.42.61).
Métro: Les Sablons.
Last orders taken at 2 P.M.
  and 10 P.M.
Closed Saturday, Sunday,
  August, and New Year's.
Credit cards: AE, V.
Air-conditioned.
English spoken.
295-franc menu. A la carte,
  350 francs.

Consistency and stability are two important traits in a restaurant, and two of the hardest to maintain over the years. As customers, there are days when we are ready for potluck and days when we want to dine with a measure of security, assured that there will be no surprises, thank you. One restaurant that continues to deliver that sort of day-to-day reliability is Jacqueline Fénix, a cozy and tranquil restaurant just outside the city limits in Neuilly. As soon as you enter, you know you're in good hands. The decor is both elegant and homey, with sprays of fresh flowers, a sparkling chandelier, richly colored oil paintings, gigantic mirrors, and Jacqueline Fénix's handmade chintz chair coverings. The blond and attentive Fénix is there to greet you, take your order, and urge you to take just one last bite of cheese or dessert. You are equally secure with chef Michel Rubod's menu, which over the

SPECIALTIES:
Seasonal: millefeuille de lapereau à l'aubergine (layered rabbit and eggplant), bar braisé aux poires à la crème de Cassis (braised sea bass with pears and black currant liqueur), daube de lapereau au basilic et aux culs d'artichauts (stew of young rabbit, basil, and artichoke hearts).

years has changed in content but never in concept. Dishes are orchestrated, are composed, and appear complex by nature; but the end result, in tasting, proves the opposite. Simplicity and freshness remain his trademark. And you never have to guess about what's on your plate. No matter what combinations Rubod dreams up, they have a refreshing springtime air about them. Take his *daube de lapereau.* Many parts join to form a basic Provençal stew: moist, tender rabbit with mounds of fresh artichokes, sprinkled with fresh basil and a nicely acidic tomato *confit.* One of his prettiest seasonal specials is the perchlike fish called *sandre,* sprinkled with tender green asparagus and bathed in a chive-

SABLES DE POMMES CHAUDES, CONFITURE DU TEMPS
SHORTBREAD COOKIES WITH WARM APPLES AND SEASONAL FRUIT JAM

Many Paris restaurants are returning to simpler, homey desserts such as this one of warm shortbread topped with sautéed apple slices and a dollop of homemade apricot jam. This version comes from Michel Rubod, chef at Jacqueline Fénix, a refreshing little restaurant in Neuilly (see entry, above). Note that the dough must be prepared the day before it is being served.

Shortbread:
⅓ cup (50 g) almonds, ground to a fine powder
¼ cup (50 g) sugar
2 egg yolks
⅓ cup (3 ounces; 90 g) unsalted butter, softened
1 cup (140 g) all-purpose flour (do not use unbleached flour)

Apple slices:
1 tablespoon (½ ounce; 15g) unsalted butter
4 tart cooking apples, peeled, cored, cut into thin slices
1 tablespoon sugar

Apricot jam

1. Prepare the shortbread dough: In the bowl of a food processor, blend the ground almonds, sugar, and egg yolks. Add the butter and flour and process until well blended. Remove the dough from the bowl and shape it into a 6 x 2-inch (15 x 5-cm) roll, wrap in plastic wrap, and refrigerate for 24 hours.

2. Prepare the oven to 375°F (190°C).

3. Roll the cookie dough to a ¼-inch (7-mm) thickness, then cut into 18 2½-inch (6-cm) rounds. Place on a baking sheet and bake until golden, about 10 minutes.

4. Prepare the apple slices: While the cookies are baking, melt the tablespoon of butter in a medium-size skillet over moderate heat. Add the apples and sugar, and cook, stirring occasionally, just until the apple slices are cooked through, about 10 minutes.

5. To serve, place 3 warm cookies on each plate, top with a portion of apples, and serve immediately with a dish of jam alongside.

Yield: 6 servings.

flecked *beurre blanc*. The dish has the look of a fresh
May garden: many tints of greens, soft flavors, and
textures that soothe and satisfy. Soup lovers will
adore his full-flavored *pistou,* a thick, deep green,
plentiful soup, sparkling with garlic, basil, and
tender chunks of *langoustines.* If none of this sounds
simple and all that really appeals is a tossed salad,
then that's what you'll get, with a choice of dressings. For dessert gourmands, Jacqueline Fénix
presents a multicourse symphony. Among personal
favorites are two likely to inspire memories of
childhood. There is a warm chocolate soufflé served
with hot chocolate sauce and toasted *broiche*; and a
platter of puffy lemon tea cakes and crisp shortbread served with a dollop of rich apricot marma-
lade (see recipe, page 97).

On my last visit, the only flaw was in the
seasoning. Many dishes could have used just a last-
minute perking up, an infinitesimal sprinkling of
salt, a turn of the pepper mill, to give them a final
boost as they came from kitchen to dining room.

RESTAURANT JAMIN
32 Rue de Longchamp,
    Paris 16.
(47.27.12.27).
Métro: Trocadéro.
Last orders taken at 2:15 P.M.
    and 10:15 P.M.
Closed Saturday, Sunday, and
    July.
Credit cards: AE, DC, V.
Private dining room for 18.
Air-conditioned.
English spoken.
690- and 790-franc menus.
    A la carte, 800 francs.

SPECIALTIES:
*Seasonal: galette de truffes aux
oignons et lard fumé (truffle cake
with onions and bacon), foie gras
chaud à la crème de lentilles
(warm foie gras with creamy
lentil sauce).*

Not since Paul Bocuse has a chef won the hearts
and palates of a nation as Joël Robuchon has.
This timid, quiet, serious, and hardworking chef is
an unlikely superstar, for his joy lies in creation and
execution, not in wandering about the dining room
to gather kudos and compliments. In fact, he seems
almost embarrassed by the fuss made over him and
the restaurant, and often I wonder if he didn't wish
all the fanfare would calm down so he'd have more
quiet time to spend creating.

What's so special about Robuchon? Quite
simply, he is the most uncompromising chef I've
ever seen, and one of the most intelligent. He has
redefined modern French cuisine. He offers luxury,
but never excess. He provides imaginative, original
food that is never bizarre. Each dish is a well-
conceived, well-constructed work of art, as pleasing
to the eye as it is to the palate. And no one, but no
one, in France cares as much about raw ingredients:
He selects the freshest and most fragrant of black
truffles and uses them with generous abandon. He
makes regular trips around the country, visiting his
fishermen in Brittany, his truffle merchants in the

Southwest, the specialist who raises his veal in the Auvergne. My favorite dishes here include anything Robuchon showers with black truffles (particularly his truffle cake with onions and bacon), his foie gras with a cream of lentils, the superbly fresh fish preparations, and his always appealing, ever-changing assortment of desserts. (A recipe for his Puff Pastry Pineapple Tart appears on page 197.) In a very brief time, many of his dishes have become classics, including his superb *rôti d'agneau aux herbes en croûte de sel* (roasted lamb with herbs cooked in a salt crust; see recipe, following page), and he still makes his own bread and rolls (see recipe, page 222). There's no question that Robuchon is at the peak of his career, and it's likely he'll stay there for many years to come. The biggest problem here, of course, is securing a table: There are only 45 spots, so patience is the name of the game.

BRASSERIE STELLA
133 Avenue Victor-Hugo, Paris 16.
(47.27.60.54).
Métro: Victor-Hugo.
Last orders taken at 2:30 P.M. and 1 A.M.
Closed Thursday and August.
Credit card: V.
Some English spoken.
150 to 180 francs.

SPECIALTIES:
Brasserie: plateau de fruits de mer (platter of fish and shellfish); petit salé aux lentilles (salt-cured pork with lentils); choucroute (sauerkraut, pork, and sausages); steak tartare (chopped raw beef); plats du jour (changing daily specials).

Brasserie Stella is so stunningly old-fashioned that it's authentically back in style. The glaring neon lights and helter-skelter decor are as tacky as they are nostalgically soothing, and the stylish clientele, squashed elbow-to-elbow along faded banquettes, make this a perfect place to settle back and people-watch. In truth, Stella is just another neighborhood hangout, but when you consider the neighborhood—the very fashionable 16th—you understand its appeal. Service here is surprisingly democratic, the food's all right, and you can always find a table late at night, long after other restaurants have closed their doors. I love their *steak tartare*—which waiters prepare tableside with great fanfare and flourish—served with decent *frites* or a simple green salad.

ROTI D'AGNEAU AUX HERBES EN CROUTE DE SEL JAMIN
JAMIN'S ROASTED LAMB WITH HERBS COOKED IN A SALT CRUST

This remarkably simple and flavorful dish is a popular item at chef Joël Robuchon's Restaurant Jamin (see entry, page 98). The lamb roasts in a thyme-infused salt crust, which actually serves as a hermetic, flavorful roasting shell. The crust is discarded after cooking.

Salt Crust:
½ cup (150 g) table salt
1 cup (240 g) coarse
  (kosher) salt
1 egg, separated
3¾ cups (525 g) all-
  purpose unbleached
  flour
4 tablespoons fresh
  thyme leaves, or 2
  tablespoons dried
  thyme, mixed with
  1¼ cups (310 ml)
  water

Lamb:
2 pounds (1 kg)
  boneless roasting
  lamb (a portion of
  leg of lamb works
  very well)
Freshly ground black
  pepper
1 teaspoon fresh thyme
  leaves, or ½
  teaspoon dried
  thyme
Pinch of salt
1 teaspoon coarse
  (kosher) salt

1. Preheat the oven to 400°F (205°C).

2. Prepare the salt crust: In a large bowl, blend together the two salts, the egg white, flour, and thyme and water mixture. Knead until well blended. It is essential that the dough be firm, not too moist or sticky, or the lamb will steam, not roast. If necessary, knead in additional flour for a firm dough. Roll out the dough so it is large enough to wrap the lamb.

3. Season the lamb with the pepper and thyme. Completely wrap the lamb in the salt crust, pressing all the seams together and checking to make sure it is well sealed, and place on a baking sheet.

4. Just before roasting, combine the egg yolk with the pinch of salt and ½ teaspoon water to make a glaze. With a pastry brush, brush the glaze over the surface of the crust. Sprinkle all over with coarse salt.

5. Place the lamb in the oven and roast for 25 to 30 minutes for rare (or until the interior of the lamb is cooked to 112°F, or 45°C, when measured with a meat thermometer). For well-done lamb, cook an additional 5 to 10 minutes. The crust should be a deep golden brown. Let the lamb rest in the crust for 1 hour before serving. (The lamb will remain warm.)

6. To serve, cut open the crust at one end, remove the lamb, and cut the meat on the diagonal into very fine slices. Discard the crust. Serve with buttered fresh pasta or a potato gratin.

Yield: 4 servings.

ARC DE TRIOMPHE, PLACE DES TERNES, PORTE MAILLOT

17th arrondissement

APICIUS
122 Avenue de Villiers,
    Paris 17.
(43.80.19.66).
Métro: Péreire.
Last orders taken at 2:15 P.M.
    and 10 P.M.
Closed Saturday, Sunday,
    August, and Christmas
    week.
Credit cards: AE, V.
Private dining room for 25.
Air-conditioned.
English spoken.
310-franc lunch menu, 390-
    franc dinner menu. A la
    carte, 450 francs.

S P E C I A L T I E S :
Seasonal: foie gras de canard,
poêlé, en aigre doux (sweet and
sour sautéed duck liver), grand
dessert au chocolat amer (assorted
chocolate desserts).

I like chef Jean-Pierre Vigato's sense of style. His food is unfussy, and he's not afraid to offer very, very simple fare. But that's not to say his food is bland or unstylish. On my last visit, I fell in love with his flawless *fricassée de champignons*—a beautiful, fragrant mix of the freshest wild mushrooms—served in generous portions from a lovely silver saucepan; and his fine ravioli of *langoustines* and lobster, a regal, full-flavored dish that's as fresh as a sea breeze. Those who savor more substantial fare will love his manly *"plats bourgeois,"* including veal kidneys, lamb chops, beef, and pig's feet, all prepared in a modern, satisfyingly simple style. The pastel decor leaves me a bit cold, and service can be awkward and uneven.

LA COQUILLE
6 Rue du Débarcadère,
    Paris 17.
(45.74.25.95).
Métro: Porte Maillot.
Last orders taken at 2 P.M.
    and 10:30 P.M.
Closed Sunday, Monday,
    August, and Christmas
    week.
Credit card: V.
Air-conditioned.
English spoken.
About 300 francs.

S P E C I A L T I E S :
Elegant bistro: scallops in season
(October to May), fricassée de
poulet aux morilles (chicken with
wild morel mushrooms), soufflé au
praslin de noisettes (hazelnut
soufflé).

O ver the years, some of my most pleasant Parisian dinners have taken place at La Coquille, a small, cozy restaurant that for years was run by the outgoing Paul Blache and his daughter, Catherine. They have retired but the current owners, Clément and Marie-Thérèse Lausecker, are doing justice to La Coquille's fine tradition. Best of all, the menu is still filled with dishes I've learned to love, like the well-seasoned *boudin noir* (blood sausage) served with a variety of mustards; the perfect grilled fish (try the *turbotin,* served with a chive and butter sauce), the very warming, satisfying *fricassée* of chicken with fresh cream and morel mushrooms (see recipe, page 111), and the fragrant hazelnut soufflé (see recipe, page 104). From October through May, they continue to serve the superb classic *coquilles Saint-Jacques,* simply baked in their shells with a touch of herbs and butter, and during the fall and winter months, Monsieur Lausecker brings in wild game from his native Alsace.

LE BISTRO D'A COTE
10 Rue Gustave-Flaubert,
   Paris 17.
(42.67.05.81).
Métro: Ternes.
Last orders taken at 2 P.M.
   and 11 P.M.
Closed Saturday lunch,
   Sunday, holidays, and the
   first two weeks in
   August.
Credit cards: EC, V.
Sidewalk terrace.
English spoken.
180 francs.

SPECIALTIES:
Lyonnais: saladier lyonnais aux pieds d'agneau (green salad with bacon, soft-cooked egg, and sheep's foot), salade tiède de lentilles et cervelas de Lyon (warm lentil salad with sausage), andouillette tirée à la ficelle (poached chitterling sausage).

Michel Rostang seems to have the right idea. Just as diners were beginning to say they were fed up with four-hour meals and 600-franc bills, he gave them a chance to push back the carpets, roll up their sleeves, and dive into sensuous food that revives and satisfies. Right around the corner from the grander restaurant that bears his name, he opened Le Bistro d'à Côté (The Bistro Next Door), and it was an instant success. Rostang began with impeccable material: The adjacent 1900s *épicerie* was in perfect condition, with tin ceilings, mirrored walls, and thick shelves (marble on one side, for the cream, butter, and eggs, and elegant wood on the other side, to stock the dry goods). Rostang and his wife, Marie-Claude, have filled these shelves with treasures gathered at Paris's flea markets over a month of Sundays: colorful asparagus plates and pitchers, Art Deco clocks and radios, and an enormous collection of well-worn, familiar red Michelin guides. In all, it makes an ideal, even idyllic backdrop for a traditional Lyonnais bistro, for hearty platters of he-man fare—meltingly tender chicken in red wine vinegar and creamy potato gratins, salads of curly endive, a superbly fresh and well-

The Bistro Next Door, a former épicerie.

On May 26, 1791, the Restaurant Méot opened, and soon won an extraordinary reputation. It boasted of bathtubs full of Champagne, and 22 varieties of red wine and 27 varieties of white on the extensive menu, which offered more than 100 different dishes.

Chef Michel Rostang at his Bistro d'à Côté.

seasoned terrine of chicken livers, crisp green lentils topped with *cervelas* sausages, and a marvelous terrine of duck *confit* accompanied by wilted green cabbage. I've been less enthusiastic about the rather dry ham and cheese gratin of macaroni and dry *manchons*, or legs of duck; and I remain unconvinced of the gastronomic merits of most French beef—which is bland and tough, served here as thick, beautiful, yet unimpressive *côte de boeuf*.

There is also a collection of modern dishes that do not seem out of place: Rostang offers a stunning terrine of red peppers, tomatoes, and fresh anchovies; an unusual *galette*, or thick corn pancake, filled with salmon and bathed in a fine curry sauce; and a serviceable carpaccio of tuna, thinly sliced tuna marinated in oil and served with grilled country bread. The wine list offers some well-priced bottles, including their house red, a fruity, pure syrah red from the *collines Rhodaniennes* in the northern part of the Rhone Valley; a super white Savoie, the Chignin from René Quenard; Léon Beyer's pinot d'Alsace; and Georges Duboeuf's omnipresent but welcoming Brouilly.

SOUFFLE AU PRASLIN DE NOISETTES LA COQUILLE
LA COQUILLE'S HAZELNUT SOUFFLE

La Coquille is a favorite neighborhood bistro (see entry, page 101), and this is its signature dessert. I sampled the soufflé the first time I dined there one cold wintry evening. As my love for La Coquille grew, so did my fondness for this light, hazelnut-filled dessert.

Praline powder:
¾ cup (100 g)
   hazelnuts
½ cup (100 g) sugar
1 teaspoon unsalted
   butter for buttering a
   cookie sheet

Pastry cream:
1 cup (250 ml) milk
½ vanilla bean
6 eggs, separated
3 tablespoons sugar
¼ cup (30 g) all-
   purpose flour (do
   not use unbleached
   flour)
Pinch of salt
1 tablespoon (½ ounce;
   15 g) unsalted butter,
   for buttering a 4-cup
   (1-liter) soufflé mold

¼ cup (60 ml) kirsch

1. Preheat the oven to 300°F (150°C).

2. Toast the hazelnuts on a baking sheet in the oven for 5 minutes. While they are still warm, rub them in a dish towel to remove as much skin as possible. Cool, then chop coarsely by hand.

3. In a medium-size saucepan over low heat, melt the sugar until it dissolves and becomes slightly rust-colored. Add the nuts and stir until they are thoroughly coated with sugar. This is now your praline.

4. Turn the praline out onto a cool buttered cookie sheet and allow to harden, about 5 minutes. When hard, place the praline in a food processor and grind to a powder. Set aside. (The praline powder can be made in advance and stored in an airtight container. It can be refrigerated for a week or frozen indefinitely.)

5. Prepare the pastry cream: In a medium-size saucepan over medium heat, bring the milk and vanilla bean to a boil. Remove from the heat, cover, and allow to steep for 5 minutes.

6. In a medium-size mixing bowl combine 4 of the egg yolks with the sugar, then the flour. Remove the vanilla

CHEZ FRED
190 bis Boulevard Pereire,
   Paris 17.
(45.74.20.48).
Métro: Pereire.
Last orders taken at 2 P.M.
   and 10:30 P.M.
Closed Saturday lunch,
   Sunday, and August.
Credit cards: AE, DC, V.
Sidewalk terrace.
English spoken.
145-franc menu, including
   wine. A la carte, about
   200 francs.

SPECIALTIES:
Bistro: changing daily specials.

A good-natured sort of bistro where handsome, chatty young waiters serve up a fine and well-priced litany of daily specials, such as *pot-au-feu, boeuf à la mode, gigot, sauté d'agneau*, and *petit salé*. The decor here is *grand-mère* 1930—the walls covered with mirrors, old china, and a collection of umbrellas left behind by absent-minded customers. I love the fact that they've kept to the traditional daily specials: if *boeuf mode*'s on the menu, this must be Thursday!

bean from the milk and whisk the milk into the egg mixture. (You may rinse the vanilla bean and reserve it for another use.) Place the mixture in a medium-size saucepan and cook over medium heat, stirring constantly, until it begins to boil. Continue cooking for 2 minutes, stirring constantly. Remove from the heat and add the 2 additional egg yolks, whisking until well blended. (The soufflé can be prepared ahead up to this point.)

7. Preheat the oven to 325°F (165°C).

8. To finish the soufflé, in a large bowl add half the praline powder to the pastry cream and mix until well blended.

9. In another large bowl beat the egg whites with a pinch of salt until stiff but not dry. Add one-third of the egg white mixture to the pastry cream mixture and fold in gently but thoroughly. Then gently fold in the remaining whites. Don't overmix, but be sure that the mixture is well blended.

10. Butter the soufflé mold. Gently pour the soufflé mixture into the mold and sprinkle the remaining praline powder on top of the soufflé. This will form a golden crust when the soufflé is baked. Bake for 12 to 15 minutes.

11. Remove the soufflé from the oven, sprinkle with the kirsch, and serve immediately.

Yield: 4 servings.

CHEZ GEORGES
273 Boulevard Pereire,
　　Paris 17.
(45.74.31.00).
Métro: Porte Maillot.
Last orders taken at 2:30 P.M.
　　and 11:30 P.M.
Closed August.
Credit card: V.
Terrace dining.
Private dining room for 35.
English spoken.
250 francs.

S P E C I A L T I E S :
Bistro: changing daily specials,
gigot rôti aux flageolets (roast leg
of lamb with white beans).

Since 1926 the Mazarguil family has kept this classic bistro intact, with its banquettes, mirrors, lace curtains, and waiters rushing about at a furious pace. The place is always lively, with its old-fashioned air, and although the food has some very uneven moments, this is a convenient, low-key spot to know about for those weekend nights when so many other establishments close their doors. Best bets include their fresh oysters from the Charentes (try the tiny, mild *papillons*), the leg of lamb—sliced right at the table from a rolling cart—served with white beans, the roast beef and potato gratin, and a rather respectable *tarte Tatin.* I'm less impressed with the *petit salé aux choux* (salt-cured pork with cabbage)—on my last visit the cabbage tasted old and bitter—and with the gigantic profiteroles, which offer more quantity than quality. The wine list offers some very good selections, including Tollot-Beaut's Chorey-lès-Beaune, Domaine Parent's Côtes-de-Beaune, and Dauvissat's Chablis.

LE GOURMET DES TERNES
87 Boulevard de Courcelles, Paris 17.
(4.27.43.04).
Métro: Ternes.
Last orders taken at 2:30 P.M. and 10 P.M.
Closed Saturday, Sunday, and August.
No credit cards.
Sidewalk terrace.
150 francs.

SPECIALTIES:
Bistro: grilled meats with French fries.

Anyone looking for a superb grilled steak or lamb chops in totally unpretentious surroundings should reserve at Le Gourmet des Ternes, a modest bistro near the Place des Ternes. The *complet* sign appears in the window around eleven each morning, meaning that all tables are already reserved. The neighborhood businessmen know a good deal when they find it. This is a well-worn spot, recently improved with a coat of paint, and although none of the chairs or light fixtures match and the waitresses lost interest a long time ago, the regulars keep returning, enjoying the chic and lively crowd, the solid, simple fare. In the summertime, you can enjoy a meal on the small sidewalk terrace.

MICHEL ROSTANG
22 Rue Rennequin, Paris 17.
(47.63.40.77).
Métro: Ternes.
Last orders taken at 2 P.M. and 10 P.M.
Closed Saturday lunch (and dinner April to August), Sunday, holidays, and the first two weeks in August.
Credit cards: EC, V.
Private dining room for 10.
Air-conditioned.
English spoken.
230- and 400-franc lunch menus; 460-franc tasting menu. A la carte, 600 francs.

SPECIALTIES:
Seasonal: tarte tiède et croustillante de saumon sauvage cru (warm fresh raw salmon tart), galette d'artichauts aux truffes fraîches (thin cake of artichokes and truffles) in season.

Over the years I've had very on-again, off-again feelings about Michel Rostang's restaurant. I always find the decor wildly overdone, even oppressive, and the food has varied from dull to spectacular. If my last visit is any indication, however, Rostang and his staff are in better form than ever, despite the fact that he divides his time between Paris and New York and has the added responsibility of his next-door bistro, Le Bistro d'à Côté. Rostang seems to be one happy survivor of the *nouvelle cuisine* popularity of the 1970s, and his current cuisine shows maturity and fine attention to detail. Who could complain about the very freshest, first-of-season scallops sliced paper thin, set on a bed of lamb's lettuce, drizzled with fragrant olive oil, then showered with diced scallops, chervil, and tomatoes? Or how about the thickest, freshest, fattest *raie* (skate wing) quickly pan-fried to a golden brown, set atop bright green savoy cabbage? His ingredients are first-rate, and his very attentive and professional staff know how to make diners feel at home. A note of warning: Over the past few years I've received many complaints from Americans who felt waiters showed an anti-American bias.

GUY SAVOY
18 Rue Troyon, Paris 17.
(43.80.40.61).
Métro: Charles-de-Gaulle/
Etoile.
Last orders taken at 2 P.M.
and 10:45 P.M.
Closed Saturday lunch (and
dinner in summer) and
Sunday.
Credit cards: EC, V.
Private dining room for 20.
Air-conditioned.
English spoken.
400-franc menu. A la carte,
300 to 600 francs.

SPECIALTIES:
Seasonal: anguilles fumées et petits
poireaux tièdes en vinaigrette
émulsionée (smoked eel with warm
leeks in vinaigrette).

For nearly ten years, Guy Savoy has remained one of my favorite Parisian chefs. He serves the sort of food I could eat every night of the week—a variety of uncomplicated fish and shellfish preparations topped with light and vibrant sauces, along with an ever-changing repertoire of daily specials that match the mood of the season. Now in his new surroundings (the large, airy space occupied by Maguy and Gilbert Le Coze, before they took their popular Le Bernardin to New York), Guy Savoy has a restaurant to match his culinary talents. The welcome is always warm, there is an appealing assortment of wines to choose from (and a charming *sommelier* to help you wend your way through the list), and the crisp new green and white decor is sure to put you in a properly restful, cheerful mood.

TIMGAD
21 Rue Brunel, Paris 17.
(45.74.23.70).
Métro: Porte Maillot.
Last orders taken at 2:30 P.M.
and 11 P.M.
Open daily.
Credit cards: AE, DC, EC, V.
Air-conditioned.
200 francs.

SPECIALTIES:
North African: couscous, tajines
(meat and poultry stews), méchoui
(whole grilled lamb).

Combining the rich gastronomic traditions of Morocco, Algeria, and Tunisia, Timgad offers some of the most refined and elegant couscous in Paris, the best spicy *merguez* lamb sausage, along with impeccably seasoned *tajines,* meat and poultry stews cooked over a wood-fired stove. Timgad's fantasy interior—decorative white walls of intricately carved plaster, brightened with sprays of fresh fruit and a flowing fountain—puts everyone in a festive mood, eager to enjoy plate after plate of buttery couscous, garnished with vegetables, raisins, chick-peas, and a luscious broth. As in most Parisian restaurants, the staff is all male, save for one important employee: the couscous lady. As chef Ahmad Laasri insists, only women have the patience for rolling the delicate grains of couscous, or semolina. So each morning a young Moroccan woman rolls some thirty pounds (about fifteen kilos) of the delicate grain, enough to feed the restaurant's customers for the day. Favorites here— along with the couscous and mandatory second helpings of their homemade *merguez*—include the coriander-laced chicken with olives and any version of their full-flavored lamb, grilled over an open wood fire.

SAINT-OUEN, LA VILLETTE, BELLEVILLE, PERE LACHAISE

19th and 20th arrondissements and Saint-Ouen

AU COCHON D'OR
192 Avenue Jean-Jaurès,
 Paris 19.
(46.07.23.13).
Métro: Porte de Pantin.
Last orders taken at 2:30 P.M.
 and 10:30 P.M.
Open daily.
Credit cards: AE, DC, EC, V.
Private dining room for 40.
Air-conditioned.
English spoken.
350 francs.

SPECIALTIES:
Grilled meats, shellfish.

The old stockyards that made this and other bistros along Avenue Jean-Jaurès so famous are no more, but that doesn't stop the crowds from filling this old-fashioned two-story restaurant. Go on a Sunday afternoon, order a steak (I think they serve the very best beef in town) and a bottle of Bordeaux, and sit back to watch the happy Parisian families feasting with *grand-mère* on snails, oysters, grilled meats, and plenty of wine.

LE COQ DE LA MAISON
 BLANCHE
37 Boulevard Jean-Jaurès,
 93400 Saint-Ouen.
(40.11.01.23).
Métro: Mairie de Saint-Ouen.
Last orders taken at 2:30 P.M.
 and 10 P.M.
Closed Sunday and May Day.
Credit cards: AE, V.
Terrace dining.
Private dining room for 120.
English spoken.
250 francs.

SPECIALTIES:
Bistro: jambon persillé (parsleyed ham), coq au vin (chicken in red wine), game in season.

Just across the Paris city line north of town sits the rambling Coq de la Maison Blanche, a bustling place that gives you the feeling of dining in a popular country restaurant, not a corner bistro near Paris. The house specialty is *coq au vin*, here prepared with an honest curmudgeonly bird and served up in a good, thick red wine sauce from a huge copper vessel. Other dishes worth sampling include the *salade folle*, made with fresh foie gras, crayfish, and green beans; *escargots aux noisettes*, a hearty platter of snails seasoned with parsley and hazelnuts; and a classically good *jambon persillé*. The wine list is small but well chosen. There's always a carefully selected Beaujolais, along with inexpensive, little-known wines, such as Ménétou-Salon, from the Loire Valley.

CHEZ LOUISETTE
136 Avenue Michelet,
 Marché Vernaison, 94300
 Saint-Ouen.
(40.12.10.14).
Métro: Porte de Clignancourt.
Open Saturday, Sunday, and
 Monday, from noon until
 6 P.M. only.
No credit cards.
100 francs.

When I'm in Paris for the weekend, my very favorite Sundays begin with a long run in Parc Monceau, followed by an afternoon combing Paris's vast flea market at the Porte de Clignancourt. During my run, I think about the platters of mussels at Chez Louisette, and about the great Edith Piaf songs that Emmanuelle—a dark, buxom, energetic Piaf-style *chanteuse*—will sing that afternoon as she woos the very mixed group of regulars

Bistro: moules (steamed mussles), poulet rôti (roast chicken); petit salé aux lentilles (salt pork with lentils).

that crowd into this crazy-as-a-loon bistro. Chez Louisette is a riot, with sawdust on the floor, a dime-store mix-and-match decor (take a look at the ceiling, with its dozen or so chandeliers, obvious flea market rejects), and Christmas decorations that stay up year-round. The happy drinking crowd is always just short of rowdy, and I find that I tend to order the same thing each time: giant bowls of steamed mussels—a dish that the Duchess of Windsor is said to have eaten here, ever so daintily, with her fingers. I have a 1950s guidebook to Paris that quotes one client: "Chez Louisette's is the only place in the flea market where you get your money's worth!" If you stay well into the afternoon, you'll note there's barely a dry eye in the house as Emmanuelle (and others) sing on about "La Vie en Rose." You won't regret a thing: a scene, in the best old-fashioned sense.

MERE-GRAND
20 Rue Orfila, Paris 20.
(46.36.03.29).
Métro: Gambetta.
Last orders taken at 2 P.M. and 9 P.M.
Closed Saturday, Sunday, and July.
Credit card: V.
46- to 98-franc lunch menus (including wine), 66- to 129-franc dinner menus.

SPECIALTIES:
Home cooking: confit de canard maison (preserved duck), ris de veau à l'estragon (sweetbreads with tarragon), lapin aux pruneaux (rabbit stew with prunes), poule au pot Mère-Grand (poached chicken and vegetables).

This homey neighborhood restaurant may not merit a detour on its own, but anyone looking for a place to eat before or after a visit to the historic Père Lachaise cemetery will want to make plans to lunch at Mère-Grand, a charming spot decorated in shades of mauve, with little copper saucepans hanging from the walls. Everyone here orders from one of the three simple menus, which include such classic bistro fare as *lapin à la moutarde* and grilled *tournedos* of beef. There's a varied assortment of fresh-flavored first courses, among them a rugged country *pâté du Périgord*, and better than average *fromage de tête* (headcheese). The house wine is drinkable and service is friendly. Reservations are not accepted, so if you plan on lunch get there at noon. By 12:05, every table is taken.

PARIS ENVIRONS: VERSAILLES

LA BOULE D'OR
25 Rue du Maréchal-Foch,
  78000 Versailles.
(39.50.22.97).
Last orders taken at 3 P.M.
  and 10 P.M..
Closed Sunday dinner and
  Monday.
Credit cards: AE, DC, EC, V.
English spoken.
138-franc lunch menu
  weekdays, 180-franc
  lunch menu daily. A la
  carte, 300 francs.

SPECIALTIES:
Authentic classic French dishes
ranging from the eighteenth
century to the present, specialties of
the Jura; agneau de lait (milk-fed
spring lamb) from mid-January to
April.

Diners who want to remain historic to the core should visit La Boule d'Or, founded in 1674 and billed as the oldest inn in Versailles. Under the reign of Louis XIV, this was only one of 400 inns to be found in Versailles, and today it serves as a living culinary museum, offering dozens of thoroughly classic preparations, some dating back to 1383. I highly recommend La Boule d'Or for a Sunday lunch, when you can follow the lead of the well-heeled locals: doing a bit of marketing in the morning, spending a few hours at table, reserving the afternoon for the Versailles gardens.

LE POTAGER DU ROY
1 Rue du Maréchal-Joffre,
  78000 Versailles.
(39.50.35.34).
Last orders taken at 1:45 P.M.
  and 9:45 P.M.
Closed Sunday and Monday.
Credit card: V.
Air-conditioned.
English spoken.
105- and 150-franc menus.
  A la carte, 300 francs.

SPECIALTIES:
Seasonal: poissons crus marinés
(marinated raw fish).

Le Potager du Roy is one of Versailles' best dining bargains, and so it comes as no surprise to find the restaurant full at both lunch and dinner. The fare ranges from the most traditional—foie gras, filet of beef, *jarret de veau*, and *oeufs à la neige*— to more contemporary fare. Some dishes we sampled on the last visit included a light salad of marinated sardines served with a ramekin of tabouli; a cold fresh pasta salad in a creamy but light zucchini sauce; and a fine *charlotte d'aubergines* (eggplant charlotte filled with chunks of flavorsome lamb). The orange and brown decor won't exactly cheer you up, but service is swift and friendly.

LA FRICASSEE DE POULET AUX MORILLES LA COQUILLE
LA COQUILLE'S FRICASSEE OF CHICKEN WITH MORELS

I must have visited La Coquille (see entry, page 101) a dozen times before sampling this thoroughly satisfying bistro dish. I always seemed to be ordering the game or the boudin *(blood sausage) or the beautifully cooked scallops, and just ignored the chicken. Now it is a favorite, and one that is particularly welcoming on a cold wintry evening. This version is lighter than most, though for a richer dish, one could substitute cream for the morel cooking water, reducing it as instructed in the recipe.*

1 ounce (30 g) dried
  morels
3 tablespoons extra-
  virgin olive oil
1 tablespoon (½ ounce;
  15 g) unsalted butter
1 chicken (about 3 to 4
  pounds; 1.5 to 2 kg),
  cut into serving
  pieces and brought
  to room temperature
Salt and freshly ground
  black pepper to taste
2 shallots, finely minced
¼ teaspoon sweet
  paprika
1 cup (250 ml) *crème
  fraîche* (see page 237)
  or heavy cream
Small handful of parsley
  or chervil, minced,
  for garnish

1. Combine the morels with 2 cups (500 ml) of water in a medium saucepan. Bring to a boil over high heat, then allow to cook away vigorously, uncovered, until the liquid is reduced by half. This should take about 20 minutes. Strain the liquid through dampened cheesecloth. Rinse the morels, return them to the strained liquid, and reserve.

2. Melt the oil and butter in a large, deep-sided 12-inch (30-cm) skillet over high heat. (If you do not have a pan large enough to hold all the chicken pieces in a single layer, cook the chicken in several batches.) Season the chicken liberally with salt and pepper, and when the fats are hot but not smoking, brown the chicken on one side until the skin turns an even, golden brown, about 5 minutes. Carefully regulate the heat to avoid scorching the skin. Turn the pieces and brown them on the other side for an additional 5 minutes.

3. Remove the chicken pieces to a large platter. Discard all but 1 tablespoon of the fat remaining in the pan. In the pan, over medium heat, brown the shallots. Then mix in the paprika.

4. Combine the *crème fraîche*, morels, and strained liquid, stir well, and add to the skillet. Return the chicken to the skillet and cook, covered, over low heat, until the chicken is cooked to desired doneness, about 20 minutes.

5. Serve with cooked rice or steamed new potatoes, sprinkling each serving with fresh parsley or chervil.

BRASSERIE DU THEATRE
15 Rue des Réservoirs,
    78000 Versailles.
(39.50.03.21).
Last orders taken at 3 P.M.
    and 1:30 A.M.
Closed December 25.
Credit card: V
Terrace dining.
English spoken.
150 francs.

SPECIALTIES:
Choucroute (sauerkraut, various sausages, bacon, and pork, served with potatoes), grilled meats.

My first choice for lunch in Versailles is the lively Brasserie du Théâtre, a charmingly decorated turn-of-the-century spot featuring classic bistro and brasserie fare: *choucroute* and *cassoulet*, salads of herring and *céleri rémoulade*, and a litany of daily specials that might include lamb with white beans or simple grilled sole. This neighbourhood brasserie is billed as the Lipp of Versailles, and one can see why. The setting is right out of the movies, with a cast that includes a tall, handsome *maître d'hôtel* who resembles Roger Moore, and slim mustachioed waiters sporting white aprons that reach down to their toes. Travel posters, antique enamel advertising plaques, and autographed celebrity posters line the walls, while an enormous vase of bright fresh flowers welcomes you as you enter the dining room.

RESTAURANTS: AN ALPHABETICAL LISTING

(WITH ARRONDISSEMENTS)

Chez Albert, Paris 14

Allard, Paris 6

Ambassade d'Auvergne,
    Paris 3

L'Ambroisie, Paris 4

L'Ami Louis, Paris 3

Chez André, Paris 8

Androuët, Paris 8

Chez Les Anges, Paris 7

Apicius, Paris 17

L'Aquitaine, Paris 15

Artois, Paris 8

L'Assiette, Paris 14

Astier, Paris 11

Brasserie Balzar, Paris 5

Benoit, Paris 4

Le Boeuf sur le Toit, Paris 8

Bofinger, Paris 4

La Bonne Table des Fés,
    Paris 6

La Boule d'Or, Versailles

La Boutarde,
    Neuilly-sur-Seine

Bristol, Paris 8

La Cagouille, Paris 14

Le Caméléon, Paris 6

Carré des Feuillants, Paris 1

Cartet, Paris 11

Caviar Kaspia, Paris 8

Chardenoux, Paris 11

Charlot, Le Roi des
    Coquillages, Paris 9

Aux Charpentiers, Paris 6

Chiberta, Paris 8

Au Cochon d'Or, Paris 19

Au Cochon d'Or des Halles,
    Paris 1

Le Coq de la Maison Blanche,
    Saint-Ouen

La Coquille, Paris 17

Le Bistrot d'à Côté, Paris 17

La Coupole, Paris 14

Le Divellec, Paris 7

Dodin Bouffant, Paris 5

Le Duc, Paris 14

L'Epi d'Or, Paris 1

Jacqueline Fénix,
    Neuilly-sur-Seine

La Fermette du Sud-Ouest,
    Paris 1

Brasserie Flo, Paris 10

La Fontaine de Mars, Paris 7

Chez Fred, Paris 17

La Galoche d'Aurillac,
    Paris 11

Chez Georges, Paris 2

Chez Georges, Paris 17

Gérard et Nicole, Paris 14

Le Globe d'Or, Paris 1

Le Gourmet des Ternes,
Paris 17

Le Grand Véfour, Paris 1

Le Gueuze, Paris 5

Brasserie de l'Ile Saint-Louis,
Paris 4

Restaurant Jamin, Paris 16

Chez Jenny, Paris 3

Julien, Paris 10

Lescure, Paris 1

Louis XIV, Paris 1

Chez Louisette, Saint-Ouen

La Lozère, Paris 6

Lucas-Carton, Paris 8

Aux Lyonnais, Paris 2

La Maison Blanche, Paris 15

La Maison du Valais, Paris 8

Chez Maître Paul, Paris 6

Mère-Grand, Paris 20

Moissonnier, Paris 5

Le Restaurant d'Olympe,
Paris 15

Chez Pauline, Paris 1

Perraudin, Paris 5

Le Petit Marguery, Paris 13

Le Petit Zinc, Paris 6

Pharamond, Paris 1

Chez Philippe, Paris 11

Au Pied de Cochon, Paris 1

Pierre Traiteur, Paris 1

Pile ou Face, Paris 2

Polidor, Paris 6

Le Potager du Roy, Versailles

Chez René, Paris 5

Ritz-Espadon, Paris 1

Le Roi du Pot-au-Feu, Paris 9

Michel Rostang, Paris 17

Le Ruban Bleu, Paris 1

Guy Savoy, Paris 17

La Sologne, Paris 7

A Sousceyrac, Paris 11

Brasserie Stella, Paris 16

La Table de Jeannette, Paris 1

Taillevent, Paris 8

Tan Dinh, Paris 7

La Tchaïka, Paris 6

La Tchaïka, Paris 11

Brasserie du Théâtre,
Versailles

Terminus Nord, Paris 10

Thoumieux, Paris 7

Timgad, Paris 17

La Tour d'Argent, Paris 5

La Tour de Montlhéry, Paris 1

Chez Toutoune, Paris 5

Le Train Bleu, Paris 12

Au Trou Gascon, Paris 12

Le Trumilou, Paris 4

Vaudeville, Paris 2

Jules Verne, Paris 7

Chez la Vieille, Paris 1

RESTAURANTS LISTED BY ARRONDISSEMENTS

**Palais-Royal, Les Halles,
Opéra, Bourse**
1st and 2nd arrondissements

Carré des Feuillants

Au Cochon d'Or des Halles

L'Epi d'Or

La Fermette du Sud-Ouest

Chez Georges

Le Globe d'Or

Le Grand Véfour

Lescure

Louis XIV

Aux Lyonnais

Chez Pauline

Pharamond

Au Pied de Cochon

Pierre Traiteur

Pile ou Face

Ritz-Espadon

Le Ruban Bleu

La Table de Jeannette

La Tour de Montlhéry

Vaudeville

Chez la Vieille

**République, Bastille, Les
Halles, Ile Saint-Louis**
*3rd, 4th, and 11th
arrondissements*

Ambassade d'Auvergne

L'Ambroisie

L'Ami Louis

Astier

Benoit

Bofinger

Cartet

Chardenoux

La Galoche d'Aurillac

Brasserie de l'Ile Saint-Louis

Chez Jenny

Chez Philippe

A Sousceyrac

La Tchaïka

Le Trumilou

**Latin Quarter, Luxembourg,
Sèvres-Babylone**
5th and 6th arrondissements

Allard

Brasserie Balzar

La Bonne Table des Fés

Le Caméléon

Aux Charpentiers

Dodin Bouffant

La Gueuze

La Lozère

Chez Maître Paul

Moissonnier

Perraudin

Le Petit Zinc

Polidor

Chez René

La Tchaïka

La Tour d'Argent

Chez Toutoune

**Faubourg Saint-Germain,
Invalides, Ecole Militaire**
7th arrondissement

Chez Les Anges

Le Divellec

La Fontaine de Mars

La Sologne

Tan Dinh

Thoumieux

Jules Verne

**Madeleine, Saint-Lazare,
Champs-Elysées**
8th arrondissement

Chez André

Androuet

Artois

Le Boeuf sur le Toit

Bristol

Caviar Kaspia

Chiberta

Lucas-Carton

La Maison du Valais

Taillevent

**Grands Boulevards, Place de
Clichy, Gare du Nord**
9th and 10th arrondissements

Charlot, Le Roi Des
     Coquillages

Brasserie Flo

Julien

Le Roi du Pot-au-Feu

Terminus Nord

**Gare de Lyon, Vaugirard,
Montparnasse,
Denfert-Rochereau**
*12th, 13th, 14th, and 15th
arrondissements*

Chez Albert

L'Aquitaine

L'Assiette

La Cagouille

La Coupole

Le Duc

Gérard et Nicole

La Maison Blanche

Le Restaurant d'Olympe

Le Petit Marguery

Le Train Bleu

Au Trou Gascon

**Arc de Triomphe, Trocadéro,
Bois de Boulogne,
Neuilly-sur-Seine**
*16th arrondissement,
Neuilly-sur-Seine*

La Boutarde

Jacqueline Fénix

Restaurant Jamin

Brasserie Stella

**Arc de Triomphe, Place des
Ternes, Porte Maillot**
17th arrondissement

Apicius

La Coquille

Le Bistro d'a Côté

Chez Fred

Chez Georges

Le Gourmet des Ternes

Michel Rostang

Guy Savoy

Timgad

**Saint-Ouen, La Villette,
Belleville, Père-Lachaise**
*19th and 20th
arrondissements and
Saint-Ouen*

Au Cochon d'Or

Le Coq de la Maison Blanche

Chez Louisette

Mère-Grand

Paris Environs: Versailles

La Boule d'Or

Le Potager du Roy

Brasserie du Théâtre

Cafés
CAFES

Au Petit Fer à Cheval (see entry, page 123).

It is impossible to imagine Paris without its cafés. Parisians are sun-worshippers, and the attraction of an outdoor sidewalk stopping place perfectly suits their inclination. Sometimes around the first week of February, sunshine or not, café doors open wide, chairs and tables tumble out, and the season begins. The city has some 12,000 cafés varying in size, grandeur, and significance. As diverse as Parisians themselves, the cafés serve as an extension of the French living room, a place to start and end the day, to gossip and debate, a place for seeing and being seen.

No book on Paris literary, artistic, or social life is complete without details of café life, noting who sat where, when, and with whom—and what they drank. One wonders how writers and artists accomplished as much as they did if they really whiled away all those hours at sidewalk tables sipping *café au lait,* Vichy water, and *ballons* of Beaujolais.

When did it start? The café billed as the oldest in Paris is Le Procope, opened in 1686 by a Sicilian, Francesco Procopio dei Coltelli, the man credited with turning France into a coffee-drinking society. He was one of the first men granted the privilege of distilling and selling wines, liqueurs, *eaux-de-vie,* coffee, tea, and chocolate, with a status equal to a baker or butcher. Le Procope attracted Paris's political and literary elite, and its past is filled with history. It has been reported that it was there that Voltaire drank forty cups of his favorite brew each day: a blend of coffee and chocolate, which some credit with inspiring his spontaneous wit. When Benjamin Franklin died in 1790 and the French assembly went into mourning for three days, Le Procope was entirely draped in black in honor of France's favorite American. Even the young Napoleon Bonaparte spent time at Le Procope: When still an artillery officer, he was forced to leave his hat as security while he went out in search of money to pay for his coffee. Le Procope still exists at the original address, 13 Rue de l'Ancienne Comédie, but as a restaurant, not a café.

By the end of the 18th century, all of Paris was intoxicated with coffee and the city supported some 700 cafés. These were like all-male clubs, with many serving as centers of political life and discussion. It is no surprise to find that one of the speeches that precipitated the fall of the Bastille took place outside the Café Foy at the Palais-Royal.

By the 1840s the number of Paris cafés had grown to 3,000. The men who congregated and set the tenor of the times included journalists, playwrights, and writers who became known as *boulevardiers*. Certain cafés did have special rooms reserved for women, but in 1916 a law was passed that prohibited serving women sitting alone on the terraces of those along the boulevards.

Around the turn of the century, the sidewalk cafés along Boulevard du Montparnasse—Le Dôme, La Rotonde, and later, La Coupole—became the stronghold of artists; those along Boulevard Saint Germain—Aux Deux Magots, Flore, and Lipp—were the watering holes and meeting halls for the literary. When the "lost generation" of expatriates arrived in Paris after World War I, they established themselves along both boulevards, drinking, talking, arguing, and writing.

Cafés still serve as picture windows for observing contemporary life. The people you see today at Aux Deux Magots, Café de Flore, and Lipp may not be the great artists of the past, but faces are worth watching just the same. Linger a bit and you will see that the Paris stereotypes are alive and well: the surly waiters and red-eyed Frenchmen inhaling Gitanes; old men in navy berets; *clochardes* (bag ladies) hauling bright pink Monoprix shopping bags holding all their earthly possessions; ultra-thin, bronzed women with hair dyed bright orange; and schoolchildren decked out in blue and white seersucker, sharing an afternoon chocolate with mother.

If you know how to nurse a beer or coffee for hours, café-sitting can be one of the city's best buys. No matter how crowded a café may be, waiters will respect your graceful loafing and won't insist that you order another round just to hold the table. Drinks are usually less expensive if you are willing to stand at the bar. At mealtime, if you see a table covered with a cloth or even a little paper placemat, that means the table is reserved for dining. If it is bare, you are welcome to sit and just have a drink. Note that the service charge is automatically added to all café bills, so you are required to pay only the final total and need not leave an additional tip, although most people leave any loose change.

The following listing offers a brief glimpse of Paris café life, suggesting the grand and famous cafés along with some lesser-known neighborhood favorites.

CHATELET, LES HALLES, PONT-NEUF

1st, 2nd, and 4th arrondissements

CAFE BEAUBOURG
100 Rue Saint-Martin,
Paris 4.
(48.87.63.96).
Métro: Châtelet.
Open daily, 8 A.M. to 2 A.M.
Credit cards: AE, DC, V.

The new double-decker Café Beaubourg over-looks the circus-like atmosphere of the Centre Pompidou museum plaza, which year-round is filled with bagpipe players, guitarists, actors, fat men who sit on beds of nails, and now Le Génitron, an enormous clock that counts down the seconds remaining until the year 2000. Yet if you spend just a few moments at one of the upstairs tables, you'll realize that the ultra-modern Café Beaubourg fills an age-old Parisian need, for cafés are places where you can be alone in public. Look around and you'll see table after table filled with lone individuals—puffing on a cigarette, drinking a beer, writing, reading, or carefully perfecting the art of doing nothing. And while at first glance the Café Beaubourg's decor is shocking—the adjectives that come to mind are giant, cold, overmodern—the place works. The huge metal armchairs are surpris-ingly comfortable, the double-decker setting offers room to breathe in a neighborhood that can be utterly stifling, and the train-station voluminosity serves to shelter us, and separate us, from that world just outside the door. Food here is an afterthought: The generous *crudités* platter is fine, but sandwiches tend to be dreadfully dry. This can be remedied if you order a tomato salad on the side and create your own sort of city picnic, a great choice on a rainy Paris day, when the colors of the brightly clothed crowd below jump out at you beneath the sobering gray sky.

Cafés—for looking cool or for reading.

LE COCHON A L'OREILLE
15 Rue Montmartre, Paris 1.
(42.36.07.56).
Métro: Les Halles.
Open 4 A.M. to 4:30 P.M.
   Closed Sunday.
Hot meals at lunch only.
English spoken.

This is the most beautiful workingman's bar in Paris. It houses great murals, fresh flowers on the tiny bistro tables, workers in blue overalls five deep at the zinc bar, and peanut shells on the floor. If you happen to be up and about at 6 A.M., you may want to toss back a few drinks with the local merchants, who still keep this end of Les Halles busy in the early morning hours.

CAFE COSTES
4 Rue Berger, Paris 1.
(45.08.54.39).
Métro: Les Halles.
Open daily, 8 A.M. to 2 A.M.

Café Costes, which opened near the end of 1984, has been billed "the first modern café in Paris." This huge peach-toned double-decker Art Deco space would look right at home in Los Angeles or Manhattan. Yet everything about Café Costes has that totally and distinctly Parisian air, albeit the 1980s Les Halles version. The menu, thank goodness, could not be more classic (there's a pretty good *croque-monsieur* made with *pain Poilâne*), the light French music adds a romantic touch, and it appears that at last Paris has a café that bridges the gap between the classicism of Aux Deux Magots and the pinball atmosphere of the corner café.

UN CAFE, S'IL VOUS PLAIT

Cafés are, of course, for more than just coffee. Although café fare has not changed drastically since the early days, food, like fashion, goes in and out of style. During the 19th century, one popular drink was *fond de culotte* ("seat of your pants"), so named since supposedly it could only be drunk while sitting down. It was a mixture of gentian liqueur and *crème de Cassis*. During the same period, other popular drinks included the *mêle-Cassis*, half Cassis and half Cognac; the *bicyclette*, a blend of Champagne and vermouth; and the *pompier*, or "fireman," a blend of vermouth and Cassis.

Today, coffee, beer, and anise-flavored *pastis* are the staple drinks, along with various fruit juices sweetened with sugar. The *croque-monsieur*—a ham sandwich topped with grated cheese, then grilled—and the *sandwich mixte*—a thickly buttered *baguette* filled with Gruyère cheese and thin slices of *jambon de Paris*—are favorite café snacks. For larger meals, there are often meaty *plats du jour*, pork *rillettes*, pâtés, platters of raw vegetables known as *crudités*, *salade niçoise*, and even hot dogs.

Coffee and other hot drinks come in many forms. This small glossary should help you order what you want.

Café noir or *café express:* plain black espresso

Double express: a double espresso

Café serré: extra-strong espresso, made with half the normal amount of water

Café allongé: weak espresso, often served with a small pitcher of hot water so clients may thin the coffee themselves

Café au lait or *café crème:* espresso with warmed or lightly steamed milk

Grand crème: large or double espresso with milk

Décaféiné or *déca:* decaffeinated espresso

Café filtre: filtered American-style coffee (not available at all cafés)

Chocolat chaud: hot chocolate

Infusion: herb tea

Thé nature, thé citron, thé au lait: plain tea, tea with lemon, tea with milk

"*I* was often alone, but seldom lonely: I enjoyed the newspapers and books that were my usual companions at table, the exchanges with waiters, barmen, booksellers, street vendors . . . the sounds of the conversations of others around me, and finally, the talk of the girls I ended some evenings by picking up."

—A. J. Liebling

Inside Aux Deux Saules.

AUX DEUX SAULES
91 Rue Saint-Denis, Paris 1.
(42.36.46.57).
Métro: Les Halles.
Open daily, 10 A.M. to
    midnight.

This is a popular spot for the young-and-chic-but-impoverished, and comes as a small breath of fresh air amid a sea of sex shops and fast-food eateries. Most of the action here goes on outdoors, where the trendy crowd hangs out at the large communal picnic tables set along this busy pedestrian *passage.* There are no willows *(saules)* left here, but the café serves a rather decent bowl of onion soup *gratinée* and drinkable red wine. Do save time for a trip inside: You can down a quick coffee at the bar, facing the fabulous ceramic murals depicting life in old Les Halles.

LA SAMARITAINE CAFE
19 Rue de la Monnaie,
    Paris 1.
(Go to Magasin 2, 5th floor,
    and follow signs.)
(45.08.33.33).
Métro: Pont-Neuf.
Bar open 9:30 A.M. to 7 P.M.
    (Tuesday and Friday until
    8:30 P.M.). Food service
    begins 11:30 A.M. Closed
    Sunday.
English spoken.

The popular slogan of this well-known department store is *"On Trouve Tout à la Samaritaine,"* or "One Finds Everything at La Samaritaine." That everything includes one of the most spectacular views of the Paris cityscape. Visit on a sunny afternoon, order up a *citron pressé* (lemonade) or a beer, and relax before or after a visit to this mammoth, confusing department store.

MARAIS, HOTEL-DE-VILLE, REPUBLIQUE, GARE DE L'EST, ILE SAINT-LOUIS

4th, 10th, and 11th arrondissements

MA BOURGOGNE
19 Place des Vosges, Paris 4.
(42.78.44.64).
Métro: Saint-Paul.
Open daily, 8 A.M. to 1 A.M.
   Closed February.

This is the best, and most active, café in the Marais, and it's set under the arcades of Paris's oldest square. Sit outdoors on the traditional beige and red rattan chairs, absorbing the beauty of the architecture dating back to 1407. The café is calm in the morning, and packed with local office workers at lunchtime. The *pommes frites* are not bad, just ask for them *bien cuites*—well cooked. Writer Georges Simenon's inspector Maigret spent a lot of time here, perhaps inspecting the varied clientele, which ranges from old locals to tourists to the chic young residents of one of Paris's most sought-after addresses.

Tête-à-tête at Ma Bourgogne.

LE FLORE EN L'ILE
42 Quai d'Orléans, Paris 4.
(43.29.88.27).
Métro: Pont-Marie.
Open daily, 10 A.M. to 2 A.M.
Hot meals served
   continuously until 1 A.M.
English spoken.

This combination café/restaurant/tea salon on Ile Saint-Louis is nothing special on the outside, but if you can secure a seat at the open-air windows along the sidewalk, the view of Notre Dame, just across the bridge, is breathtaking. Settle in to read one of the French or English publications that hang from bamboo racks along the *caisse*, and enjoy one of the famous and fabulous Berthillon sorbets or ice creams sold here. Tea does not come from a tea bag but is freshly brewed and steaming hot, and the classical music in the background helps one enjoy a moment of peace and a nice breeze on a warm day.

LE PETIT CHATEAU
    D'EAU
34 Rue du Château–d'Eau,
    Paris 10.
(42.08.72.81).
Métro: République.
Open 7:45 A.M. to 8 P.M.
    Closed Saturday, Sunday,
    and August.

This is a perfect neighborhood café, just down the street from the old-fashioned little Château d'Eau covered market. The barrel-chested *patron* with a deep, booming voice is usually decked out in Wrangler jeans and red suspenders and holds court with locals as he tends his zinc-covered half-moon bar. Le Petit Château d'Eau also offers one of the city's classic interiors: Beveled glass doors lead to the spotless and cheery little café, with its fresh coat of paint and bright bouquets of market-fresh flowers. Large mirrors rimmed in antique green and white tiles make the room even cozier, as you sit back in an upholstered booth to read one of the newspapers or magazines set out for the clientele.

A BIT OF PARISIAN COFFEE HISTORY

When Louis XIV first tasted coffee in 1664, he was not impressed. But Parisian high society fell in love with the intoxicating brew, enjoying it at lavish and exotic private parties arranged by the Turkish ambassador, who arrived in 1669.

By 1670, the general public got a taste of the rich caffeinated drink when an Armenian named Pascal hawked it at the Saint-Germain fair in the spring. He hired formally dressed waiters to go out among the crowds and through the streets, crying as they went, *"Café. Café."* Later Pascal opened a little coffee boutique like those he had seen in Constantinople. It was not a smashing success, but he survived with the help of his wandering waiters, who even went door to door with jugs of the thick black brew. Their only competition was *"le Candiot,"* a cripple who sold coffee in the streets of Paris for a meager two *sous,* sugar included.

Then, as now, doctors discussed the merits and drawbacks of coffee. Those who favored the drink argued that it cured scurvy, relieved smallpox and gout, and was even recommended for gargling, to improve the voice. *Café au lait* was lauded for its medicinal qualities, and in 1688, Madame de Sévigné, whose letters record the life of the period, noted it as a remedy for colds and chest illness.

By the time the city's first café, Le Procope, opened in 1686, coffee was well on its way to winning the Parisian palate.

AU PETIT FER A CHEVAL
30 Rue Vieille-du-Temple,
Paris 4.
(42.72.47.47).
Métro: Hôtel-de-Ville.
Open 7:30 A.M. to 2 A.M.
Closed Sunday.
Hot meals served at lunch,
until 3 P.M.
English spoken.

A tiny, popular neighborhood café that dates back to 1903, when the Combes family opened it as the Café de Brésil. Today the café still boasts a fabulous marble-topped horseshoe (*fer à cheval*) bar, mirrored walls, and the original patchwork tile floor. The *patron* has embellished the room a bit but retained a feeling of authenticity by adding another mirror, a giant chandelier, and shelves of glass and brick. Instead of bothersome pinball machines, so popular lately in cafés, there is soothing classical music. The back room, always packed at lunchtime, boasts a giant Métro map and booths made up of old wooden Métro seats.

LATIN QUARTER, LUXEMBOURG, SAINT-GERMAIN, SEVRES-BABYLONE, QUAI D'ORSAY

5th, 6th, and 7th arrondissements

BRULERIE DE L'ODEON
6 Rue de Crébillon, Paris 6.
(43.26.39.32).
Métro: Odéon.
Open 10 A.M. to 6:45 P.M.
Tuesday through Friday;
10 A.M. to noon and
1:45 P.M. to 6:45 P.M.
Saturday. Closed Sunday,
Monday, and August.

O ne of Paris's oldest coffee roasting houses, this tiny coffee boutique and tasting spot is not a café per se, but for those of us in search of an honest cup of coffee (not a bitter compromise), this is the spot. Right off the Place de l'Odéon and near the Luxembourg Gardens, the Brûlerie de l'Odéon is an intimate, quiet corner to rest one's tired feet. There are just six little tables, where you can order about a dozen different brews and blends of coffee, plus an equal number of tea varieties. There's nothing flashy here—in fact you may feel as though you're sipping tea in the front of a coffee warehouse. But it's a beautiful spot, really, decorated with great posters and displaying shelves filled with biscuits, honeys, and teas.

AUX DEUX MAGOTS
170 Boulevard Saint-
Germain, Paris 6.
(45.48.55.25).
Métro: Saint-Germain-des-
Prés.
Open daily, 8 A.M. to 2 A.M.
Closed the second week
in January.
English spoken.

T he ultimate Paris café, great for observing the current fashion scene and restoring yourself with a steaming cup of good hot chocolate on a chilly afternoon. Aux Deux Magots offers more than twenty-five different whiskies, and coffee is still served in thick white cups. Sidewalk entertainment varies from fire eaters to organ grinders to junior Bob Dylans. The interior is calm and appealing, with its mahogany-red banquettes and brass-

Aux Deux Magots.

CAFE DE FLORE
172 Boulevard Saint-
Germain, Paris 6.
(45.48.55.26).
Métro: Saint-Germain-des-
Prés.
Open daily, 7:45 A.M. to 1:30
A.M.
English spoken.

edged tables, walls of mirrors, and waiters attired in white floor-length aprons and neat black vests. You can sit under the famous wooden statues of the two Chinese dignitaries—the *deux magots,* who gave their name to the café. (The café's name does not, as some writers have suggested, translate as "two maggots"!) The owner recalls watching Jean-Paul Sartre indoors from ten to twelve-thirty each day, writing while smoking cigarette after cigarette. Hemingway came, too, after World War I, for "serious talk" and to read aloud the poetry he'd written.

The rival of Aux Deux Magots next door, this was always more of a literary hangout, popular with Sartre, Simone de Beauvoir, and Albert Camus. During the Occupation, the cafés in Montparnasse were full of German soldiers, and so Parisians preferred Flore, where not only were there no German soldiers, there was even a small stove. After the war in the late 1940s, when most artists still gathered in Montparnasse, Picasso used to come here every night, sitting at the second table in front of the main door, sipping a glass of mineral water and chatting with his Spanish friends. Little has changed since. There's still the simple and classic Art Déco interior: red banquettes, walls of mahogany and mirrors, and a large sign suggesting that, while pipe smoking is not forbidden, *"l'odeur de certains tabacs de pipe parfumés incommode la plupart de nos clients."* In other words, "courteous clients don't smoke pipes here." The large sidewalk café is neither as pleasant nor as accessible as that at Aux Deux Magots, yet it is equally popular.

Café de Flore.

CROQUE-MONSIEUR
(GRILLED HAM AND CHEESE SANDWICH)

The croque-monsieur *is the most Parisian of sandwiches. It's really no more than a grilled ham sandwich topped with grated cheese, but it appears in many different guises. One could spend weeks hopping from café to café, taking notes on variations and favorites. Sometimes a* croque-monsieur *is topped with a thick cheese béchamel sauce, or transformed into a* croque-madame *with the addition of an egg, but frankly, few Parisian cafés do justice to the sandwich. All too often, a* croque-monsieur *is made with airy, factory-made white bread, second-rate ham, and the cheese, well, it's not always Gruyère. (Parisian supermarkets even sell frozen* croque-monsieurs, *ready for popping in the oven!) If you want a great* croque-monsieur, *make it yourself, with exceptional homemade* pain de mie, *the slightly buttery white bread that's been unjustly distorted by industrialization.*

3 tablespoons (1½ oz; 45 g) unsalted butter
12 small, thin slices homemade *pain de mie* (see recipe, page 216)
7 ounces (200 g) or 6 thin slices best-quality ham, cut to fit bread
4½ ounces (140 g) Gruyère cheese, grated

1. Preheat the broiler.

2. Butter the slices of bread on one side. Place one slice of ham on 6 of the buttered sides, and cover with the remaining bread slices, buttered side out.

3. Place the sandwiches under the broiler, and grill on the buttered side until golden. Remove the sandwiches, turn, and cover each with grated Gruyère. Return to the broiler and grill until the cheese is bubbling and golden.

Yield: 6 sandwiches.

Note: To transform a *croque-monsieur* into a *croque-madame,* grill a *croque-monsieur* until it is almost bubbling and golden, then cut a small round out of the top piece of cheese-covered bread, exposing the ham. Reserve the round. Break a small egg into the hole and place under the broiler for 2 or 3 more minutes. To serve, top the egg with the cheese-covered round.

One French cookbook even offers a recipe for a sandwich named after the food critic Curnonsky. To prepare a *croque-Curnonsky,* blend equal amounts of butter and Roquefort cheese, spread on thin slices of *pain de mie,* top with ham and another slice of bread, and grill on both sides.

CAFE DES HAUTEURS
(Musée d'Orsay)
62 Rue de Lille, Paris 7.
(45.49.48.14).
Métros: Quai d'Orsay or
    Solférino.
Open 10:30 A.M. to 6 P.M.
    Tuesday, Wednesday,
    Friday, and Saturday;
    until 10 P.M. Thursday;
    9 A.M. to 6 P.M. Sunday.
    Closed Monday. Entry
    fee, about 21 francs.

BRASSERIE LIPP
151 Boulevard Saint-
    Germain, Paris 6.
(45.48.53.91).
Métro: Saint-Germain-des-
    Prés.
Open 8 A.M. to 1 A.M. Closed
    Monday, July, and major
    holidays.
Hot meals served
    continuously until
    12:45 A.M.
English spoken.

How many cafés—anywhere in the world—can boast of Toulouse-Lautrec murals on the wall and a view of the white domes of Sacré Coeur in the distance? The rooftop café of the Musée d'Orsay (a lively museum fashioned out of a 19th-century railroad station) is one of the finest spots for viewing the city. The café is situated right next to the museum's famed Impressionist collection, and through chunks of glass cut around a mammoth railway clock, one views a vast expanse of the cityscape, out over the slow-moving Seine, across to the Tuileries Gardens, and on beyond to the hills of Montmartre. In good weather one can relax on the small outdoor terrace.

One of the city's most famous café-restaurants, still a late-night spot for politicians such as François Mitterrand, designers such as Yves Saint-Laurent, and editors from houses such as Gallimard and Hachette. During the day, the rather cramped and airless terrace is filled with American, German, and English tourists drinking the delicious Alsatian beers and sharing platters of *jambon* and *fromage*. The walls of the interior are classically dark and dingy, but in a felicitous way. Colorful ceramic tiles painted with parrots and cranes give the main floor dining room a lighter feel, and the bright lights of the old-fashioned chandeliers turn night into day. Despite the fact that the food is barely edible—the famous *choucroute* is third rate, the popular *gigot* tasteless, and the pastries soggy and tired—Lipp packs them in night after night. They don't take reservations by telephone, and a good deal of fuss is made of securing a table on the main floor. Those who dine upstairs don't talk about it.

Time for a café lunch.

SNACKS

The most popular café snacks are sandwiches, made either on the long and narrow *baguette;* on *pain de mie,* the square white bread; or on *pain Poilâne,* Paris's most popular country-style loaf. Poilâne's bread is often served as a *tartine,* an open-face sandwich with various toppings.

Here are some of the most popular sandwich ingredients, followed by other popular snacking items.

Jambon de Paris: cooked ham

Jambon de pays: country ham, usually salt-cured

Saucisson sec or ***saucisson à l'ail:*** dried sausage, plain or with garlic

Rillettes: soft, spreadable pork or goose pâté

Pâté de campagne: pork pâté

Sandwich mixte: Gruyère cheese and ham on a *baguette*

Cornichons: small French pickles or gherkins

Oeuf dur: hard-cooked egg

Carottes rapées: grated carrot salad, usually with vinaigrette dressing

Crudités: variety of raw vegetables in a salad, usually including grated carrots, beets, and tomatoes

Assiette de charcuterie: a combination plate of dried sausage, pâté, and *rillettes*

CAFE MOUFFETARD
116 Rue Mouffetard, Paris 5.
(43.31.42.50).
Métro: Monge.
Open 7 A.M. to 8:30 P.M.
   Closed Sunday afternoon
   and Monday.

The big sign outside reads *"Brasserie"* in bold burgundy lettering, but this rather earthy little, spot set right in the middle of the busy Rue Mouffetard market is one of the homier cafés in Paris. A smoky little worker's hangout, it was brought to my attention by an American colleague, Martha Rose Shulman, who was lured here by the homemade pastries, dense and buttery *croissants,* and delicious, almost creamy, *brioches.* This is probably the only café in town where the *patron* and his wife make their *croissants* and *brioches,* working through the night so the market workers will have something fresh and warm to sustain them through a long morning's labor. In wintertime, they also make little *chaussons aux pommes,* hot apple tarts, perfect for eating with a giant *café crème.*

An animated moment.

LA PALETTE
43 Rue de Seine, Paris 6.
(43.26.68.15).
Métro: Mabillon.
Open 8 A.M. to 2 A.M. Closed
    Sunday, one week in
    February, and August.
Hot meals served at lunch,
    until 3 P.M.
English spoken.

This artist's hangout is perfect on a sunny summer's afternoon, when the tables fill as much of the sidewalk as law and reason will allow. Everyone is in a light mood and seems to know everyone else, so La Palette has a particularly intimate, Parisian air. The *patron* wanders about shaking hands and chatting with the brightly dressed clientele, who come for hearty cups of coffee and to snack on open-face sandwiches made with fresh *pain Poilâne.*

AU PETIT CAFE CLUNY
20 Boulevard Saint-Michel,
    Paris 5.
(43.26.68.24).
Métro: Saint-Michel.
Open daily, 6:30 A.M. to
    2 A.M. (all night Friday
    and Saturday). Closed
    three weeks in August
    and two weeks in
    February.

This is one of those large and rambling cafés of the main streets of the Latin Quarter, where people don't go for the decor or the food, but simply to people-watch and relax. It's a few steps from the Cluny Museum and at one of the city's busiest crossroads, the corner of Boulevard Saint-Michel and Boulevard Saint-Germain.

LE PRE AUX CLERCS
30 Rue Bonaparte, Paris 6.
(43.54.41.73).
Métro: Saint-Germain-des-
Prés.
Open daily, 7 A.M. to 2 A.M.

On weekends, when I go wandering about the Left Bank's antique and decorator shops, I love to stop for a quick bite at this very ordinary-looking corner café. What lures me in is the *croque-monsieur* made with Lionel Poilâne's incomparable sourdough bread, a generous grilled ham and cheese sandwich that demands to be washed down with a chilled and foamy draft beer, right from the tap.

OPERA, CHAMPS-ELYSEES

8th and 9th arrondissements

LE FOUQUET'S
99 Avenue des Champs-
Elysées, Paris 8.
(47.23.70.60).
Métro: George-V.
Open daily, 8:30 A.M. to
2 A.M.
English spoken.

This is one of the most popular Right Bank cafés, perfect for observing the ever-changing scene on the Champs-Elysées. Le Fouquet's is always making society news, as starlets and journalists talk and write about their rendezvous here. James Joyce used to dine at Le Fouquet's almost every night, and today well-known French chef Paul Bocuse stops in whenever he's in town. Most don't come for the scene or the food, but to grab a snack before or after viewing one of the dozens of first-run films playing at movie houses along the avenue. Sexism lives at Le Fouquet's, where a sign warns,

A solitary café moment.

Au Petit Fer à Cheval (see entry, page 123), a place for coffee and classical music.

POPULAR APERITIFS

Absinthe, the highly alcoholic anise-flavored drink invented by a Frenchman in 1797, was banned in 1915 because of its harmful effects on the nerves. It was quickly replaced by another popular though less dangerous drink, *pastis*, which has much in common with absinthe, but is lower in alcohol. Wormwood, the ingredient which caused absinthe to be banned, is omitted.

Pastis: anise-seed-flavored aperitif that becomes cloudy when water is added (the most famous brands are Pernod and Ricard)

Suze: bitter liqueur distilled from the root of the yellow mountain gentian

Picon and *Mandarin:* bitter orange-flavored drink

Pineau des Charentes: sweet fortified wine from the Cognac region

Kir: dry white wine mixed with *crème de Cassis* (black currant liqueur)

Kir royal: Champagne mixed with *crème de Cassis*

"Les dames seules ne sont pas admises au bar" ("Women who are alone are not allowed at the bar"). The management insists that the sign, which has been up at the seven-stool bar since the restaurant opened at the turn of the century, was put there to protect women, not insult them. Most women see it otherwise. Incidentally, Le Fouquet's is pronounced to rhyme with "bets" not "bays," a remnant of the fashionable fascination with English early in the century.

CAFE DE LA PAIX
12 Boulevard des Capucines, Paris 9.
(42.68.12.13).
Métro: Opéra.
Open daily, 10 A.M. to 1:30 A.M.
English spoken.

This open, expansive café near the Opéra represents a sort of gaiety of days past. The building has been declared a historic monument, and the café is not a bad place to sip your lemonade while sitting under the crisp green-and-white-striped umbrellas that line the sidewalk. You should enjoy the spectacle of the passing show, including international tourists as well as Parisians.

MONTPARNASSE

6th and 14th arrondissements

LA CLOSERIE DES LILAS
171 Boulevard du
Montparnasse, Paris 14.
(43.26.70.50).
Métro: Port-Royal.
Open daily, 9 A.M. to 2 A.M.
English spoken.

The lilacs are long gone, but the romance of days when men like Henry James and Ernest Hemingway gathered here is still very much alive at this popular café-restaurant. Beneath the colorful green and white awnings amid a garden of greenery, you can sit outdoors and sip coffee, or move to the enclosed terrace for an authentic *salade niçoise*. La Closerie des Lilas is still a hangout for French film stars and chic young Frenchmen, and a spot where one can linger while reading the copies of *L'Express* and *Paris Match* provided for the clients.

LA COUPOLE
102 Boulevard du
Montparnasse, Paris 14.
(43.20.14.20).
Métro: Vavin.
Open daily, 8 A.M. to 2 A.M.
Closed August (and until early 1989).

This Montparnasse café-restaurant (see also page 87) is still a favorite meeting place for artists, models, and tourists, and the haunt of young Americans since its opening in 1927. Though today few artists can afford to live in this popular district, little seems to have changed over the past five decades. Artists still come and sit at the left, under the posters of current exhibitions, while the chic set dines on the right. Sunday is for family lunches, when reservations are at a premium. During off hours, the old-timers fill the large, cavernous hall, sitting at the same tables they've occupied for decades and reading the papers that hang from bamboo frames. Try the briny Belon oysters, the grilled lamb chops, the moist pistachio-studded sausages, or the Baltic herring served with mounds of *crème fraîche* and chunks of fresh apples. This is

---

OTHER ALCOHOLIC DRINKS

Calvados: apple brandy

Marc de Bourgogne: pronounced "mar," an *eau-de-vie* distilled from pressed grape skins and seeds

Pippermint Get: bright green alcoholic mint drink

Cidre: hard apple cider

one place you can always go for a snack or a full meal and never have a sense of being rushed.

LE DOME
108 Boulevard du
   Montparnasse, Paris 14.
(43.35.25.81).
Métro: Vavin.
Open 8 A.M. to 1 A.M. Closed
   Monday.
Hot meals served
   continuously from noon
   to 1 A.M.

When Le Dôme first opened at the turn of the century, it was just a drinking shack and Montparnasse was a suburb of the Latin Quarter. Today, this well-populated neighborhood is a mix of young and old, and the fern-filled terrace of Le Dôme is a fine place for lingering over coffee, a *ballon* of *rosé*, a *croque-monsieur*, or a *sandwich mixte*.

POPULAR NONALCOHOLIC DRINKS

Orangina: carbonated orange soda, the most popular nonalcoholic café drink

Citron, orange, or *pamplemousse pressé:* lemon, orange, or grapefruit juice served with a carafe of tap water and sugar, for sweetening to taste

Gini: bitter lemon

Limonade: 7-Up-style drink

Diabolo: lemonade with a variety of sweet fruit syrups

Menthe: sweet, bright-green mint-flavored syrup, drunk with water

Diabolo menthe: mint syrup and lemonade

Coca: Coca-Cola

Schweppes: tonic water

LA ROTONDE
105 Boulevard du
   Montparnasse, Paris 6.
(43.26.68.84).
Métro: Vavin.
Open daily, 8 A.M. to 2 A.M.
English spoken.

Lenin and Trotsky sipped their *café crème* here in 1915, along with others of the international intelligentsia who made the café famous. It has all been remodeled, and much of its charm has been lost, but in the afternoon La Rotonde gets the sun, so the Montparnasse crowd camps out here, sipping Ricard and smoking Gitanes.

BOIS DE BOULOGNE

16th arrondissement

LA GRANDE CASCADE
Near the Longchamp
  racetrack, Bois de
  Boulogne, Paris 16.
  (45.27.33.51).
Not accessible by Métro.
Open daily, 9 A.M. to
  midnight. Closed last ten
  days in December and
  first three weeks in
  January.
English spoken.

This grand old *Belle Epoque* café-restaurant serves coffee and tea in the afternoons, on the open-air terrace right in the middle of the Bois de Boulogne. At one time the restaurant probably had some of the best service in town; now the single aging waiter makes no attempt to hide his boredom, and the rather skimpy menu of coffee, tea, and ice cream offers little imagination. But if you

A daily Parisian ritual.

happen to be hiking through the Bois on a sunny day, this is the place to sit, amid bright geraniums on a pretty tiled patio, and share the moment with old French couples offering their lumps of sugar to the birds.

LES JARDINS DE BAGATELLE
Parc de Bagatelle, Bois de Boulogne, Paris 16.
(40.67.98.29).
Not accessible by Métro.
Open daily, 9 A.M. to 1 A.M.
English spoken.

The Bagatelle is one of Paris's prettiest parks, famous for its stunning rose gardens. The café, set at the edge of the woods some distance from the gardens, is the perfect place to relax after a Sunday's stroll through the park. This is the only Paris café I know where you get to press your own lemons and oranges for *citron* or *orange pressé*. Gruff, overworked waiters bring the old-fashioned clear glass citrus press right to the table, along with the neatly halved fruit.

BEER

Beer *(bière)* comes in many sizes and can be ordered by the bottle, *bouteille*, or on tap, *à la pression*.

Demi—8 ounces (25 centiliters)

Sérieux—16 ounces (50 centiliters)

Formidable—1 quart (1 liter)

LE VICTOR HUGO
4 Place Victor-Hugo, Paris 16.
(45.00.87.55).
Métro: Victor-Hugo.
Open 7 A.M. to 8:30 P.M.
Closed Sunday.

Le Victor Hugo is not mentioned here because of its ambience, its history, or the people who have sipped here over the years. Rather, it's noted for its location, overlooking the fountains of the classic and well-heeled Place Victor-Hugo. I have to admit that, on Saturday afternoons, I love nothing better than to position myself here, sort of trying to read the daily paper but all the while noticing the beautiful and fashionable folk who wander past. Truly, this is one of the city's best seats for authentic Parisian people-watching, and the *garçons* could not be more typical: They'll forget what you've ordered and are sure to disappear after you request the check, but in the end they add to the charm of the entire experience.

Salons de Thé
TEA SALONS

The Art Deco allure of Brocco (see entry, page 138).

Golden *pains au chocolat,* lush ruby red strawberry tarts, and moist, dark chocolate cakes form a multicolored still life in the sparkling window. When gazing through, one senses an air of calm, repose, contentment. The door opens, revealing a mysterious blend of jasmin tea, vanilla-scented apple tart, and Haydn. At a far table, elderly women in veiled hats sit *tête-à-tête,* immersed in gossip and frothy hot chocolate, while nearby a well-dressed businessman flirts with a slender, chic Parisienne who seems more involved in her *tarte abricot* than in his advances. This is the daily life of the Parisian *salon de thé*—cozy, intimate affairs designed to indulge France's insatiable sweet tooth and flair for guiltlessly whiling away hours at the table.

Though teatime is associated more closely with London, Paris supports dozens of full-fledged *salons de thé,* most of them distinctly French. Parisians don't fool around with frail cucumber sandwiches and dry currant buns—they get right to the heart of the matter, dessert.

In Paris, as in London, tea salons reached the height of popularity at the turn of the century, providing matrons of standing with well-appointed surroundings for entertaining guests outside the home, and offering women a respectable career opportunity.

During the 1920s, tea and dance salons became popular along the Champs-Elysées and in restaurants in the Bois de Boulogne: Here aging *grandes dames* came alone, as did young men. They met, they danced, they drank tea, then went their separate ways.

Thanks to a renaissance during the 1970s, Paris now offers an unlimited variety of tea salons, each with a distinctive decor, menu, and ambience that follow the whim and passion of the owner. A cup of coffee or pot of tea will be more expensive here than in a run-of-the-mill café, but the atmosphere is usually calmer (no noisy pinball machines) and the food generally superior. Lunch, and sometimes dinner, is available at most *salons de thé,* but more often than not, the food is an afterthought. An early morning or late afternoon visit for tea and pastry will, in the end, be more rewarding. Tea salons are, by the way, places where one feels perfectly comfortable alone.

PALAIS-ROYAL, PLACE DES VICTOIRES, LOUVRE

1st and 2nd arrondissements

A PRIORI THE
35 Galerie Vivienne, Paris 2.
(42.97.48.75).
Métro: Bourse.
Open noon to 7 P.M.
Hot meals served at lunch
   only.
Credit card: V.
English spoken.

Galerie Vivienne is Paris's prettiest turn-of-the-century *passage*—the arched, romantic forerunner of the shopping mall. Leave it to a group of Americans to turn this sleepy but elegant area into a lively meeting spot. Here, the chic set that haunts the *avant-garde* shoe and clothing shops that encircle the nearby Place des Victoires come for classical music, brownies or corn muffins, and lots of English tea. Welcoming wicker chairs spill into the brightly tiled arcade year round, no matter what the weather.

ANGELINA
226 Rue de Rivoli, Paris 1.
(42.60.82.00).
Métro: Tuileries.
Open daily, 10 A.M. to
   6:30 P.M. Closed August.
Credit cards: AE, DC, V.
English spoken.

One almost expects a troupe of Proustian characters to wander into this turn-of-the-century salon just across the street from the Jardin des Tuileries. Up until 1948, this was the old and celebrated Rumpelmayers, where as a child A. J. Liebling downed ersatz American ice cream sodas and began his love affair with Paris. Today—with its green-veined marble-topped tables and walls embellished with murals and mirrors—it's still snobbish, expensive, and ever-popular, and about the only place in town where they melt real chocolate bars for their lethally rich, delicious hot chocolate.

FANNY TEA
20 Place Dauphine, Paris 1.
(43.25.83.67).
Métro: Pont-Neuf.
Open 1 P.M. to 7:30 P.M.
  Tuesday through Friday;
  3:30 P.M. to 8 P.M.
  Saturday and Sunday.
  Closed Monday.
Credit card: V.
English spoken.

The world of Fanny Tea, on the diminutive Place Dauphine near the Pont-Neuf, is so strange and mystical you almost expect a palm reader to sit down, gently, beside you. Books of poetry and old French novels vie for table space with flickering candles, giant Victorian pewter teapots, and delicious vanilla-scented warm apple tarts. There's seldom a table free, but this is the perfect place to escape the damp on a rainy Parisian afternoon, and to listen to classical music as you write your memoirs. If you're lucky, film star Yves Montand, who lives on the square, will wander by.

MUSCADE
36 Rue de Montpensier,
  Paris 1.
(42.97.51.36).
Métro: Palais-Royal.
Open daily, noon to 8:30 P.M.
  in winter; 11 A.M. to
  11 P.M. in summer; tea,
  coffee, and desserts only
  from 3:30 P.M. to 7 P.M.
Credit cards: AE, DC, V.
English spoken.

You don't have to book a table at the costly Grand Véfour to enjoy the romantic pink rose garden of the Palais-Royal. From May to September, Muscade expands to the garden terrace, one of the city's most tranquil, elegant outdoor spots for people-watching or just resting weary bodies. The Palais-Royal garden is an honest neighborhood park as well, filled with old ladies sharing their *baguettes* with the pigeons, maids and mothers pushing infants in pristine navy prams, and children at play in the sandbox. Stop off before or after a visit to the Louvre or the Comédie Française, ignore the less than professional service, and enjoy the fresh fruit tarts and *café crème.*

VERLET
256 Rue Saint-Honoré,
  Paris 1.
(42.60.67.39).
Métro: Louvre.
Open 9 A.M. to 7 P.M. Closed
  Sunday and August.
English spoken.

The rich aroma of freshly roasted coffee mingling with teas from China, Ceylon, India, and Japan draws passersby to the door of Verlet, one of the most reputable and helpful coffee and tea merchants in Paris. Here, not far from the Place du Palais-Royal and the Louvre's Musée des Arts Décoratifs, you enter a casual, cosmopolitan world, crammed with open sacks of roast coffee from all corners of the globe, mounds of dried fruits and nuts, and colorful tins of tea blended on the spot to your liking.

There's always a line continuing outside the door for Verlet's products, but if there's some table

space, settle down for a few minutes in this unadorned 1930s setting for the famous coffee, or tea
served from silver-plated teapots with handles covered by bright felt mittens. There are always four or
five rich cakes and pastries made on the premises,
including a luscious apricot tart (see recipe, page
140) that goes so well with a warming cup of
jasmine tea.

MARAIS, BASTILLE, REPUBLIQUE, BEAUBOURG

3rd and 4th arrondissements

BROCCO
180 Rue du Temple, Paris 3.
(42.72.19.81).
Métro: République.
Open daily, 7 A.M. to
    7:30 P.M. Closed August.
Hot meals served at lunch
    only.
Credit card: V.

The aromas of freshly baked *croissants* and thick
black espresso lure visitors into Brocco, an
impressive, impeccable Art Deco *pâtisserie* and *salon
de thé* just off the Place de la République. Here,
amid marble and mirrors and theatrical strips of
fluorescent lighting, matronly waitresses often buzz
about, defending themselves and *la maison* against a
client's complaint over less than perfect *pains au
chocolat.* But the little cane chairs and triangular oak
tables, the pretty white china and thick foam of
milk atop the *café crème* allow one to ignore the
pastry chef's momentary lapses.

At Brocco, it's café crème.

TARTE AU CITRON LE LOIR DANS LA THEIERE
LE LOIR DANS LA THEIERE'S LEMON TART

A ritual at this cozy tea salon in the Marais is to wander over to the counter where all the pastries are displayed to see what's fresh and what looks appealing. The only problem is that as soon as you sit down, another fresh dessert arrives from the kitchen, looking even better than the one you ordered. I love lemon (but not as much as chocolate), and this tart really hit the spot the first time I visited Le Loir dans la Théière. It also brought back Proustian memories of a lemon cookie I used to make as a child. The pastry, with a hint of lemon and almonds, is easy and versatile. You can, if you like, make it several days ahead and refrigerate it.

Pastry:
1 cup plus 2
    tablespoons (160 g)
    unbleached all-
    purpose flour
¼ cup (50 g) sugar
¼ cup (35 g) almonds,
    ground to a fine
    powder
Zest (peel) of 1 lemon,
    grated
Pinch of salt
½ cup (4 ounces; 115 g)
    unsalted butter,
    cubed, at room
    temperature
1 egg
1 teaspoon rum
1 teaspoon milk
1 teaspoon unsalted
    butter, for buttering
    tart pan

Filling:
4 eggs
½ cup (100 g) sugar
Zest (peel) of 3 lemons,
    grated
Juice of 3 lemons
1 cup (140 g) almonds,
    ground to a fine
    powder
¾ cup (6 ounces; 170 g)
    unsalted butter,
    melted

1. Prepare the pastry: In a medium-size bowl, combine the flour, sugar, ground almonds, lemon zest, and salt and mix until well blended. Make a well and add the butter, egg, rum, and milk. Knead until well blended. The pastry should have the consistency of a soft cookie dough. Wrap the pastry with plastic wrap and let it rest in the refrigerator at least 1 hour. Butter a 10½-inch (27-cm) tart pan. Flour your hands and use them to press the pastry into the buttered pan. Set aside.

2. Preheat the oven to 400°F (205°C).

3. Prepare the filling: In a medium-size mixing bowl, combine the eggs, sugar, lemon zest, lemon juice, and ground almonds, and mix until well blended. Add the melted butter, mix again, then pour the filling into the pastry shell.

4. Bake in the center of the oven for 30 to 40 minutes. Serve at room temperature.

Yield: One 10½-inch (27-cm) tart.

DATTES ET NOIX

4 Rue du Parc-Royal, Paris 3.
(48.87.88.94).
Métro: Saint-Paul.
Open noon to 7 P.M. in
    winter; noon to midnight
    beginning in April.
Credit cards: AE, V.
English spoken.

Dattes et Noix—"dates and nuts"—is one of the Marais's best *salons de thé*, situated across from the bright gardens of the Parc-Royal and the Musée Carnavalet. The decor consists of stark white tiled floors and contemporary graphics, the service is super-casual, and the *tarte Tatin* and chocolate cake are definitely worth making a detour for. Just before lunchtime, French women in the neighborhood stop in with their children for ice cream and *sorbet* treats to take home with them.

TARTE ABRICOT VERLET
VERLET'S APRICOT TART

Verlet is a tiny tea and coffee shop that also serves good homemade pastries. Anyone who loves apricots will love this simple, homey pie, which takes about twenty minutes to make. Be sure to use fresh, not canned, apricots.

Pastry:
½ cup (4 ounces; 125 g)
    unsalted butter,
    melted
½ cup (100 g) sugar
2 cups (260 g) all-
    purpose flour (not
    unbleached)
1 teaspoon (5 g)
    unsalted butter, for
    buttering tart pan

Filling:
5 tablespoons *crème
    fraîche* (see recipe,
    page 237) or heavy
    cream, preferably not
    ultra-pasteurized
1 egg
¼ cup (50 g) sugar
1 tablespoon all-
    purpose flour
1 teaspoon vanilla
    extract
1 pound (500 g) fresh
    apricots, pitted and
    halved
1 tablespoon
    confectioners' sugar

1. Preheat the oven to 350°F (175°C).

2. Prepare the pastry: In a medium-size bowl mix the butter and sugar together thoroughly, then add the flour and knead by hand until well blended. The pastry will be very crumbly. Butter a 10½-inch (27-cm) tart pan. Using your hands, press the pastry into the buttered pan and bake in the preheated oven for 10 minutes.

3. Meanwhile, prepare the filling: In a small bowl combine the *crème fraîche* and egg, and mix until well blended. Add the sugar, mix well, then add the flour and vanilla. Pour the mixture into the prebaked pastry shell and arrange the apricots, cut side down, on top of the cream mixture.

4. Bake until a knife inserted in the cream comes out clean, about 45 minutes. Cool and serve at room temperature, preferably within an hour of baking. Sprinkle with confectioners' sugar just before serving.

Yield: One 10½-inch (27-cm) tart.

**LE LOIR DANS
   LA THEIERE**
3 Rue des Rosiers, Paris 4.
(42.72.90.61).
Métro: Saint-Paul.
Open noon to 7 P.M. Tuesday
   through Saturday; 11 A.M.
   to 7 P.M. Sunday. Closed
   Monday.

Le Loir dans la Théière, recalling Lewis Carroll's dormouse in the teapot, doesn't pretend to be anything more than a comfortable place to pass the time of day. The loftlike space, with huge overstuffed Art Deco leather chairs, long wooden tables to share with neighbors, and a fresh daily assortment of homemade tarts, cakes, and pastries, doubles as an art and photo gallery. It's faded and slightly worn, but honest and casual, the kind of place you can take your mother or your children for a most affordable lunch or an unhurried afternoon snack. The lemon tart was deliciously lemony, perfectly fresh. So good, in fact, I asked for the recipe to include in this book (see page 139).

MARIAGE FRERES
30-32 Rue de Bourg-
   Tibourg, Paris 4.
(42.72.28.11).
Métro: Saint-Paul.
Open 11 A.M. to 7:30 P.M.
   Tuesday through
   Saturday; noon to
   7:30 P.M. Sunday.
   Closed Monday.

In the trendy yet still very old-fashioned Marais, one of France's oldest and most respected tea importers has opened a combination tea boutique and tasting salon. As you wander down the rather scruffy Rue de Bourg-Tibourg you have no idea what is in store. But as soon as you approach Mariage Frères, your senses are transported to an appealing, pleasurable world. The aroma of a mingling of exotic teas from China, Japan, and Brazil invades the senses, sounds of Wagner's *Tristan und Isolde* fill the air, as your eyes focus on a plant- and

A tea break at Mariage Frères.

wicker-filled neoclassical space bathed in delicate light and decorated in pale ocher and white. There are some 300 varieties of teas from 20 countries, as well as an astonishingly complete selection of tea paraphernalia, including about 200 teapots, a charming individual tea service, even a series of wicker picnic sets that will make you want to pack up and take off at the next opportunity. Smokers and nonsmokers are discreetly segregated, as smokers are directed to a second room upstairs. All the available teas are described in painstaking detail in the dictionary-like menu, and even tea experts are likely to feel overwhelmed. But one can always cop out and order one of the more familiar teas, among them a delicately perfumed Darjeeling, a penetrating, flinty Keemun, or a rich and pungent Assam. With such pleasant surroundings, it's a shame the food is not better. But the salad combinations are simply silly, and tea-infused specialties barely have the taste of tea. Better to come at breakfast- or tea-time, for the flaky currant-filled scones, served with a variety of tea jellies, or the soothing *tarte aux fraises des bois:* excellent *pâte sablée* smothered with a blend of pastry cream and wild strawberries, all topped with a crackling caramel crust.

Mariage Frères, a tea lover's paradise.

LATIN QUARTER, LUXEMBOURG, ODEON, ECOLE MILITAIRE

5th, 6th, and 7th arrondissements

A LA COUR DE ROHAN
59-61 Rue Saint-André-des
  Arts, Paris 6.
(43.25.79.67).
Métro: Odéon.
Open noon to 7:30 P.M.
  Tuesday through Friday;
  2 P.M. to 7:30 P.M.
  Saturday and Sunday.
  Closed Monday and the
  last two weeks of August.
English spoken.

At first glance A la Cour de Rohan, in a *passage* near the Odéon Métro, looks more like a chic decorating boutique than a tea salon. But wander inside and you'll find a superb English-country-style salon decorated in white and various shades of green. The aromas of Darjeeling and *gâteau Opéra,* and the soothing sounds of classical music, make you want to settle in for the afternoon. If it happens to be available that day, sample the fine pear tart flavored with almonds, selected from a round table in the center of the room. A La Cour de Rohan offers live classical music concerts on occasional Friday evenings.

DALLOYAU-PONS
2 Place Edmond-Rostand,
  Paris 6.
(43.29.31.10).
Métro: Luxembourg.
Open 9:30 A.M. to 7:15 P.M.
  Closed Monday during
  July and August.
Hot meals served at lunch
  only.
Credit card: V.
English spoken.

After a walk through the Luxembourg Gardens, settle in at Dalloyau-Pons, an aristocratic, old-world tea salon with a rambling terrace facing the park greenery and the stunning fountain at Place Edmond-Rostand. The snooty young waitresses act as though they'd rather be elsewhere, but overlook that, because in the summertime this is one of the classiest people-watching spots in town. In winter, go at about 10 A.M., mount the curving stairway to the tearoom, take a table overlooking the gardens, order up a steaming cup of smoky Chinese tea, and enjoy a yeasty little *brioche* in stately silence.

L'HEURE GOURMANDE
22 Passage Dauphine,
  Paris 6.
(46.34.00.40).
Métro: Odéon.
Open 11 A.M. to 7 P.M. Closed
  Sunday and the first
  three weeks of August.
Hot meals served
  throughout the day.
  Brunch served from
  11 A.M. to 3 P.M.
Credit cards: AE, V.
English spoken.

Bright, airy, and loft-like, this Left Bank tea salon is a real find. It's one Parisian *salon de thé* that serves real food—everything from *steak tartare* to assorted cheese platters, a wide range of salads, and a scrambled egg, salmon, and cheese brunch. L'Heure Gourmande is a lively spot designed to appeal to all tastes, an attraction that's obvious if you wander in any day at noon. It's also a nice place to pop into in the afternoon, for tea, coffee, or a sip of rosé. Note that L'Heure Gourmande is a bit tricky to find: The "passage" is right between Rue Mazarine and Rue Dauphine.

The tea boutique at Mariage Frères (see entry, page 141).

LA MOSQUEE DE PARIS
1 Rue Daubenton and 39
 Rue Geoffroy-Saint-
 Hilaire, Paris 5.
Métro: Censier-Daubenton.
Open daily, 11 A.M. to 8 P.M.
 Closed August.
English spoken.

From a brilliant tree-shaded garden move into darkness, entering a mysterious, atmospheric Moorish-style tearoom. As a single waiter makes the rounds, carrying trays filled with tiny glasses of sweet mint tea and flaky pastries, settle back on one of the fabric-covered banquettes and soak in the ambience. It doesn't pay to be in a hurry, so bring a book or a friend to help you admire the marble-tiled floors, colorful glass windows, and otherwise exotic decor. The salon is attached to the first mosque to be erected in France.

LE PETIT BOULE
16 Avenue de la Motte-
 Picquet, Paris 7.
(45.51.77.48).
Métro: La Tour-Maubourg.
Open 1:30 A.M. to 7 P.M.
 Wednesday through
 Sunday; 2:30 P.M. to 7 P.M.
 Tuesday. Closed Monday
 and August.
Hot meals at lunch only.
English spoken.

Near the Ecole Militaire, Le Petit Boulé is one of Paris's more refreshingly original tea salons. Every detail is attended to with tasteful care, and it's no surprise to find that this Russian-accented tea and pastry shop is in the hands of the Petrossian family of salmon and caviar fame, who impart a flair and perfection to everything they touch.

Here, in a sun-kissed atmosphere peppered with Victorian wicker chairs, tiny marble-topped tables, mirrored walls, and frosted glass Art Deco chandeliers, pastries are displayed like jewels. Mounds of golden glazed *croissants,* bamboo trays filled with hearty round *piroshki* (meat and cabbage-filled turnovers), and tiny fruit tarts form an inviting window display. At lunchtime there is, of course, salmon and blinis, caviar and vodka. After relishing the house specialties and admiring the refined decor, take home one of the more than thirty varieties of tea, superb *miel de sarrasin* (buckwheat honey), or the unusual and delicious *confiture de kumquat,* just a few of the dozens of jams, vegetable purées, and rustic dishes from France's southwest prepared under the Petrossians' direction.

CONCORDE, MADELEINE, PIGALLE
8th and 9th arrondissements

CASTA DIVA
27 Rue Cambacérès, Paris 8.
(42.66.46.53).
Métro: Miromesnil.
Open 11:30 A.M. to 6:30 P.M.
   Closed Sunday.
Hot meals served
   throughout the day.
English spoken.

Opera music, teas from Mariage Frères, coffees from Verlet—who could ask for anything more? Casta Diva is classy, lovely, lively, with a soothing pale green decor and Empire-style mahogany tables. At lunchtime, Casta Diva fills up with the chic crowd from the Rue du Faubourg Saint-Honoré, while later in the day it's an ideal place to settle in with tea and catch up on the morning paper. They offer huge salads that bound off the plate, and an assortment of not-so-terrific pastries. The lemon tart and *tarte Tatin* cry out for improvement, but the superb service, pleasant surroundings, and exquisite teas make up for it all.

LADUREE
16 Rue Royale, Paris 8.
(42.60.21.79).
Métro: Madeleine.
Opens 8:30 A.M. to 7 P.M.
   Closed Sunday and
   August.
Hot meals served at lunch
   only.
English spoken.

Until I discovered the delights of Ladurée one day at ten in the morning, I could not have cared less about morning *croissants.* But after visiting some sixty *salons de thé* throughout Paris, it's the frothy cup of *café au lait* and the flaky, yeasty *croissants* of Ladurée near the Place de la Madeleine that return in my dreams.

Can there be any early morning atmosphere more elegantly Parisian in tone? There's the hushed and intimate turn-of-the-century decor, with pale olive wood-paneled walls, straightback chairs, tiny marble-topped tables, curt waitresses in frilly white aprons, and a clientele that's equally at home at Cartier and the Ritz. The air is not snobbish, just a bit blasé, and while the sandwiches wouldn't keep a bird alive, the pastries are deliciously fresh and I've not found a better cup of *café au lait* in Paris. The chewy, almondy, almost marzipan *financiers* (almond cakes) are a little taste of heaven.

Before leaving, examine the ceiling mural in the main-floor salon: Angels float through the pastel clouds, as one pink-faced cherub wearing a chef's white toque bakes his pastries by the intense heat of the sun.

MARQUISE DE SEVIGNE
32 Place de la Madeleine,
Paris 8.
(42.65.19.47).
Métro: Madeleine.
Open 10 A.M. to 6:30 P.M.
Closed Sunday.
Credit cards: EC, V.
English spoken.

Next door at Fauchon, the "tearoom" has all the atmosphere and charm of a Greyhound bus station coffee counter. In contrast, Marquise de Sévigné, a combination chocolate shop and tearoom, is subdued and tranquil, a fine spot for resting with a superb cup of coffee and one of a dozen or so different desserts, most of them chocolate. Avoid the *gâteau au chocolat:* To me it tasted of cooked milk. Have instead the outstanding chocolate praline cake or the plain macaroons, which have little competition in this pastry-filled capital.

PARIS-VIERZON
24 Rue Boissy d'Anglas,
Paris 8.
(47.42.90.12).
Métros: Concorde or
Madeleine.
Open noon to 11 P.M. Closed
Sunday.
Credit card: V.
English spoken.

Whether you've just finished a hard day of shopping along the Rue du Faubourg-Saint-Honoré or only wish you had, this is the place to stop for brownies and English fruitcake, an original assortment of teas, and wonderful hot chocolate. A favorite is *thé noël,* a lovely blend of rose petals, cinnamon, and vanilla. I also love the idea of preparing your own hot chocolate: You're offered a cup of hot milk and a pitcher of steaming pure chocolate, to blend to taste. Unless you love elbow-to-elbow affairs, however, avoid Paris-Vierzon at lunchtime.

PENY
3 Place de la Madeleine,
Paris 8.
(42.65.06.75).
Métro: Madeleine.
Open 8 A.M. to 8:30 P.M.
Closed Sunday.
English spoken.

The best tables at Peny (also known as Penny) are the ones out on the sidewalk facing the Place de la Madeleine. Although this popular summertime spot looks more like an ordinary café, it merits tea salon status thanks to its fresh sweet coconut cake, a nostalgic favorite among Americans transplanted to Paris.

TEA FOLLIES
6 Place Gustave-Toudouze,
 Paris 9.
(42.80.08.44).
Métro: Saint-Georges.
Open noon to 7 P.M. Monday
 through Saturday;
 12:30 P.M. to 7 P.M. Sunday.
Hot meals served at lunch
 only.
English spoken.

Bright, friendly, casual, a stop at Tea Follies is like having an impeccable afternoon tea on a front porch, strewn with stacks of local newspapers and magazines and fresh flowers. The contemporary red, white, and gray tea salon opens out onto the tree-filled Place Gustave-Toudouze in the 9th *arrondissement,* and in good weather tables spread out onto the sidewalk for sunning, gossip, and delicious lemon curd tarts. There's also a nice selection of wines, and on Sunday brunch is offered.

TORAYA
12 Rue Saint-Florentin,
 Paris 8.
(42.60.13.00).
Métro: Concorde.
Open 10 A.M. to 7 P.M. Closed
 Sunday.
Credit card: V.

The miniature pastries and handmade ceramics are displayed like diamonds in a jeweler's window; the spotless decor is a sober, modern blend of black, gray, and white. Toraya is an authentic, contemporary Japanese tea salon, complete with white ceramic cups used for *matcha* (the ceremonial Japanese green tea), which is frothy, almost bitter, and whisked to a foam. To most Western palates the pastries look much better than they taste, but the adventuresome will want to try the tiny multi-colored variations made of *adzuki* bean purée, or the little leaf-wrapped balls of sticky rice. It's a lot cheaper than a trip to Tokyo, and a nice exotic touch for those with little enthusiasm for pastries laden with Western cream and sugar.

TROCADERO

16th arrondissement

CARETTE
4 Place du Trocadéro,
 Paris 16.
(47.27.88.56).
Métro: Trocadéro.
Open 8 A.M. to 7 P.M. Closed
 Tuesday and August.
Hot meals served until 4 P.M.
 only.
English spoken.

By nine in the morning this spacious terraced tea salon facing the Trocadéro swarms with handsome male joggers who come for a little after-run nourishment. It's not unusual to see a trim, well-muscled Frenchman down two *pains au chocolat,* a couple of glasses of freshly squeezed orange juice, and a *café au lait* in record time, as he buries his nose in the French sporting journal *l'Equipe.* The *pain au chocolat* is yeasty and fresh and the smoky Chinese tea first-rate, but the *financier* is better left to someone else. Don't bother in the afternoons, unless you enjoy being asphyxiated by a cigarette-induced haze.

TERNES, VILLIERS

17th arrondissement

CHOCOLAT VIENNOIS
118 Rue des Dames,
  Paris 17.
(42.93.34.40).
Métro: Villiers.
Open 11 A.M. to 11 P.M.
  Closed Sunday.
Hot meals served
  throughout the day.
Credit cards: AE, DC, V.
English spoken.

**LA PATISSERIE
  VIENNOISE**
11 Rue Poncelet, Paris 17.
(42.27.81.86).
Métro: Ternes.
Pastry shop open 8:30 A.M.
  to 7:30 P.M. Monday
  through Saturday; 9 A.M.
  to 12:30 P.M. Sunday. Tea
  salon open 9 A.M. to
  6:30 P.M. Monday through
  Saturday; 9 A.M. to
  12:30 P.M. Sunday. Both
  closed Sunday afternoon.
Credit card: V.
Some English spoken.

This adorable tea salon not far from the Rue de Lévis market is worth a detour for anyone who loves great *café viennoise* (half whipped cream, half bracing black coffee), rich and beautiful linzertorte, warm and fragrant apple strudel. The waitresses are charming, speaking French with a lovely Austrian accent, and the salon itself is out of a fairy tale. It's especially beautiful at Christmastime, when the entire building is covered with lights and greenery.

Many a morning I take my newspaper and my string bag to the Poncelet market, head for this quiet, very private tea salon overlooking the bustling market, and grab a few moments to myself. The coffee here is exceptional—always served with a miniature pitcher of cream—and the pastries are the sort that even the strongest among us must struggle to resist. I am in love with their mile-high cheesecake and the flaky fruit-filled strudels. (See also Pâtisseries).

Tea and snacks, L'Heure Gourmande (see entry, page 143).

Bistros à Vin
WINE BARS

A toast to good times.

Enter into the land of bread and Beaujolais, cheese and *charcuterie*. Known as *bistros à vin* (wine bars), most of these cozy neighborhood spots open about the time much of Paris is rising for breakfast. From the exterior many resemble ordinary cafés, yet once you've entered and sipped a glass of silky, scented Fleurie or fresh and fragrant Sancerre, and sampled an open-face sandwich of garlic-and-thyme-flecked *rillettes* (spreadable pork or goose pâté) on thick sourdough bread, you understand the difference.

There is always food and conviviality, but more important, there is wine—by the glass, the carafe, the bottle. Light and fruity Beaujolais is king, but one also finds delicate Bourgueil from Touraine; young wines from Bordeaux, Chinon, and Côtes-du-Rhône; the Atlantic Coast's delicious Muscadet; the Jura's white and pleasant Arbois; and Provence's heady, vigorous Gigondas. Obviously, not every wine bar stocks every wine, but most offer from a dozen to thirty wines at from four to about twenty francs a glass, along with—at the very least—cold platters of cheese or *charcuterie* designed to complement the house selection. Most are casual affairs with no printed menu, but wine selections and daily specials are usually handwritten on blackboards set behind the bar.

Is there any reason to go to a wine bar rather than a café for a glass of wine? Categorically, yes. The wine sold in most cafés is mass-produced and banal, and much of it watery and undrinkable. The wine sold in wine bars is usually carefully chosen by the *bistrotiers* (owners), most often dedicated men who are passionate about wine. When not behind the bar, many of them are traveling the country in search of good little wines. Often their selections are shipped directly to the wine bar in barrels (it's cheaper that way) and the *bistrotier* bottles them himself, storing the excess in basementlike caves beneath the bar.

The food—simple and unpretentious as it may be—is chosen with the same care. Most offer platters of French cheese, several kinds of hams, sausages, pâtés, and bread, often either Lionel or Max Poilâne's famous country loaf (see recipe, page 208), redolent of sourdough and fresh from their huge wood-fired ovens. Sometimes, homey pâtés, *quiches,* or dessert tarts—all dishes chosen to go perfectly with the house wines—are prepared by the owner's wife. Some wine bars offer even heartier fare, such as wintry *daubes* (stews), platters of cooked sausages, and *confit d'oie* (preserved goose). As one *bistrotier* put it, "Wine is made to go with food. Tasting wine alone should be left to the experts."

Best of all, wine bars serve as a tasting and testing ground for wines yet to be discovered, as well as for familiar favorites. Since many wine bars offer little-known, small production wines by the glass, this is the time to acquaint oneself with those such as Montlouis or Quarts de Chaume, both whites from the Loire; or to sample several of the nine *cru* Beaujolais, perhaps a Moulin-à-Vent, a Juliénas, and a Chiroubles, side by side.

While years ago most wine bars specialized in the young, inexpensive quaffing wines, today the trendier, more formal "English style" wine bars—such as Willi's, the Blue Fox Bar, and L'Ecluse—offer a wider selection, including older vintages and those from more noble vineyards.

Dozens of wine bars pepper the streets of Paris. Here are a few special ones, a choice selection for a quick lunch, a pleasant afternoon interlude, or a late-night snack. They present a good alternative to a full-fledged meal. One should lunch well for 75 to 150 francs depending on selections. The most popular spots are crowded at lunchtime, but if you go early, at noon, or late, at 2:30, you're likely to get a seat and still enjoy the atmosphere.

LES HALLES, PALAIS-ROYAL, LOUVRE

1st, 2nd, and 3rd arrondissements

LA CLOCHE DES HALLES
28 Rue Coquillière, Paris 1.
(42.36.93.89).
Métro: Les Halles.
Open 8 A.M. to 9 P.M. Closed
   Saturday evening and
   Sunday.
English spoken.

WINES:
Morgon, Brouilly, Beaujolais,
Côtes-du-Rhône, white Sancerre,
Sauternes.

SPECIALTIES:
Jambon à l'os (ham with the
bone), homemade charcuterie,
quiche lorraine, and fruit tarts,
including tarte Tatin in winter.

This pleasant little wine bar takes its name from the *cloche* (bronze bell) that once was used to note the opening and closing of the neighboring Les Halles wholesale market, which was demolished in the 1970s. But the area is as lively as ever, and La Cloche des Halles still serves as the neighborhood wine bar for the many meat, vegetable, and poultry merchants who prefer to remain in the area.

HEART OF THE MATTER

Most wine bars open early in the morning to accommodate the nearly 5 percent of the population who indulge in a spiritous breakfast, a practice known as *tuer le ver,* or "killing the worm."
   According to legend, a certain madame, the wife of Monsieur de la Varende, died suddenly as a result of a worm gnawing away at her heart. An autopsy was performed, the worm was still alive, and all attempts to kill the creature failed. Finally, someone doused the worm with white wine, bringing about its quick demise. Quite logically, the moral of the story is: A glass of wine early in the day will keep the worms at bay.

L'ECLUSE
120 Rue Rambuteau,
   Paris 1.
(40.26.30.73).
Métro: Les Halles.
Open noon to 2 A.M.
Hot meals served all day.
Credit cards: AE, V.
English spoken.

WINES:
Red and white Bordeaux, from
châteaux grand and small.

SPECIALTIES:
Daily plat du jour, steak tartare,
mixed salads, chocolate cake.

If you ever wondered whether members of a food chain of any sort can remain charming, chic, and retain at least a semblance of authenticity, the answer is yes. Over the past several years, little L'Ecluses have popped up all over Paris, following the same formula that made the first L'Ecluse, on Quai des Grands-Augustins, a success.
   The decor, menu, and style are the same in each, and each appeals to a largely well-heeled international business clientele. Belle Epoque posters, converted gas lamps, a long wooden bar, and mirrored walls give L'Ecluse a turn-of-the-century atmosphere, though the food and wine are

totally up-to-date. Note, however, that a meal here will not be cheap. Service tends to be slow, perhaps intentionally. The first glass of wine comes quickly, and it's likely to be consumed by the time your snack or meal arrives. So if you think you might want more than one glass, order a carafe or a bottle—it will be less expensive in the long run.

Don't come here looking for Beaujolais; this is Bordeaux country. You may choose from more than seventy *château*-bottled Bordeaux, with some eighteen of these wines offered by the glass on a list that changes every three weeks. Good bets: a slice of foie gras and a glass of either Sauternes or Barsac; a plate of *carpaccio* with a young red Bordeaux; and then a slice of fudgy *gâteau au chocolat* with a cup of thick, black *express*. Open into the early morning hours, L'Ecluse is good for late-night snacks, especially after the theater, opera, or movies.

JUVENILES
47 Rue de Richelieu, Paris 1.
(42.97.46.49).
Métro: Palais-Royal.
Open 11 A.M. to 11 P.M.
   Closed Sunday.
Hot meals served all day.
Credit card: V.
English spoken.
Wines may be purchased to
   take home.

WINES:
French country and château,
Spanish, Australian, Californian.

SPECIALTIES:
Tapas, mixed salads, sandwiches.

Serious wine bar enthusiasts will not want to miss Mark Williamson and Tim Johnston's newest endeavor, Juveniles, the little brother to the well-established Willi's Wine Bar, just off the fashionable Place des Victoires. Juveniles is an unadorned café turned wine bar, and it has quickly become a great place to get a quick, good bite to accompany sips of an astonishingly good selection of wines. Best bets here are the hefty sandwiches—try the *filet de boeuf*, with thick slices of rare beef, watercress,

Raising a glass with a friend.

tomatoes, and mustard dressing between two slices of grilled buttered toast; and the chicken salad, with big chunks of chicken topped with olives, carrots, tomatoes, and dressing. There's always a good selection of wines by the glass, as well as a variety of good lesser-known wines at very good prices.

MEILLEUR POT

The annual "Meilleur Pot" award designates the elite in Parisian wine bars. The traveling trophy —named after the traditional half-liter (about 17-ounce) Beaujolais *pot*, or jug—is awarded to *bistrotiers* who carry on the tradition of searching out and buying good French wines direct from the producer. The *bistrotier* then bottles the wines himself and serves them over the counter, by the glass or by the bottle.

The award, begun in Paris in 1957, is given to the *bistrotier* himself, not his establishment. If he sells or moves on, the title goes with him, right into retirement. Only one award is given each year.

Judging takes place from April to December, when a jury of ten makes anonymous visits to various Parisian wine bars. At the end of December or beginning of January, a formal award ceremony is held and the current title holder relinquishes the trophy, handing it to the new season's winner.

TAVERNE HENRI IV
13 Place du Pont-Neuf,
    Paris 1.
(43.54.27.90).
Métro: Pont-Neuf.
Open 11 A.M. to 9:30 P.M.
    Closed Saturday, Sunday,
    August, and holidays.
English spoken.
Wines may be purchased to
    take home.

WINES:
Beaujolais-Villages, Morgon,
Fleurie, Loire Valley, Sancerre,
Muscadet-sur-Lie.

SPECIALTIES:
Charcuterie and cheese platters.

Opposite the statue of its namesake, Henri IV, this tobacco shop offers that certain grubby, old-fashioned Parisian charm, where men sit reading *Le Monde* or *France Soir* as they munch on *tartines* of goose *rillettes* and sip a glass of hearty Morgon. This is the place to stop and sample such seldom-found wines as the sweet Montlouis or golden Quarts de Chaume, both Loire Valley whites. Meilleur Pot winner in 1960.

LE RUBIS
10 Rue du Marché-Saint-
    Honoré, Paris 1.
(42.61.03.34).
Métro: Tuileries.
Open 7 A.M. to 10 P.M. Closed
    Saturday, Sunday, and
    August.
Hot meal at lunch.

WINES:
Beaujolais, Brouilly, Morgon,
Chiroubles, Juliénas,
Côtes-du-Rhône, Bordeaux,
Muscadet, Anjou, Bourgeuil.

SPECIALTIES:
Tartines (open-face sandwiches),
rillettes, charcuterie, cheese, and
ham and cheese omelets. Hot daily
special.

A classic, happy sort of bustling wine bar, where lunch is a free-for-all as clients stand five and six deep at the bar, dodging waiters and nudging neighbors. In good weather you can lunch outside, standing at the huge wine barrels that serve as makeshift tables. Meilleur Pot winner in 1963.

Le Rubis, a lunchtime portrait.

WILLI'S WINE BAR
13 Rue des Petits-Champs,
    Paris 1.
(42.61.05.09).
Métro: Pyramides.
Open 11 A.M. to 2:30 P.M. and
    7:30 P.M. to 11:30 P.M.
    Closed Sunday.
Hot meals served at lunch
    and dinner.
English spoken.
Wines may be purchased to
    take home.

WINES:
Rhône Valley, Italian,
Californian, and Spanish wines.
A dozen selected wines, available
by the glass and by the bottle, are
featured each week.

SPECIALTIES:
Change daily.

Willi's is bright, airy, and pleasantly decorated with a highly polished wood bar, and just a block from the tranquil 18th-century gardens of the Palais-Royal and a few minutes' walk from the Louvre and Place de l'Opéra. It is the most refined and chic wine bar in Paris, with the snobbiest clientele. But if you're seeking an introduction to the delights of the many undiscovered wines of the Côtes-du-Rhône, take a deep breath and cut through the crowd of sheepdogs and bronzed and beautiful people to sample the bold, rich, well-balanced Hermitage of Gérard Chave, or Georges Bernard's dry, fruity Tavel, the rosé many consider the best in the world. Food here serves simply as a background for the wines, though some care is taken to provide an ever-changing selection of hot daily specials and a good variety of salads. The delicious bread comes from one of Paris's best bakers, Jean-Luc Poujauran.

MARAIS, BASTILLE, ILE SAINT-LOUIS

4th, 11th, and 12th arrondissements

AU FRANC PINOT
1 Quai de Bourbon, Paris 4.
(43.29.46.98).
Métro: Pont-Marie.
Open 11:30 A.M. to 2:30 P.M.
and 6 P.M. to 11:30 P.M.
Closed Sunday and
Monday.
Hot meals served at lunch
and dinner.
Credit cards: DC, V.
English spoken.
Wines may be purchased to
take home.

WINES:
Beaujolais, Sancerre, Graves,
Rully, Côtes-du-Jura.

SPECIALTIES:
Platters of cheese, dried or smoked
meats, salmon, and salads.

Jacques Mélac, a proud, outgoing
patron *(see entry, following page).*

AU LIMONAIRE
88 Rue de Charenton,
Paris 12.
(43.43.49.14).
Métro: Ledru-Rollin.
Open 11 A.M. to midnight.
Closed Sunday, Monday
evening, and Christmas
week.
Hot meals served at lunch
and dinner.
Wines may be purchased to
take home.

WINES:
Côtes-du-Rhône.

SPECIALTIES:
Charcuterie, salads, terrines,
cheese. Hot daily special.

This landmark wine bar, hidden behind black wrought-iron gates, is a bit dark and often deserted, but it's a nice, quiet place to rest after wandering about Ile Saint-Louis, the Marais, or Notre-Dame. Service is friendly and the daily selection of wines and luncheon items is chalked up on a big blackboard. Good choices: the simple *tartine* of Crottin de Chavignol goat cheese, or the delicious salad of sliced lamb and greens tossed with walnut oil dressing.

Au Limonaire is one of those wonderfully haphazard affairs, the kind of place you walk into and feel immediately at home. Take its zinc bar, decorative etched-glass windows, *saucisse sèche,* and *jambon de pays,* and you're in the land of nostalgia. The food is an afterthought (and not always too fresh, at that), but the Rhône wine selection is pretty good and the atmosphere is terrific. On Saturday afternoons Au Limonaire is a real neighborhood hangout, where the locals come with their children and their shopping carts to sip, to chat, and to read the Paris daily *Libération.* Most evenings—generally Wednesday through Saturday—there's live music, and sometimes even dancing, just to remind you that you're in an authentic old-fashioned *bistro du quartier.*

JACQUES MELAC
42 Rue Léon-Frot, Paris 11.
(43.70.59.27).
Métro: Charonne.
Open 9 A.M. to 7:30 P.M.
    (11 P.M. Tuesday and
    Thursday). Closed
    Sunday, Monday, and
    mid-July through mid-
    August.
Hot meal served at lunch,
    and at dinner Tuesday
    and Thursday.
Wines may be purchased to
    take home.

WINES:
Beaujolais, Chinon, Saint-Joseph,
Gigondas, Cahors, red Rully,
Sancerre, Sauternes,
Côtes-du-Jura, Vin Jaune, Lirac.

SPECIALTIES:
Auvergnat, including hot daily
specials and regional cheeses, such
as Bleu des Causses,
Saint-Nectaire, Laguiole.

The most authentic and one of the liveliest wine bars in Paris. Found just west of the Place de la Bastille, in the 11th *arrondissement,* a workingman's quarter filled with cabinetmakers and artisans, this bar is run by Jacques Mélac, an outgoing, energetic *patron.* A proud Auvergnat, he could have walked right out of central casting, with his handlebar mustache, non-stop chatter, and genuine pride in the food and wine offered in his tiny five-table establishment. He obviously has such a great time doing what he does that no one could leave this corner bar feeling sad.

If there's any question about what you're to do at Jacques Mélac's, signs that hang on the walls will tell you: "If you want water, you must place your order the day before," advises one handwritten poster. Another reminds clients that "Water is reserved for cooking potatoes." Coffee is sold reluctantly and lemonade is reserved for children under eleven years of age.

At lunchtime, the place takes on the frenzy of the stock exchange at the height of trading as workers, businessmen, and secretaries crowd about the bar or vie for a rickety stool around one of the red oilcloth-covered tables in order to take in the day's meaty specials. One day the dish might be a rustic platter of boiled beef tongue, accompanied by tiny potatoes in a delicate mustard sauce. The omelets are creamy and delicious, and Jacques Mélac offers several regional wines not easily found outside France, including the Jura's sherrylike Vin Jaune.

The wine bar, which won the Meilleur Pot in 1982, serves as a wine shop as well. Diners can pick a bottle right off the shelf for sampling, and if it suits their taste, they can buy a bottle or a case as they leave. Mélac's is also the only Paris wine bar with its own "vineyard"—vines rise along the exterior walls of the bar, and a celebratory harvest is held each fall.

Jacques Mélac takes a break with the crew (see entry, facing page).

LA TARTINE
24 Rue de Rivoli, Paris 4.
(42.72.76.85).
Métro: Saint-Paul.
Open 8 A.M. to 10 P.M. Closed
Tuesday, Wednesday
morning, and August.

W I N E S :
*Beaujolais, Touraine, Anjou,
Loire Valley, Burgundy,
Côtes-du-Rhône.*

S P E C I A L T I E S :
*Tartines (open-face sandwiches) of
charcuterie, and Crottin de
Chavignol goat cheese.*

If this was in the United States, not Paris, you'd call La Tartine a luncheonette. But this is Paris and La Tartine is a wine bar in the oldest sense of the word. (In fact, La Tartine has been called a "café for wine drinkers.") It's an authentic working-man's hangout—meaning men and women—and at lunchtime the crowds gather to share modest platters of wafer-thin slices of *jambon de Paris*, the pale-colored ham that's cured in a salt brine, then cooked. It's the ham most commonly found in Paris cafés and usually goes into the *sandwich mixte*, a ham and cheese sandwich served on a French *baguette*.

Everyone here seems to know the red-haired waitress who singlehandedly coordinates the orders from the twenty or so tables bunched together in this dim, antique bar. Above the general din can be heard shouts of "Suzette, Suzette," as workers call out for a *double express* before rushing back to the streets and the office. La Tartine offers a broad range of wines, with some 30,000 bottles stashed away in the downstairs *cave*. More than thirty wines are available by the glass, all noted on the little board that hangs behind the bar. Worth sampling here: firm and fragrant Crottin de Chavignol, the young goat cheese from the Loire Valley, best enjoyed with the crisp white Sancerre wine. Nice before or after a visit to the Marais: This is the neighborhood once frequented by Eastern European refugees, and Trotsky lived right around the corner, on Rue Ferdinand Duval. Meilleur Pot winner in 1965.

LUXEMBOURG, SAINT-MICHEL, SEVRES-BABYLONE, ECOLE MILITAIRE

5th, 6th, and 7th arrondissements

L'ECLUSE
15 Quai des Grands-
    Augustins, Paris 6.
(46.33.58.74).
Métro: Saint-Michel.
Open noon to 1:30 A.M.
    Closed Sunday.
(See L'Ecluse, 1st
    arrondissement, page
    151.)

*Sampling the new Beaujolais at
Au Sauvignon (see entry, page
160).*

**CAFE DE LA NOUVELLE
    MAIRIE**
19 Rue des Fossés-Saint-
    Jacques, Paris 5.
(43.26.80.18).
Métro: Luxembourg.
Open noon to 9 P.M. Closed
    Saturday and Sunday.

W I N E S :
*Beaujolais, Chinon, Cabernet de
Touraine, Saint-Nicolas-de-
Bourgeuil, Gamay.*

S P E C I A L T I E S :
*Tartines (open-face sandwiches) of
pâté de foie de porc (pork liver
pâté), saucisson (dried sausage),
jambon cru (salt-cured ham), and
Camembert.*

This is Paris's quintessential wine bar, set on one of the prettiest neighborhood squares on the Left Bank. A bright cream and burgundy awning—proudly announcing owner Bernard Pontonnier's 1983 Meilleur Pot award—will lure you over, and once inside you'll find a democratic blend of workers, journalists, musicians, and even the popular neighborhood *boulanger* from right across the street. This place is real and unpretentious—all is very simple and straightforward, from the hearty fresh *tartines* of *pâté de foie de porc* to the lively, fruity young Beaujolais. In the summertime, tables are moved onto the sidewalk, and though the official closing time is 9 P.M., regulars often stay on well beyond that. Be forewarned: Many come for one drink and never leave.

LE PETIT BACCHUS
13 Rue du Cherche-Midi,
   Paris 6.
(45.44.01.07).
Métro: Sèvres-Babylone.
Open 10 A.M. to 8 P.M. Closed
   Monday from 1 P.M. to
   3 P.M., Sunday, and the
   week of August 15.
Hot meal served at lunch.
Credit card: V.
English spoken.
Wines may be purchased to
   take home

WINES:
*A wide selection of French,
Californian, Spanish, and Italian
wines, by the glass and by the
bottle.*

SPECIALTIES:
*Saucisson chaud (warm pork
sausage), pot-au-feu irlandais
(Irish stew).*

In this neighborhood of *bon chic, bon genre*—a B.C.B.G. is the French equivalent of a yuppie—this tiny wine shop/wine bar serves as a friendly meeting spot, where you can sample many of Steven Spurrier's selected wines on the spot, as you browse in cramped quarters for that special bottle.

SANCERRE
22 Avenue Rapp, Paris 7.
(45.51.75.91).
Métro: Ecole-Militaire.
Open 8 A.M. to 9 P.M. Monday
   through Friday, 9 A.M. to
   4 P.M. Saturday. Closed
   Sunday and August.
Hot meals served all day.
Some English spoken.
Wines may be purchased to
   take home.

WINES:
Sancerre.

SPECIALTIES:
*Andouillette au Sancerre
(chitterling sausage in Sancerre),
omelets, Crottin de Chavignol goat
cheese.*

This is a low-key, casual little wine bar, with the folkloric decor of the wonderful little wine village of Sancerre, about 125 miles from Paris. The dry, flinty white Sancerre wine from Domaine la Moussière is featured here, along with its perfect mate, the dry, sometimes sharp Crottin de Chavignol goat cheese. The wine bar is popular with workers from the French television studios located nearby.

AU SAUVIGNON
80 Rue des Saints-Pères,
   Paris 7.
(45.48.49.02).
Métro: Sèvres-Babylone.
Open 9 A.M. to 11 P.M. Closed
   Sunday and August.

W I N E S :
Beaujolais, Burgundy, Saint-
Emilion, Rosé Sancerre, Rosé
d'Anjou, Quincy, Riesling.

S P E C I A L T I E S :
Charcuterie platters, jambon
d'Auvergne (dry-cured country
ham), dried sausages, Cantal.

Au Sauvignon is one of the city's tiniest and most chic wine bars, just steps from the popular Bon Marché department store and Left Bank boutiques. Like many other bars, it's high on Beaujolais hype come November 15, the first day of sale of Beaujolais *primeur,* the year's new Beaujolais. Walls are plastered with maps of wine routes throughout France and posters reading "Vive le Beaujolais." Walking into the newly decorated Au Sauvignon is like walking up against a stage set: The place is so narrow and small you walk four steps inside the door and you hit the back wall. In summer, there is rarely a seat available on the enclosed terrace. Still, this is a good place to stop for a quick lunch or late-afternoon snack, to sample Beaujolais or wines from Alsace and Saint-Emilion with *pâté de porc* or *jambon d'Auvergne.* Meilleur Pot winner in 1961.

MADELEINE, CHAMPS-ELYSEES, GRANDS BOULEVARDS
8th arrondissement

BLUE FOX BAR
25 Rue Royale (Cité Berryer;
   enter between 23 and 25
   Rue Royale), Paris 8.
(42.65.10.72).
Métro: Madeleine.
Bar open 11 A.M. to 11 P.M.
   Restaurant open noon to
   3 P.M. and 7 P.M. to 11 P.M.
   Both closed Saturday
   evening and Sunday.
Hot meal at lunch in winter.
Credit card: V.
English spoken.

W I N E S :
Fifteen different French wines each
day, by the glass.

S P E C I A L T I E S :
Mixed salads, cheese, desserts.

One of my favorite wine bars: chic without being pretentious, offering simple salads, an exciting selection of not-too-expensive wines by the glass, and always a high-fashion international crowd, ideal for people-watching. Service here is often so casual that it borders on nonexistent, but go when you're in a patient mood, and a good glass of wine will help you put on a happy face.

L'ECLUSE
64 Rue François Ier, Paris 8.
(47.20.77.09).
Métro: Franklin-D.-
 Roosevelt.
Open daily, noon to
 1:30 A.M.
(See L'Ecluse, *1st
 arrondissement,* page
 151.)

L'ECLUSE
15 Place de la Madeleine,
 Paris 8.
(42.65.34.69).
Métro: Madeleine.
Open noon to 1:30 A.M.
 Closed Sunday.
(See L'Ecluse, *1st
 arrondissement,* page
 151.)

MA BOURGOGNE
133 Boulevard Haussmann,
 Paris 8.
(45.63.50.61).
Métro: Miromesnil.
Open 7 A.M. to 8:30 P.M.
 Closed Saturday, Sunday,
 and July.
Hot meal served at lunch.
Credit card: V.
 Wines may be purchased to
 take home.

WINES:
*Mâcon, Sancerre, Chablis,
Pouilly-Fumé, Beaujolais,
Burgundy, Bordeaux.*

SPECIALTIES:
*Coq au vin (chicken in red wine),
boeuf bourguignon (beef in red
wine), andouillette au Pouilly
(chitterling sausage in white
wine). Hot daily special.*

Above: A wine bar lunch.

*At Au Sauvignon, it's smiles and
toasts when the new Beaujolais
arrives (see entry, facing page).*

Well-dressed businessmen and -women stand elbow to elbow at the bar at lunchtime, when you won't be able to sit down without a reservation. This is a solid, serious wine bar. Serious, that is, about wine, but not about daily cares; the atmosphere is comfortable and happy, just the way you ought to feel when you're standing in a room filled with sausages and hams hanging from the rafters. The friendly, chatty *patron,* one Louis Prin, was a winner of the Meilleur Pot in 1962.

BISTROT DU SOMMELIER
97 Boulevard Haussmann,
  Paris 8.
(42.65.24.85).
Open noon to 3 P.M. and
  7:30 P.M. to 10:30 P.M.
  Closed Saturday evening,
  Sunday, and one week at
  Christmas.
Hot meals served at lunch
  and dinner.
Credit cards: AE, DC, V.
English spoken.
Wines may be purchased to
  take home.

WINES:
*A wide selection of French,
Californian, Spanish, and Italian
wines, by the glass and bottle.*

SPECIALTIES:
Navarin d'agneau (lamb stew).

LE VAL D'OR
28 Avenue Franklin-D.-
  Roosevelt, Paris 8.
(43.59.95.81).
Métro: Saint-Philippe-du-
  Roule.
Open 8 A.M. to 9 P.M. Monday
  through Friday, 8 A.M. to
  6 P.M. Saturday. Closed
  Sunday.
Hot meal served at lunch.
Credit card: V.
English spoken.

WINES:
*Beaujolais-Villages,
Côte-de-Brouilly, Fleurie, Morgon,
Juliénas, Côte-de-Nuits-Villages,
Aloxe-Corton, white Mâcon,
Sancerre, Pouilly-Fumé.*

SPECIALTIES:
*Jambon (ham), terrine de foies de
volailles (chicken liver terrine),
quiche, tarte Tatin, and Cantal,
Brie, and goat cheese. Hot daily
specialties.*

The *"Complet"* sign—all tables taken—goes up around noon at the Bistrot du Sommelier, a trendy, lively wine bar along the Right Bank's Boulevard Haussmann. The café-style decor is ultra-simple (bare tables and tile floors), food and service are unremarkable, but then what you go for is the good wine and Parisian ambience, and there's plenty of that. There's an extensive selection of wines by the glass, the carafe, the bottle, and one could hardly go wrong with Guigal's heady and hard-to-find Côte-Rôtie or the vibrant Bandol, Domaine de Terrebrune.

Géraud Rongier's bustling wine bar off the Champs-Elysées is great any time of year, but particularly fun from November 15 to the end of the year, because one generally finds some of the best Beaujolais in town. Packed at lunch, when office workers line up at the bar, it looks like any ordinary corner café, but Rongier, who won the Meilleur Pot in 1973, makes Le Val d'Or worth a detour. He can be found each morning at the Rungis wholesale market on the outskirts of Paris, shopping for ingredients for the *plats du jour* he serves to the crowds of well-dressed businessmen in his small downstairs dining room. If the sturdy *boeuf bourguignon* is on the menu, go for it, or the platter of *saucissons* cooked in the full-bodied Côte de Brouilly. The *tarte Tatin* isn't always available, but when it is, don't pass it by. This irresistible upside-down apple tart is prepared on the premises and served with a huge pot of thick *crème fraîche*.

On the main floor, Rongier serves a hearty ham and cheese *quiche*, abundant platters of excellent *charcuterie*, and *baguettes* filled with thick slices of superb *jambon à l'os* (a flavorful ham cured with the bone intact). When you order wine, they'll bring the whole bottle to the table, and charge you only for what you consume.

GARE MONTPARNASSE, DENFERT-ROCHEREAU
14th and 15th arrondissements

LE PERE TRANQUILLE
30 Avenue du Maine,
  Paris 14.
(42.22.88.12).
Métro: Montparnasse.
Open 10 A.M. to 8 P.M. Closed
  Sunday, Monday, and at
  the owner's discretion
  (but never in August).
Hot meal served at lunch.
Béarnais and Auvergnat
  spoken.
Wines may be purchased to
  take home.

WINES:
Loire valley: white Saumur,
Sauvignon de Touraine, red
Gamay de Touraine, Bourgeuil,
Champigny, Chinon; and
Beaujolais primeur until
Christmas.

SPECIALTIES:
Daily traditional dishes including
blanquette de veau (poached veal
in a cream and egg yolk-thickened
sauce), sauté d'agneau (lamb
stew).

This truly misnamed wine bar is for any lover of quirky behavior, for the owner, Jean Nouyrigat, Meilleur Pot winner in 1979, is far from a "tranquil father." If he doesn't like the looks of you, he may throw you out on your ear. On the other hand, if he takes a liking to you, you may well spend the day there, drinking his wines and sampling his hearty *plat du jour* (you won't know what it is until it's set before you). The wine list behind the bar means nothing, for some of the wines haven't been available for ages. Since Mr. Nouyrigat opens and closes at his convenience, it's best to call before setting out.

BEAUJOLAIS

In Paris, the third Thursday of November—the first day of sale of Beaujolais *primeur,* the new Beaujolais—signals the beginning of a season-long fête that doesn't cease until after the holiday revelry has cleared sometime in January.

It really doesn't matter if the year's crop happens to be overabundant, short on acidity, or even lacking in that special fruitiness associated with Beaujolais. It doesn't matter that almost everyone in Paris agrees that the publicity surrounding the wine is beyond proportion to its real worth. The fact is that Beaujolais is a "happy" wine, one that is there to enjoy; you don't have to take it too seriously.

Wherever wine bars sell Beaujolais, it is available by the glass, year round. Although the terms *primeur* and *nouveau* are used interchangeably, technically *primeur* is served only from the third Thursday of November to December 15. The term *nouveau* is technically reserved for the wines released for sale December 15, to be drunk through the next November.

LE RALLYE
6 Rue Daguerre, Paris 14.
(43.22.57.05).
Métro: Denfert-Rochereau.
Open 9:30 A.M. to 8 P.M.
   Closed Saturday, Monday,
   and August.
Wines may be purchased to
   take home at adjacent
   boutique.

WINES:
Beaujolais cru, red and white
Loire Valley.

SPECIALTIES:
Charcuterie, Cantal, Bleu
d'Auvergne, goat cheese.

A plain little workers' bar, on the lively Rue Daguerre market street. The food is simple and the wines well chosen, with a small wine shop right next door. The owner, Bernard Péret, won the 1967 Meilleur Pot award.

SCENTS OF PARIS

"It was the Camembert above all that they could smell. The Camembert with its gamey scent of venison had conquered the more muffled tones of Maroilles and Limbourg....Into the middle of this vigorous phrase the Parmesan threw its thin note on a country flute, while the Brie added the dull gentleness of damp tambourines. Then came the suffocating reprise of a Livarot. And the symphony was held for a moment on the high, sharp note of an aniseed Gérôme, prolonged like the note of an organ."—Emile Zola, *Le Ventre de Paris.*

ARC DE TRIOMPHE

17th arrondissement

LE PAIN ET LE VIN
1 Rue d'Armaillé, Paris 17.
(47.63.88.29).
Métro: Ternes.
Open daily, 11:30 P.M. to
   1 A.M.
Hot meals served all day.
Credit card: V.
English spoken.
Wines may be purchased to
   take home at adjacent
   boutique.

WINES:
All regions of France, with
particularly good Madiran,
Gigondas, Cahors, and various
Loire selections, as well as
Bordeaux and Burgundies.

SPECIALTIES:
Tartines (open-face sandwiches)
and salads; hot daily specialties.

With its smashing view of the Arc de Triomphe, this bustling little wine bar is run by four Parisian chefs—Alain Dutournier of Au Trou Gascon, Bernard Fournier of Le Petit Colombier, Jean-Pierre Morot-Gaudry of Restaurant Morot-Gaudry, and Henri Faugeron of Faugeron—and here they offer a wine list better than you'll find in most restaurants. There is a changing *plat du jour,* as well as salads, plates of smoked salmon or cheese, and open-face sandwiches of duck *rillettes, foie gras,* or York ham.

PETRISSANS
30 bis Avenue Niel, Paris 17.
(42.27.52.03).
Métro: Ternes.
Open 9:30 A.M. to 1:30 P.M.
and 3 P.M. to 9 P.M. Closed
Saturday evening,
Sunday, and August.
Hot meal served at lunch.
Credit cards: AE, V.
English spoken.
Selected wines may be
purchased to take home.

WINES:
Cahors, Madiran, Chinon,
Burgundies, and young Bordeaux.

SPECIALTIES:
Tartines (open-face sandwiches),
poitrine d'oie fumée (smoked goose
breast).

This was the neighborhood "Petit Café" of 20th-century French dramatist and novelist Tristan Bernard. Now it is a little neighborhood bar down the street from a branch of the Printemps department store. Sometimes peaceful, sometimes animated, Petrissans is a genteel spot, with a cozy men's club atmosphere, mirrored walls, and mahogany-colored banquettes. The menu is simple, and minimal, offering a variety of wines by the glass and small platters of ham, cheese, and sausage. On Saturdays, men are there "baby-sitting" the children while their wives shop at the nearby Rue Poncelet open-air market.

SAINT-OUEN

CHEZ SERGE
7 Boulevard Jean-Jaurès,
93400 Saint-Ouen.
(40.11.06.42 and
40.12.42.07).
Métro: Mairie de Saint-
Ouen.
Open 7 A.M. to 9 P.M. Closed
Sunday and August.
Hot meal served at lunch.
Credit card: V.
English spoken.
Selected wines may be
purchased to take home.

WINES:
Beaujolais, Chénas, Brouilly, red
Poitou, white Graves,
Pouilly-Fuissé, Sauternes.

SPECIALTIES:
Foie gras frais au Sauternes (duck
and goose foie gras), morue à
l'orange (codfish in orange sauce).

You have to love wine and adventure to make the trip to this workers' village just across the city line. But the active neighborhood wine bar is authentic, the homemade foie gras is good, and so is the cooking done by owner Serge Cancé's wife, Michelle. Do try the delicious dry white Graves. Meilleur Pot winner in 1975.

Marchés
MARKETS

Rue Mouffetard: a daily ritual (see entry, page 172).

Most mornings, after an early jog around Paris's Parc Monceau, I extract a string bag from my sweatshirt pocket and head straight for Rue Poncelet, the lively open-air street market a few blocks away. Marketing is best in the morning, when the vegetable man is in good temper (and is sober), the crowds thin, and the produce at its freshest.

The cluttered, colorful market—one of many scattered about Paris—opens precisely at 9 A.M., when most days the sky is thick, somber, and a dozen shades of gray, and the city is just beginning to wake up. A tour of Paris's markets offers a rare glimpse of an immensely important French ritual—one that should even be of interest to those not particularly passionate about food—since it allows one to examine the authentic fabric and texture of contemporary Gallic society.

Parisians devote a good part of their day to marketing, and it's obvious that what many Frenchmen do between meals is make shopping lists, market, and talk about meals past and meals future. Daily marketing is still the rule in Paris, where everything from Camembert to cantaloupe is sold to be eaten that day, preferably within a few hours. I still smile appreciatively when the cheese man asks if the Camembert will be savored that afternoon, or perhaps that evening, then shuffles through his larder, touching and pinching to come up with one that's perfectly ripe and properly creamy.

Most of the merchants are fiercely proud people, and though some may be rough and peasantlike, they display a refined sense of aesthetics. The vegetable man admirably attacks his *métier* like an artist: Each morning, beginning around 7 A.M., he painstakingly arranges the fruits and vegetables in orderly rows, paying careful attention to shapes, textures, and shading. The result is a colorful, vibrant mosaic: Fat stalks of celery rest next to snow-white cauliflower, the ruffled green leaves of Swiss chard stand beside them, followed by yellow-white Belgian endive, pale green artichokes, then—zap!—rosy tomatoes or ruby red peppers. Across the aisle, green Granny Smith apples line up alongside the sweet Italian oranges, called *sanguines* (favored for their juice, which runs the color of a brilliant sunset), while bananas from Martinique and walnuts from Grenoble fill out the palette.

Mastering the intricacies and etiquette of French marketing is no simpler than learning French, and easily as frustrating. And it requires patience. A serious marketing trip—which will only get you through the next meal—can take a good hour, and often takes more, if you want to do it right.

The selection at even the smallest markets is amazing. A large *rue commerçante* (merchant street) such as Rue Poncelet might include half a dozen *boulangeries* and *pâtisseries;* two supermarkets; a good dozen fruit and vegetable merchants; a coffee, tea, and spice shop; three fishmongers; four or five cafés; two wine shops; three flower shops; four poultrymen; two *triperies* for tripe, kidneys, sweetbreads, and liver; three *fromageries;* one butcher for horsemeat; five other *boucheries;* four *charcuteries* for cold cuts; two or three regional or foreign specialty shops; and half a dozen restaurants. Depending on the length of the lines and the merchants' chatter, each individual purchase can take five to ten minutes.

French merchants, it must be noted, are not just merchants. They're philosophers, songsters, comics, tutors, and culinary counselors. Parisian housewives don't need cookbooks. The butcher, poultryman, and fishmonger all willingly dispense verbal recipes with each purchase. (Otherwise, merchants are not known for their generosity. The concept of a baker's dozen is not generally put into practice in France, though the fishmonger will, on occasion, throw in a bunch of dill with the salmon.)

Booming voices and shrill cries fill the air throughout the day, as merchants hawk their finest produce, selling from rickety wooden pushcarts or narrow stalls. One piercing voice boasts of *"la très belle salade"* (very beautiful lettuce), while another shouts *"Jetez un petit coup d'oeil"* (take a little look) at the *"canette de Barbarie extra"* (extra-special duckling). Another ruddy-faced butcher holds out a fresh, plump *boudin* (blood sausage) for a shopper to inhale, announcing that it offers *"une véritable symphonie"* of lively aromas.

Meanwhile, at one corner, you may trip over a donkey tended by a trader selling an exotic array of herbs and essences, while nearby a jazzy brass band plays on.

The chatter is often amusing. One fall, I looked on as a shopper requested a kilo of *raisins de Hambourg,* France's popular muscat grape. Then, by accident, she noticed that the plump purple grapes came from Provence, in the south of France. "But I thought they came from Germany," she said in confusion. "But Madame," the merchant replied with a serious wink and a broad smile, "you know that in France, agriculture is very, very complicated."

I always begin at one end of the street—flanked by indoor and outdoor stalls—and tour the entire market before buying a thing, making mental notes of what's fresh, stopping to wave at the flower lady (who, due to my affinity for red tulips, calls me "Madame Tulipe"), reading the price and origin of each item chalked on little blackboards that dangle above the stalls.

Lots of things here work on what one friend calls the *"pas possible"* principle, meaning "it isn't done this way here, so tough luck for you if you want it otherwise." Merchants bristle at any atypical request, particularly from foreigners. One friend worked for weeks to get her pork butcher to cut the *poitrine fumée,* or smoked slab bacon, thin enough to fry American-style. The butcher finally won, insisting that if he sliced the bacon any thinner, she'd end up with lace.

Once I ordered two kilos of fresh jalapeño peppers for pickling, and the vegetable merchant looked as though he'd seen a mirage. He asked, "How do you eat them?" "Just like this," I responded, pretending to bite into a fiery raw pepper. The merchant smiled, turned to a colleague, and playfully whispered, "She comes by every morning, buys two kilos at a time!"

And it took a long time to wean myself of the democratic American form of marketing: self-service. Here, the law is *ne touchez pas*—don't touch—and anyone caught selecting his own pears and peaches will be forcefully admonished.

The full flavor of the market varies according to the time of day. It's as much fun to tour markets at morning's close, promptly at 1 P.M., as it is when they first open. One o'clock is the hour when a sudden hush falls over all of Paris. Shoppers scurry home to lunch while merchants sing, chant, and shout like schoolchildren let free for recess. A few minutes later the streets are deserted, save for a few *clochardes* (bag ladies) rifling through the rejected produce that tumbles to the gutters.

Sometimes, the population density in markets can be just too much. On a rainy Saturday around six in the afternoon, Poncelet is a veritable obstacle course. Families with strollers, slow-moving old ladies pulling metal shopping carts, dogs, and long lines make passage all but impossible.

But no matter the time of day, the season, or the market, Paris is ever a moveable feast.

The city's markets, like its neighborhoods, reflect a variety of cultures and classes, and a tour of one or several will tell you much about the daily life of the city, and of the habits of those who live in each neighborhood.

There are three basic sorts of markets: The *rues commerçantes,* or merchant streets, are stationary indoor-outdoor street markets, generally large, rambling, and open six days a week. Paris has fourteen *marchés couverts,* or covered food markets, large, open affairs with a total of 740 merchants; while the fifty-seven *marchés volants,* or roving markets, include more than 5,000 independent merchants moving from neighborhood to neighborhood on given days.

RUES COMMERCANTES
Merchant Streets

Standard hours are 9 A.M. to 1 P.M. and 4 P.M. to 7 P.M. Tuesday through Saturday; 9 A.M. to 1 P.M. Sunday. Most are closed Monday, and the number of merchants is substantially reduced during the months of July and August.

RUE DES BELLES-FEUILLES
Beginning at Avenue Victor-Hugo, Paris 16.
Métro: Victor-Hugo.

What the street lacks in character is made up for in the quality of produce—among the best in Paris, attracting some of the wealthiest customers. Shops to look into include Lillo Fromagerie (No. 35), a spotless, friendly store with an exceptionally beautiful assortment of cheese; and Herrier (No. 39), one of the city's finest fish markets.

RUE CLER
Beginning at Avenue de la Motte-Picquet, Paris 7.
Métro: Ecole Militaire.

This is one of Paris's tidiest high-class markets, with a broad pedestrian street that makes for comfortable browsing. Since many Americans live in the quarter, merchants are used to curious stares and constant questioning about unusual items. Take a look at Charcuterie Gonin (No. 40), a brilliantly spotless corner shop with a huge assortment of carry-out items, including *moussaka, couli-biac* of salmon, and tarts; and Davoli (No. 34), one of the city's few real Italian markets, all mirrors and black marble, with an amusing clutter of hams and sausages. Off Rue Cler on Rue du Champ-de-Mars, Marie-Anne Cantin (No. 12) offers a remarkable selection of goat cheese, as well as extraordinary Camembert.

RUE DE LEVIS
Beginning at Boulevard des Batignolles, Paris 17.
Métro: Villiers.

A lively market street not far from the tiny, elegant Parc Monceau, where you can picnic on the market's offerings. Begin at No. 21, the Couasnon Boulangerie, where Louis Couasnon, a dedicated young baker, offers superb *Belle Epoque* brand *baguettes,* made with a touch of rye flour, and *pain paillasse,* a rustic sourdough country loaf. Further along, at No. 24, the Jean Carmès et Fils *fromagerie* offers more than 100 varieties of French cheese, all aged in its own cellars.

> *"The air was laden with the various smells of the city and its markets: The strong smell of leeks mingled with the faint but persistent scent of lilacs, all carried along by the pungent breeze which is truly the air of Paris."*
> —Jean Renoir

RUNGIS WHOLESALE MARKET

France's largest food market—south of Paris, near Orly airport—covers some 440 acres of blacktopped surface, with 864 wholesalers and 1,050 producers selling everything from fresh fruits and vegetables to whole sides of rosy beef, to basket upon basket of fresh Brittany coast oysters. To feed the city's 10 million inhabitants, the Rungis wholesale market annually processes some 700,000 tons of potatoes, 500 million eggs, 560,000 tons of meat, and 750 million liters of wine.

There's no question that Rungis, open since 1969, lacks the romantic, grubby charm of the old Les Halles market it replaced. The modern-day wholesale market is spacious and sanitary, with hangar upon hangar of sober gray buildings. Fishmongers open the market at 3 A.M. and action continues until about 11 A.M., when the flower merchants move into the scene.

Rungis is open only to professionals, and casual onlookers are not welcomed openly. There are, however, two public tours. Each Thursday at 11 A.M. the Rungis market offers a tour, in French, which can be arranged in advance for individuals or groups by calling 46.87.35.35. Rungis is accessible via Paris bus numbers 183, 185, 285, and 131.

Robert Noah, an American who runs the Paris en Cuisine cooking school, conducts guided tours, in English, beginning at 5:30 A.M. and ending around 9 A.M. The tour takes visitors through all of the major markets. Write Paris en Cuisine, 49 Rue de Richelieu, 75001 Paris. Telephone 42.61.35.23.

RUE MONTORGUEIL
Beginning at Rue
  Rambuteau, Paris 1.
Métro: Les Halles.

Les Halles, Paris's most famous market, is no more, but Rue Montorgueil remains. It is authentic, grubby, and run-down, but many of the city's finest chefs still do their marketing here, sharing chores as one chef markets for fish, another goes after the meat, still another for the produce, then all meeting for coffee before heading back to their restaurants. While in the neighborhood, visit the majestic 16th-century Saint-Eustache church, where you will find a little chapel dedicated to the fruit and vegetable merchants of Les Halles.

RUE MOUFFETARD
Beginning at Rue de l'Epée-
de-Bois, Paris 5.
Métro: Monge.

Parisians complain of high prices, poor-quality produce, and too many tourists, but Rue Mouffetard remains one of the city's classic and most popular merchant streets. Begin at the top of the market just before noon to get a feel of the spirit and texture of the street, which has an honest sort of beaten-down charm. There's a lot of hawking and jostling here as tough merchants sell out of wooden crates balanced on tattered wooden sawhorses.

A detour to Passage Passé Simple leads into a tiny flower market and two exceptional Auvergnat shops, selling every cut of pork imaginable, along with dried beans and nuts sold from overflowing gunnysacks. Farther down, off Rue de l'Arbalète, there's a lively African market, selling all sorts of dried fish, baskets, and sandals. Back on Rue Mouffetard at No. 116, stop in at Café Mouffetard for the dense and buttery *croissants* and rich *brioche*. Also take a quick look at the Facchetti Italian market, No. 134, with its four-story mural of animals wandering through the forest.

Taking time for the news between sales.

RUE PONCELET
Beginning at Avenue des
Ternes, Paris 17.
Métro: Ternes.

Highlights include La Fromagerie Alléosse (No. 13), for its impeccable assortment of cheeses, and Le Moule à Gateau (No. 10), with delicious *chaussons aux pruneaux* (prune turnovers) and other pastries. If you're in the market on Tuesday, Saturday, or Sunday, peek in the little alley between Nos. 25 and 29 Rue Poncelet. No doubt there will be a line, and at the front of it you'll find a lively

Flowers, anyone?

maraîcher, a market gardener, who trucks in the freshest local farm produce. Around the corner on Avenue des Ternes (No. 16), the glass front of Maison Pou shields one of the neatest neighborhood *charcuteries.*

LES MARCHES BIOLOGIQUES (ORGANIC MARKETS)

These are food markets unlike others in Paris— more like old-fashioned country farmer's markets. On weekends, from thirty to fifty independent "organic" farmers set up stalls along one of the main streets of Boulogne and Joinville, two Parisian suburbs. They sell organically grown fruits and vegetables; homemade breads; dried fruits and nuts; *charcuterie,* farm-raised chickens, ducks, and geese; and even wine that's guaranteed to be "natural." The organic, or *biologique,* movement in France is active and well-organized, and this market is a shining example of its success. On a given weekend you might also find one stand selling freshly made pizza, and another rustic whole-wheat breads. There is also homemade apple or pear cider, a huge variety of artisanal goat cheeses, sausages, and beer, and even one merchant offering bright and glorious sprays of dried flowers. For all markets, it is best to go early in the day for a good selection.

Le Marché Boulogne, 140 Route de la Reine, 92 Boulogne-sur-Seine. Métro: Boulogne–Pont de Saint-Cloud, or accessible via Paris's No. 72 bus. Open 8 A.M. to 4 P.M. first and third Saturday of each month.

Le Marché Joinville-le-Pont, Place Mozart, 94 Joinville. Métro: RER Line B to Joinville, then via the suburban No. 106 and 108N buses. Open 8:30 A.M. to 1 P.M. second and fourth Saturday of each month.

Le Marché Sceaux-Robinson, Rue des Mouille-Boeuf. Métro: RER Line B to Robinson. Every Sunday, 8:30 A.M. to 1 P.M.

For further information on these markets, call Nature et Progrès, 47.00.60.36.

RUE DU POTEAU
Beginning at Place Jules-
    Joffrin, Paris 18
Métro: Jules-Joffrin.

One of the prettiest and most pristine markets in Paris, set high above Sacré-Coeur along a series of charming winding streets. The market's worth a detour simply to get an idea of what a real Paris neighborhood might have looked like a few decades ago. Start out early in the morning at Place Jules-Joffrin, then go to No. 81 Rue du Mont-Cenis, where, at Pâtisserie de Montmartre, you'll find some of the best *croissants* and *pains au chocolat* in Paris. Take your time peeking into the shops along Rue du Poteau, where the spotless turn-of-the-century storefronts will amaze you. A real find is the Fromagerie de Montmartre, at No. 9, where you'll be certain to find something appealing among the forty varieties of goat cheese and 100 other cow's- and sheep's-milk varieties.

RUE DE SEINE/BUCI
Beginning at Boulevard
    Saint-Germain, Paris 6.
Métro: Odéon.

This is considered Paris's most expensive market street, and it is certainly one of the most densely populated. The vendors are a close-knit group, changing stations from day to day. One morning the diminutive blond-haired lady with the husky voice might try to sell you a kilo of *mandarines,* while the next day she's positioned behind a pile of leafy greens. It's a bit disconcerting: Just when you've got a standing joke with the orange merchant he gets transferred to the tomatoes. At No. 81, note the Hamon Fromagerie, offering some of the best goat cheese in the neighborhood. It's also one of the few Paris *fromageries* to sell *fromage frais bien égoutté,* a fresh curd cheese and key ingredient in Americanlike cheesecake. A big stall on the corner of Rue de Seine and Rue de Buci offers a variety of exotic produce, including mounds of fresh wild mushrooms. At the adjoining stall, there's a gruff old merchant who prides himself on his beautiful celery, black radishes, and fresh herbs. Take a right onto Rue de Buci, where at No. 6 the Boudin *boulangerie* offers an unusual puff pastry *fougasse,* a flaky, satisfying lacy bread. It's available on Wednesdays only, and can be special-ordered—perfect for an afternoon snack with coffee. Their other breads and pastries are best forgotten.

MARCHES COUVERTS
Covered Markets

Standard hours are 8 A.M. to 1 P.M. and 4 P.M. to 7:30 P.M. Tuesday through Saturday. Many of these markets have lost merchants and clients over the years, and so tend to be quieter and more subdued than either the merchant streets or the roving markets. They're great for visiting on a rainy day.

**MARCHE
CHATEAU-D'EAU**
At Rue du Château-d'Eau
and Rue Bouchardon,
Paris 10.
Métro: Château-d'Eau.

This is the real thing: an earthy, historic, old market, with lower-quality and less exotic produce, but one that certainly gives a hint of what the old Les Halles was like. You'll find butchers washing sweetbreads in the market's central fountain, while grandmotherly French women with tattered metal carts toddle by. Take the time to walk through the nearby Passage du Marché: It's reminiscent of old France.

ENFANTS ROUGES
39 Rue de Bretagne, Paris 3.
Métro: Filles-du-Calvaire.

For Paris history buffs, this market will easily take you back in time. The produce is far from prime, but the atmosphere is thick as the Paris sky in winter. Stop and examine the old coffee merchant's shop, which looks like a stage set for a turn-of-the-century film. Two nearby spots worth noting: Boulangerie Onfroy at 34 Rue de Saintonge (with absolutely the best rye bread in town) and the lovely Square du Temple park, where you can have a nice picnic lunch.

MARCHE DE PASSY
Corner of Rue Bois-le-Vent
and Rue Duban,
Paris 16.
Métro: La Muette.

A great little market with wonderful skylights, superb *charcuterie* from Lyons, a nice little Italian market, and top-quality cheese at Monsieur Gay's stand. If there's time, take a walk down Rue de l'Annonciation, one of the city's fine merchant streets.

MARCHE SAINT-GERMAIN
At Rue Mabillon and Rue
Lobineau, Paris 5.
Métro: Mabillon.

Clean, quiet, and still full of character, this market offers lots of little stalls with fresh, fresh produce and friendly merchants. Best days are Tuesday, Thursday, and Saturday, when new shipments of produce come in.

*A*t No. 16 Rue Montmartre, there's a curiously named alley, the Queen of Hungary Passage (Passage Reine de Hongrie). Sometime during the 18th-century reign of Marie Antoinette, the queen was passing through the alley and was handed a petition by a woman who ran a market stall. The queen commented on the merchant's likeness to the queen of Hungary, and soon the alley was renamed.

TO MARKET, TO MARKET

*P*aris's first food market was established during the 5th century, on what is now the Ile de la Cité. As the city expanded, other small markets were created, first at the city gates, then beginning in the 13th century, at the old iron works between Rue Saint-Denis, Rue Saint-Honoré, and Rue Croix-des-Petits-Champs, the site of the present Forum des Halles shopping mall.

At the time, the big *halles,* or market, was shared by merchants, craftsmen, and peddlers offering an international array of goods. To encourage trade here, other city merchants and craftsmen were ordered to close their shops two days each week. It was not until the 16th century, when Paris had 300,000 inhabitants, that produce and other food-stuffs came to dominate the market.

By 1546, Paris boasted of four major bread markets and one live animal market. In the 17th century, the Quai de la Mégisserie along the Seine's Right Bank—now the site of the live bird market, then known as the "valley of misery"—was the chicken, wild game, lamb, goat, and milk-fed pig market; Rue de la Poissonnière was established as the fish market; and the wine market was installed on the Left Bank's Quai Saint-Bernard.

The French Revolution of 1789 put an end to the royal privilege of authorizing markets, and transferred the power to the city. By 1860, Paris had fifty-one markets, twenty-one of them covered and the rest open-air affairs.

By the mid-19th century the central Les Halles was badly in need of repair, so a new hall with iron girders and skylight roofs—reminiscent of the still-existing Gare de l'Est—was built by the architect Baltard between 1854 and 1866. The design, complete with vast underground storehouses and linked by roofed passages and alleys, became a model for markets throughout France and the rest of the world. As the city's population grew, the market space eventually became inadequate, and in 1969 the market was moved to Rungis, south of Paris, near Orly airport. Les Halles was torn down to make way for a major modern shopping complex, now a lively neighborhood of parks, restaurants, and shops.

**MARCHE
SAINT-QUENTIN**
Corner of Boulevard de
Magenta and Rue de
Chabrol, Paris 10.
Métro: Gare de l'Est.

This huge renovated market is one of the most spotless and liveliest of the turn-of-the-century covered markets. Excellent offerings of cheese, wine, and *charcuterie,* perfect for a stop before taking the train from the nearby Gare du Nord or Gare de l'Est. One of the city's green Wallace Fountains stands in the center of the market.

MARCHES VOLANTS

Roving Markets

Note that these markets are open from 7 A.M. to 1:30 P.M. only on the days listed. These tend to be less expensive than the other markets, and often you'll find fresher, more unusual produce here, but sometimes less variety. They are usually set up on sidewalks or along the islands of major boulevards and offer a full range of products, including fruits and vegetables, meats, poultry, fish, cheese, and fresh flowers.

5th arrondissement

CARMES
Place Maubert.
Métro: Maubert-Mutualité.
Tuesday, Thursday, and
    Saturday.

MONGE
Place Monge.
Métro: Monge.
Wednesday, Friday, and
    Sunday.

6th arrondissement

RASPAIL
Boulevard Raspail, between
    Rue du Cherche-Midi
    and Rue de Rennes.
Métros: Rennes or Sèvres-
    Babylone.
Tuesday and Friday.

7th arrondissement

BRETEUIL
Avenue de Saxe, from
    Avenue de Ségur to Place
    Breteuil.
Métro: Ségur.
Thursday and Saturday.

8th arrondissement

MADELEINE
Place de la Madeleine
Métro: Madeleine.
Tuesday and Friday.

11th arrondissement

CHARONNE
Boulevard de Charonne,
    between Rue de
    Charonne and Rue
    Alexandre-Dumas.
Métro: Alexandre-Dumas.
Wednesday and Saturday.

MENILMONTANT
Boulevard de Belleville and
    Boulevard de
    Ménilmontant.
Métro: Ménilmontant.
Tuesday and Friday.

POPINCOURT
Boulevard Richard-Lenoir,
    between Rue Oberkampf
    and Rue de Crussol.
Métro: Oberkampf.
Tuesday and Friday.

12th arrondissement

BEAUVEAU
Place d'Aligre.
Métro: Ledru-Rollin.
Tuesday through Sunday.

BERCY
Boulevard de Reuilly,
  between Rue de
  Charenton and Place
  Félix-Eboué.
Métro: Daumesnil.
Tuesday and Friday.

COURS DE VINCENNES
Cours de Vincennes,
  between Boulevard de
  Picpus and Avenue du
  Docteur-Arnold-Netter.
Métro: Nation.
Wednesday and Saturday.

13th arrondissement

GOBELINS
Boulevard Auguste-Blanqui,
  from Place d'Italie to Rue
  Barrault.
Métro: Place d'Italie.
Tuesday, Friday, and Sunday.

14th arrondissement

ALESIA
Rue d'Alésia, from Rue de la
  Santé to Avenue René-
  Coty.
Métro: Glacière.
Tuesday and Saturday.

BRUNE
Boulevard Brune, beginning
  at No. 49.
Métro: Porte de Vanves.
Thursday and Sunday.

EDGAR QUINET
Along Boulevard Edgar-
  Quinet, beginning at Rue
  de Départ.
Métro: Edgar-Quinet.
Wednesday and Saturday.

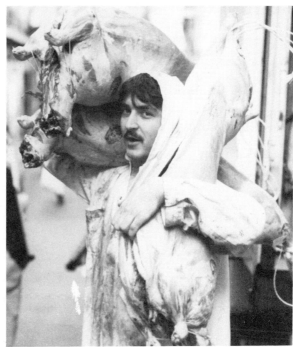

15th arrondissement

CONVENTION
Rue de la Convention,
    between Rue Alain-
    Chartier and Rue de
    l'Abbé-Groult.
Métro: Convention.
Tuesday, Thursday, and
    Sunday.

DUPLEIX
Boulevard du Grenelle,
    between Rue Lourmel
    and Rue du Commerce.
Métros: Dupleix or La
    Motte-Picquet-Grenelle.
Wednesday and Sunday.

16th arrondissement

AUTEUIL
Place Jean-Lorrain.
Métro: Michel Ange–
    Auteuil.
Wednesday and Saturday.

COURS LA REINE
Avenue Président Wilson
    between Rue Debrousse
    and Place Iéna.
Métro: Alma Marceau or
    Iéna.
Wednesday and Saturday.

EXELMANS
Place de la Porte Molitor.
Métro: Porte d'Auteuil.
Tuesday and Friday.

SAINT-DIDIER
Corner of Rue Mesnil and
    Rue Saint-Didier.
Métro: Victor-Hugo.
Tuesday, Thursday, and
    Saturday.

Pâtisseries
PASTRY SHOPS

Demonstrating appropriate madeleine technique.

The Parisian pastry chef is truly a man to be admired. Imagine his responsibility. Day in and day out, season after season, he must attend to the care and feeding of the formidable Parisian sweet tooth.

Everywhere you turn in Paris, someone—man, woman, or child— seems to be either munching on a *pain au chocolat,* peering wide-eyed into the window of a pristine, wondrous pastry shop, savoring the last lick on an ice cream cone, or carrying, with admirable agility, a beribboned white box filled with the day's dessert.

Perhaps the city's per capita consumption of butter, sugar, cream, and eggs is not the highest in the world, but if a population won prizes simply on its level of enthusiasm for all things sweet and satisfying, I think that Parisians would win. I have watched reed-thin women heartily down three and four dessert helpings in a row—unashamedly, unabashedly, with no remorse. I have eaves-dropped as a pair of businessmen huddled at lunchtime, talking in hushed, animated tones. The subject was not politics, not Euromis-siles, not racing cars, but chocolates. Chocolates! I have listened as one enthusiastic *pâtissier* explained what went on when several of Paris's pastry chefs gathered together: "I love éclairs, but I don't make them in my shop. So when I visit my buddies, I have an éclair feast. Seven is my limit. And I usually meet my limit."

French regional and ethnic pastries, of course, are important in Paris. The cheese-filled Alsatian *gâteau au fromage blanc* and the just-sweet-and-buttery-enough *kougelhopf* are everywhere; from Basque country in the southwest comes the cream-filled *gâteau basque;* from Normandy, the simply perfect apple tart. Don't miss at least a visual tour of Rue des Rosiers, the main street of the Jewish quarter, where there are almost as many pastry shops as street numbers, or a peek inside one of Gaston Lenôtre's several elegant shops, where a look is just about (but not quite) as good as a taste.

Everywhere, one finds *croissants* (along with the chocolate-filled version known as *pain au chocolat); brioche* (the *mousseline* variety is more buttery and typically Parisian); the *madeleine,* a lemony tea cake that Proust made famous; and the *financier* (a personal favorite), the almondy rectangle that is part cake, part cookie, and absolutely satisfying when fresh and carefully made.

For many—Parisians as well as those passing through—a day in this town without a pastry is a day not worth living. Why this is so would be the subject of a major treatise, but suffice it to say that they climb the sweet mountain because it is there.

LES HALLES, BASTILLE

2nd and 4th arrondissements

FINKELSZTAJN
27 Rue des Rosiers, Paris 4.
(42.72.78.91).
Métro: Saint-Paul.
Open 9 A.M. to 1:30 P.M. and
2:30 P.M. to 7:30 P.M.
Closed Monday, Tuesday,
and July 1 through mid-
August.
English spoken.

This is the best of the many pastry shops that line Rue des Rosiers, the heart of Paris's Jewish quarter. Finkelsztajn's cheesecake (better known as *vatrouchka*) rivals anything you'll find in New York, especially when it comes fresh and warm from the

French fruit tarts: always luscious.

oven in the afternoon. Their *gâteau aux figues* helps you understand where the Fig Newton began, and the assortment—poppy seed cakes, hazelnut cakes, and strudels filled with apples and raisins, honey and citrus peel, even dates—is enough to make one weep real tears. Throw discipline to the winds for a day, and enjoy.

PATISSERIE POTTIER
4 Rue de Rivoli, Paris 4.
(48.87.87.16).
Métro: Saint-Paul.
Open 8 A.M. to 1 P.M. and
   3 P.M. to 7:30 P.M. Closed
   Monday, Tuesday (except
   in December), and
   August.

The windows of this pristine, jewellike shop not far from the Places des Vosges is filled with minor masterpieces. Talented, ambitious young Christian Pottier is in love with his work, and it shows: His cakes and pastries are always pure, fresh, sparkling, and authoritative. All are worth trying: the shiny, buttery *brioche* that's made with only the best *beurre des Charentes;* the moist *quatre-quarts* pound cake filled with Golden Delicious apples or enhanced with a twist of lemon; and the chocolate *étoile* cake, a blend of chocolate meringue and chocolate mousse. Monsieur Pottier, who works in the neatly organized bake shop beneath the store, also prepares some 800 pure-butter *croissants* each day, brushing them lightly with a sugar syrup that gives them a hint of almonds and hazelnuts. They come out of the oven at 8:15 each morning, so get in line.

STOHRER
51 Rue Montorgueil, Paris 2.
(42.33.38.20).
Métro: Les Halles.
Open 7:30 A.M. to 8 P.M.
   Closed Monday and the
   first two weeks of August.
Credit card: V.
English spoken.

One of Louis XV's pastry chefs opened this shop in 1730, and it continues to thrill clients with its delicious individual *pithiviers*—cream-filled, flaky puff pastry decorated like a crown—little apricot or apple tarts, and superbly fresh *pains au chocolat*. Little elderly salesladies seem to swarm about the tiny shop, eager to assist in your selection. Take time to walk through the neighboring Rue Montorgueil market, which is slightly seedy but still retains the charm of old Les Halles.

LATIN QUARTER, LUXEMBOURG, SAINT-GERMAIN

5th and 6th arrondissements

PATISSERIE
   BOULANGERIE
   ALSACIENNE
(ANDRE LERCH)
4 Rue du Cardinal-Lemoine,
   Paris 5.
(43.26.15.80).
Métro: Cardinal-Lemoine.
Open 7:30 A.M. to 1:30 P.M.
   and 3 P.M. to 7 P.M. Closed
   Monday, Tuesday, and
   August.

André Lerch and his madeleines.

A jolly, super-active pastry chef/baker, André Lerch brings the best of Alsace to Paris, with his golden *kougelhopf* (see recipe, page 187), twenty different kinds of simple, family-style fruit tarts that vary with the seasons, giant rounds of fresh cheese-cake (*tarte au fromage blanc*), along with whatever new creation he dreamed up overnight. (When Monsieur Lerch can't sleep, he picks up a cookbook to inspire himself to try a new recipe the next day in the shop!) He'd like nothing better than to be able to spend four or five hours decorating a single tart, but instead he lives realistically, and feeds his creative urgings by changing his repertoire with the seasons. He's busiest from November to March, when wintry Alsatian baked good are most in demand: *springerle, quiche lorraine,* and the delicious spice bread *pain d'épices* are all there. Year-round, he sells *kougelhopf* (along with the folkloric Alsatian molds for making them at home) and the famous plump tea cakes known as *madeleines*.

MADELEINES
LEMON TEA CAKES

While researching this book, I became fixated, absolutely fanatical, about madeleines, *the plump and golden tea cakes shaped like tiny scallop shells. They were something to boost my spirits on the days when I walked for miles sleuthing in search of culinary jewels. I tasted dozens of* madeleines, *but only a few that were "just right."*

The best, freshest madeleine *has a dry, almost dusty taste when taken on its own. One of my favorite versions is made by André Lerch, an Alsatian baker with a bread and pastry shop on the Left Bank.*

*To be truly appreciated—to "invade the senses with exquisite pleasure" as they did for Marcel Proust—*madeleines *must be dipped in tea, ideally the slightly lime-flavored* tilleul, *which releases the fragrant, flavorful lemon essence of the little tea cake. Special* madeleine *tins can be found in all the French restaurant supply shops, and in the housewares section of department stores. The following is a recipe I developed.*

4 eggs
1 cup (200 g) sugar
Grated zest (peel) of 2
 lemons
1¾ cups (225 g) all-
 purpose flour (do
 not use unbleached
 flour)
¾ cup (6 ounces;
 185 g) unsalted
 butter, melted and
 cooled, plus 1
 tablespoon (½ oz;
 15 g) unsalted butter,
 for buttering
 madeleine tins

1. Place the eggs and sugar in a large bowl, then using a whisk or electric mixer, beat until lemon colored. Add the zest. Fold in the flour, then the ¾ cup butter.

2. Refrigerate the batter for 1 hour.

3. Preheat the oven to 375°F (190°C).

4. Butter the *madeleine* tins, then spoon in the batter, filling each well about three-fourths full. Bake 10 to 12 minutes, or until *madeleines* are golden brown.

5. Remove the *madeleines* from their tins as soon as they're baked and cool them on a baking rack. Note: Wash tins immediately with a stiff brush and hot water but no detergent, so they retain their seasoning. The *madeleines* are best eaten as soon as they've cooled. They may, however, be stored for several days in an airtight container.

Yield: Thirty-six 3-inch (8-cm) *madeleines*.

BOUDIN
4 Rue de Buci, Paris 6.
(43.26.04.13).
Métro: Saint-Germain-
 des-Prés.
Open 6:30 A.M. to 8 P.M.
 Closed Monday and
 August.
Some English spoken.

Thérèse and Claude Boudin have been baking breads and pastries here since the 1950s, and there is one good reason to pay them a visit. This is perhaps the only pastry shop in Paris to offer a lacy *fougasse* made of puff pastry, rather than the traditional bread dough. They make about thirty or forty large rectangles each day, mostly in the winter months, simply because Claude Boudin enjoys creating them. Made from *croissant* dough without added yeast, his *fougasse* is flaky, buttery, and irresistible when it comes out of the oven at around 10:30 A.M. (If the *fougasse* sells well that day, and there's time, he makes a second batch in the afternoon.) The Boudins' other products—particularly the breads—are less than inspiring.

LE MOULE A GATEAU
111 Rue Mouffetard, Paris 5.
(43.31.65.45).
Métro: Censier-Daubenton.
Open 9 A.M. to 7:30 P.M.
 Tuesday through
 Saturday; 9 A.M. to
 1:30 P.M. Sunday. Closed
 Monday.

Le Moule à Gâteau's ever-changing array of French family-style and regional cakes and pastries is welcoming and refreshing. This little chain store, with several shops around Paris, uses quality ingredients, the staff is friendly and well-trained, and some of the cakes and pastries are baked right before your eyes in this small but attractive wood and glass boutique. Their idea is to make it simple, make it fresh, and the crowds will form. They're right. Best of all, you can buy just about everything by the slice, so sampling is in order. Good bets are the *chaussons aux pruneaux* (prune turnovers) and fine, moist *pensées aux myrtilles,* cakes of blueberries and almond cream set on a shortbread crust. If you're there early, around 9 or 9:30, try a *pain au chocolat* fresh from the oven: They're warm and buttery, and the two generous sticks of chocolate inside will melt in your mouth. (If they're not warm, or not obviously fresh from the oven, try something else.)

André Lerch's kougelhopf (for recipe, see facing page.)

KOUGELHOPF ANDRE LERCH
ANDRE LERCH'S ALSATIAN COFFEE CAKE

In Paris, André Lerch, an outgoing Alsatian baker (see entry, page 184), runs a popular bread and pastry shop where he bakes forty to fifty kougelhopf each day, using well-seasoned molds a half-century old. There's a curious story behind these molds: Apparently, before World War II there was an Alsatian bakery where his now is. The baker went off to war, leaving behind his molds, buttered and prepared with whole almonds. He never returned, and when Monsieur Lerch moved in decades later, he found the molds stashed behind the ovens. He insists that well-seasoned molds are the secret to good kougelhopf. "The mold isn't good until it's been used 200 times," he warns. Since most of us won't make 200 kougelhopf in two and a half lifetimes, Monsieur Lerch offers a shortcut: Thoroughly butter a new mold, and place it in a low oven for several hours, re-buttering every fifteen minutes or so. The mold will take on a seductive essence of browned butter, and will be ready to produce fragrant, golden loaves.

½ cup (80 g) white raisins
2 tablespoons kirsch (cherry brandy) or other fruit-based *eau-de-vie*
1 cup (250 ml) milk
1 tablespoon or 1 package dry yeast
3¾ cups (525 g) unbleached all-purpose flour
2 eggs, beaten
½ cup (100 g) sugar
1 teaspoon salt
¾ cup (6 ounces; 185 g) unsalted butter, at room temperature
1 tablespoon (½ oz; 15 g) unsalted butter, for buttering the *kougelhopf* mold
½ cup (70 g) whole almonds
1 tablespoon confectioners' sugar

1. In a small bowl combine the raisins and kirsch.

2. Heat the milk to lukewarm, add the yeast, stir well, and set aside for 5 minutes.

3. Place the flour in a large bowl and make a well in the center. Add the dissolved yeast and milk, the eggs, sugar, and salt, mixing well after each addition. The dough will be quite sticky. Knead by hand for 10 minutes by slapping the dough against the side of the bowl, or knead by machine for 5 minutes. Add the butter, bit by bit, and knead until the dough is smooth or until the dough comes cleanly off the sides of the bowl. Drain the raisins and knead them into the dough.

4. Place the dough in a large clean bowl and cover securely with plastic wrap. Let rise at room temperature, about 1 hour. The dough will rise slightly.

5. Punch down, knead gently, cover, and let rise again, about 1 hour. The dough will rise slightly.

6. Preheat the oven to 350°F (175°C).

7. Heavily butter a 2-quart (2-liter) earthenware *kougelhopf* mold or bundt pan and place an almond in the well of each of the mold's indentations. Place the dough in the mold and let rise until it reaches the top, about 1 hour.

8. Bake 1 hour, or until *kougelhopf* is golden brown.

9. Unmold and when cool, sprinkle with confectioners' sugar. *Kougelhopf* tastes best the day after it's baked, when it's been allowed to "ripen."

Yield: 1 *kougelhopf*.

SEVRES-BABYLONE, ECOLE MILITAIRE, LA TOUR-MAUBOURG

7th arrondissement

CHRISTIAN CONSTANT
26 Rue du Bac, Paris 7.
(47.03.30.00).
Métro: Rue du Bac.
Open daily, 8 A.M. to 8 P.M.
Credit card: V.
English spoken.

If you'd like to see how *nouvelle cuisine* has inspired French pastries, stop in at Christian Constant's all-white, contemporary shop, where exotic kiwi tarts and tiny boutique-size chocolates fill the display window. Not all his creations inspire respect, but Christian Constant does offer a few pleasant classics: His warm individual *tarte Tatin* goes down well in the morning with a bracing cup of thick *express,* and they can be enjoyed, in tranquility, in the little tea salon that adjoins the shop.

LENOTRE
44 Rue de Bac, Paris 7.
(42.22.39.39).
Métro: Rue du Bac.
Open 9 A.M. to 8 P.M. Monday through Saturday; 9 A.M. to 1 P.M. Sunday. Closed August.
Credit cards: AE,V.
English spoken.

A small boutique featuring a selection of Lenôtre's famous pastries and chocolates. See 16th *arrondissement.*

Irresistible, buttery croissants.

LA MAISON CHAVINIER
39 Avenue Rapp, Paris 7.
(47.05.41.48).
Métro: Ecole Militaire.
Open 7 A.M. to 8 P.M. Closed Sunday.

If you're wandering about the neighborhood, stop in for a good, lemony *madeleine* or their fresh and famous *gâteau basque,* filled with delicious almond cream. Breads here are cooked in a wood-fired oven: Try the *pain de seigle aux raisins,* hearty rye and raisin.

A BAKER'S DOZEN

In the 17th century, butlers were charged with buying the wine and bread for their households. A contract would be signed with the local baker for a year's worth of bread. For every twelve loaves bought for the household, the butler got to keep the thirteenth for himself.

PATISSERIE MILLET
103 Rue Saint-Dominique, Paris 7.
(45.51.49.80).
Métro: La Tour-Maubourg.
Open 9 A.M. to 7 P.M. Tuesday through Saturday; 9 A.M. to 1 P.M. Sunday. Closed Monday, one week in February, and August.
English spoken.

A classic, spotless pastry shop offering pure honey *madeleines:* almond-flavored *financiers;* buttery, egg-rich *brioche mousseline* (see recipe, page 198); some twenty different varieties of cakes and tarts; and twenty flavors of ice cream. Their *croissants* are some of the best in town, and Denis Ruffel, Miller's energetic pastry chef, tucks two delicious sticks of chocolate into his remarkable *pain au chocolat.* Upstairs, behind the scenes, there's a good-size chocolate "factory," while on the main floor a small tea salon provides the perfect spot for sampling everything that tempts the palate.

PELTIER
66 Rue de Sèvres, Paris 7.
(47.34.06.62 or 47.83.66.12).
Métro: Vaneau.
Open 9:30 A.M. to 8 P.M. Tuesday through Saturday; 8:30 A.M. to 7 P.M. Sunday. Closed Monday.
Credit cards: DC, EC, V.
Will ship internationally.
English spoken.

Since 1961, the Peltier name has stood for quality pastry in Paris. Today, the family's spacious, pristine shop offers some of the most beautiful tarts and cakes in Paris, along with superb *croissants* and lovely frozen fruit soufflés. Sample their special cakes and tarts—one covered with seven different fresh fruits, another a mango-flavored *charlotte*—at the counter in the corner of the shop. Then take home a *princesse,* a meringue cake with almonds, vanilla cream, and grains of *nougatine.*

AU PONT ROYAL
18 Rue du Bac, Paris 7.
(42.61.27.63).
Métro: Rue du Bac.
Open 7 A.M. to 8 P.M. (7 P.M. Sunday). Closed Monday and August.
Credit card: V.
Will ship selected specialties internationally.

For the person who has everything: a made-to-order, detailed, ice cream bust in the flavor of your choice. For a mere 7,000 to 8,000 francs, Jean Saffray will make a life-size mold of your head, then fill it with ice cream surrounded by white chocolate. For a bit less—about 150 francs—you can order an ice cream likeness of François Mitterrand. (His bust is already in stock.) If you've only a few francs to spend, and aren't interested in celebrity-studded ice cream, console yourself with Monsieur Saffray's delicious and almondy *financiers.*

FINANCIERS
ALMOND CAKES

The little rectangular almond cakes known as financiers *are sold in many of the best pastry shops in Paris. Perfect* financiers *are about as addictive as chocolate, and I'd walk a mile or two for a good one. The finest have a firm, crusty exterior and a moist, almondy interior, tasting almost as if they were filled with almond paste. Next to the* madeleine, *the* financier *is probably the most popular little French cake, common street food for morning or afternoon snacking. The cake's name probably comes from the fact that a* financier *resembles a solid gold brick. Curiously, as popular as they are,* financiers *seldom appear in recipe books or in French literature.*

The secret to a good financier *is in the baking: For a good crust, they must begin baking in a very hot oven. Then the temperature is reduced to keep the interior moist. Placing the tins on a thick baking sheet while they are in the oven is an important baking hint from the Left Bank pastry chef Jean-Luc Poujauran, who worked for months to perfect his* financiers, *among the best in Paris. The special tin* financier *molds, each measuring 2 x 4 inches (5 x 10 cm), can be found at restaurant supply shops. Small oval* barquette *molds or even muffin tins could also be used.*

1 cup (140 g) almonds
1⅔ cups (210 g) confectioners' sugar
½ cup (70 g) unbleached all-purpose flour
¾ cup (185 ml) egg whites (5 to 6)
¾ cup (6 ounces; 185 g) unsalted butter, melted and cooled, plus 1 tablespoon (½ oz; 15 g) unsalted butter, for buttering 18 *financier* molds

1. Preheat the oven to 450°F (230°C).

2. Toast the almonds on a baking sheet until browned, about 5 minutes. Remove but leave the oven on. When the almonds are cool, grind them to a fine powder in a food processor.

3. In a medium-size bowl, combine the sugar, ground almonds, and flour, then sift or force the mixture through a fine mesh sieve into a second bowl. The mixture should be very fine. Stir in the unbeaten egg whites until thoroughly blended, then stir in the ¾ cup butter until well blended.

4. Butter the *financier* molds (or *barquette* molds), then fill each mold almost to the rim. Place the tins on a thick baking sheet (or a broiler pan) and place in the center of the oven. Bake for 7 minutes, then reduce heat to 400°F (205°C) and bake another 7 minutes. Turn off the heat and let the *financiers* rest in the oven another 7 minutes.

5. Remove the *financiers* from the oven and unmold as soon as they've cooled. Serve with tea, coffee, ice cream, or *sorbet*. (Note: Wash molds immediately with a stiff brush and hot water but no detergent, so they retain their seasoning.) The *financiers* may be stored in an airtight container for several days.

Yield: Eighteen 2- x 4-inch (5- x 10-cm) *financiers*.

POUJAURAN
20 Rue Jean-Nicot, Paris 7.
(47.05.80.88).
Métro: La Tour-Maubourg.
Open 8:30 A.M. to 8:30 P.M.
Closed Sunday and
August.

You can't help but love Jean-Luc Poujauran—he's young, feisty, ambitious, and a solid success. His charming shop tucked away on a nowhere street in the 7th *arrondissement* is chock-a-block full of goodies: a regional *gâteau basque,* pizzas, heady spice cake, fresh *financiers* (see recipe, facing page), and coffee- and nut-flavored pound cakes. (See also Boulangeries.)

MADELEINE, SAINT-PHILIPPE-DU-ROULE

8th arrondissement

DALLOYAU
99-101 Rue du Faubourg
  Saint-Honoré, Paris 8.
(43.59.18.10).
Métro: Saint-Philippe-du-
  Roule.
Open 9:30 A.M. to 7:15 P.M.
  Monday through
  Saturday; 8:45 A.M. to
  1:45 P.M. and 3 P.M. to
  6:45 P.M. Sunday. From
  July 10 to August 25,
  closed Sunday afternoon
  and Monday.
Credit card: V.
English spoken.

Since 1802, when Napoleon ruled the republic, Dalloyau has done its best to satisfy the Parisian palate. Today, the company's activities are incredibly diverse, offering pastries, chocolates, *charcuterie,* and fully catered meals and banquets. Best bets, though, are the coffee macaroons and the cake *mogador,* composed of chocolate cake, chocolate *mousse,* and a fine layer of raspberry jam. (See also Chocolateries.)

LADUREE
16 Rue Royale, Paris 8.
(42.60.21.79).
Métro: Madeleine.
Open 8:30 A.M. to 7 P.M.
  Closed Sunday and
  August.
English spoken.

Ladurée is one of Paris's most elegant and traditional shops—a tea salon and pastry shop of note. Press your nose against the window and dream on. The choice is not a simple one. Shall it be a buttery early morning *croissant,* a lunchtime strawberry tart, or a mid-afternoon chocolate macaroon? If there's time—and a table free—also stop for a cup of *café au lait,* one of the best in the city. On your way out, buy a delicate *brioche mousseline* or a raisin-filled *brioche* called *cramique,* to lure you out of bed the next morning. (See also Salons de Thé.)

PASTEUR

15th arrondissement

HELLEGOUARCH
185 Rue de Vaugirard, Paris 15.
(47.83.29.72).
Métro: Pasteur.
Open 8:30 A.M. to 7:30 P.M.
  Closed Monday and August.

Several years ago I conducted a blind tasting, in search of the best of Paris's *croissants*. Hellegouarch won hands down, and their *croissants*—when fresh from the oven around 9 A.M.—are still among the best in town. Their *pains au chocolat* are equally appealing: everything the buttery, flaky, chocolate-filled pastry should be, and even a little more.

VICTOR-HUGO, PASSY, AUTEUIL

16th arrondissement

PATISSERIE ALSACIENNE (C. BROCARD)
91 Avenue Raymond-Poincaré, Paris 16.
(45.00.56.55).
Métro: Victor-Hugo.
Open 8 A.M. to 7:30 P.M.
  Closed Monday and mid-July through first week of September.

A fine little shop just off Place Victor-Hugo, for sampling superb Alsatian pastries, including a fresh and buttery *kougelhopf, quiche lorraine,* onion tarts, Christmas *stollen,* and anise bread.

COQUELIN AINE
67 Rue de Passy, Paris 16.
(45.24.44.00).
Métro: Muette.
Open 9 A.M. to 7 P.M. Tuesday through Saturday; 9 A.M. to 1 P.M. Sunday. Closed Monday.
Credit Card: V
English spoken.

Take a break while visiting the Rue de l'Annonciation market and get in line with all the genteel ladies of this very chic *quartier.* They know where the good things are, like fresh and yeasty *brioche,* almond-rich *financiers,* and dozens of other sweets to excite even the stoic. The few tables in back are almost always taken, but if it's a warm and sunny day, take your snacks out to a park bench on the square, and enjoy.

LENOTRE
44 Rue d'Auteuil, Paris 16.
(45.24.52.52).
Métro: Michel-Ange/Auteuil.
Open daily, 9 A.M. to 9 P.M.
Credit cards: AE, V.
English spoken.

LENOTRE
49 Avenue Victor-Hugo,
   Paris 16.
(45.01.71.71).
Métro: Victor-Hugo.
Open daily, 9 A.M. to 9 P.M.
Credit card: V.
English spoken.

One wonders how Gaston Lenôtre does it. He and his band of pastry chefs are all over the world, turning out cakes and pastries, chocolates and ice creams, full-course meals and light snacks by the thousands. Yet throughout, everything stamped "Lenôtre" has that certain incomparable quality that can't be beat. His chocolates are still among the best in town, and no one makes a *gâteau Opéra* or meringue and chocolate mousse-filled *concorde* like Lenôtre's. (See also Boulangeries and Chocolateries.)

TERNES, WAGRAM

17th arrondissement

LENOTRE
121 Avenue de Wagram,
   Paris 17.
(47.63.70.30 and
   40.54.94.13).
Métros: Ternes or Wagram.
Open 9 A.M. to 8 P.M. Monday
   through Saturday; 9 A.M.
   to 1 P.M. Sunday.
See Lenôtre, 16th
   arrondissement.

LE MOULE A GATEAU
10 Rue Poncelet, Paris 17.
(47.63.06.49).
Métro: Ternes.
Open 9 A.M. to 7:30 P.M.
   Tuesday through
   Saturday; 9 A.M. to 1:30
   P.M. Sunday. Closed
   Monday.
See Le Moule à Gâteau, 5th
   arrondissement, page 186.

Warm bread, at any hour.

Always a crowd at Berthillon.

ICE CREAM WORTH WAITING FOR

The line stretches right around the corner, and neither subzero temperatures nor pouring rain can deter the hearty souls who queue up for a taste of Berthillon, Paris's finest ice creams, sorbets, and *granites*. There's always a lot of good-natured grumbling about the wait, while perfect strangers trade tales of past visits or argue passionately about which of the sixty-plus Berthillon flavors is best, purest, most authentic, most decadent.

There's always a lot of "place saving" as customers race up to the front of the line to check the list of current seasonal offerings. Once you reach the window you'd better have your choice well in mind—there is no time for hemming, hawing, asking advice, or questions. Will it be *glace au chocolat amer,* bitter chocolate ice cream rich with cream and eggs or maybe *nougat au miel,* a crunchy, heavenly blend of nuts and smooth, smooth honey? Or perhaps the glistening black currant *sorbet (Cassis)* that tastes so much like the real thing you can't believe you're not nibbling blackberries.

Berthillon, 31 Rue Saint-Louis-en-l'Ile, Paris 4. (43.54.31.61). Métro: Pont-Marie. Open 10 A.M. to 8 P.M. Closed Monday, Tuesday, July, August, and during Easter break.

If the thought of waiting in line is discouraging, don't despair. Berthillon ice cream and *sorbets* are sold in many Paris cafés:

Restaurant Cadmios, 17 Rue des Deux-Ponts, Paris 4. (43.25.50.93) (cones only).

Le Flore en l'Ile, 42 Quai d'Orléans, Paris 4. (43.29.88.27).

Lady Jane, 4 Quai d'Orléans, Paris 4. (46.33.08.36).

Le Mandarin, 148 Boulevard Saint-Germain, Paris 6. (46.33.98.35).

Le Petit Châtelet, 39 Rue de la Bûcherie, Paris 5. (46.33.53.40).

Le Reveille, 29 Boulevard Henri-IV, Paris 4. (42.72.73.26).

Rostand, 6 Place Edmond-Rostand, Paris 6. (43.54.61.58).

La Rotonde, 105 Boulevard Montparnasse, Paris 6. (43.26.68.84 and 43.26.48.26).

**LA PATISSERIE
    VIENNOISE**
11 Rue Poncelet, Paris 17.
(42.27.81.86).
Métro: Ternes.
Pastry shop open 8:30 A.M.
    to 7:30 P.M. Monday
    through Saturday; 9 A.M.
    to 12:30 P.M. Sunday. Tea
    salon open 9 A.M. to 6:30
    P.M. Monday through
    Saturday; 9 A.M. to 12:30
    P.M. Sunday. Both closed
    Sunday afternoon.
Credit card: V.
Some English spoken.

A very special shop on one of Paris's most lively market streets. Like taking a trip to old Vienna, La Pâtisserie Viennoise is sheer fantasy. At Christmastime, every inch of this tiny shop (and a few feet outdoors) is filled with marzipan snowmen and chocolate Santas, neatly packaged assortments of spice cookies, sugar cookies, anise cookies, and fruit-studded, frosted *stollen.* All year round, the window tempts shoppers with flaky apple or cherry strudels, dark lattice-top *Linzer tortes,* and the thick walnut-packed *engadine,* Europe's answer to the pecan pie. There's a coffee bar along the side of the shop and a tea salon upstairs, so pull up a stool or settle into a booth, order a *petit crème,* and indulge.

MONTMARTRE

17th and 18th arrondissements

**PATISSERIE DE
    MONTMARTRE**
81 Rue du Mont-Cenis,
    Paris 18.
(46.06.39.28).
Métro: Jules-Joffrin.
Open 9 A.M. to 7:45 P.M.
    Monday through
    Saturday; 8 A.M. to
    6:30 P.M. Sunday.
Credit card: V.
Will ship chocolates
    internationally.

T ake a walk along the charming Rue du Poteau market street, then stop in for a crisp and buttery *croissant,* a fine *pain au chocolat,* superb *brioche,* or a hazelnut-scented *financier.* There's a small tea salon in back, where a light lunch can also be had.

VAUDRON
4 Rue de la Jonquière,
    Paris 17.
(46.27.96.97).
Métro: Guy-Moquet.
Open 7:45 A.M. to 1 P.M. and
    2 P.M. to 7:30 P.M. Tuesday
    through Saturday; 7:45
    A.M. to 5:15 P.M. Sunday.
Closed Monday.

A large and spotless pastry shop dedicated to quality and simplicity at affordable prices. Vaudron has been around since 1931, catering to its faithful Parisian clientele and their births, baptisms, and weddings, generation after generation. Since 1969, Roland Indrière, now assisted by his son, has continued the tradition, aspiring to offer simple, unfussy, appealing cakes and pastries made with the highest-quality ingredients. Try their chocolates, their honey-sweetened *financiers,* and their deliciously fresh buttercream-filled caramel macaroons. They prepare giant apple turnovers (*chaussons aux pommes*) each Wednesday and pear-filled pound

> *"Make your pastry; when it is ready and you have added whatever you please, give it whatever shape and name you consider suitable."*
>
> —*Advice to French pastry cooks*

cakes (*quatre-quarts aux poires*) each Thursday, not to mention beautiful *brioches*, *madeleines*, twenty flavors of ice cream, and other cakes and tarts.

MÉNILMONTANT

20th arrondissement

GANACHAUD
150 Rue Ménilmontant, Paris 20.
(46.36.13.82).
Métro: Pelleport.
Open 2:30 P.M. to 8 P.M. Tuesday; 7:30 A.M. to 8 P.M. Wednesday through Saturday; 7:30 A.M. to 1:30 P.M. Sunday. Closed Monday and either July or August.
English spoken.

I can't imagine that anyone who has made the voyage to Ganachaud has gone away disappointed. Even before you get inside the shop, you're impressed. Most mornings, the pastry chef is there in the window, folding his *croissant* dough in a neat, orderly fashion. Later, he forms *croissant* after *croissant* as your tummy rumbles. Once inside, you need to decide: Will you wait for the moist, wheaty *croissants* to be fetched on a paddle from the wood-fired oven, or will you go for the prune turnovers or a slice of *bostock* (a recycled slice of *brioche*, miraculously given new life with a touch of almonds and a sprinkling of kirsch), or, like me, give in to the ever-irresistible *pain au chocolat*? (See also Boulangeries.)

TARTE FEUILLETEE A L'ANANAS JAMIN
JAMIN'S PUFF PASTRY PINEAPPLE TART

Pineapple is an often-ignored fruit in France, although it has been around since the 18th century. Louis XIV pricked his tongue the first time he tried pineapple (not knowing it should be peeled), but Louis XV loved the sweet fruit. At Restaurant Jamin (see entry, page 98), chef Joël Robuchon found that, at first, he had a hard time convincing diners that a simple little pineapple tart could be so delicious. Until, of course, they tasted it. It's especially easy to make if you've a stash of tart shells in the freezer. The tart must be assembled at absolutely the last minute, or it turns soggy and you lose the wonderfully fresh and fruity flavor of the pineapple. Monsieur Robuchon uses a very thin puff pastry base for this tart, but any good homemade pastry crust may be used.

1 cup (250 ml) milk
2 egg yolks
¼ cup (50 g) sugar
3 tablespoons
    unbleached all-
    purpose flour
1 tablespoon cornstarch
2 teaspoons kirsch
    (cherry brandy) or
    other fruit-based *eau-
    de-vie*
1 prebaked 10½-inch
    (27-cm) pastry shell,
    cooled
6 slices fresh pineapple,
    each ½ inch
    (1½ cm) thick
2 tablespoons quince or
    red currant jelly

1. Place the milk in a small saucepan over medium-high heat and scald it.

2. Meanwhile, in the bowl of an electric mixer, combine the egg yolks and sugar, and beat until thick and pale yellow. Slowly incorporate the flour and cornstarch. Slowly blend the scalded milk into the egg mixture.

3. Return the mixture to the pan and bring it to a boil over medium heat, stirring constantly. Remove from heat and whisk in the kirsch. Spread the warm pastry cream over the pastry shell.

4. Cut the pineapple slices into wedges. Arrange the wedges in a sunburst pattern on the pastry cream, starting from the outside and working in.

5. In a small saucepan melt the jelly over low heat. Strain. Brush the warm jelly over the pineapple and serve the tart immediately.

Yield: One 10½-inch (27-cm) tart.

BRIOCHE MOUSSELINE DENIS RUFFEL

Paris bakeries offer many variations on the classic brioche, *a buttery, egg-rich yeast bread that's enjoyed for luxurious breakfasts or snacks, appearing in various forms and sizes. This* brioche, *known as* brioche mousseline *because it is richer in butter than* brioche ordinaire, *is incredibly golden and delicious.* Brioche mousseline *is typically Parisian, and the light and sticky dough is often baked in tin coffee cans. Denis Ruffel, from the Left Bank pastry shop Pâtisserie Millet (see entry, page 189), offers his personal version, baked in a rectangular loaf pan. Ruffel's special glaze gives all sweet breads a certain glow.*

Brioche:

1 tablespoon or 1 package dry yeast

¼ cup (60 ml) lukewarm milk

⅓ cup (65 g) sugar

1 teaspoon salt

4 cups (560 g) unbleached all-purpose flour

8 eggs

1¼ cups (10 ounces; 310 g) unsalted butter at room temperature, plus 2 teaspoons unsalted butter, for buttering the loaf pans

Glaze:

1 egg

1 egg yolk

Pinch of salt

Pinch of sugar

1 teaspoon milk

1. In the bowl of an electric mixer combine the yeast, milk, and sugar, stir by hand, and set aside for 5 minutes until the yeast has dissolved.

2. Stir in the salt, then with the mixer at low speed add the flour, cup by cup, then the eggs, one by one, mixing well after each addition.

3. Add the 1¼ cups butter, bit by bit, incorporating it smoothly into the dough. The dough will be very soft and sticky. Cover securely with plastic wrap and let rise, at room temperature, until doubled in bulk, about 1 hour.

4. With a wooden spoon, stir the dough to deflate it, cover again, refrigerate, and let rise until doubled in bulk, 1½ to 3 hours.

5. Preheat the oven to 350°F (175°C).

6. Stir down the dough again and pour equal portions of the dough into two well-buttered 6-cup (1.5-liter) loaf pans. The dough will remain very soft and sticky. Cover and let rise until almost doubled in bulk, about 1 hour. Don't worry if it doesn't double in bulk. It will rise more during the baking.

7. Combine the ingredients for the glaze and brush all over the top of the *brioches.* Bake until golden brown, about 35 minutes. Unmold immediately and cool on a rack. The *brioches* can easily be frozen.

Yield: 2 loaves.

Boulangeries
BAKERIES

Fresh bread daily—in France it's a must.

Of the hundreds of Parisians I've interviewed over the years, I love the bakers best. Most often they are roly-poly men in worn white T-shirts, who came to Paris from little French towns and villages to make their way; they are men who love their wives, who never seem to have enough time to sleep, and who are passionate — almost crazily, over-the-edge, off-the-wall passionate—about bread. So am I.

One of my greatest gastronomic Parisian treats is to walk into a favorite *boulangerie* around noon, my stomach growling with hunger. I order a crusty *baguette "bien cuite,"* and before I've set down my two francs and ninety centimes I've bitten off the heel. Chewy, yeasty ecstasy. Bread *is* life. It's food that makes you feel good, feel healthy; food that goes with everything, and goes especially well with the things we love most about France—fine cheese, great wine.

Bread baking is hard, tedious, lonely work, and unfortunately few young Frenchmen still aspire to be bakers when they grow up. Working through the night in a suffocatingly hot basement holds little glamour for them. The truth is, the romantic notion of the frail French baker slaving through the night to provide breakfast fare is basically a memory these days, though there are still a few diligent souls who do labor through the darkest hours.

How does one tell the good loaf from the bad, and what makes the difference? The good French loaf is made with a respect for the simple nature of the ingredients: wholesome stone-milled wheat or rye flour; fresh yeast (*levure*) or a fresh sourdough starter (*levain*); pure water and a minimum of salt. This is true whether it's a thin, crisp, and golden *baguette* or *ficelle;* a plump round country-style *pain de campagne;* or a made-to-eat-with-cheese loaf studded with hazelnuts, walnuts, or raisins. In the best bakeries, ovens are fired all day long, ensuring that customers can purchase loaves just minutes old throughout the day. (Most French bread contains no fat and thus quickly goes stale.) All dough is now kneaded mechanically, but the best is done slowly, so the flavor is not killed by overkneading. Good dough is allowed to rise slowly, several times, with plenty of rest between kneadings. At the finest bakeries every loaf is formed by hand. Good bread has a thick crust, a dense and golden interior with lots of irregular air holes, and a fresh wheaty aroma and flavor.

During the past few years, many bakers have joined the "good bread campaign," a nationwide, loosely organized attempt to bring back the kind of bread made before World War II brought modernization to the corner bakery. At the same time, there is a renewed interest in all things natural, and *biologique* (organic) breads are popping up all over. The back-to-the-country movement is strong here today, and the words *campagne* (country) and *paysanne* (peasant) appear everywhere.

The French loaf is still one of the city's best buys. "There used to be a saying that the daily newspaper, a liter of milk, and the *baguette* all had equal value and importance in French daily life, and all should cost the same," explained Didier Vacher, a young Paris baker committed to making an honest *baguette*. While it may have been true at one time, the *baguette* is today an incredible bargain when you consider that daily newspapers cost four francs fifty centimes and a liter of fresh whole milk costs four francs seventy centimes.

LES HALLES

1st and 2nd arrondissements

ANDRE CLERET
4 Rue des Lavandières-
 Sainte-Opportune, Paris 1.
(42.33.82.68).
Métro: Châtelet
 Open: 7 A.M. to 8 P.M..
 Closed Sunday, Monday,
 and either July or
 August.

André Cléret is a baker who seems to work in his own little world, dreaming up different breads for each day of the week, filling his fine sour bread dough with black olives or dried fruits, offering "cake" (a French sort of everyday fruit-cake) to the customers who stream in and out of his shop in droves. His bakery, which also features a handy stand-up counter for sampling and sipping coffee, is situated right behind the Châtelet group of theaters, near the lively bird and plant markets on and around the quais. Also worth sampling are the delicious apple tart and the thin sourdough *baguettes au levain*.

G. LABBE
25 Rue l'Arbre Sec, Paris 1.
(42.60.11.05).
Métro: Louvre or Pont-Neuf.
Open 8 A.M. to 8 P.M. Closed
 Saturday, Sunday, and
 holidays.

I first discovered Monsieur Labbé's state-of-the-art *baguette* while lunching one day at Chez la Vielle, Adrienne Biasin's homey bistro down the street (see page 28). When I left the restaurant, I stopped in at this nondescript bakery to take a dense, heavy *baguette* home for dinner. As it turned out I didn't stay home that evening, but there the *baguette* was, fresh as ever, for breakfast the next day.

J. P. LE LEDIC
16 Rue des Petits-Carreaux,
 Paris 2.
(42.36.54.29).
Métro: Sentier.
Open 6:30 A.M. to 8 P.M.
 Closed Sunday and
 Monday.

Just an ordinary-looking bakery offering great artisanal *pain paillasse*—giant deep-brown coun-try loaves—great for tucking under your arm as you wind your way through this crowded market street. Tasting Monsieur Le Ledic's loaf, I got excited about bread once again!

BOULANGERIE
  MONTMARTRE
149 Rue Montmartre,
  Paris 1.
(42.36.14.69).
Métro: Montmartre.
Open 7 A.M. to 8 P.M. Closed
  Sunday, Monday, and
  holidays.

A plain old-fashioned neighborhood *boulangerie*, making superbly crispy, dense, and chewy classic *baguettes*. You'll find them served at the small bistro Aux Lyonnais, near the Bourse.

BOURSE, REPUBLIQUE, ILE SAINT-LOUIS

2nd, 3rd, 4th, and 11th arrondissements

JACQUES DUBOS
103 Avenue Parmentier,
  Paris 11.
(43.57.53.27).
Métro: Parmentier.
Open 7 A.M. to 8 P.M. Closed
  Sunday.

I f you're looking for a great classic *baguette*—dense, chewy, heavy—to go with your *charcuterie*, to prepare a ham and cheese sandwich, or simply to eat "as is," stop by this good neighborhood *boulangerie*. His bread is served at the lively family bistro Astier, nearby.

ONFROY
34 Rue de Saintonge,
  Paris 3.
(42.77.56.46).
Métro: Filles-du-Calvaire.
Open 8:15 A.M. to 1:30 P.M.
  and 3 P.M. to 8 P.M. Closed
  Saturday afternoon,
  Sunday, and mid-July
  through August.

T his is one baker I almost thought of keeping a secret. I am wild about rich, sour rye bread, the sort of hearty Eastern European loaf on which you could survive forever. And this is what comes out of Fernand Onfroy's old-fashioned wood-fired oven. This unflappable Normandy baker—whose first childhood memory is of the Americans landing on Omaha Beach—works quietly and diligently, also producing a fine *baguette biologique* from organically grown flour, a whole wheat *baguette complète*, as well as the everyday *baguette*. When Monsieur Onfroy opened his modest little shop not far from Place de la République in 1965, he discovered the remains of an old underground Roman oven, then a more recent, though still ancient, oven at another level. Rue de Saintonge was first opened in 1628, and most likely there's been a bakery at No. 34 for several centuries.

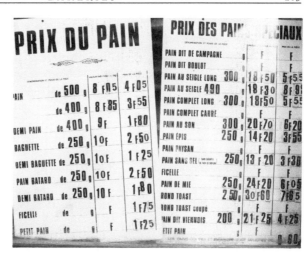

AU PANETIER
10 Place des Petits-Pères,
 Paris 2.
(42.60.90.23).
Métro: Bourse.
Open 8 A.M. to 7 P.M. Closed
 Saturday, Sunday, and
 either July or August.

By eight most mornings there's a line of customers streaming in to buy Bernard Lebon's *baguette au levain* (sourdough *baguette*), still baked in a sturdy, oak-fired, brick-lined oven built around the turn of the century. Up at five each day, he travels just a few stories from his apartment above the shop to a flour-dusted but impeccably tidy cellar, where his assistant has been working since midnight. Monsieur Lebon gets right to work, ready to greet the first crackling batch of bread as it comes from the oven at 6 A.M. Working steadily, he continues to mix, knead, and form additional loaves for later bakings at 9 A.M. and noon. The 250 *baguettes* they form each day are crisp and chewy, and like the baker, authentic and honest. But Monsieur Lebon and his wife, Yvette, don't stop there: They offer some fifty different shapes of bread (not all of them available each day), including giant *couronnes* (rings) of wheat and rye, special *baguettes moulées* baked in molds to yield even crisper crusts, in all preparing eight different kinds of dough. What's the hardest thing about his job? "Getting the various breads to rise evenly, so they're ready for baking at the same time," says the agile, square-jawed baker. Does he love his own bread? He eats it three meals a day. Plus, every afternoon he enjoys one of his pastry chef's apple tarts, warm from the oven. Decorated breads can be made to order. The shop's restored Belle Epoque interior is worth a detour.

LES PANETONS
47 Rue Saint-Louis-en-l'Ile,
Paris 4.
(43.26.77.11).
Métro: Pont-Marie.
Open 10 A.M. to 2 P.M. and
4 P.M. to 8 P.M. Closed
Monday.

This bright, cheery contemporary bake shop right in the middle of Ile Saint-Louis offers appealing displays of fine, fresh breads in a variety of sizes and shapes, including gluten bread, giant round *boules biologiques*, good rye breads flavored with nuts or raisins, and tiny, delicate sesame rolls.

SAINT-GERMAIN, LATIN QUARTER, PLACE D'ITALIE
5th and 13th arrondissements

GERARD BEAUFORT
6 Rue Linné, Paris 5.
(47.07.10.94).
Métro: Jussieu.
Open 7:30 A.M. to 8 P.M.
Closed Saturday and
Sunday.

An ordinary-looking bakery near the Jardin des Plantes (and the Rue des Boulangers), offering a marvelous assortment of serious breads: wonderful *baguettes au levain*, and tiny raisin and walnut loaves with just a hint of cinnamon.

BOULANGERIE LE CARDINAL
68 Rue du Cardinal-
Lemoine, Paris 5.
(43.26.34.62).
Métro: Cardinal Lemoine.
Open 7:15 A.M. to 1:15 P.M.
and 4 P.M. to 7:30 P.M.
Closed Sunday, Monday,
and either July or
August.

At one time, Michel Perruche had the largest wood-fired oven in Paris, built near the Place de la Contrescarpe on the Left Bank. Even a documentary film, "La Boulangerie de la Contrescarpe," was made about his modest Art Deco *boulangerie*. Monsieur Perruche has newer gas-fired ovens now, but his country-style *baguette de campagne*—made from regular *baguette* dough but dusted with flour— remains a delight. The calm, quiet little baker is up at three each morning, and with the help of a single assistant produces some 800 loaves of bread a day, with the first batch ready just after seven in the morning.

R. CLEMENT
123 Rue L. M. Nordmann,
Paris 13.
(47.07.12.78).
Métro: Glacière.
Open 7:30 A.M. to 1:30 P.M.
and 4 P.M. to 8 P.M. Closed
Sunday and Monday.

A near-perfect *baguette:* with a wonderfully crunchy, almost nutty crust, and a dense, moist, golden *mie*, or interior. It stays fresh for hours—that is, if you can keep it that long.

**BOULANGERIE
MODERNE**
16 Rue des Fossés Saint-
Jacques, Paris 5.
(43.54.12.22).
Métro: Luxembourg.
Open 7 A.M. to 8 P.M. Closed
Saturday and Sunday.

There's nothing modern about the Belle Epoque storefront of this tiny neighborhood *boulangerie* set on the active Place de l'Estrapade near the Panthéon. They sell an "American-style" *baguette* that tastes as though it's made with gluten-rich American flour. It's a neighborhood favorite, with a crisp crust and denser than average, chewy interior.

LES PANETONS
113 Rue Mouffetard, Paris 5.
(47.07.12.08).
Métro: Censier-Daubenton.
Open 7:30 A.M. to 7:30 P.M.
Tuesday through
Saturday; 7:30 A.M. to 1
P.M. Sunday. Closed
Monday.
See Les Panetons, 4th
arrondissement, facing
page.

PLACE MONGE MARKET
Stall at 61 Place Monge,
Paris 5.
Métro: Monge.
Open 7 A.M. to 1 P.M.
Wednesday, Friday, and
Sunday.

Three mornings each week, when the Place Monge open-air market is in full swing, you can find these truly classic big, round sourdough rye loaves carefully stacked on wooden tables. Buy this dense and chewy *pain de seigle* on Friday and it will still show plenty of spunk on Tuesday. The loaves are baked in wood-fired ovens in the outskirts of Paris.

MAISON PLANE
53 bis Boulevard Arago,
Paris 13.
(47.07.14.58).
Métro: Glacière.
Open 7:30 A.M. to 2 P.M. and
4 P.M. to 8 P.M. Closed
Wednesday and
Thursday.

Try to get here right about lunchtime, when the crisp and crunchy *petits pains* are fresh from the oven. This little neighborhood *boulangerie* also offers a nice variety of unusual decorative breads, beautiful *kougelhopf*, and delicious, tangy sourdough *pain au levain*.

J. C. VANDERSTICHEL
31 Boulevard Arago,
Paris 13.
(47.07.26.75).
Métro: Gobelins.
Open 6:30 A.M. to 8 P.M.
Closed Sunday, Monday,
and either July or
August.

Wonderful organic loaves that come from the oven around eleven in the morning. Try the hearty, crusty *baguette biologique*—you won't regret it. This is a simple, straightforward bakery, which also offers beautiful classic *baguettes* and *ficelles*.

Saint-Germain-des-Pres, Sevres-Babylone, La Tour-Maubourg

6th and 7th arrondissements

AVENUE DE BRETEUIL MARKET
Stall at 21 Avenue de Saxe, Paris 7.
Métro: Sèvres-Lecourbe.
Open 7 A.M. to 1 P.M. Saturday.

Each Saturday, when the Avenue de Breteuil market attracts hundreds of local shoppers, you can find big, hearty rounds of country sourdough rye. Ask for the *pain de seigle* that is baked in wood-fired ovens in Vincennes, outside of Paris.

GOUDENHOOFT
175 Rue de Grenelle, Paris 7.
(45.51.94.71).
Métro: La Tour-Maubourg.
Open 7 A.M. to 8 P.M. Closed Sunday.

If you wander in on a day they've got crisp and lacy *fougasse* fresh from the oven, go for it! Covered with a sheer egg glaze, the crust of this beautiful rectangular white bread is both crisp and chewy at the same time. The pastries here are also quite respectable.

GERARD MULOT
2 Rue Lobineau, Paris 7.
(43.26.85.77).
Métro: Mabillon.
Open 6:45 A.M. to 8 P.M. Closed Wednesday.

In the shadow of the Marché Saint-Germain, Gérard Mulot tempts the entire neighborhood with his superb *pain aux noix* (walnut bread), a rye bread loaded with raisins, and some of the most fantastic almond macaroons in Paris.

LIONEL POILANE
8 Rue du Cherche-Midi, Paris 6.
(45.48.42.59).
Métro: Sèvres-Babylone.
Open 7:15 A.M. to 8:15 P.M. Closed Sunday.
English spoken.

Pain Poilâne... need one say more? There is no question that Lionel Poilâne makes the most famous bread in France, perhaps the world. Thousands of Parisians buy his moist sourdough loaf each day. It's sold at more than 600 shops around Paris, more than 300 restaurants. Each day, airplanes take off for Manhattan and Tokyo, delivering fresh-baked loaves for those willing to pay a very steep price. Each giant, round wholesome loaf is made with a pungent sourdough starter, all-French flour, and fragrant sea salt. Each is formed by hand, rising in rustic—yet practical—fabric-lined wicker baskets. The loaves are baked in wood-fired ovens, one of which was built by the *patron* himself. But Poilâne bread is far from perfect, as Monsieur Poilâne readily admits. "People complain that it is uneven," he notes, suggesting that "with *levain*,

The line flows out the door at Poilâne.

that's the name of the game. No two batches are ever the same; a simple storm can ruin an entire baking."

And he's right. There are days Poilâne bread is so dry, so lacking in authority and flavor, you know something's gone wrong. I've also tasted the bread so rich, dense, so properly acidic and authoritative, that every other loaf, before or after, is pale in comparison. Criticism aside, no one's yet attempted to meet the Poilâne challenge. Rarely imitated—never successfully—he remains *"le roi du pain."* The Poilâne loaf has set the contemporary standard for bread, the loaf against which almost all others are judged (see recipe, following page).

Visitors to the family shop on Rue du Cherche-Midi are almost always welcome to visit the wonderfully fragrant, flour-dusted cellar, to watch the famous bread being mixed, kneaded, and baked in the ancient wood-fired oven set beneath the street. Large personalized *pain décoré* can be ordered several days in advance. On busy Saturday afternoons, they often pass out butter cookies to soothe those waiting in line!

Pain Poilane au Levain Naturel
POILANE'S NATURAL SOURDOUGH BREAD

This is the recipe that Paris's most famous baker, Lionel Poilâne, created for the French housewife, and the closest I've come to re-creating his superb and popular loaf at home. I also call it "Patience Bread," because it takes almost a week to make the first batch of this natural, slightly sour loaf. Anyone who loves bread-baking should give it a try, for it is really rather miraculous that such wonderful flavors can come from the simple blend of salt, water, and flour, and not a touch of yeast.

To bakers accustomed to the fast-acting whoosh one gets from yeast doughs, Poilâne's dough is a real sleeper. This dough really takes its time expanding, but the reward for your patience is a very fine-grained, mildly acidic, gentle loaf. It's the most subtle and delicious bread I know, at the same time sophisticated and countryish. When you bite into it, you'll say, "Now, this is bread!" A great crust, with a moist, chewy, wheaty-brown interior.

In developing this recipe, Susan Herrmann Loomis, who is my associate, and I baked at least 100 loaves, no two of which turned out exactly alike, nearly all of which offered a vibrantly acidic interior and an irresistible chewy crust. We worked with different kinds of flours, rising times, and water proportions, and found the following combination the most foolproof.

5 ½ to 6 cups (770 to 840 g) unbleached flour
2 ⅓ cups (580 ml) lukewarm water
1 tablespoon sea salt

1. To make the starter, or *chef:* In a small bowl combine 1 cup (140 g) flour with ⅓ cup (80 ml) water. Stir until well blended, then transfer the dough to a floured work surface and knead into a smooth ball. It should be fairly soft and sticky. Return the starter to the bowl, cover with a damp cloth, and let sit at room temperature for 72 hours. It should rise slightly and take on a fresh, acidic aroma.

2. After 72 hours, uncover the starter and transfer it to a medium-size mixing bowl. Add ½ cup (125 ml) lukewarm water to the starter and stir. Add an additional 1 ½ cups (210 g) flour and stir to blend. Transfer the dough to a floured work surface and knead into a smooth ball. It should be firm but not stiff. Return the dough to the bowl, cover with a damp cloth, and let sit in a warm place for 24 to 48 hours. (The length of time really depends on your schedule. A longer rise will produce a slightly more acidic bread.)

3. To complete the dough: Transfer the dough to a very large shallow bowl. Add 1 ½ cups (375 ml) water and the sea salt. Stir until the mixture is fairly well blended, then begin adding the remaining 3 to 3 ½ cups (420 to 490 g) flour cup by cup, mixing well after each addition. Continue folding the dough over itself to incorporate air—it may actually be too soft to knead—for 10 minutes, adding additional flour as necessary to keep the dough from being too sticky. The final dough

should be rather soft, but not so soft it sticks to your fingers. Cover with a damp cloth and let sit in a warm place for 1 hour.

4. To form the loaf: Cut off a handful of dough, about 1 cup (250 g), to set aside for the next loaf. Transfer the remaining dough to a very heavily floured work surface. Shape it into a tight ball by folding it over itself. Do not be disturbed if the dough is softer than ordinary bread dough. Place a large floured towel in a round shallow bowl or basket—one about 9½ inches (24 cm) wide and 4 inches (10 cm) deep works well—and place the dough in the towel-lined bowl or basket. Loosely fold the towel over the dough. Let sit in a warm place for 8 to 12 hours.

5. Preheat the oven to 375°F (190°C).

6. Heavily dust the loaf with flour. Place a shallow round cake pan (about 10 inches; 25½ cm), on top of the basket and flip the pan and basket over together so the loaf falls out upside down onto the cake pan. Slash the top of the bread several times with a razor blade to a depth of about ¼ inch (7mm), so it can expand regularly during baking. Bake in the cake pan until golden brown, 1 to 1½ hours. The loaf should have a very hard crust and sound hollow when the bottom is tapped. Remove to a baking rack to cool.

Do not be concerned if the dough does not rise substantially—a normal loaf will rise to about 2 to 3 inches (5 to 8 cm) in the center. With a new *chef* it usually takes several loaves before there is a substantial rise. The ideal loaf should have an interior with large irregular air holes throughout, and should be very moist and taste slightly acidic. The crust should be very crisp and dense.

Note: After you have made your first loaf and have saved the *chef*, begin at step 2 for subsequent loaves. Proceed normally through the rest of the recipe, always remembering to save a *chef* which can be stored at room temperature, covered with a damp cloth, for two or three days, or refrigerated for up to two weeks. After about three days, add 2 tablespoons flour and 2 tablespoons water and stir, to keep *chef* active. The night before you plan to make the bread, remove *chef* from the refrigerator and add 2 tablespoons flour and 2 tablespoons water, to reactivate.
Yield: 1 loaf.

POUJAURAN
20 Rue Jean-Nicot, Paris 7.
(47.05.80.88).
Métro: La Tour-Maubourg.
Open 8:30 A.M. to 8:30 P.M.
   Closed Sunday and
   August.
English spoken.

Young Jean-Luc Poujauran, an energetic, ideal-istic baker from France's southwest, claims he was the first in Paris to turn out a *baguette biologique,* made with organically grown, stone-ground, all-French flour. That was more than a decade ago, and his honey-colored, dense, and chewy *baguette* is unquestionably one of the best in Paris. A native of the rich and rustic southwest, Monsieur Poujauran is always trying new ideas: He once made a *biologi-que croissant,* using organic eggs, butter, and flour, in memory of his grandmother, who brought him up on pure and healthy foods. He's the sort of young man who inspires confidence: When he was first starting out and had little money, faithful customers chipped in to help him buy his first bread mixer. Try his earthy sourdough *pain de campagne,* along with the delightful and delicious pastries that fill this charming turn-of-the-century *boulangerie.* High-quality French pastry and bread flour can also be purchased in the shop. (See also Pâtisseries.)

Poujauran's special boutique (above), and baker Jean-Luc (right) with his antique delivery truck.

GRANDS BOULEVARDS, GARE SAINT-LAZARE, CLICHY

8th and 9th arrondissements

FEYEUX
56 Rue de Clichy, Paris 9.
(48.74.37.64).
Métro: Liège or Place de
 Clichy.
Open 7:15 A.M. to 7:30 P.M.
 Closed Monday.

A combination tea room, bakery, and chocolate shop, this unpretentious *boulangerie* offers a timeless array of thoroughly Parisian fare, including good country bread, or *pain de campagne,* and some of the flakiest *croissants* in the entire city.

LENOTRE
3 and 5 Rue du Havre,
 Paris 9.
(42.22.22.59).
Métro: Saint-Lazare.
Open 9:30 A.M. to 7 P.M.
 Tuesday through Friday;
 10 A.M. to 7 P.M. Saturday
 and Monday. Closed
 Sunday.
Credit card: V.
English spoken.

Not content to reign as the king of pastries, Gaston Lenôtre, with the help of his professional crew, has greatly improved and increased his bread selection to include a remarkable *baguette,* along with a dozen different shapes and varieties of old-time regional breads and decorated, rustic country loaves to be personalized and ordered in advance. (See also Chocolateries.)

Crusty baguettes

BAGUETTES

The crackling crisp, slender *baguette*—the name comes from the French for wand—is not as old as most people think. And it wasn't born; it evolved essentially out of consumer demand. According to Raymond Calvel, one of France's more respected bread experts, the *baguette* came into being just before World War I, when the classic French loaf had two shapes: the round *miche,* weighing about 5 pounds (2.5 kilos), and the *pain long,* an 8-inch by 30-inch (20.5-cm by 76-cm) loaf of the same weight. The *mie,* or interior, of the *pain long* was dense and heavy, the crust crisp and flavorful. Most consumers preferred the crust and bakers accommodated, making the bread thinner and thinner to obtain maximum crust, reducing the loaf's volume until they came up with the traditional 30-inch (76-cm) *baguette,* weighing 8 ounces (250 grams).

Other historians suggest that the *baguette* evolved from the *viennois,* a long, thin Austrian-type loaf popular around the turn of the century. The loaf has the same form as the *baguette,* but the dough is sweetened with sugar and softened with milk.

RENE SAINT-OUEN
111 Boulevard Haussmann,
    Paris 8.
(42.65.06.25).
Métro: Miromesnil.
Open 8 A.M. to 7 P.M. Closed
    Sunday and one month
    in summer.

More like a museum devoted to *pain de fantaisie*, the windows of this rather ill-kept shop are filled with breads shaped like rabbits and bicycles, chickens and stars. The bread is inedible, but if you want a humorous souvenir to hang on your wall, this is the place to buy it.

**BOULANGERIE SAINT-
    PHILIPPE**
73 Avenue Franklin-D.-
    Roosevelt, Paris 8.
(43.59.78.76).
Métro: Saint-Philippe-deu-
    Roule.
Open 7:30 A.M. to 7:30 P.M.
    Closed Saturday.

There's always a line out the door at the popular Boulangerie Saint-Philippe, where office workers of the *quartier* seem to spend a good portion of their day, lunching in the back room or waiting to sample the breads or pastries. Their superbly classic *baguette* is dense, chewy, properly crisp (one could easily polish off a loaf without noticing it was gone). I'm also a big fan of their delightful lemon tart.

BIR-HAKEIM, MONTPARNASSE, PORTE DE VANVES, PLAISANCE

14th and 15th arrondissements

**BOULANGERIE
    BRULAND**
64 Rue Daguerre, Paris 14.
(43.22.08.08).
Métros: Gaîté or Denfert-
    Rochereau.
Open 6:45 A.M. to 8 P.M.
    Closed Sunday and
    Monday.

Wow! Great country bread with staying power. That is, good substantial sourdough country bread that seems to stay fresh-tasting for days. I first discovered the bread at Gérard Allemandou's La Cagouille, then later visited Monsieur Bruland's *boulangerie*, where the incredible assortment of breads will make you want to eat nothing but bread for a week! This is sort of a candy store for bread lovers, with breads flavored with anchovies and black olives, with cheese, and a *pain complet plus*, seasoned with sunflower seeds and wheat germ.

**LE MOULIN DE LA
    VIERGE**
105 Rue Vercingétorix,
    Paris 14.
(45.43.09.84).
Métros: Pernety or
    Plaisance.
Open 8 A.M. to 8 P.M. Closed
    Sunday, Monday, and
    August.

During the past few years, young Basile Kamir has become the darling baker of many of the city's best chefs, including José Lampreia at La Maison Blanche. It's no surprise, for Monsieur Kamir's delicious, dense, golden counry bread, baked with organically grown wheat, is some of the best in town. The breads come in many fantasy shapes, include tiny round *boules*, slender *flûtes*, and giant loaves of *pain de campagne*. His *boulangerie* is

LE MOULIN DE LA VIERGE
166 Avenue de Suffren, Paris 15.
(47.83.45.55).
Métro: Cambronne.
Open 7 A.M. to 8 P.M. Closed Sunday, holidays, and either July or August.

one of the most strangely situated in town: The adorable old-fashioned turn-of-the-century bakery sits as a historical monument in the middle of block after block of impersonal modern high-rise buildings at the southern edge of town. Don't give up in trying to find it!

LIONEL POILANE
49 Boulevard de Grenelle, Paris 15.
(45.79.11.49).
Métros: Bir-Hakeim or Grenelle.
Open: 7:15 P.M. to 8:15 P.M. Closed Monday.
English spoken.
See Lionel Poilâne, 6th *arrondissement,* page 206.

A BREAD MUSEUM

The Musée Français du Pain, installed in the *grenier* (grain loft) of a still active flour mill just southeast of Paris at the edge of the Bois de Vincennes, is like a toy store for bread lovers. Thousands of bread-related trinkets and memorabilia line the spotless rooms that are filled with cartoons and drawings, carefully preserved bread boards and knives, wicker rising baskets and shiny copper molds—all there to celebrate the nobility of bread in history. There are façades and signs from Belle Epoque bakers; Saint-Honoré, the 7th-century "patron saint" of bakers, is represented paddle in hand; there are 17th-century metal molds, designed for making hosts used for religious celebrations; fascinating tin spice-cookie molds, ancient bread-related manuscripts, as well as miniature models of brick-lined, wood-fired ovens.

Musée Français du Pain, 25 bis Rue Victor-Hugo, 94220 Charenton-le-Pont. (43.68.43.60). Métro: Charenton-Ecoles. Open 2 P.M. to 4 P.M. Tuesday and Thursday. Closed July and August.

MAX POILANE
87 Rue Brancion, Paris 15.
(48.28.45.90).
Métro: Porte de Vanves.
Open 7:15 A.M. to 8 P.M. Monday through Friday; 7:30 A.M. to 1:30 P.M. Saturday. Closed Sunday.
English spoken.

One of Paris's best-kept secrets is that there is more than one Poilâne: famous brother Lionel, and less famous brother Max. Working with the same ingredients and huge woodfired ovens, they produce essentially the same large, round country loaf, with slight variations. Max's shop on the edge of town is worth a detour: The charming turn-of-the-century *boulangerie*, with its marble floors, glistening chandelier, and beautiful crusty loaves arranged like still lifes in wicker baskets around the room, is one of the most romantic little bakeries in town. Lean, intense, and poetic, Max Poilâne is a fanatic about bread: "I love bread, I eat bread with bread. One day I even found myself eating bread with *sorbet*—that was too much." When he goes to restaurants, he brings a little sack of his own bread with him. Like Lionel, he has managed to keep his operation simple, artisanal, despite the fact that five huge wood-fired ovens are kept going twenty-four hours a day. Large personalized *pain décoré* (decorated country loaf) can be ordered several days in advance.

A Ganachaud assortment (see entry, page 221).

THE DAILY LOAF

The following are just a few breads—of various sizes, flours, *fantaisie* shapes—found in the Parisian *boulangerie*.

Baguette: in Paris, this is legally a loaf weighing about 8 ounces (250 grams) and made from flour, water, and yeast. It may also contain fava bean flour and ascorbic acid, or vitamin C. *Baguettes* dusted with flour may be sold as *baguette de campagne, baguette à l'ancienne,* or *baguette paysanne.* There are also two "brand name" *baguettes,* the Belle Epoque and the Banette, sold in various bakeries. The bakers guarantee that these are made without the addition of fava bean flour or ascorbic acid, and are made according to old-fashioned methods.

Baguette au levain: (also sold by other names, sometimes called *baguette à l'ancienne*): sourdough *baguette.*

Boule: ball, or round loaf, either small or large.

Chapeau: small round loaf, topped with a little *chapeau,* or hat.

Couronne: ring-shaped *baguette.*

Bernard Ganachaud, master baker (see entry, page 221).

Le fer à cheval: horseshoe-shaped *baguette.*

Ficelle: very thin, crusty *baguette.*

Fougasse: generally, a crusty, flat rectangular-shaped, lacy bread made of *baguette* dough; can be filled with onions, herbs, spices, or anchovies, or can be made of puff pastry dough.

Miche: large round country-style loaf.

Pain de campagne: there is no legal definition for the country loaf, which can vary from a white bread simply dusted with flour to give it a rustic look (and fetch a higher price) to a truly hearty loaf that may be a blend of white, whole wheat, and perhaps rye flour with added bran. It comes in every shape, from a small round individual roll to a large family loaf.

Pain complet: bread made partially or entirely from whole wheat flour, with bakers varying proportions according to their personal tastes.

Pain de fantaisie: generally, any odd or imaginatively shaped bread. Even *baguette de campagne* falls into the *fantaisie* category.

Pain de mie: the rectangular white sandwich loaf that is nearly all *mie* (interior crumb), and very little crust. It is made for durability, its flavor and texture developed for use in sandwiches. Unlike most French breads, it contains milk, sugar, and butter, and may contain chemical preservatives.

Pain aux noix and *pain aux noisettes:* bread, most often rye or wheat, filled with walnuts or hazelnuts.

Pain polka: bread that is slashed in a criss-cross pattern; usually a large country loaf cut in this manner.

Pain aux raisins: bread, most often rye or wheat, filled with raisins.

Pain de seigle: bread made from 60 to 70 percent rye flour and 30 to 40 percent wheat flour.

Pain de son: legally, a dietetic bread that is quality-controlled, containing 20 percent bran mixed with white flour.

Pain viennois: shaped like a *baguette,* with regular horizontal slashes, this loaf usually contains white flour, sugar, powdered milk, water, and yeast.

PAIN DE MIE DENIS RUFFEL
DENIS RUFFEL'S SANDWICH LOAF

This is France's firm, fine-grained sandwich loaf: milky, just slightly sweet, and delicious when fresh and toasted. Denis Ruffel, from Pâtisserie Millet (see entry, page 189), the Left Bank pastry shop, manages to turn a single loaf of pain de mie *into an entire buffet, making dozens of tiny, highly decorated, open-face sandwiches. He'll top some with caviar or smoked salmon and lemon triangles, others with a blend of Roquefort, walnuts and butter, and still others with thin slices of sausages topped with piped butter rosettes. The* mie, *by the way, is the crumb, or non-crusty portion of any bread, and since this bread has virtually no crust, it's called* pain de mie. *Some Paris bakers advertise* pain de mie au beurre, *to distinguish their bread from those made with margarine. The loaf is usually made in a special pan fitted with a sliding cover, which helps mold the bread into a tidy rectangle. The molds are available at many cookware shops, although the bread can be made in any straight-sided loaf pan. To obtain a neat rectangular loaf, cover the dough-filled loaf pan with foil and a baking sheet, then weight the sheet with a brick or other heavy object and bake.*

1 cup (250 ml) lukewarm milk
3 tablespoons unsalted butter, (1½ oz; 45 g), at room temperature, plus 1 tablespoon (½ oz; 15 g) for buttering the bowl and loaf pan
1 tablespoon or 1 package dry yeast
2 tablespoons sugar
2 teaspoons salt
2¾ cups (385 g) unbleached all-purpose flour

1. In a large bowl, combine the milk, the 3 tablespoons butter, yeast, and sugar, stir, and set aside for 5 minutes to proof the yeast.

2. Once proofed, stir in the salt, then add the flour, cup by cup, mixing well after each addition. Knead by hand for 2 or 3 minutes, or until the dough forms a smooth ball. Place in a well-buttered, large bowl (use some of the remaining 1 tablespoon butter) and cover securely with plastic wrap. Let rise in a warm place until double in bulk, approximately 1 to 1½ hours.

3. Butter a 6-cup (1.5-liter) loaf pan, or the mold and cover of a 6-cup (1.5-liter) *pain de mie* pan. If using a loaf pan, butter a piece of aluminum foil to use as a lid. Punch down the dough, knead for 1 minute, then transfer it to the pan or mold. Press down the dough smoothly, being sure it fills the corners, and cover. Let rise until double in bulk, another 1 to 1½ hours.

4. About 30 minutes before the dough is ready to be baked, preheat the oven to 375°F (190°C).

5. Bake until the loaf is golden brown, about 45 minutes. (If using a loaf pan cover with buttered foil and a baking sheet, then weight the sheet with a brick or other heavy object.) Unmold immediately and cool on a rack. The bread will stay fresh for several days, wrapped and stored at room temperature. *Pain de mie* also freezes well.

Yield: 1 loaf.

VICTOR-HUGO, AUTEUIL

16th arrondissement

LENOTRE
44 Rue d'Auteuil, Paris 16.
(45.24.52.52).
Métro: Michel-Ange/Auteuil.
Open daily, 9 A.M. to 9 P.M.
Credit cards: AE, V.
English spoken.
See Lenôtre, 9th
   arrondissement, page 211.

LENOTRE
49 Avenue Victor-Hugo,
   Paris 16.
(45.01.71.71).
Métro: Victor-Hugo.
Open daily, 9 A.M. to 8 P.M.
Credit card: V.
English spoken.
See Lenôtre, 9th
   arrondissement, page 211.

DECORATED BREAD

One of the most beautiful and festive breads in Paris is the *pain decoré*, generally a large, round, decorated loaf that is personalized with one's name, a favorite symbol or saying, or most classically, a bunch of grapes or sheaves of wheat. The following *boulangeries* will prepare decorated breads to order, though all must be ordered in advance. The breads, by the way, are not simply decorative, they're edible when fresh.

Lenôtre, 3 and 5 Rue du Havre, Paris 9. (45.22.22.59); 49 Avenue Victor-Hugo, Paris 16. (45.01.71.71); 44 Rue d'Auteuil, Paris 16. (45.24.52.52); 121 Avenue de Wagram, Paris 17. (47.63.70.30). Three days in advance.

Lionel Poilâne, 8 Rue du Cherche-Midi, Paris 6. (45.48.42.59). Two days in advance.

Max Poilâne, 87 Rue Brançion, Paris 15. (48.28.45.90). Two days in advance.

LA PETITE MARQUISE
3 Place Victor-Hugo,
   Paris 16.
(45.00.77.36).
Métro: Victor-Hugo.
Open 8:45 A.M. to 7:30 P.M.
   Closed Sunday and
   August.
Credit card: V.
English spoken.

When La Petite Marquise's bread is fresh, it's chewy, pleasantly acidic, and full of flavor. They make several different shapes of bread from the same dough, including a wonderful flat *galette*.

Lacy fougasse on display.

ARC DE TRIOMPHE, PORTE MAILLOT, VILLIERS

17th arrondissement

AUX ARMES DE NIEL
29 Avenue Niel, Paris 17.
(47.63.62.01).
Métro: Ternes.
Open 6:30 A.M. to 8:30 P.M.
  Monday, and Wednesday
  through Saturday;
  6:30 A.M. to 1:30 P.M. and
  4 P.M. to 8 P.M. Sunday.
  Closed Tuesday.

For a good, solid sourdough *baguette* (ask for a *ficelle au levain*) with deep and dark brown crust, a yeasty aroma, and honey-colored interior. Also huge, round, beautiful decorative loaves made to order.

The hearty Poilâne loaf.

BOULANGERIE BELEM
47 Rue Boursault, Paris 17.
(45.22.38.95).
Métro: Rome.
Open 10 A.M. to 8:30 P.M.
  Closed Monday.

The Portuguese make some of the most marvelous bread in the world, and here, tucked away in a working-class corner of the 17th *arrondissement*, you'll find some classic Portuguese corn bread—dense, delicious round loaves, great to slice for grilling and coating with sweet butter.

BOUTIQUE DU PAIN
11 Rue Gustave-Flaubert,
  Paris 17.
(47.63.75.68).
Métro: Ternes.
Open 7 A.M. to 8 P.M. Closed
  Sunday.

Honest, authentic breads from a friendly, dedicated baker named Marcel Pain. Both his *baguette de campagne* and *baguette biologique* are good and crusty, and the hazelnut and raisin rye is perhaps the best of its kind in Paris. Monsieur Pain and his charming wife are an ambitious pair, and each week there seems to be a new kind of bread or pastry to tempt passersby.

LENOTRE
121 Avenue de Wagram,
    Paris 17.
(47.63.70.30 and
    40.54.94.13).
Métros: Ternes or Wagram.
Open 9 A.M. to 8 P.M. Monday
    through Saturday; 9 A.M.
    to 1 P.M. Sunday.
See Lenôtre, 9th
    arrondissement, page 211.

*Satisfied customer, Moulin de la
Vièrge (see entry, page 212).*

BOULANGERIE QUENTIN
21 Rue de Lévis, Paris 17.
(43.87.28.27).
Métro: Villiers.
Open 7 A.M. to 8 P.M. Tuesday
    through Saturday; 7 A.M.
    to 1:30 P.M. and 3 P.M. to
    8 P.M. Sunday. Closed
    Monday and either July
    or August.
Some English spoken.

BOULANGERIE VACHER
55 Boulevard Gouvion-
    Saint-Cyr, Paris 17.
(45.74.04.50).
Métro: Porte Maillot.
Open 7 A.M. to 8 P.M. Closed
    Wednesday, Thursday,
    and either July or
    August.

In 1982 Louis Couasnon began making the Belle Epoque, a brand-name *baguette* prepared by about eighty French bakers working to promote a return to artisanal breads. Monsieur Couasnon makes only about 100 such *baguettes* each day, using special flour. His sourdough loaf, made from 4 percent rye flour and white flour reinforced with special gluten, is mixed at 2:30 A.M. and comes out of the oven around 9 A.M. It is fat and thick-crusted, with an almost charcoal crust and a light, airy interior.

"It doesn't take any longer to make good bread than bad bread, so why not make good bread?" asks young Didier Vacher, who grew up across the street, above his parents' old *boulangerie*. Now he lives above his own shop, a little corner *boulangerie* he bought at the age of 24. Since the opening, he's been making the Banette, a sort of brand-name sourdough *baguette* made according to old-fashioned methods. It's a classic, and worth a visit if you're in the neighborhood. Also note the gigantic rectangular country loaves.

BOSTOCK BERNARD GANACHAUD

Bostock is a terrific way to recycle day-old brioche, *which on its own is already quite marvelous. One of my favorite Parisian bakers, Bernard Ganachaud, kindly shared the recipe for this kirsch-and-almond-flavored pastry. Superb fresh from the oven,* bostock *is still delicious a few days later. Eat it for breakfast or dessert. (See Ganachaud entry, facing page.)*

1¼ cups (170 g) whole almonds
1 cup (250 ml) water
1⅜ cups (275 g) sugar
10 slices day-old *brioche*
2 large eggs
3 tablespoons kirsch *eau-de-vie* (cherry brandy)

1. Preheat the oven to 375°F (190°C).

2. Toast the almonds on a baking sheet until browned, about 5 minutes. Remove but leave the oven on. When cooled, grind ¾ cup (100 g) of the almonds to a fine powder in a food processor. Coarsely chop the remaining almonds.

3. In a medium-size saucepan over medium heat, combine the water and ⅝ cup (125 grams) sugar and stir until dissolved. Remove the syrup from the heat.

4. Dip the slices of *brioche* in the syrup and drain them on a wire rack. Once drained, arrange the slices on a baking sheet.

5. In a small mixing bowl combine the eggs, finely ground almonds, and remaining sugar and blend to a thick paste. Spread the mixture on the *brioche*.

6. Sprinkle the *brioche* with kirsch, then the coarsely chopped almonds. Bake for 15 minutes or until golden brown.

Yield: 10 servings.

MÉNILMONTANT

20th arrondissement

GANACHAUD
150 Rue Ménilmontant,
   Paris 20.
(46.36.13.82).
Métro: Pelleport.
Open 2:30 P.M. to 8 P.M.
   Tuesday; 7:30 A.M. to
   8 P.M. Wednesday through
   Saturday; 7:30 A.M. to
   1:30 P.M. Sunday. Closed
   Monday, and either July
   or August.
English spoken.

Sincere, hard-working Bernard Ganachaud is one of my favorite Paris bakers. Son of a baker, the dapper, white-haired man has been working with bread since the age of eight, when he began helping his father. Nowadays at seven each night he or one of his crew lights up the gigantic wood-fired oven that dominates his shop, and by 4 A.M. the oven is put to work, baking 1,000 or so crusty loaves each day. Monsieur Ganachaud was the first bread baker in France to win the coveted Meilleur Ouvrier de France award, and one look at his *boutique*, one bite of his bread, and you understand why. He offers thirty different shapes and varieties of bread, from eight different flours, including a hearty *seigle noir*, or black rye. He also makes a wonderful *bostock*, a pastry made from day-old *brioche* (see recipe, facing page). Ganachaud is located out in the middle of nowhere, but the best things in life are always worth a detour. (See also Pâtisseries.)

Bread by the armful is almost a one-day supply for an enthusiastic eater.

PETITS PAINS PARISIENS JAMIN
JAMIN'S CRUSTY OVAL-SHAPED ROLLS

These rolls are so favored at Jamin (see entry, page 98), the popular restaurant on Rue de Long-champ, that each diner consumes an average of three rolls per meal. Chef Joël Robuchon bakes them fresh for both lunch and dinner, in a small convection oven fitted with a vaporizing attachment to help develop a good crust. Equally good results can be obtained at home.

2 ½ cups (625 ml) lukewarm water
2 tablespoons or 2 packages dry yeast
6 to 7 cups (840 to 980 g) unbleached all-purpose flour
2 teaspoons salt

1. Combine the water, yeast, and 1 cup (140 g) of the flour in a large mixing bowl, and set aside for 5 minutes to dissolve the yeast.

2. Once the yeast has dissolved, add the salt; then begin adding the remaining flour, cup by cup, until the dough is too stiff to stir. Place the dough on a lightly floured wooden board and begin kneading, adding additional flour as necessary. The dough should be fairly stiff and firm. Knead until the dough is smooth and satiny, 10 to 15 minutes. Place the dough in a bowl, cover securely with plastic wrap, and let rise at room temperature until doubled in bulk, about 1 hour.

3. When the dough has doubled, punch down and let rise again, covered, until doubled in bulk, 1 hour.

4. Punch down again, then separate the dough into 18 equal portions, each weighing about 3 ounces (95 g). Form into neat ovals, and place on a baking sheet. Mist with water (a household flower mister works well), cover with a clean cloth, and let rise until almost doubled in bulk, about 45 minutes.

5. Preheat the oven to 450°F (230°C). Just before putting the rolls in the oven, place a shallow baking pan filled with 2 cups (500 ml) boiling water on the bottom of the oven to create a steamy atmosphere for baking, which will give the rolls a good crust.

6. Bake until the rolls are a rich golden brown, 20 to 25 minutes. Mist with cold water several times during the first 3 minutes of baking.

7. Remove the rolls from the oven and transfer to a cooling rack. Because there is no fat in this recipe, the rolls will not stay fresh for long. They should, ideally, be consumed within two hours of baking. (Alternatively, the rolls, once baked, may be frozen. To serve, take the rolls directly from the freezer, place unwrapped in a cold oven, set oven to 400°F/205°C, and bake 15 to 20 minutes to thaw and refresh.)
Yield: 18 rolls.

Fromageries
CHEESE SHOPS

Fromagerie de Montmartre (see entry, page 238).

If all France had to offer to the world of gastronomy was bread, cheese, and wine, that would be enough for me. Of the trinity, it is cheese that links one to the other. I cannot imagine a more understated, unified French meal than one perfectly fresh *baguette*, a single Camembert, so ripe and velvety it won't last another hour, and a glass or two of young, fruity, well-balanced red wine. And I can't imagine a better place to discover French cheese than in Paris, where dozens of *fromageries* line the streets, each shop as different and distinctive as the personality of its owner, each offering selections that vary with the seasons.

Only the French produce so many varieties of cheese, so graphically reflecting their regional landscape and the many kinds of soil, climate, and vegetation. From the milk of cows, goats, and sheep; from the green, flat lands of Normandy, the steep mountain Alps, and the plains of Champagne east of Paris comes a veritable symphony of aromas, textures, colors, and forms. Cheese fresh from little farms and big cooperatives, cheese to begin the day and to end it. The French consume a great deal of cheese—about forty-two pounds per capita per year, compared to the American's twenty pounds—and of all the varieties, Camembert is the undisputed favorite.

How many varieties of French cheese are there, really? The French are not a people given to simple agreement. When Winston Churchill said, "A country that produces 325 varieties of cheese can't be governed," he was, undoubtedly, responding to a bit of cheese hype. The real figure, say experts, is more like 150 to 200 serious varieties, with perhaps an additional 100 cheeses that are minor variations.

There's an old *New Yorker* magazine cartoon that describes the confusion perfectly: An elderly woman is sitting on the sofa, poring over maps of France. She looks up at her husband and says: "Has it ever occurred to you, dear, that most of the villages and towns in France seem to have been named after cheeses?"

Don't let anyone convince you that the cheese you eat in France and the French cheese you eat in the United States are necessarily the same. A major reason they don't taste the same has to do with United States Department of Agriculture regulations barring the importation of cheese made from unpasteurized milk that has been aged less than sixty days. Pasteurization may make cheese "safe," but in the process it kills all the microbes that give the cheese its character and flavor, that keep it a live, ever-changing organism. There is no question that pasteurized milk produces uniformly bland, "dead" cheese. The regulation rules out the importation of France's finest fresh young cheese, including raw-milk Camembert and Brie, and the dozens of varieties of lively, delicate goat cheese, although on occasion a few may slip through.

Yet even in France, cheese made from pasteurized milk is increasingly common. For instance, less than 5 percent of the 160,000 tons of Camembert produced in France each year is made from raw milk. The advantage, of course, is that cheese made with pasteurized milk can be made available year-round, and will have more stable keeping qualities. When in France, take the time to get a true taste of fresh French cheese: Specify raw-milk cheese by asking for *fromage fermier* or *au lait cru*. These cheeses are produced in limited quantities, the result of traditional production methods.

Paris has dozens of *fromageries* that specialize in raw-milk cheese, with some shops offering as many as 200 different varieties. Before living in Paris I thought that cheese merchants only bought and sold cheese. Wrong. The best, most serious cheese people actually age the cheese they sell. That is, they buy the cheese ready-made from the farmer, then, following a sensitive and tricky aging process, they take the cheese from its young, raw state to full maturity, refining the cheese in underground cellars that are usually humid and cold. The process is called *affinage,* and it can last from days to months, depending on the cheese. As each cheese matures, it takes on its own personality, influenced by the person responsible for its development. Maturing cheese needs daily attention: Some varieties are washed with beer, some with a blend of salt and water, some with *eau-de-vie.* Some are turned every day, moved from one cellar to another as the aging process continues. Each merchant has his own style of aging, and there are varying opinions on how cold and how humid the cellar should be; whether the cheese should be aged on clean straw or old straw, paper, or even plastic; or whether the cheese should be turned daily or just every now and then. And each merchant has a different opinion on when a cheese is ripe, and thus ready to be put on sale.

I adore watching the dedicated *fromagers,* whose love for cheese is totally infectious. In their cellars they are in heaven, as they vigorously inhale the heady, pungent aromas that fill the air and give the cheese little "love taps," the same way bakers give their unbaked loaves a tender touch before putting them in the oven. Now, having toured most of the various aging cellars that exist beneath the streets of the city, I see what a single individual can do to change the course of a cheese's life, ultimately determining taste and texture. Henry Voy's cheese, from La Ferme Saint-Hubert, has a lusty, almost over-the-hill quality about it that at times can be quite appealing. Cheeses from Lillo and Alléosse are refined and elegant, always in perfect, presentable shape.

A few words on selecting cheese: Be sensitive to the seasons. For instance, don't expect to find Vacherin in the middle of summer. When in doubt, ask to know the seasonal specialties in a given shop. In selecting cheese for a *dégustation* (a cheese tray or sample selection for tasting), either at home or in a restaurant, choose three to four varieties, generally including a semi-soft cheese, a goat cheese, and a blue. Eat the mild cheese first, then move on to the stronger varieties.

Be wary of cheese wrapped in plastic. Like us, cheese has to breathe to maintain life and vigor. Don't be afraid of a bit of mold. Generally the bluish film on goat's milk cheese is a sign that the cheese is made with raw milk and has been ripened on fresh straw. Cheese that won't mold, and won't spoil, is already too dead to bother about.

Be open-minded and adventurous. The first months I lived in Paris I rarely bought Brie or Camembert—I'd had so many disappointing pasteurized-milk varieties that I lost my enthusiasm for these wonderful cheeses. Then one day, I happened to sample a perfect Camembert and "click," I instantly understood what the fuss was all about.

OPERA, PALAIS-ROYAL

1st arrondissement

LA MAISON DU BON FROMAGE
35 Rue du Marché-Saint Honoré, Paris 1.
(42.61.02.77).
Métro: Pyramides.
Open 9 A.M. to 2 P.M. and 4:15 P.M. to 8 P.M. Closed Sunday, Monday, and August.
Credit card: V.
English spoken.

Owners Michèle and Alain Eletufe are true perfectionists, and that perfection shows even before you've entered their tiny *fromagerie,* boasting some 200 different varieties of cheese. Look out for their lovely *chèvres* (all guaranteed to be made with fresh, never frozen, goat's milk), the superb Reblochon from the Savoie, an exceptional Brie de Meaux, and an aged Brillat-Savarin, with its rosy, reddish glow. They also offer a good selection of breads, perfect for a Tuileries Gardens picnic.

CHEZ TACHON
38 Rue de Richelieu, Paris 1.
(42.96.08.66).
Métro: Palais-Royal.
Open 9:30 A.M. to 1:30 P.M. and 4 P.M. to 7:30 P.M. Closed Sunday, Monday, July, and August.

A truly classic old-fashioned neighborhood *fromagerie,* near the Louvre and the Palais-Royal. Little handwritten signs tell you about the origin and history of many cheese varieties, and there is even an advisory list noting which ones are currently at their ripest. Tachon presents some wonderful finds, including many small-production raw-milk farm cheeses: the best-ever Burgundian Epoisses, from the Laiterie de la Côte in Gevrey-Chambertin; superb Swiss Tête de Moine du Bellelay; a better than average farm-fresh Saint-Nectaire, mild, sweet, and tangy, and aged a full two months on beds of rye straw; and Livarot, from Normandy farms, strong, spicy, and elastic, the sort of cheese that sticks agreeably to your teeth. Also try the Roquefort Maria-Grimal, the Camembert from the Coopérative d'Isigny, and the earthy, air-dried, smoked pork sausages from the French Alps.

LUXEMBOURG

5th arrondissement

FERME SAINTE-SUZANNE
4 Rue des Fossés-Saint-
  Jacques, Paris 5.
(43.54.90.02).
Métro: Luxembourg.
Open 8 A.M. to 1 P.M. and
  4 P.M. to 7:30 P.M. Closed
  Saturday, Sunday, and
  August.
Restaurant open 11:30 A.M.
  to 2:30 P.M. Monday
  through Friday, and
  Thursday evenings from
  7:30 P.M. to 9:30 P.M.

A pretty little shop off the active Left Bank Place de l'Estrapade, with a pleasant little cheese restaurant in back (see *Dégustation* box, page 240). This shop is typical of a good, standard, neighborhood *fromagerie,* where there is a fine, classic selection, mostly of raw-milk cheese that is carefully aged. The owners seem more interested in the little restaurant than in the *fromagerie,* and from time to time there's a slip in quality. But it's worth a look inside if you're in the neighborhood. Good bets: fresh and creamy Chabichou goat cheese; nicely aged Camembert from La Ferme d'Antignac in Normandy; and a fine Brie.

BAC, SEVRES-BABYLONE, ECOLE MILITAIRE

7th arrondissement

BARTHELEMY
51 Rue de Grenelle, Paris 7.
(45.48.56.75).
Métro: Bac.
Open 8:30 A.M. to 1 P.M. and
  4 P.M. to 7:15 P.M. Tuesday
  through Friday; 8:30 A.M.
  to 1:30 P.M. and 3 P.M. to
  7:15 P.M. Saturday. Closed
  Sunday and Monday.
Credit card: V.
English spoken.

Everyone from the president of the French Republic to actress Catherine Deneuve shops here, and even without that recommendation this Paris landmark deserves a visit. Barthelemy offers some of the finest Swiss Vacherin (from October to March), well-aged Epoisses, Camembert from the Coopérative d'Isigny, as well as Gabriel Coulet's exceptional Roquefort.

CHEESE TO GO

If you are planning to tuck a selection of French cheeses into your suitcase for your welcome-back meal in the United States, be careful. U.S. Customs observes very strict government rules on foods coming into the country. Technically, no cheese, unless it is commercially sealed, can be brought by tourists into the U.S. This rules out virtually all French cheese.

STREET NAME MENU

It should come as no surprise to find that in Paris, a city so devoted to food, dozens of street names have a food connection. Here are a few, with the *arrondissement,* or neighborhood, in which they are now located:

Rue des Boulangers, 5th *arrondissement*: When the street was named in 1844, it was lined with numerous bakeries. Today there's not a loaf of bread for sale on "Bakers' Street."

Passage de la Brie, 19th *arrondissement*: named for the region east of Paris, known for its wheat, pastures, butter, and of course, cheese.

Rue Brillat-Savarin, 13th *arrondissement*: named in honor of the gastronome and author of the famous *Physiology of Taste.*

Rue Brise-Miche, 4th *arrondissement*: During the Middle Ages, it was on this street that clergymen distributed bread to the needy. *Brise-miche,* named in 1517, literally means "break bread."

Rue Curnonsky, 17th *arrondissement*: named in memory of the gastronome Maurice-Edmond Sailland, who took on the Russian-sounding pseudonym around the turn of the century, when everything Russian was fashionable in Paris. The author of the multi-volume *La France Gastronomique* died in 1956, and the street was later named in his honor.

Rue des Eaux, 16th *arrondissement*: In 1650, when this road was opened in the Passy district, workers had discovered the area's mineral waters. (Passy is now one of the more fashionable Paris neighborhoods.) The source dried up during the 18th century, but the name, "Street of the Waters," remained. Who knows, if the source still existed, we could all be drinking Passy water instead of Perrier.

Rue de la Faisanderie, 16th *arrondissement*: A pheasant preserve, or *faisanderie,* once existed here, near the *château* of the Muette.

Rue des Fermiers, 17th *arrondissement*: There are no farmers, or *fermiers,* left here today, but in the 1800s there were still a few farms in this now-citified neighborhood not far from Parc Monceau.

The street was named in 1840, when the area became part of Paris.

Rue des Jeûneurs, 2nd *arrondissement*: The name, perhaps, comes from a sign that hung above one of the houses in 1715, during the reign of Louis XV. It read: "Aux Déjeuners," or "Lunches Here."

Rue des Maraîchers, 20th *arrondissement*: During the 18th century, vegetable garden markets, or *maraîchers,* bordered the region. The street was named in 1869.

Impasse Marché aux Chevaux, 5th *arrondissement*: There are many Paris streets named after past or still-existing markets, but this is one story I particularly enjoy. Beginning in 1687, this was a major market site. Early each Wednesday and Saturday, pigs were brought to market for sale, then later in the day mules, donkeys, and horses *(chevaux)* were sold, giving the street its name. On Sundays, they sold wagons and dogs.

Rue des Meuniers, 12th *arrondissement*: The street of the millers takes its name from the flour mill that existed here during the 18th century. Today there's no sign of a mill.

Rue des Morillons, 15th *arrondissement*: Morillon is the name of a grapevine that flourished in the Parisian climate, at a time when Parisians and those living on the outskirts still had room to grow grapes. The path that led from the vineyard was declared a road in 1730 and a street in 1906. Vineyards have once again been planted in the nearby Parc Georges-Brassens, but they're of the Pinot Noir variety, not Morillon.

Impasse de la Poissonerie, 4th *arrondissement*: This street was built in 1783 when the Sainte-Catherine market first opened. It bordered a fish shop, thus its name.

Boulevard Poissonière, 9th and 10th *arrondissements*: Opened at the beginning of the 17th century, this street served as a *passage* for fish merchants coming direct from the Port of Calais, delivering their fish to the Paris central market, Les Halles. It was named in 1685.

LA MAISON DU FROMAGE
(Alain Quatrehomme)
62 Rue de Sèvres, Paris 7.
(47.34.33.45).
Métro: Sèvres-Babylone.
Open 8:45 A.M. to 1 P.M. and
    4:15 P.M. to 7:45 P.M.
    (Saturday open without
    interruption.) Closed
    Sunday and Monday.

This popular Left Bank shop supplies some of the best restaurants in town, including Alain Senderen's Lucas-Carton. Look out for superb Beaufort from the Savoie; a Parmesan aged 2½ years; a Saint-Marcellin aged as in Lyons, until it's creamy and runny. Also try their Swiss Fribourg, a superb cheese to sample with the sweet wines of the Jura; and from November to March, the Swiss Vacherin.

MARIE-ANNE CANTIN
12 Rue du Champ-de-Mars,
    Paris 7.
(45.50.43.94).
Métro: Ecole Militaire.
Open 8:30 A.M. to 1 P.M. and
    4 P.M. to 7:30 P.M. Closed
    Sunday afternoon.
English spoken.

One of Paris's prettiest cheese boutiques, just off the bustling Rue Cler open-air market. Marie-Anne is the daughter of Christian Cantin, whose cheese shop at 2 Rue de Lourmel, in the 15th *arrondissement,* has long been a Paris landmark. Now, along with her husband, Antoine Dias, Madam Cantin is operating her own boutique, offering 80 to 100 remarkably well-aged varieties from France, Switzerland, and the Netherlands. They're both passionate about cheese ("We never stop eating it," says Monsieur Dias), and their excitement carries over into the neatly organized, appealing little store. Their pride and joy are the aging cellars beneath the shop, with one for goat cheese (very dry) and one for cow's-milk cheese (very humid). The floor of the cow's-milk cellar is lined with rocks, which are "watered" regularly to provide proper humidity. All cheese is aged on natural straw, and varieties such as Munster and Maroilles get a daily washing of beer or salt water, to turn mild, timid little discs into strong, forceful cheese. The true cheese lover, says Monsieur Dias,

"Browsing" at Marie-Anne Cantin's.

is someone who invariably selects Camembert, Brie, or Livarot as part of his cheese course. The best varieties sampled here include a classic and elegant Camembert; a dusty, creamy little Bouton-de-Chèvre (farm-made goat cheese); and perhaps the best Charolais goat cheese in the world: creamy, refined, clean, and full-flavored. If you're in the mood for a mercilessly pungent cheese, try the northern Vieux Lille ("old Lille")—strong and rugged, it's a cheese that almost attacks your palate. More soothing and Cheddar-like is Salers, a mild and nutty cooked cheese from the Auvergne, and Comté, France's version of the well-known Swiss Gruyère. And do not ignore the "runny" Saint-Marcellin, aged as in Lyons. The shop will prepare packages for traveling abroad.

GARE SAINT-LAZARE, MADELEINE

8th arrondissement

ANDROUET
41 Rue d'Amsterdam,
  Paris 8.
(48.74.26.90).
Métro: Liège.
Open 8 A.M. to 7 P.M. Closed
  Sunday.
Credit cards: AE, DC, V.
English spoken.

In Paris, the name Androuët (pronounced ahn-drew-ett) has been synonymous with cheese since the shop on Rue d'Amsterdam opened its doors in 1909. The boutique has now been sold, and though this is still the spot to go to create a lovely cheese tray, a picnic, or a package of cheeses to take home with you, the selection is not nearly as spectacular as it was years ago. The lovely assorted boxes of cheese—ready-made cheese trays with a fine variety, all labeled and ready to serve—are still available, but what you'll see displayed in the window is not the real thing, but plastic models!

When I first moved to Paris, I came here every Saturday to sample new varieties, using the shop as a mini-university of cheese. Today there are still some special Androuët cheeses I count among my favorites, including the triple-cream Lucullus; the smooth Soumaintrain, full of flavor as well as character; and the Arôme au Gêne from the Lyonnais region, pungent discs fermented in *marc de Bourgogne*, an *eau-de-vie* distilled from pressed grape skins and seeds. In the fall, sample the Munster, aged two or three months at large farms and given a daily splash of white wine; Pierre-Qui-Vire, an elegant, smooth Burgundian cow's-milk cheese, full of character and aged two months in a cool, humid cellar; Epoisses, an autumn specialty that's brushed with *marc de Bourgogne* to give it a rare pungency and a rind the color of fresh fall leaves; and Rollot, the smooth and spicy cow's-milk cheese from Picardy, aged two months and washed daily with a salt and water brine. Through much of the fall they also offer the rare, delicate, and subtle Brie de Melun Frais, a chalky white and delicately flavored young Brie. Androuët's Roquefort is often disappointing, and from time to time certain varieties of goat cheese are highly over-salted.

CREPLET-BRUSSOL
17 Place de la Madeleine,
    Paris 8.
(42.65.34.32).
Métro: Madeleine.
Open 9 A.M. to 7 P.M. Closed
    Sunday, Monday, and
    August.
Credit cards: AE, V.
English spoken.

Because of its location—near the famous Fauchon and Hédiard food shops—this is one of the city's best-known cheese shops. The windows are filled with a lot of processed, packaged varieties of cheese, but inside there is a solid, classic collection, including a fine raw-milk Camembert from the Isigny Cooperative in Normandy; nicely aged Brie; and a good variety of cheeses from the north of France.

LA FERME SAINT-HUBERT
21 Rue Vignon, Paris 8.
(47.42.79.20).
Métro: Madeleine.
Open 8:30 A.M. to 7 P.M.
    Closed Sunday.
Credit cards: AE, DC, V.
English spoken.

Just around the corner from Fauchon, this small, compact shop offers extraordinary cheese varieties, including what's probably the best and most carefully selected Roquefort in Paris; a spectacular Beaufort, aged at least two years in special cellars; and a vigorous Maroilles, from Flanders, aged for four months and dosed daily with a sprinkling of beer. They also offer the Swiss Tête de Moine—a fabulous, fruity cylinder of cheese that resembles Gruyère but has more punch, depth, and character. It's a good traveling cheese, and will last for weeks refrigerated. Also worth sampling are the delicate, pale goat's-milk butter and a rather unusual goat's-milk yogurt. Many varieties of cheese are somewhat rough and rustic, like the shop's owner, Henry Voy. For my taste, some cheeses have been aged too long, losing a bit of their charm. (See also the *Dégustation* box, page 240.)

CAMBRONNE

15th arrondissement

LA FERME DU HAMEAU
223 Rue de la Croix Nivert,
   Paris 15.
(45.32.88.70).
Métro: Porte de Versailles
Open 8:30 A.M. to 1 P.M. and
   3:30 P.M. to 7:30 P.M.
Closed Sunday, Monday,
   and July.

A tidy cheese shop that offers a little bit of everything, from delicious-looking *cassoulet* or *poule aux riz* in glass jars to lovely packages of macaroons. In the cheese department, they offer a superb Coulommiers—a marvelous cheese, generally overshadowed by often-bland Brie. Here the Coulommiers is a delight, well aged, and tasting faintly of almonds. Although it's often called "Brie's little brother," this bloomy, fat disc of cow's-milk cheese is worth going out of one's way to find. Other cheeses of note: a rare Beaufort *d'alpage,* a nicely aged Saint-Nectaire, and in the fall and winter months, Vacherin Mont d'Or. From March 15 to October 15, look out for their special selection of goats-milk cheeses.

FROMAGE DE CHEVRE MARINE A L'HUILE D'HERBES
GOAT CHEESE MARINATED IN OIL WITH HERBS

This is a traditional method of storing and extending the life of a goat cheese, particularly useful for chèvre that has become very firm and dry. It's great to have on hand for days when you haven't had time to market. After the cheese has been consumed, you can continue adding more cheese and herbs to the oil, or use it for cooking or for salad dressings.

6 small goat cheeses
   (Picodon, Crottin, or
   Cabécou)
1 clove garlic, peeled
1 teaspoon fresh or ½
   teaspoon dried
   thyme
1 teaspoon fresh or ½
   teaspoon dried
   rosemary
2 bay leaves
12 whole black
   peppercorns
12 whole white
   peppercorns
12 whole coriander
   seeds
2 cups (500 ml) olive oil

1. Cut each cheese in half horizontally. In a wide-mouth pint (500-ml) jar place the cheese, then the garlic and herbs and spices. Cover with oil. Close securely and store in a cool place for at least 1 week.

2. To serve, remove the cheese from the jar, and drain off the oil. Broil the cheese just until warm, and serve with a tossed green salad and slices of fresh bread. Use cheese within 1 month.

Yield: 12 servings.

VICTOR-HUGO

16th arrondissement

LILLO
35 Rue des Belles-Feuilles,
   Paris 16.
(47.27.69.08).
Métro: Victor-Hugo.
Open 8 A.M. to 1 P.M. and
   4 P.M. to 7:30 P.M. Closed
   Monday.
English spoken.

An elegant, sparkling little shop near the Place Victor-Hugo on one of Paris's most chic market streets, Rue des Belles-Feuilles. This is a neighborhood where quality is taken for granted, and no one need worry about Monsieur Lillo letting his clients down. Though few cheeses are actually aged here, many of the 200 or so varieties are "finished" for five or six days in the neat cellars beneath the shop. Almost all are raw-milk small-production cheeses, and among the best varieties sampled was a remarkable Pavin d'Auvergne, a flat disc of mildly tangy, soft and supple cow's-milk cheese from the Auvergne region. The cheese is similar to Saint-Nectaire. Also excellent: raw-milk Brie, Munster, and Roquefort.

THE RIND

The million dollar question: Should you eat the rind or shouldn't you? Even the experts don't agree. According to *Larousse des Fromages,* the French cheese bible, it is all a question of personal taste. Larousse advises, however, not to leave a messy plate full of little bits of crust. Pierre Androuët, the former dean of Paris cheese merchants, is more definite. Never eat the rind, he says, because it harbors all the cheese's developing molds and yeast and can emit an alkaline odor. The truth? It's really up to you, though let logic rule. The rinds of soft-ripened cheese such as Brie and Camembert are definitely edible, and when the cheese is perfectly ripe, the thin, bloomy *croûte* adds both flavor and texture. However, with another soft cheese, Vacherin, the rind is always removed, and the creamy cheese is scooped out with a spoon. The rinds of semi-soft cheese, such as Reblochon, can have a very nutty flavor. The crust is always discarded when eating hard mountain cheeses, such as Emmenthal, Gruyère, and Tête de Moine.

COURCELLES, VILLIERS

17th arrondissement

ALLEOSSE
13 Rue Poncelet, Paris 17.
(46.22.50.45).
Métro: Ternes.
Open 9 A.M. to 1 P.M. and
4 P.M. to 7 P.M. Closed
Sunday afternoon and
Monday.

Say "cheese," it's Alléosse.

The Alléosse family runs one of the most sparkling, spectacular cheese shops in all of Paris. Every time I wander in here, I have to exert a good deal of self-discipline, or I am likely to wander out with a dozen varieties, with never the time to sample them all. The Alléosse cheeses are aged in a series of *caves* beneath the shop, and although the selection varies according to the season, some very special varieties to note include a beautifully aged Langres, a soft, smooth, pungent cheese from just north of Burgundy; a smooth and super-rich sheep's-milk farm cheese, or *brebis fermier,* from the Pays Basque; discs of goat's-milk cheese aged with a coating of ground walnuts; and a supple raw-milk blue-veined Fourme d'Ambert, aged with Sauternes. There is generally a good selection of very fresh goat's-milk cheeses from Burgundy, always good Beaufort, delicious Coulommiers, and at times a well-aged Saint-Marcellin.

JEAN CARMES ET FILS
24 Rue de Lévis, Paris 17.
(47.63.88.94).
Métro: Villiers.
Open 8 A.M. to 1 P.M. and
4 P.M. to 7:30 P.M. Closed
Sunday afternoon,
Monday, and August.
English spoken.

Situated right in the middle of the hectic Rue de Lévis market, Carmès is a big, open, family-run cheese shop, with "Dad," Jean Carmès, behind the cash register while son, Patrick, rushes about with a nervous sort of vigor, keeping an eye on incoming deliveries, and checking out the progress of the 200 or so varieties of cheese aging in humid rooms below and above the shop. These people are passionate about cheese, taking the care to label each variety, happy to help you select a single cheese or an entire platter. Eighty percent of their cheese is bought fresh from farms. Most varieties spend an average of three to four weeks in the Carmès cellars, aging on fresh, clean straw mats until the cheese is ready to be put on sale. Some specialties here: l'Ecume, a triple cream so rich it easily replaces butter; Tanatais goat cheese, much like a Charolais, dry and delicious with a bloomy crust; and a Petit-Suisse *"comme autrefois"* ("like the old days"), a fragile cheese that stays fresh just four or five days. Real fresh *crème Chantilly* (sweetened *crème fraîche*) and Fontainebleau (a creamy dessert cheese) are sold here as well.

**FROMAGERIE
COURCELLES**
79 Rue de Courcelles,
  Paris 17.
(46.22.22.36).
Métro: Courcelles.
Open 8:30 A.M. to 1 P.M. and
  4 P.M. to 7:30 P.M. Closed
  Sunday, Monday
  morning, and August.

A bright new renovation of a classic, quality *fromagerie*. There's always a line out the door at this tiny, spotless shop, where raw-milk Camembert (the Grand Béron can be remarkable), Pyramide goat cheese, Alsatian Munster, Epoisses from Burgundy, and Roquefort are always in perfect form.

ALAIN DUBOIS
80 Rue de Tocqueville,
  Paris 17.
(42.27.11.38).
Métro: Villiers.
Open 8 A.M. to 1 P.M. and
  4 P.M. to 7:30 P.M. Tuesday
  through Saturday; 9 A.M.
  to 1 P.M. Sunday. Closed
  Monday.
Credit card: V.
Some English spoken.

Young Alain Dubois turned the family *crémerie* into a full-fledged *fromagerie* in the early 1970s. The shop is artfully and tastefully arranged, and Dubois is proudest of his Epoisses de Bourgogne, washed with *marc de Bourgogne* every day or so and aged according to his own "secret" process; his

Cheese from the mountains, an Alléosse assortment (see entry, page 235).

Two types of Emmental, first Savoyard, then Swiss, and two types of Comté cheese from the Jura region of France, first aged, next to it, young.

Fribourg, a softer Swiss Gruyère, aged in cellars in the Jura region for at least two years; and his Swiss Vacherin Mont d'Or, still made in chalets and available from the end of fall into the early spring. Dubois offers some seventy varieties of goat cheese, according to the season. The current goal is to persuade restaurants to take the cheese course more seriously. He dines anonymously in restaurants, studies the cuisine, then approaches the chef with suggestions for a selection that fits the personality of the restaurant. Dubois is categorically opposed to aging certain cheese, such as Brie, Camembert, or Saint-Nectaire, in Paris *caves.* "Certain varieties must taste of the soil and air of the region in which they were made, and they can't be aged in small batches in the city," insists the smiling, outgoing Dubois. "For a truly great Brie, you need an enormous amount aged in the same spot." His argument is convincing, for his Camembert—aged in Normandy at the Coopérative d'Isigny—is creamy, refined, and delicious. Eighty percent of his cheese comes direct from the farm, since, as he puts it, "farm cheese is what gave France its great reputation for cheese." He and his wife love visiting farms in search of good cheese and are avid restaurant-goers, feeling that one can't be a good *fromager* without being a dedicated *gastronome.*

CRÈME FRAÎCHE

Where would French cuisine be without crème fraîche, *that thick and slightly tangy cream that lies somewhere between heavy cream and sour cream? Every* crémerie *in France sells* crème fraîche *in bulk, usually ladled out of giant round crockery bowls. It's versatile and nearly indispensable, showing up in hot and cold sauces, and is perfect for whipping with a touch of sugar to dab on a mound of fresh wild strawberries.*

2 cups (500 ml) heavy cream (you cannot use ultra-pasteurized)

2 tablespoons cultured buttermilk

1. Mix the heavy cream and buttermilk together in a medium-size bowl. Cover loosely with plastic wrap and let stand at room temperature overnight, or until fairly thick.

2. Cover tightly and refrigerate for at least 4 hours, to thicken it even more. The *crème fraîche* will keep for up to 1 week in the refrigerator, where the tangy flavor will continue to develop.

Yield: 2 cups (500 ml).

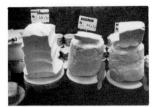

Creamy blocks of butter.

BUTTER

France produces 10 percent of the world's butter, most of it unsalted. Though Normandy, with its shining green pastures and fawn-colored cows, produces a high-quality product, the best butter comes from Charentes, in the southwest of France. Charentes butter, sold in packets under the label *"beurre d'Echiré"* or *"beurre de Ligueil,"* is favored by French pastry chefs because it is firmer and less watery than other varieties and makes superior pastry.

In cheese shops you often see huge creamy blocks of butter behind the counter. They are usually labeled *"beurre des Charentes," "beurre de Normandie,"* or *"beurre demi-sel." Demi-sel* is Brittany's lightly salted butter. Rarely used in cooking, it finds its place on the table. (While the bulk butters look good and fresh, beware: They sit all day absorbing the mingled odors of the cheeses and are not always terribly fresh.)

The French don't usually butter their bread, so whether or not butter appears on the home or restaurant table is really a matter of personal taste. Butter is always served with *charcuterie* (cold cuts), with radishes, anchovies, sardines, and with the rye bread that comes as part of any order of oysters or other shellfish. If you don't see butter on a restaurant table, it is perfectly proper to ask for it, though in more casual restaurants you may be charged a *supplément* of a few francs. Butter is usually included with the cheese course, and is used to soften the effect of strong and salty cheeses such as Roquefort.

MONTMARTRE

18th arrondissement

FROMAGERIE DE MONTMARTRE
9 Rue du Poteau, Paris 18.
(46.06.26.03).
Métro: Jules-Joffrin.
Open 8:45 A.M. to 12:30 P.M. and 4 P.M. to 7:30 P.M.
Closed Sunday and Monday.
English spoken.

If you just love looking at beautiful cheese displays, don't miss this spacious *fromagerie,* typical of the pretty food shops along Rue du Poteau. It offers a sparkling variety of farm-fresh raw-milk cheeses from all over France, and the owner, Madame Delbey, is happy to let you "window shop" as you wander about the well-organized store, examining the flawless selection of cheese displayed on

trays of straw and aged in her own cellars. Goat cheese is one of their best features—they offer more than forty different varieties. Outstanding cheese sampled here includes a beautifully aged Comté from the Jura; Auvergnat Cantal aged more than 18 months; and their creamy Fontainebleau "maison."

FONTAINEBLEAU

This creamy, white, succulent dessert cheese is found, from time to time, in Paris fromageries. Usually sold in little white containers lined with cheesecloth, the fresh cheese takes its name from the town of Fontainebleau, south of Paris. Although Fontainebleau is far from rare, this elegant cheese is seen less and less frequently in Paris shops: It stays fresh for just twenty-four hours, and it is not economical for most cheese shops to handle. But since this appealing dessert is easy to make, there's no reason not to serve it often. In France, Fontainebleau is made at home with fromage blanc, sort of a "curdless" cottage cheese, but I found that yogurt is an excellent substitute. This version is similar to coeur à la crème, but since it is lightened with egg whites, Fontainebleau is less rich. It is an ideal dessert for a large group, because the recipe can easily be doubled or tripled. And since it is made a day in advance, it takes no last-minute preparation. Fontainebleau is particularly beautiful when made in a white ceramic coeur à la crème mold, but it can be formed in a strainer as well. I serve Fontainebleau with a fresh raspberry sauce and the little almond cakes, financiers (see recipe, page 190). It is also delicious with strawberries, fresh figs, or blueberries.

2 cups (500 ml) low-fat
    yogurt
1 cup (200 g) sugar
2 cups (500 ml) heavy
    cream (preferably
    not ultra-
    pasteurized) or *crème*
    fraîche (see recipe,
    page 237)
3 egg whites

1. In a large mixing bowl, combine the yogurt and all but 2 tablespoons of the sugar.

2. In a second bowl, whip the cream or *crème fraîche* until stiff and fold into the yogurt mixture.

3. In yet another bowl, whip the egg whites until stiff, add the reserved 2 tablespoons of sugar, and whip until glossy, about another 20 seconds. Gently fold the egg whites into the yogurt-cream mixture.

4. Transfer mixture to a 6-cup (1.5-liter) cheesecloth-lined, perforated mold (or use two or more smaller molds). Cover the mold, and place it in a bowl in the refrigerator. Refrigerate for 24 hours, draining off the liquid from time to time. The cheese should become fairly firm and dry, almost like a whipped cream cheese.

5. To serve, unmold the Fontainebleau onto a platter, unwrap, and surround with a colorful fresh fruit sauce or fresh berries. Serve immediately.

Yield: 8 to 10 servings.

"The Roquefort, with its blue and yellow marbling, looks diseased, like rich people who have eaten too many truffles."
—Emile Zola,
Le Ventre de Paris

DEGUSTATION

A favorite way to enjoy French cheese is to take a tour of France through a *dégustation* (tasting) of the country's more than 180 varieties of cheese. The following restaurants, most of which are also *fromageries,* offer a *dégustation* of cheeses on their menus.

Androuët, 41 Rue d'Amsterdam, Paris 8. (48.74.26.93). Métro: Liège. Restaurant open noon to 2:30 P.M. and 7 P.M. to 9:30 P.M. Closed Sunday. Credit cards: AE, DC, V. 180-franc *dégustation.* Reservations advised.

Once one of my favorite spots for sampling cheese—in seven heavenly courses—Androuët has changed ownership and style. The cozy, rustic dining room has been transformed into a cold, modern restaurant. The seven-course *dégustation* is still on the menu, and though it's not nearly up to the quality of years past, it's still the biggest show in town. Be sure to come with a very hearty appetite, and plenty of time!

La Boutique à Sandwiches, 12 Rue du Colisée, Paris 8. Métro: Franklin-D.-Roosevelt. (43.59.56.69). Open noon to 4 P.M. and 6 P.M. to midnight. Closed Sunday and August. About 100 francs. Credit card: V.

For an unusual cheese experience, wander up to the first floor of this simple delicatessen to sample *raclette,* a hearty, filling Swiss dish that includes firm, buttery melted cheese, potatoes boiled in their skins, pickled onions, and *cornichons.* Huge wheels of several varieties of Swiss cheese are split in half, then the exposed portion is placed under a special *raclette* broiler. As the cheese melts, it is scraped off—crispy, bubbling brown crust and all—and brought to the table. You will hardly be able to finish the tangy melted cheese before the waiter is back, ready to scrape another serving onto your plate. With the *raclette,* savor the delicate white Apremont wine, from the Savoie.

La Ferme Saint-Hubert, 21 Rue Vignon, Paris 8. (47.42.79.20). Métro: Madeleine. Restaurant open 11:30 A.M. to 3 P.M. and 6:45 P.M. to 10 P.M. Closed Sunday and Monday. 64-franc *dégustation.*

Next door to La Ferme Saint-Hubert *fromagerie*

A selection of Cantal.

you'll find a tiny, casual little lunchroom serving abbreviated *dégustations* suited to cheese enthusiasts with limited time. Their most popular platter is made up of seven varieties, representing the seven major types of French cheese. At La Ferme Saint-Hubert, they are aged to the borderline of perfection, while reflecting the owner's preference for ripe, full-flavored cheese. Platters of goat cheese and salads are also available. There's a small wine selection, and little pots of pure white goat's-milk butter are served with a fresh country loaf from baker Lionel Poilâne. The cheese is not labeled, so you'll have to make good mental notes, then slip into the shop next door after the meal to identify the cheese you have just tasted. *Raclette* is served every evening.

Ferme Sainte-Suzanne, 4 Rue des Fossés-Saint-Jacques, Paris 5. (43.54.90.02). Métro: Luxembourg. Restaurant open 11:30 A.M. to 2 P.M. Monday through Friday; 7:30 P.M. to 9 P.M. Thursday and Friday. Closed Saturday, Sunday, and August. 46- and 92-franc *dégustations.*

A lively, skylit neighborhood lunch spot, with a simple cheese-based menu featuring savory *crêpe tourtes;* salads that combine greens, goat cheese, and walnuts; and nicely labeled *dégustation* platters served with the fabulously crusty *baguettes* from the nearby Boulangerie Moderne. The melted Swiss Raclette cheese is served with tiny boiled potatoes and slices of delicious smoked ham. There's a small wine list, including an excellent Côtes-du-Rhône.

La Maison du Valais, 20 Rue Royale, Paris 8. (42.60.23.75). Métro: Madeleine. Open 12:15 P.M. to 2:30 P.M. and 7:15 P.M. to 10:30 P.M. *Raclette,* 81 francs. Credit cards: AE, V.

My favorite spot in Paris for sampling platter after platter of warm, creamy-white Swiss *raclette.* Here, in a rustic chalet-like setting, the superb—and filling—*raclette* is served with plenty of boiled potatoes and a marvelously piquant condiment of onions and mustard, as well as puckery *cornichons.* With it sample a light white Swiss Fendant from—where else—Valais.

Charcuteries
PREPARED FOODS
TO GO

Decisions are easy, if you know what you want.

To lovers of all things earthy, hearty, rib-sticking, and aromatic, the Paris *charcuterie* is a touch of heaven. Literally meaning the shop where you buy *chair cuite*—cooked meat—the city has hundreds—some museumlike with carved marble counters and hanging brass racks, others modern and spotless with wares displayed like diamonds in a jeweler's window. There you can buy fragrant sausages and mosaic pâtés, salted and smoked hams, and strange-sounding *grattons, fritons, rillettes,* and *rillons.* Who else but the French could manage to make so much of the lowly pig? And where else but Paris can you find one shop with eighteen different kinds of *boudin* sausage made right on the premises; another with more than a dozen different kinds of ham; still others that sell not just pork products, but also caviar and *foie gras,* fresh country breads and smoked salmon, and even the vodka, Champagne, or Sauternes to go with them?

You need not go beyond Paris to sample the wonders of the French world of *charcuterie*—my favorite regional shops feature rustic products from the rugged Auvergne region in south-central France, and offer farm-fresh goat and sheep's milk cheese, a heady

Bleu d'Auvergne, dozens of kinds of hams, sausages, and pâtés of so many different names, colors, and shapes it makes the mind spin. There are also Alsatian-owned shops redolent with the pungent warmth of cooked sauerkraut, mounds of pork chops, and colorful assorted sausages, plus some of the finest farm Munster cheese and romantic heart-shaped gingerbread cookies.

Shops with a Breton accent are likely to feature Brittany's prune-filled flan known as *far breton,* while those from the Savoie region bordering Switzerland will offer mountain-cured hams and sausages, and local white wines, such as the pale, delicate Apremont or fizzy, light Crépy.

The size and selection available vary widely from shop to shop, neighborhood to neighborhood. Run-of-the-mill *charcuteries* make only a small portion of the products themselves (75 percent of the products sold in *charcuteries* nationwide are industrially produced), but the finest shops, such as those mentioned here, either produce most of their own sausages, hams, pâtés, and *terrines* or buy them direct from independent farmers in various regions of France.

Many but not all Paris *charcuteries* also offer hot meals at lunch and dinnertime, a concept that to most of us seems essentially modern. It's not, for ever since *charcuteries* were first established in 1475, their very reason for existence was to sell cooked pork products. In days when a large percentage of Parisians lived without cooking facilities, the *charcuterie* served as a kitchen away from home, ready with hot, carry-out meals all week long.

Along with the hundreds of different meat products, most *charcuteries* also sell *escargots* (snails) ready for popping in the oven, a variety of pastry-topped pâtés or *terrines* to be eaten warm or cold, pizzas and *quiches,* and dozens of salads, ranging from those of ivory-colored celery root or bright red beets to a julienne of carrots showered with vinaigrette. Condiments such as olives, pickles, and *cornichons* can almost always be found, along with many kinds of regional packaged cakes, cookies, and pastries.

Today the Parisian definition of *charcuterie* is a broad one, and major shops such as Fauchon, Lenôtre, Dalloyau, Hédiard, and Flo Prestige (all listed elsewhere in this guide) perform the services of *charcuterie* and caterer, offering, as well, pastries, breads, chocolates, wines, liquors, and condiments. What follows here, then, is a choice selection of the smaller shops, most of them family-run, with unique personalities all their own. In each case, a sampling of this, a slice of that, will help make a picnic lunch or snack a true Parisian feast.

TUILERIES

1st arrondissement

CHEDEVILLE
12 Rue du Marché-Saint-
  Honoré, Paris 1.
(42.61.11.11).
Métro: Tuileries.
Open 7 A.M. to 1:30 P.M. and
  3 P.M. to 7 P.M. Closed
  Sunday.
Credit cards: DC, V.
Some English spoken.

One of the city's major *charcuteries*, famous for the pâtés, sausages, and hams that find their way into some of Paris's better restaurants. A place full of character, where you are welcome to watch the half dozen butchers hard at work preparing for the day's labors.

ORDERING CHARCUTERIE

The best way to visit a Paris *charcuterie* is armed with a little knowledge and a hearty appetite. The following are some of the most commonly found products:

Andouille: cold smoked chitterling (tripe) sausage.

Andouillette: smaller chitterling (tripe) sausage, usually served grilled.

Ballotine: usually poultry, boned, stuffed, and rolled.

Boudin blanc: white sausage, of veal, chicken or pork.

Boudin noir: pork blood sausage.

Cervelas: garlicky cured pork sausage.

Confit: duck, goose, or pork cooked and preserved in its own fat.

Cou d'oie farci: neck skin of goose, stuffed with meat and spices, much like a sausage.

Crépinette: small sausage patty wrapped in caul fat.

Fritons: coarse pork *rillettes*, or a minced spread, that includes organ meats.

Fromage de tête: headcheese, usually pork.

Galantine: cooked, boned poultry or meat stuffed

and rolled, classically glazed with gelatin, and served cold.

Grattons: crisply fried pieces of pork, goose, or duck skin; cracklings.

Hure (de porc or *de marcassin):* a headcheese prepared from the head of a pig or boar.

Jambon (ham)

   d'Auvergne: salt-cured ham.

   de Bayonne: raw dried, salt-cured ham.

   de Bourgogne: also *persillé:* cold cooked ham, cubed and preserved in parsleyed gelatin, usually sliced from a terrine.

   cru: any raw cured ham.

   cuit: any cooked ham.

   fumé: any smoked ham.

   de montagne: any mountain ham.

   à l'os: ham with the bone in.

   de Paris: pale, lightly salted, cooked ham.

   de Parme: Italian *prosciutto* from Parma.

   du pays: any country ham.

   persillé: also *de Bourgogne;* cold cookd ham, cubed and preserved in parsleyed gelatin, usually sliced from a terrine.

   sec: any dried ham.

   de Westphalie: German Westphalian ham, raw-cured and smoked.

   de York: smoked English-style ham, usually poached.

Jambonneau: cured ham shank or pork knuckle.

Jésus: smoked pork sausage from the Franche-Comté.

Lard: bacon

Lardons: cubes of bacon.

Merguez: small spicy sausage.

Museau de porc: vinegared pork muzzle.

Oreilles de porc: cooked pig's ears, served grilled, with a coating of egg and bread crumbs.

Pâté (seasoned, chopped meats that are molded, baked, and served hot or cold)

> *de campagne:* coarse country-style.

> *de canard:* with duck.

> *de chevreuil:* with venison.

> *en croûte:* baked in pastry.

> *de foie:* with liver.

> *de grive:* with thrush, or songbird.

> *de lapin:* with rabbit.

> *de lièvre:* with wild hare.

> *maison:* in the style of the house or *charcuterie.*

> *d'oie:* with goose.

Pied (foot)

> *de cochon:* pig's foot.

> *de mouton:* sheep's foot.

> *de porc:* pig's foot.

Poitrine fumée: smoked bacon.

Poitrine d'oie fumée: smoked goose breast.

Rillettes (d'oie): minced spread of pork (goose); also can be made with duck, fish, or rabbit.

Rillons: pork belly, cut up and cooked until crisp, then drained of fat; can also be made of duck, goose, or rabbit.

Rosette (de boeuf): dried pork (or beef) sausage, usually from Beaujolais.

Saucisse (most often, small fresh sausage, which is cooked in liquid and/or broiled, and eaten warm)

> *chaude:* warm sausage.

> *de Francfort:* hot dog.

> *de Morteau:* smoked pork sausage from the Franche-Comté.

> *de Strasbourg:* red-skinned hot dog.

> *de Toulouse:* mild country-style pork sausage.

Saucisson (most often, a large air-dried sausage, such as salami, eaten sliced as a cold cut. When fresh, usually called *saucisson chaud*—hot sausage)

"*Drink wine when you eat ham.*

Soup is for ordinary hunger; roasts make a meal festive.

Venison pâté is too good for disobedient children."

—Lesson from a 17th-century French schoolbook.

Coils of boudin.

à l'ail: garlic sausage, usually to be cooked and served warm.

d'Arles: dried, salami-type sausage.

de campagne: any country-style sausage.

en croûte: sausage cooked in pastry crust.

de Lyon: air-dried pork sausage, flavored with garlic and pepper, and studded with chunks of pork fat, sometimes flavored with pistachio nuts or truffles.

sec: any dried sausage, or salami.

Terrine (actually the earthenware container used for cooking meat, game, fish, or vegetable mixtures. It also refers to the pâté served in the vessel. It differs from a pâté proper in that the *terrine* is actually sliced out of the vessel, while a pâté has been removed from the terrine)

d'anguille: eel.

de caille: quail.

de campagne: country-style.

de canard: of duck.

du chef: in the chef's special style.

de faisan: of pheasant.

de foie: of liver.

de foies de volaille: of chicken liver.

de grives: of thrush, or songbird.

maison: in style of the *charcuterie* or house.

de perdreau: of partridge.

de volaille: of chicken.

MARAIS, BASTILLE

4th and 11th arrondissements

LA GALOCHE D'AURILLAC
41 Rue de Lappe, Paris 11.
(47.00.77.15).
Métro: Bastille.
Open 10 A.M. to midnight.
   Closed Sunday, Monday,
   and the last week in July
   through the first week in
   September.

This always lively local bistro also sells regional hams, sausages, breads, cheese, and wine; a nice spot to know about late at night or at lunchtime, when other neighborhood *charcuteries* tend to be closed.

Sausage and frites.

PRODUITS HONGROIS
11 Rue de Sévigné, Paris 4.
(48.87.46.06).
Métro: Saint-Paul.
Open 9 A.M. to 1 P.M. and
   3 P.M. to 7 P.M. Closed
   Sunday, Monday, and
   August.

A tidy, tiny shop near the Place des Vosges, full of fresh, aromatic, and delicious Hungarian sausages. A special, spicy treat: the beef and pork sausage seasoned with hot peppers.

LE SAVOYARD
39 Rue Popincourt, Paris 11.
(No telephone).
Métros: Voltaire or Saint-
   Ambroise.
Open 9 A.M. to 8 P.M. Closed
   Monday, August, and the
   first week in September.

This out-of-the-way *charcuterie* is worth a detour. Perfectly aged Reblochon; fresh, smoked, and dried sausages right from the Savoie mountains; Savoie wines and even a little bar at which to enjoy them.

CHEZ TEIL
6 Rue de Lappe, Paris 11.
(47.00.41.28).
Métro: Bastille.
Open 9 A.M. to 1 P.M. and
   3 P.M. to 8 P.M. Tuesday
   through Saturday; 9 A.M.
   to 1 P.M. Sunday. Closed
   Monday and August.

Even though the face of the neighborhood is changing, there is hardly an earthier, more authentically old-fashioned street in all of Paris than Rue de Lappe. Dance halls for tangos; neighborhood bistros for dining; and *charcuterie* after *charcuterie* for sausages, cheese, country bread, and *foie gras*. This tiny shop is a treasure not to be missed.

A LA VILLE D'AURILLAC
34 Rue de Lappe, Paris 11.
(48.05.94.85).
Métro: Bastille.
Open 8:30 A.M. to 1:30 P.M.
and 3:30 P.M. to 8 P.M.
Tuesday through
Saturday; 10:30 A.M. to
1:30 P.M. Sunday. Closed
Monday and August.
Some English spoken.

A LA VILLE DE RODEZ
22 Rue Vieille-du-Temple,
Paris 4.
(48.87.79.36).
Métro: Saint-Paul.
Open 8 A.M. to 1 P.M. and
3 P.M. to 7:30 P.M. Closed
Sunday, Monday, and
mid-July through August.

Be prepared to take a deep, deep breath when you enter this modest Auvergnat *charcuterie,* filled with the heady, mingling aromas of well-seasoned sausages, fine aged hams, plus honest Saint-Nectaire and mountain-fresh Cantal cheese. The friendly Bonal family also sells walnut oil and shiny patent *galoches,* the wooden shoes with leather uppers, direct from the country.

The long, hearty loaves of country bread come up from Aurillac in south-central France four times a week. While the fragrant sausages and hams that hang from the rafters of this spotless shop all have the wholesome Auvergnat stamp. You will also find buckwheat flour for earthy *crêpes; fouace* (an extra-buttery regional *brioche* studded with candied fruits); *boudin noir* (blood sausage); rough red regional wines; and that delicate, straw-yellow, Cantal-like cheese, Laguiole. You can select an entire picnic or a simple snack, then buy a hand-made wicker basket in which to carry your treasures.

Carefully slicing into a terrine.

SAINT-GERMAIN-DES-PRES, ODEON

6th arrondissement

CHARCUTERIE
  ALSACIENNE
10 Rue de Buci, Paris 6.
(43.54.93.49).
Métro: Saint-Germain-des-
  Prés.
Open daily 8 A.M. to 8 P.M.

Oh boy, sausage-lover's heaven! I'm a real fan of Alsatian food, especially the incredible collection of sausages one finds in this charming, fragrant boutique, a new offshoot of a company founded in Mulhouse back in 1876. Try the cumin-flecked pork sausages, the *boudin* blood sausages, or the thin smoked Montbéliards. The word "cute" must have been coined to describe the interior of this bright and modern shop, decorated with woodwork painted with bright folkloric floral designs.

CHARCUTERIE COESNON
30 Rue Dauphine, Paris 6.
(43.26.56.39).
Métro: Odéon.
Open 8:30 A.M. to 1:15 P.M.
  and 3 P.M. to 8 P.M. Closed
  Sunday, Monday, one
  week at Easter, and
  August.
English spoken.

One of the city's most respected family *charcuteries,* run by the friendly Coesnon family, who came to Paris from Normandy nearly thirty-five years ago. Their specialties include homemade French sausages, with more than eighteen different varieties of *boudin* including boudin *noir* (blood sausage), some filled with raisins, chestnuts, apples, or herbs; and *boudin blanc* (pork and veal sausage); along with *andouillettes* (chitterling sausages). In the winter months, the *boudin* is made fresh each Tuesday and Thursday. Also game terrines, home-smoked bacon, and *foie gras cru* (fresh fattened goose and duck liver), all year round.

PORTE D'ORLEANS

14th arrondissement

DUCREAUX PRODUITS
  REGIONAUX
5 Rue de Sarrette, Paris 14.
(43.27.06.05).
Métro: Alésia.
Open 8 A.M. to 1 P.M. and
  4 P.M. to 8 P.M. Tuesday
  through Saturday. Closed
  Sunday afternoon,
  Monday, and August.

Walking into this shop is like being transported to a family farm in Brittany. This rather funky, spotless *charcuterie* is filled with the salty aroma of fresh-cured hams, while the local prune-filled *far breton* compete for your palate's attention.

VICTOR-HUGO, ARC DE TRIOMPHE, VILLIERS
16th and 17th arrondissements

**CHARCUTERIE
ALSACIENNE**
37 Rue de Belles-Feuilles,
Paris 16.
(47.27.33.74).
Métro: Victor-Hugo.
Open 7:30 A.M. to 1 P.M. and
3:30 P.M. to 8 P.M. Closed
Sunday afternoon and
Monday.
See Charcuterie Alsacienne,
6th *arrondissement*, facing
page.

Oh là là!

CORDIER
129 Avenue Victor-Hugo,
Paris 16.
(47.27.97.74).
Métro: Victor-Hugo.
Open 8:45 A.M. to 1:15 P.M.
and 3:30 P.M. to 7:45 P.M.
Closed Sunday.
Credit card: V.
English spoken.

Cordier is a solid, traditional, neighborhood *charcuterie,* with a touch of luxury. Fine smoked salmon, and fresh raw fattened duck and goose liver (*foie gras*) at holiday time.

JEAN-CLAUDE ET NANOU
46 Rue Legendre, Paris 17.
(42.27.15.08).
Métro: Malesherbes.
Open 9 A.M. to 1 P.M. and
4:30 P.M. to 8 P.M. Closed
Sunday afternoon,
Monday, and mid-July
through August.

Chic, friendly, and outgoing, the young Jean-Claude and Nanou run a tidy family *charcuterie,* filled with impeccably fresh sausages and hams, pâtés and *foie gras* shipped up from the Auvergne region every few days. A respectable assortment of regional cheeses and extraordinary dried and smoked sausages can be bought here as well.

BOUCHERIE LAMARTINE
172 Avenue Victor-Hugo,
Paris 16.
(47.27.82.29).
Métro: Victor-Hugo or
Pompe.
Open 7 A.M. to 7:30 P.M.
Closed Saturday
afternoon and Sunday.

Boucherie Lamartine, one of the best butcher shops in Paris, also sells the products made in Lyons by René Besson, better known as Bobosse. They carry his delicate *quenelles de brochet,* or pike dumplings, and the famous pistachio-studded pork sausage, *saucisson de Lyon.*

MAISON POU
16 Avenue des Ternes,
    Paris 17.
(43.80.19.24).
Métro: Ternes.
Open 9:30 A.M. to 1:15 P.M.
    and 3:30 P.M. to 7:15 P.M.
    Closed Sunday and
    Monday.
Credit cards: DC, V.
Some English spoken.

A "press-your-nose-against-the-window" shop: elegant, upscale, and spotless, filled with fragrant sausages, steaming sauerkraut, pâtés, and hams, not to mention a wide selection of wines, cheeses, preserved and dried wild mushrooms, and truffles.

SCHMID
41 Rue Legendre, Paris 17.
(47.63.31.04).
Métro: Villiers.
Open 8 A.M. to 2 P.M. and
    4 P.M. to 7:45 P.M. Closed
    Sunday and holidays.
Credit card: V.
Some English spoken.

Almost as good as a trip to Alsace: windows filled with heart-shaped Alsatian spice cookies; golden farm-aged Munster; sausages for slicing or poaching; plus wines, liqueurs, and *foie gras* from the region.

FOIE GRAS

Foie gras—a crown jewel of French gastronomy—is the smooth and buttery liver from a fattened duck or goose. Seasoned lightly with salt and pepper, then cooked gently in a white porcelain terrine, this highly perishable delicacy demands no further embellishment than a slice of freshly toasted country bread and a glass of chilled sweet Sauternes. At its best, *foie gras* is one of the world's most satisfying foods. Earthy and elegant, a single morsel of it melts slowly on the palate, invading one's senses with an aroma and flavor that's gracefully soothing, supple, and rich, with a lingering, almost organic aftertaste. Depending on its origin and length of cooking time, the color of *foie gras* ranges from a slightly golden brown to a peach-blushed rose. Rich in calories, *foie gras* is best enjoyed slowly and parsimoniously—it is also expensive.

Which is better, goose or duck liver? It is purely a matter of preference. Fattened goose liver (*foie gras d'oie*) is less common and more expensive than fattened duck liver (*foie gras de canard*) because its production requires more intensive care and feeding. Geese are very susceptible to disease or perturbation in their daily routine, so the casualty rate is high. Ducks are more hardy and less demanding, and during the past twenty years the fattened duck liver has gained popularity, as French restaurateurs and consumers have also developed a

Today's specials.

strong appetite for the breast of the fattened duck, the *magret de canard*. As for taste, goose liver is slightly subtle and mild, duck liver more forward-tasting and a bit more acidic.

What does one look for in *foie gras?* Ideally, a slice of *foie gras* should be the same color throughout, a sign that it is from the same liver and has been carefully and uniformly cooked. It should always have a fresh, appealing, liverlike aroma.

Serve *foie gras* slightly chilled, but not too cold. If possible, remove it from the refrigerator fifteen to twenty minutes before serving. When too cold, flavors are masked. When too warm, *foie gras* can turn mushy, losing its seductive charm.

The following are the legal French definitions and preparations for *foie gras*. When purchasing it preserved, look for products packed in terrines or glass jars, rather than tins, so you can see exactly what you are buying. The best *foie gras* has a fresh color, slices neatly, is generally free of blood vessels, and is not heavily surrounded with fat. Many shops also sell *foie gras* by the slice, cut from a larger terrine. This should be refrigerated, and is best eaten within a few hours. *Foie gras* that can legally enter the United States must have been sterilized—cooked at a temperature of 230°F (110°C)—and is generally marked *foie gras de conserve*.

Foie gras cru: Raw liver. If of good quality, this is the ultimate in *foie gras*. Usually found only at select Paris *charcuteries* around the end of the year, it is delicious sliced raw and spread on warm toasted bread; it can also be preserved in a terrine at home. Often sold vacuum-packed. The best are the smallest, a little over 1 pound (500 to 600 grams) for goose, a little under 1 pound (400 grams) for duck. Lobes should be supple, round, smooth rather than granular, and without spots. A good buy when purchased from a reputable merchant.

Foie gras mi-cuit or nature: The lightly cooked preserved *foie gras* of connoisseurs, and the best way to sample *foie gras* for the first time. Ideally, only the highest-quality livers are preserved in this manner. The terms *mi-cuit* and *nature* are used interchangeably with *foie gras frais,* denoting that the livers have been pasteurized at 175 to 200°F (80 to 90°C). Next to raw, this is the best way to enjoy *foie gras,* for it is barely cooked, retaining its pure, agreeably rich flavor. Sold in terrines; vacuum packed; in aluminum foil-wrapped rolls; in a can or jar; it requires refrigeration. Depending on packaging, it will last several days to several months.

Foie gras entier: Entire lobes of the fattened liver, lightly seasoned and generally cooked in a terrine or glass jar. If the container is large, additional pieces of another liver may be added to fill it in. Sold fresh *(frais),* which requires refrigeration and must be consumed within a few weeks or months (depending on length of cooking time); and *en conserve,* which requires no refrigeration and will last several years.

Foie gras en conserve: Fattened livers, whole or in pieces, that have been seasoned, then sterilized in a jar or can at 230 to 240°F (108 to 115°C). Requires no refrigeration. Carefully conserved, high-quality *foie gras* will actually ripen and improve with age. It should be stored in a cool, dry place and turned from time to time, and could be kept for up to ten years. A good buy when purchased from a reputable merchant.

Bloc de foie gras: By law, composed of either 50 percent fattened duck liver or 35 percent goose liver that must be obviously present in chunks, held together by *foie gras* that has been mechanically blended. Not the best buy, for there is also a 10 percent allowance for pork barding fat.

Foie gras truffé: Foie gras with at least 3 percent truffles. A bad buy, for the flavor of the expensive truffle is totally lost, the price greatly inflated.

Foie gras parfait: A mechanically mixed blend of usually mediocre-quality *foie gras* surrounded with stuffing of pork, veal, or chicken meat, then wrapped in barding fat. A bad buy.

Foie gras pâté, galantine, or *purée:* Various products with a base of *foie gras.* Usually composed of lowest-quality livers mixed with pork, chicken, or veal, surrounded by barding fat. The word *gras* may be missing, but the mixtures must contain a minimum of 50 percent *foie gras,* with added stuffing mixture and pork barding fat. A bad buy.

Chocolateries
CHOCOLATE SHOPS

The allure of chocolate.

The way the French fuss over chocolate, you might think they had invented it. They didn't, but as in so many matters gastronomic, they inspire envy. The French have refined the art of chocolate making, coaxing and coddling their bonbons into existence, working carefully until they've produced some of the smoothest, strongest, richest, most intoxicating, and flavorful candies to be found anywhere in the world.

The French chocolate-buying public is discriminating, and the *chocolatiers,* or chocolate makers, are fortunate to have a clientele willing to pay a premium price for confections made from the finest South American cocoa beans, the best Madagascar vanilla, the freshest Sicilian pistachios, the most expensive Dutch cocoa butter.

Before there was chocolate as we know it today—in bars and bonbons, taken as a snack or dessert—chocolate was prepared as a drink: a combination of roasted ground cocoa beans, sugar, cinnamon, and perhaps vanilla. As the brew became popular in Europe during the 17th century, it also became the subject of dispute. Was chocolate healthy? Was it lethal? Was it a dangerous aphrodisiac? The famous Madame de Sévigné wrote her daughter at the time: "It flatters you for a while, it warms you for an instant; then it kindles a mortal fever in you." But when her daughter moved from Paris, she worried about how she could "get along" without a *chocolatière,* or chocolate pot.

Paris's first chocolate shop—situated on Rue de l'Arbre-Sec in what is now the 1st *arrondissement*—was opened in 1659, when Louis XIV gave one of Queen Anne's officers the exclusive privilege to sell chocolate.

Chocolate soon became the rage of the French courts. It was served at least three times a week at Versailles, and it is said that Napoleon preferred chocolate to coffee as a morning pick-me-up. In Voltaire's later years, he consumed twelve cups a day, always between five in the morning and three in the afternoon. He lived to be eighty-four years old. Brillat-Savarin put it most concisely: "Chocolate is health."

And it was to that point that in the early 1800s two very clever Parisians figured a way around the still-raging dispute concerning the wholesomeness of chocolate. They sold it as medicine. A certain Monsieur Debauve, a *chocolatier,* and a Monsieur Gallais, a pharmacist, teamed up and opened an elegant shop at 30 Rue des Saints-Pères, just off the Boulevard Saint-Germain. Soon the nervous, the sickly, the thin, the obese, were going to Debauve & Gallais for "the chocolate treatment." It's no surprise to find that the chocolate preparations became bigger business than other pharmaceuticals, and Debauve & Gallais—still selling chocolates on the same spot today—soon became the most important chocolate shop in Paris.

Today in France, chocolate remains synonymous with *gourmandise* and comfort. But the French display a great deal of discipline when it comes to their beloved bonbons. They actually eat much less chocolate than their neighbors—the French consume about eleven pounds of chocolate per person per year, compared to twenty-two for the Swiss and fifteen for the Belgians (the Americans consume about nine pounds). But when they eat chocolate, they want plenty of it: 80 percent of all the chocolate sold in Paris is sold during the last three weeks of December!

BASTILLE

3rd and 11th arrondissements

PATISSERIE CLICHY
5 Boulevard Beaumarchais,
  Paris 3.
(48.87.89.88).
Métro: Bastille.
Open 9 A.M. to 7:30 P.M.
  Tuesday through
  Saturday; 8:30 A.M. to
  7 P.M. Sunday. Closed
  Monday.
Credit card: V.
English spoken.

Just a few steps from the Bastille, this popular old-fashioned pastry and chocolate shop also has a little tea salon in the back, for sampling their better-than-average *croissants* and *pains au chocolat,* or their chocolates, with a cup of rich black *express.* The chocolates to try here are the chunky, wonderful *mendiants,* palm-sized rounds of bittersweet chocolate filled with walnuts, hazelnuts, and gigantic raisins. At Eastertime, the whole neighborhood comes to admire chef Paul Bugat's windows, artfully arranged with hand-molded chocolate eggs and fish. Also, there are *marrons glacés* (candied chestnuts) in the fall and spectacular displays of *pâtes de fruits,* or jellied fruit, all year long.

LA PETITE FABRIQUE
12 Rue Saint-Sabin, Paris 11.
(48.05.82.02).
Métro: Bastille.
Open 10 A.M. to 1:30 P.M. and
  4 P.M. to 7:30 P.M. Closed
  Sunday and August.
Credit cards: EC, V.
Some English spoken.

A bright pink neon signs leads you to the door, and the rich, alluring aroma of chocolate calls you inside. This is a tiny shop offering a small, artisanal selection of good-quality chocolates. Try the huge *palet d'or,* deep, dark chocolate filled with cream and more chocolate; the satisfying praline-filled *rocher,* and the hearty *bûche,* a log of dark chocolate filled with bright green almond paste.

SÈVRES-BABYLONE, ECOLE MILITAIRE

6th and 7th arrondissements

DEBAUVE & GALLAIS
30 Rue des Saint-Pères,
  Paris 6.
(45.48.54.67).
Métro: Sèvres-Babylone.
Open 10 A.M. to 1 P.M. and
  2 P.M. to 7 P.M. Tuesday
  through Friday; 10 A.M.
  to 1 P.M. and 2 P.M. to 6
  P.M. Saturday. Closed
  Sunday, Monday, and the
  last week of July through
  the first week of
  September.

A little jewel—begun as a pharmacy that also dispensed chocolate—this shop has barely changed in 170 years. The sturdy pharmacy counter is now covered with glass amphoras filled with hazelnut pralines and chocolate truffles dusted with cocoa. The pharmacy shelves, flanking a huge mirror, now hold colorful tin containers filled with coffee and tea, both dispensed without prescription. And when the sun shines, it still cuts its way through the elegant *cosse d'orange* windows, arranged to form an elegant orange wedge. Like all Paris

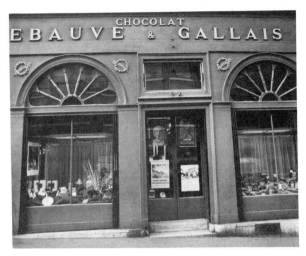

chocolate shops, Debauve & Gallais handle their wares like diamonds, wrapping each order, no matter how small, in bags decorated with gold seals and silver ribbons. Their chocolates are dark, intense, strong, and masculine. Here, flavor's the thing, not texture, for some chocolates are a bit grainy and sugary.

LENOTRE
44 Rue du Bac, Paris 7.
(42.22.39.39).
Métro: Rue du Bac.
Open 9 A.M. to 8 P.M. Monday
    through Saturday; 9 A.M.
    to 1 P.M. Sunday. Closed
    August.
Credit cards: AE, V.
English spoken.

Some of the most beautiful and ethereal chocolates in town. Ask for a 100-gram assortment and you'll find ten different chocolates, wonderfully aromatic, with a smooth and even texture. There's a good, strong burst of real chocolate flavor on the palate. The *palet d'or* and little triangles of *noisettes* (hazelnuts) are exceptional. See also Pâtisseries.

PUYRICARD
27 Avenue Rapp, Paris 7.
(47.05.59.47).
Métro: Ecole Militaire.
Open 9:30 A.M. to 1 P.M. and
    2 P.M. to 7:30 P.M. Closed
    Monday morning,
    Sunday, and August.

A sober, old-fashioned shop selling handmade chocolates from Aix-en-Provence—rich and creamy, with the intensity of good South American chocolate.

MADELEINE, ROND-POINT, ARC DE TRIOMPHE

8th and 9th arrondissements

LA BONBONNIERE SAINT AUGUSTIN
85 Boulevard Haussmann, Paris 8.
(42.65.33.18).
Métro: Saint-Augustin.
Open 9 A.M. to 7 P.M. Closed Sunday.
Credit card: V.

This pristine family-run shop near the major department stores is the sister boutique of the Bonbonnière de la Trinité (see page 263). It offers, of course, the same deep, dark, fresh-tasting chocolates, as well as a healthy assortment of packaged French regional candies, cakes, and cookies.

DALLOYAU
99-101 Rue du Faubourg Saint-Honoré, Paris 8.
(43.59.18.10).
Métro: Saint-Philippe-du-Roule.
Open 9:30 A.M. to 7:15 P.M. Monday through Saturday; 8:45 A.M. to 1:45 P.M. and 3 P.M. to 6:45 P.M. Sunday. From July 10 to August 25, closed Sunday afternoon and Monday.
Credit card: V.
English spoken.

Classic and creamy chocolates, all made in an impeccable workshop near the Opéra. The best are the cinnamon-and-praline-filled *El Dorado* and the smooth bittersweet-chocolate-covered caramels. This shop is old and traditional: Neighborhood matrons settle into cozy upholstered chairs while they wait for their pastries and boxes of chocolates to be wrapped. (See also Pâtisseries.)

LA MAISON DU CHOCOLAT
225 Rue du Faubourg Saint-Honoré, Paris 8.
(42.27.39.44).
Métro: Ternes.
Open 9:30 A.M. to 7 P.M. Closed Sunday, Monday, and the last week of July through the third week in August.
English spoken.

A chocolate-lover's dream: chocolate-colored facade, chocolate-colored blinds, even the *chocolatier* Robert Linxe in a chocolate-colored apron. You feel as though you'll gain a pound or two just walking into the shop. Monsieur Linxe is the undisputed king of chocolate in Paris, selling a sophisticated, handmade assortment made in the neat little basement workshop of this former wine and spirits shop. He's rightly proud of his *framboise* (raspberry-flavored chocolate), and his creamy *palet d'or* melts in your mouth. His latest creations include the caramel-butter-filled *rigoletto,* the superb milk chocolate *la bohème,* and *roméo,* with an interior flavored with fresh-brewed arabica coffee. There's also a good selection of wines, a fine and inexpensive house Champagne, and a remarkable choice of Armagnacs. (See also Vin, Bière, Alcool.)

**LA MAISON DU
   CHOCOLAT**
52 Rue François-ler, Paris 8.
(47.23.38.25).
Métro: Franklin-D.-
   Roosevelt.
Open 9:30 A.M. to 7:30 P.M.
   Closed Sunday.
See also page 259.

*Robert Linxe, chocolatier at La
Maison du Chocolat.*

Fans of Robert Linxe's shop on Rue du Faubourg
Saint-Honoré will be delighted to know about
his sister shop off the Champs-Elysées. Here, in a
cool, pristine, chocolate-hued boutique, chocolate
lovers can sit at the marble-topped bar or around
low round tables and indulge in one of the world's
greatest passions. One scorching day in summer I
was miraculously invigorated by a *Guayaquil frappé,*
a tall glass of iced chocolate, a whipped blend of
bitter chocolate ice cream and rich melted chocolate. The menu offers no less than five variously
flavored hot chocolates, chocolate *mousse, sorbets,* and
ice creams. The chocolate, pastries, and cakes can
be purchased to sample in the shop or to take
home. The diminutive menu offers a sampling of
appropriate gastronomic sayings, including a perti-
nent warning from Saint Ignatius of Loyola, founder
of the Jesuit order: "Gourmandise is a capital sin.
So therefore, my brothers, let us guard against
being gourmands. Let's be gourmets."

MARQUISE DE SEVIGNE
32 Place de la Madeleine,
Paris 8.
(42.65.19.47).
Métro: Madeleine.
Open 9:30 A.M. to 7 P.M.
Closed Sunday.
Credit cards: EC, V.
English spoken.

With a name like this, who could go wrong? A portrait of the famous Marquise de Sévigné—in all her abundance—appears on the chocolate box lids and on the gold-foil wrappers that envelop the shop's delicious pralines. Also sample the *coeur de Paris,* an almost solid heart of chocolate filled with a hazelnut and a touch of praline; and the fresh and creamy *palet,* dark chocolate filled with cream and chocolate.

CHOCOLATE FOR ALL SEASONS

In Paris, chocolate is always in fashion. Throughout the year, the sparkling windows of the city's chocolate shops serve as a calendar, announcing each holiday, beginning with Valentine's Day when thousands of chocolate hearts are broken.

Spring is ushered in as shop windows are aswim with chocolate fish in anticipation of *Poisson d'Avril,* April Fool's Day. Large fish with bows around their tails are filled with schools of *fritures,* tiny chocolate minnows. And little boxes filled with milk chocolate "sardines" appear everywhere.

At Eastertime chocolate bunnies, chicks, ducks, and puppies frolic in displays. They are surrounded by chocolate eggs wrapped with silvery, glittery, magical paper. On the Place de la Madeleine, Fauchon's huge, lacy chocolate egg sits in regal splendor, stopping pedestrian traffic for weeks.

Easter has hardly passed when tiny chocolate pots of *muguets,* lilies of the valley, appear as the traditional French symbol for the first of May. They keep company with the hearts and flowers that burst forth for *Fête des Mères,* Mother's Day.

Although the summer heat signals a slowdown for chocolates in Paris, chocolate shops refuse to give up. Windows are full of summer symbols, all nicely molded in chocolate—pails and shovels for playing in the sand, starfish, and shells.

Fall comes in with blustery days that announce the season for chocolate mushrooms and luscious, creamy truffles. All of this is a fanfare to Christmas, when chocolate shops split their attention between the candied chestnuts known as *marrons glacés* and *bûches de Noël,* or Christmas log cakes, homey reminders of times past, when guests offered their hosts a real log to keep the fire burning.

TANRADE
18 Rue Vignon, Paris 9.
(47.42.26.99).
Métro: Madeleine.
Open 9:15 A.M. to noon and
  1:30 P.M. to 6:30 P.M.
Closed Sunday, Monday,
and August.

A venerable establishment on Rue Vignon, Tanrade has been in business since 1820, and at its present location, just around the corner from Fauchon and the Place de la Madeleine food shops, for more than sixty years. (This is why we have included it in the 8th *arrondissement* listing.) There, in the shop's carefully preserved Art Deco interior, Pierre Tanrade makes chocolates exactly as generations of Tanrades have before him. The best are the *rochers*, little rounds of toasted almonds covered with chocolate. This firm is also known throughout the world for its *marrons glacés*, marvelous candied chestnuts, available only from November through February. Tanrade also specializes in *confitures*, or jams and jellies, which are made by hand in tiny batches in the same unlined copper basins they use to make their candied chestnuts. When visiting the shop, be sure to notice the frosted glass and black wrought iron chandeliers: Pierre Tanrade's grandmother designed them herself, working the outline of the Tanrade confiture pot into the design. (See also Spécialités Gastronomiques.)

TRINITÉ, LE PELETIER, GARE SAINT-LAZARE

9th arrondissement

**LA BONBONNIERE DE LA
  TRINITE**
4 Place d'Estienne-d'Orves,
  Paris 9.
(48.74.23.38).
Métro: Trinité.
Open 9:30 A.M. to 7 P.M.
  Closed Sunday.
Credit card: V.
Some English spoken.

A father-to-son operation since 1925, this cozy neighborhood shop offers fresh-flavored, intense chocolates, some decorated with dainty candied violets. The shop also offers dozens of varieties of teas, flavored honey, and tins of regional cakes and cookies.

*Fine chocolates listed in a fine
handwriting.*

LENOTRE
3 and 5 Rue du Havre,
    Paris 9.
(45.22.22.59).
Métro: Saint-Lazare.
Open 9:30 A.M. to 7 P.M.
    Tuesday through Friday;
    10 A.M. to 7 P.M. Saturday
    and Monday. Closed
    Sunday.
Credit card: V.
English spoken.
See Lenôtre, 7th
    arrondissement, page 258.

CANDIED CHESTNUTS

Candied chestnuts, *marrons glacés,* are fall and winter specialties sold at most of the better chocolate shops in town. They appear around the beginning of November, when the first fresh chestnuts begin arriving from the Ardèche, in southeastern France. They generally disappear at the close of the season, around the middle of January. The process of turning fresh raw chestnuts into little candied jewels is painstakingly slow, and requires immense patience.

The fresh chestnuts are first boiled several times to free them from their shells and skins. If any bits of skin remain, they are removed by hand. The chestnuts are then wrapped in cheesecloth to prevent them from falling apart during the next process—a three- to seven-hour stint in a pressure cooker. Next, they are cooked again, this time for 48 hours in a vanilla sugar syrup over very low heat. The chestnuts are often delivered to shops in this form, conserved in syrup. They are then glazed in small quantities by sprinkling them with water and baking them, a process which gives the chestnuts their characteristic sugary appearance. Finally they are wrapped in the traditional shiny gold foil paper.

A LA MERE DE FAMILLE
35 Rue du Faubourg
    Montmartre, Paris 9.
(47.70.83.69).
Métro: Le Peletier.
Open 8 A.M. to 1:30 P.M. and
    3 P.M. to 7 P.M. Closed
    Sunday, Monday
    morning, and August.
Credit cards: EC, V.
Some English spoken.

This shop comes right out of a fairy tale. Stop in at three in the afternoon, as the children are getting out of school, and watch the owners spoil the entire neighborhood with their incredible variety of sweets from all parts of France. In the chocolate department, sample the little *barquettes* of dark chocolate filled with *cassis* (black currant) or *framboise* (raspberry). (See also Spécialités Gastronomiques.)

VICTOR-HUGO

16th arrondissement

BOISSIER
184 Avenue Victor-Hugo,
    Paris 16.
(45.04.87.88).
Métro: Victor-Hugo.
Open 8 A.M. to 7 P.M. Monday
    through Friday; 9 A.M. to
    1 P.M. Saturday. Closed
    Sunday.
Credit card: V.

BOISSIER
45 Avenue Marceau,
    Paris 16.
(47.20.31.31).
Métro: Alma-Marceau.
Open 8 A.M. to 7 P.M. Monday
    through Friday; 9 A.M. to
    1 P.M. Saturday. Closed
    Sunday.
Credit card: V.

LENOTRE
49 Avenue Victor-Hugo,
    Paris 16.
(45.01.71.71).
Métro: Victor-Hugo.
Open daily, 9 A.M. to 9 P.M.
Credit card: V.
English spoken.
See Lenôtre, 7th
    arrondissement, page 258.

MARQUISE DE SEVIGNE
1 Place Victor-Hugo,
    Paris 16.
(45.00.89.68).
Métro: Victor-Hugo.
Open 9:30 A.M. to 7 P.M.
    Closed Sunday.
Credit card: V.
English spoken.
See Marquise de Sévigné,
    8th *arrondissement,* page
    261.

The discreet exterior suggests this is a bank, not a chocolate shop. Once inside, you know differently. Wander into Boissier, if only to admire the marble counter set with little trays of cakes and chocolates, looking as if someone is getting ready for a very exclusive bake sale. Many wealthy families in the neighborhood may have full-time cooks, but the woman of the house still comes in, personally, to carefully select the evening's dessert. The chocolates themselves are not terrific.

A bright, modern sister shop to the traditional chocolate shop on Victor-Hugo, offering beautifully presented chocolates and pastries, to sample in the upstairs tea room or to take with you.

CHOCOLATE SHOPS 265

Macarons Creoles
CHOCOLATE MACAROONS

One day I was exhausted and a friend suggested that what I needed was chocolate. Not just any chocolate, but something special from La Maison du Chocolat, one of the best chocolate shops in Paris. Fortunately, it just happens to be at the end of my street. I bought a chocolate-filled chocolate macaroon and was instantly cured. In gratitude and greed, I created this recipe the very next day, and have never found anyone who'd turn them down.

Macaroons:
1 cup (140 g) almonds
3 ½ ounces (110 g) bittersweet chocolate (preferably Lindt or Tobler brand)
1 teaspoon vanilla extract
2 large egg whites (2 ½ ounces; 80 g)
¾ cup (150 g) sugar
1 tablespoon (½ oz; 15 g) unsalted butter, for buttering the baking sheet

Filling:
1 ¾ ounces (50 g) bittersweet chocolate
2 tablespoons *crème fraîche* (see recipe, page 238) or heavy cream (preferably not ultra-pasteurized)

1. Preheat the oven to 275°F (135°C).

2. Toast the almonds on a baking sheet until browned, about 5 minutes. Remove, but leave the oven on. When cool, grind the almonds to a fine powder in a food processor.

3. In a small saucepan over very low heat, melt the 3 ½ ounces (110 g) chocolate with the vanilla.

4. In the bowl of an electric mixer on slow speed, mix the egg whites, almonds, and sugar until well blended. With the machine still running, add the melted chocolate mixture, and continue beating until thoroughly blended.

5. Butter a baking sheet (or line with cooking parchment paper, then butter the paper). Spoon the batter onto the baking sheet, allowing 1 heaping tablespoon of batter for each macaroon.

6. Bake just until the macaroons are set, 15 to 18 minutes. They should be slightly firm but not dry. Transfer the macaroons to a rack to cool.

7. Meanwhile, prepare the filling. In a small saucepan over very low heat, melt the 1 ¾ ounces (50 g) chocolate. Add the *crème fraîche* or heavy cream and stir until well blended. Set aside to cool.

8. When the macaroons and the filling have cooled, spread a heaping tablespoon of the filling on half the macaroons, and cover each with a second macaroon, making a sort of sandwich. The macaroons may be served immediately, though they are best if they sit for a few hours.

Yield: 10 to 12 filled macaroons.

Spécialités Gastronomiques
SPECIALTY SHOPS

The exotic world of Izraël (see entry, page 269).

The specialty shops of Paris, ranging from old-fashioned, family-owned candy and spice shops to slick and rambling food emporiums, offer a potpourri of good things at your fingertips. Whether you're looking for the best caviar or the freshest black truffle; whether you plan to indulge in thirty different kinds of honey or would like to sample a peanut-flavored mustard; or whether you just want to purchase a little sack of licorice as you wander about Paris, the following should offer some guidance. From the exotic to the commonplace, here is a hint of the things of which dreams are made.

PALAIS-ROYAL, LES HALLES, BOURSE, OPERA

1st and 2nd arrondissements

LE COQ SAINT-HONORE
22 Rue Gomboust, Paris 1.
(42.61.52.04).
Métros: Opéra or Pyramides.
Open 8 A.M. to 1:30 P.M. and 4:30 P.M. (5:30 on Fridays) to 7 P.M. Closed Saturday afternoon and Sunday.
Credit card: V.
English spoken.

Even if you aren't going to buy, wander past this incredible butcher shop—perhaps the best in Paris—to press your nose against the glass. If it's poultry or meat and grows in France, you'll find it here: baby lamb from the southwest and salt-marsh lamb from the Atlantic coast; beautiful chickens from Bresse, the Landes, and Périgord; farm-raised turkeys, Challans ducks, and in season, fabulous

SPECIALTIES:
Meat and poultry.

French game. Monsieur André-Mary Josse, the owner, is a charming man and runs a serious shop; his clients include all the best chefs in Paris.

PAUL CORCELLET
46 Rue des Petits-Champs,
    Paris 2.
(42.96.51.82).
Métros: Opéra or Pyramides.
Open 11 A.M. to 7 P.M.
    Monday; 9:30 A.M. to
    7 P.M. Tuesday through
    Saturday. Closed Sunday.
Credit cards: AE, V.
Some English spoken.

SPECIALTIES:
Teas, honeys, vinegars, mustards,
syrups, and spices.

Imagine, sixty varieties of tea, fifteen kinds of honey, twenty-five varieties of vinegar, and more than twenty-five different mustards (even a peanut-flavored version inspired by former President Carter). Along with all this you get Paul Corcellet himself—robust, rotund, and indefatigable. He'll probably introduce his friendly wife, invite you to sample a drink in the shop, then share with you his latest discovery, be it a new cocktail or a new mustard. Corcellet remains faithful to exotic fare: He first opened in 1934, specializing in North African spices and produce, and still sells a wide assortment of exotic syrups and spices. Many products are available in miniature containers, handy for sampling and for traveling.

FLO PRESTIGE
42 Place du Marché-Saint-
    Honoré, Paris 1.
(42.61.45.46).
Métros: Opéra or Pyramides.
Open daily, 8 A.M. to
    midnight.
Credit cards: AE, DC, EC, V.
English spoken.

SPECIALTIES:
Carry-out foods perfect for
picnickers.

One of Paris's more trustworthy carry-out food shops, offering a bright and fresh selection of raw-milk cheeses, beautiful smoked salmon, assorted *charcuterie, foie gras,* and salads. Everything can be purchased in individual portions (there's even bread by the slice), so put together a picnic and head for the Tuileries Gardens. Wine and pastries are also available.

GARGANTUA
284 Rue Saint-Honoré,
    Paris 1.
(42.60.63.38).
Métros: Tuileries.
Open 8 A.M. to 7:30 P.M.
    Closed Sunday.
Credit cards: AE, V.
English spoken.

SPECIALTIES:
Large-size pastries and carry-out
charcuterie.

As the name suggests, everything here is king-size. Enjoy quality *croissants, pains au chocolat,* and oversize puff pastry *palmiers,* all big enough to feed a family of four, at the small counter tucked in back of the shop. The place is casual and colorful, with a wide selection of *charcuterie,* wines, liquors, and salads, ready to take home, on a picnic, or on a plane.

LUCIEN LEGRAND
1 Rue de la Banque, Paris 2.
(42.60.07.12).
Métro: Bourse.
Open 10 A.M. to 7 P.M.
  Monday; 8:30 A.M. to
  7:30 P.M. Tuesday through
  Saturday. Closed Sunday
  and two weeks in August.
Credit card: V.
English spoken.

SPECIALTIES:
Wonderful selection of wines,
spices, and candies.

There have been few cosmetic changes here since 1890, when this combination wine shop and *épicerie* (grocery) began selling mustard and lentils, wine by the barrel, lamp oil, and the dozens upon dozens of multicolored sweets and bonbons now displayed outdoors in huge glass containers. Today, the beautiful Belle Epoque facade remains, while inside Legrand serves as one of the city's better wine shops, with more than a touch of character and history. Monsieur Legrand is a born storyteller, a source of wisdom about old Paris as well as wine.

PETIT QUENAULT
(Vieux Vins de France)
56 Rue Jean-Jacques-
  Rousseau, Paris 1.
(42.33.46.85).
Métro: Les Halles.
Open 9 A.M. to 12:30 P.M. and
  2 P.M. to 7 P.M. Tuesday
  through Friday; 9 A.M. to
  noon and 3 P.M. to 7 P.M.
  Saturday. Closed Sunday,
  and Monday morning.
Credit card: V.

SPECIALTIES:
Wild mushrooms, chocolate, and
spices in bulk.

Petit Quenault is a simple, matter-of-fact restaurant supply house, selling everying from Heinz catsup to bouillon cubes. But the shop is also open to individuals, and this is the place to go to stock up on quantities of dried wild mushrooms, including *cèpes* and *morilles*. Their prices are among the lowest in town. Also try the Le Pecq baking chocolate, the brand preferred by many of Paris's pastry chefs.

**TETREL EPICERIE/
  CONFISERIE**
44 Rue des Petits-Champs,
  Paris 2.
(42.96.59.58).
Métro: Pyramides.
Open 9 A.M. to 7:30 P.M.
  Closed Sunday.

SPECIALTIES:
Old-fashioned candies.

Apristine little shop for fine foodstuffs, the polished wood counters and sparkling windows all crowded with tins of candies, *confit,* and sardines. This is a good place to experience old Paris and pick up some old-fashioned sweets or a small gift reminiscent of the 19th century.

VERLET
256 Rue Saint-Honoré,
  Paris 1.
(42.60.67.39).
Métro: Palais-Royal.
Open 9 A.M. to 7 P.M. Closed
  Sunday, Monday, and
  August.
English spoken.

SPECIALTIES:
A fine selection of coffees and teas.

For common and uncommon coffees and teas, fresh from the world over. Stop in after a walk along the Rue de Rivoli for a pick-me-up in the homey, aromatic little lunch room. They serve a good *croque-monsieur* and fine fresh desserts. (See also Salons de Thé).

MARAIS

4th arrondissement

IZRAEL
30 Rue François-Miron,
  Paris 4.
(42.72.66.23).
Métro: Saint-Paul.
Open 9:30 A.M. to 1 P.M. and
  2:30 P.M. to 7 P.M. Tuesday
  through Friday; 9:30 A.M.
  to 7 P.M. Saturday. Closed
  Sunday, Monday, and
  August.
Credit cards: EC, V.
English spoken.

SPECIALTIES:
*North African products and also
foods imported from throughout the
world.*

Some years ago, a friendly, robust man named Israël married a woman named Izraël, hence the name of the shop. That doesn't quite make him Israël Izraël, but he does have a great sense of humor about it. The shop opened nearly fifty years ago, specializing in North African products. Today, the cluttered, delicious-smelling store features more than 3,000 products from all over the world, everything from guava paste to Fritos, delicious Polish buckwheat to woven African baskets. There's a marvelous assortment of grains, rice, flours, dried fruits, and nuts, sold out of giant sacks.

A L'OLIVIER
23 Rue de Rivoli, Paris 4.
(48.04.86.59).
Métros: Saint-Paul or Hôtel-de-Ville.
Open 9:30 A.M. to 7 P.M.
    Closed Sunday and Monday.
Credit card: V.
Some English spoken.

SPECIALTIES:
Oils of all kinds and for all purposes.

This bright old-fashioned shop offers every kind of oil imaginable, from olive, walnut, and hazelnut for the table to palm oil for frying and almond oil for massages. Although the quality of the oil is not extraordinary, the nicely packaged products make fine gifts.

LATIN QUARTER, SAINT-GERMAIN, SEVRES-BABYLONE, INVALIDES
5th, 6th, and 7th arrondissements

HEDIARD
126 Rue du Bac, Paris 6.
(45.44.01.98).
Métro: Sèvres-Babylone.
Open 9:15 A.M. to 7:30 P.M.
    Closed Sunday.
Credit cards: AE, EC, V.
See Hédiard, 8th
    arrondissement, page 275.

SARDINES

Decades ago, most self-respecting French gourmands tucked tins of fine and delicate Brittany sardines away in their *caves* (cellars), sometimes aging the tender little fish for a decade or more. Vintage, or *millésime,* sardines are again the rage in Paris, where most fine specialty shops offer a mixed assortment, tinned and carefully dated. Once they're taken home, the tins must be stored in a cool spot and turned every three or four months. As the unctuous, chewy sardines age, they become softer, more refined and delicate, ready to be consumed with a slice of crusty bread.

Sardines destined for *millésime* stardom bear no resemblance to the cheap garden-variety canned fish. Vintage sardines are always preserved fresh, while most ordinary sardines are frozen, then fried and processed. To prepare vintage sardines for processing, the fish are usually washed, grilled, and quickly deep-fried before being packed, by hand, into small oval tins. Generally the head, skin, and central backbone are removed from sardines packed for aging. Oil—usually the finest virgin olive oil—is added, perhaps a touch of spice or simply salt, then the tins are sealed and stored. They are turned regularly to ensure even aging, then put on the market one or two years after processing.

Many tins of vintage sardines include the words *première catégorie* or *extra* on the label, assuring that the sardines were prepared fresh, not frozen. Check for the processing date stamped into the bottom of the tin, so you know how long to keep them. Experts recommend the sardines be kept no more than four years.

The following are just a few of the shops offering vintage sardines. The tin or wrapper will bear the processing date.

Hédiard, 21 Place de la Madeleine, Paris 8. (42.66.44.36).

Fauchon, 26 Place de la Madeleine, Paris 8. (47.42.60.11).

Soleil de Provence, 6 Rue du Cherche-Midi, Paris 6. (45.48.15.02).

Au Verger de la Madeleine, 4 Boulevard Malesherbes, Paris 8. (42.65.51.99).

**LES HERBES DU
    LUXEMBOURG**
3 Rue du Médicis, Paris 6.
(43.26.91.53).
Métros: Luxembourg or
    Odéon.
Open 9:30 A.M. to 7:30 P.M.
    Tuesday through Friday;
    11 A.M. to 7:30 P.M.
    Saturday. Closed Sunday.
Credit card: V.
English spoken.

SPECIALTIES:
Herbs, teas, organic grains, oils.

I like to call this shop the health food general store. It offers everything from dried herbs and oils, fruits and nuts, honeys, *confitures,* and fresh whole-grain breads each Wednesday, to organic baby foods and teas, all with an eye toward health and well-being. Some special items of note: the line of L'Olivier oils, sea salt from Brittany, an assortment of miniature soaps, shampoos, and toiletries for travel, and lily- or cedar-scented paper for lining drawers.

THE GENERAL STORE
82 Rue de Grenelle, Paris 7.
(45.48.63.16).
Métro: Bac.
Open 10 A.M. to 7 P.M. Closed
    Sunday.
Credit cards: AE, DC, V.
English spoken.

SPECIALTIES:
Packaged specialty products from America, as well as home-baked American sweets and pastries.

After sampling your fill of caviar, *foie gras, croissants,* and chocolate truffles, if what you're really craving is Hershey bars and corn chips, brownies, and chocolate chips, this shop is the ticket to your dreams. The General Store is a sparkling boutique full of star-spangled goodies, all cheaper than a one-way ticket to America.

MAISON WOERLI
36 Rue Saint-André-des-
    Arts, Paris 6.
(43.26.89.49).
Métro: Saint-Michel.
Open 8 A.M. to 8 P.M. Closed
    Sunday, Monday, and
    August.

SPECIALTIES:
Assorted candy.

An authentic, old-fashioned neighborhood *épicerie* (grocery), with dozens of glass jars lined up outside, filled with mysterious sweets. Even if your purchase of licorice amounts to a few francs, the friendly shop owner will carefully select each piece with little tongs, as though you were buying diamonds. Candy shops such as Woerli are disappearing, so go before this remnant of Paris's past is no more.

PETROSSIAN
18 Boulevard La Tour-
   Maubourg, Paris 7.
(45.51.59.73).
Métro: Invalides.
Open 9 A.M. to 1 P.M. and
   2:30 P.M. to 7 P.M. Closed
   Sunday and Monday.
English spoken.

SPECIALTIES:
*The finest Russian caviar, plus
high-quality smoked salmon, foie
gras, and truffles.*

As Christian Petrossian says, "We sell dreams." And dreams are made of Russian caviar, smoked salmon, *foie gras,* truffles, and Sauternes. Everything here is of high quality, but the prices are competitive. I rarely buy caviar anywhere else in Paris—Christian himself makes regular trips to the Caspian Sea to monitor its processing. Other specialties in this elegant, well-appointed shop include Russian pastries, fresh blinis, assorted herring, vodka, and delicious black Georgian tea, along with Petrossian's own line of French products from the Périgord.

SOLEIL DE PROVENCE
6 Rue du Cherche-Midi,
   Paris 6.
(45.48.15.02).
Métro: Sèvres-Babylone.
Open 9:45 A.M. to 7 P.M.
   Closed Sunday, Monday,
   and August.
Some English spoken.

SPECIALTIES:
*Olives, olive oil, honey, herbs, and
soap.*

Make a special detour and come here for the first-rate olives, olive oil, and honey shipped direct from Paul Tardieu's organic farm in Provence. The olives are the best cured black olives France has to offer, and the light, fruity oil is first pressed, virgin. Just ask for Monsieur Tardieu's products under his name. The shop also sells a variety of oils out of giant metal vats, along with dried Provençal herbs and refreshing soaps.

TOUTOUNE
   GOURMANDE
7 Rue de Pontoise, Paris 5.
(43.25.35.93).
Métro: Maubert-Mutualité.
Open daily, 10 A.M. to 10 P.M.
Credit card: V.
English spoken.

SPECIALTIES:
*Carry-out charcuterie and
pastries, packaged delicacies.*

Charming, outgoing Colette Dejean has opened a tiny boutique right next to her popular Left Bank bistro, Chez Toutoune, so customers can carry out many of her delightful specialties. Among them, an earthy homemade *boudin* blood sausage and superb apple tart, as well as many packaged specialty items, including unusual mustards, honeys, *confitures,* and *cornichons.*

CHAMPS-ELYSEES, MADELEINE, LE PELETIER

8th and 9th arrondissements

CAVIAR KASPIA
17 Place de la Madeleine,
    Paris 8.
(42.65.33.52).
Métro: Madeleine.
Open 9:30 A.M. to 12:30 A.M.
    Closed Sunday.
Credit cards: AE, DC, V.
English spoken.

SPECIALTIES:
Caviar, smoked salmon, assorted smoked fish, blinis.

A neat, simple little boutique on the Place de la Madeleine, offering an excellent assortment of quality caviar, superb smoked salmon, and delightfully fresh blinis to take with you. There is also a nice informal restaurant upstairs, where you can sample the house specialties on the spot. (See also Restaurants.)

The window display at Fauchon.

FAUCHON
26 Place de la Madeleine,
    Paris 8.
(47.42.60.11).
Métro: Madeleine.
Open 9:40 A.M. to 7 P.M.
    Closed Sunday.
Credit cards: AE, DC, EC, V.
English spoken.

SPECIALTIES:
International selection of over 20,000 products, including imported exotic fruits and vegetables.

A visit to Fauchon is better than going to the theater. Many people even find their two shops on the Place de la Madeleine more fascinating than the Louvre. Fauchon's pristine glass windows, filled with expensive and exotic fruits and vegetables from every corner of the world, still stop traffic. Even the most jaded palates are tempted by the sheer quantity of food: more than 20,000 products including pastries, chocolates, a mammoth international selection of fresh and packaged goods, coffee, tea, spices, and a complete *charcuterie*. The famous pastry shop—with little tables for stand-up snacking—is always bustling. Certainly the best-known food shop in town, but not always the friendliest, not always the best.

At Fauchon, choosing is never easy.

HEDIARD
21 Place de la Madeleine,
    Paris 8.
(42.66.44.36).
Métro: Madeleine.
Open 9:15 A.M. to 7:30 P.M.
    Closed Sunday.
Credit cards: AE, DC.
English spoken.

SPECIALTIES:
Hédiard brand spices, oils,
vinegars, teas and coffees.

Tea, spice, everything nice, and more, Hédiard is one of the best shows in town, with one-stop shopping for everything from their famous spices to exotic blends of vinegar or oil. Many visitors make annual visits just to stock up on a few of Hédiard's thirty varieties of tea; also, their freshly roasted coffee beans are top quality. The wine cellar offers an extensive selection of Bordeaux at high prices.

LA MAISON DU MIEL
24 Rue Vignon, Paris 9.
(47.42.26.70).
Métro: Madeleine.
Open 9:30 A.M. to 7 P.M.
    Closed Sunday.
Some English spoken.

SPECIALTIES:
Unique varieties of honey (miel)
and honey products.

Even if you're not passionate about honey, put this shop on your list. The "House of Honey" is one of the few stores in the world devoted totally to honey and honey products, and it's been at Rue Vignon since 1908. The fantasylike tile decor—buzzing with bees and colorful hives—has not changed since then, nor has the founding family, the Gallands. They tend their own hives throughout France and buy selectively around the world. They sell some fifty-three tons of honey a year, producing about one-fourth of it themselves. Personal favorites include the hearty, rust-toned heather *(bruyère)*, and the delicate, mellow linden tree blossom *(tilleul)*. Sample tastings are offered in the shop, and most varieties are available in miniature jars, allowing one to sample several. Unfortunately, service can be cold and unfriendly. Honey-based soaps and health products are also sold.

*L*e Grand Véfour, near the Palais Royal, was the domain of the writer Colette, who lived just a few yards away. In later years her rheumatism kept her from walking, but about once a month the owner carried her in his arms to her regular seat, that had also been that of Napoleon's Josephine. Her menu was as constant as the seasons allowed, usually oysters and small stuffed birds, namely thrush, boned, stuffed with foie gras, and cooked in a slipper of pastry.

TRUFFLES

*D*elicate, earthy, and increasingly rare, the prized black Périgord truffle symbolizes the grand gastronomic life of Paris, past and present. The writer Colette, who devoted one day each year to eating truffles, said it best: "If I can't have too many truffles, I'll do without truffles."

The Périgord truffle—in appearance a rather inelegant, wrinkled black nugget generally the size of a walnut, although it can be as small as a pea or as large as an orange—is perhaps the world's most mysterious food. A fungus with a capricious personality, it stubbornly refuses to be cultivated. (As one Frenchman observed, "Growing truffles is not farming, it's luck.") And its flavor is just as elusive. No one has succeeded in adequately describing the taste of a truffle. Some say it's licoricelike, others find a hint of black pepper. As with many highly aromatic foods, it is the truffle's rich, pungent, and pervasive aroma that makes its flavor so singular. Eating fresh truffles makes me think of a quiet walk in the autumn woods under a slow drizzle; of freshly upturned black earth, of hazelnuts; of luxury, and pleasure.

The traditional truffle comes primarily from the southwest of France, in the Quercy and Périgord regions east of Bordeaux, though in recent years the crop has been slowly moving farther south. Truffles are also found in the Tricastin area of the Rhône Valley, and a small quantity of the truffles processed in France come from Italy and Spain.

Truffles grow three inches to a foot underground, in stony, porous soil near the roots of scrub oak trees. Gathered from November to March by farmers using dogs or pigs trained to scent out and unearth the elusive tuber, the truffle reaches its peak of flavor toward the month of January. Truffles thrive on a rainy summer and autumn, and their presence sometimes can be spotted by the burned patch around the base of the tree—the truffle's way of ensuring enough air for itself by killing the undergrowth—or by the presence of a swarm of truffle flies that hover above where the tuber is growing.

Fresh truffles *(truffes fraîches)*, are sold in Paris specialty shops from mid-November through

March. An average-size fresh truffle weighs about 3 ounces, or about 100 grams, and though one truffle can't be considered an avalanche, it's enough for a gastronomic adventure.

At Paris's La Maison de la Truffe, which sells more than 600 pounds (about 300 kilos) of fresh and preserved truffles each year, fresh truffles arrive every two or three days from November to April direct from the Périgord or the Vaucluse. Still encrusted with soil, the fragant gems are placed unwrapped in small wicker baskets, so they can breathe during the four-to five-hour train ride. A fresh truffle will last only three or four days, losing about one-twentieth of its weight by evaporation each day after it is unearthed. Meanwhile, its flavor fades rapidly. Guy Monier, owner of La Maison de la Truffe, suggests that if a fresh truffle must be kept longer than three or four days, it should be gently washed, then buried in goose or duck fat and refrigerated; otherwise it is likely to mildew. It may be stored in fat for up to six months. A fresh truffle can also be refrigerated for two or three days, locked tight in a glass jar with several raw eggs still in their shells. The pungent truffle aroma will permeate the eggs, which can then be used to prepare a truffle-laced omelet, perhaps the best way to first experience a truffle.

For most of the world, the only known truffle is a preserved one. Although fresh is best, well-preserved truffles are better than no truffles at all. What does one look for in buying a preserved truffle? First, only but truffles in a glass container, so you can see what you are getting, and buy only:

Truffes brossées au naturel: truffles that have been sterilized in water and salt, with no alcohol or spices used to mask or heighten their flavor. For the closest thing to a fresh truffle, try the whole preserved *truffe extra,* the top-grade truffle that is uniformly black and firm. If available, ask for a truffle of *premier ébullition,* that is, a truffle that has been brushed, salted, placed in its container, then sterilized. Since a truffle loses 25 percent of its weight during cooking, the weight of the *première ébullition* truffle cannot be verified on the label. Thus, processors are required to underestimate on the label the true weight of the truffle. Most common are truffles of *deuxième ébullition.* In this process the truffle is sterilized, removed from its container to verify its weight, then resterilized. All preserved truffles should be consumed within three years of being processed.

The following are other truffle gradings and other truffle preparations found on the market:

Truffes premier choix: small, irregularly shaped truffles that are more like pieces than whole truffles, and are more or less black.

Truffes en morceaux: broken pieces of truffle that must be at least ¼-inch (5-mm) thick. Considered equal in quality to *premier choix,* and generally lower in price.

Truffes en pelures: truffle peelings or shavings. Generally not worth the price.

Truffes préparées: truffles sterilized in water and salt, with liquor, alcohol, or wine added. A bad buy.

Jus de truffe: truffle juice. Not worth the price.

LA MAISON DE LA TRUFFE
19 Place de la Madeleine, Paris 8.
(42.65.53.22).
Métro: Madeleine.
Open 9 A.M. to 8 P.M. Closed Sunday.
Credit cards: AE. DC, EC, V.
English spoken.

SPECIALTIES:
Truffles (truffes), plus foie gras and charcuterie.

From November to March, come for the best fresh truffles to be found in Paris. Year-round, there are preserved truffles, goose and duck *foie gras,* exotic fruit, smoked salmon, a variety of *charcuterie,* and a respected assortment of wines and liqueurs.

A LA MERE DE FAMILLE
35 Rue du Faubourg Montmartre, Paris 9.
(47.70.83.69).
Métro: Le Peletier.
Open 8 A.M. to 1:30 P.M. and 3 P.M. to 7 P.M. Closed Sunday, Monday morning, and August.
Credit cards: EC, V.
English spoken.

SPECIALTIES:
A fine selection of candies and jams.

Walking into this spotless, sparkling candy shop—which dates back to 1791—is like wandering into the midst of a *naïf* painting. The window display and exterior are worth a trip on their own: the colorful, decorative boxes of bonbons, sugar candies, biscuits, and jams change with the seasons, but there's always a sense of organized clutter, inside and out. You'll find products from all over France, including the famous Madeleines de Commercy and caramel-coated Pralines de Montargis. (See also Chocolateries.)

TANRADE

18 Rue Vignon, Paris 9.
(47.42.26.99).
Métro: Madeleine.
Open 9:15 A.M. to noon and
1:30 P.M. to 6:30 P.M.
Closed Sunday, Monday,
and August.

S P E C I A L T I E S :
Candied chestnuts (marrons
glacés) and assorted sweets.

A jewel of a shop, still run by the friendly, outgo-ing Tanrade family. From November to Febru-ary lovers of *marrons glacés* stream out the door, as Tanrade offers some of the best and freshest can-died chestnuts in Paris. There are also fifty kinds of bonbons, fine chocolates, and revered *confitures* (jams). (See also Chocolateries.)

ARC DE TRIOMPHE, TROCADERO

16th and 17th arrondissements

FLO PRESTIGE

61 Avenue de la Grand-
    Armée, Paris 16.
(45.00.12.10).
Métro: Argentine.
Open daily, 7 A.M. to
    midnight.
Credit cards: AE, DC, V.
See Flo Prestige, 1st
    arrondissement, page 267.

HEDIARD

70 Avenue Paul-Doumer,
    Paris 16.
(45.04.51.92).
Métro: Muette.
Open 9:15 A.M. to 7:30 P.M.
    Closed Sunday.
Credit cards: AE, EC, V.
See Hédiard, 8th
    arrondissement, page 275.

CORNICHONS
TINY TART PICKLES

The cornichon, *a tiny tart pickle, is ubiquitous in France.* Cornichons *arrive at the table in squat white crocks, ready to be served with pâtés,* rillettes, *slices of salty country ham, or with pot-au-feu. The first time I made cornichons was in New York City. Picking through a bin full of garden-fresh cucumbers at the farmer's market on Union Square, I was able to come up with enough tiny cucumbers to make one precious quart. Now, frankly, I'm spoiled, for each August, the fresh cucumbers appear in abundance in Paris's open-air markets, ready for "putting up" with tiny white onions and plenty of fresh tarragon. I like them spicy and hot, so I add plenty of garlic and hot peppers.*

60 to 70 2-inch (5-cm) pickling cucumbers (about 2 pounds; 1 kg)

¼ cup (65 g) coarse (kosher) salt

1 quart (1 liter) cold water, plus an additional 1½ cups (375 ml)

3 cups (750 ml) best-quality white wine vinegar

1 tablespoon sugar

12 small white pickling onions, peeled but with ends intact

4 large sprigs fresh tarragon

6 cloves garlic, peeled

8 small hot red peppers (fresh or dried)

½ teaspoon whole black peppercorns

2 bay leaves

1. Trim off stem ends of the cucumbers, then rinse and drain. In a large bowl combine the salt with 1 quart (1 liter) water. Stir until the salt is dissolved, add the cucumbers, and let stand in a cool place for 6 hours.

2. Scald two 1-quart (1-liter) canning jars, lids, and rings with boiling water and drain well.

3. Drain the cucumbers, discarding the salted water.

4. In a medium-size saucepan over medium heat combine the vinegar, 1½ cups (375 ml) water, and the sugar, and bring to a boil.

5. Layer the jars with the drained cucumbers, the onions, herbs, and spices, making sure to divide the ingredients evenly between the jars.

6. Pour the boiling vinegar, water, and sugar mixture into the jars, letting a bit of the liquid overflow the jars; this helps seal the lids well. Wipe the rim of each jar and seal. Let stand until cool. Store in a cool place for at least three weeks before serving. Refrigerate after opening.

Yield: 2 quarts (2 liters) *cornichons.*

MONTMARTRE

18th arrondissement

LEPIC-SUR-MER
10 Rue Lepic, Paris 18.
(46.06.15.18).
Métros: Blanche or
  Abbesses.
Open 8 A.M. to 12:30 P.M. and
  4 P.M. to 7:30 P.M. Closed
  Sunday afternoon and
  Monday.

SPECIALTIES:
Fish, fresh and cured.

The one spot in Paris where you are likely to find authentic French anchovies from Collioure, the Catalan village that's considered the French anchovy capital. Since anchovies are rare, they're not always in stock here—but when they are, you can be sure of quality. Try the Roque brand anchovies cured in olive oil or in vinegar, sold whole or in fillets.

Vin, Bière, Alcool
WINE, BEER, AND
LIQUOR SHOPS

Wine, an indispensable part of a meal.

In Paris, wine and liquor shops are not designed for popping in and out of quickly. Like almost everything gastronomic in France, wine is selected with great care, after conversation and contemplation. Wine shop owners are much like restaurant *sommeliers*. Passionate about their chosen field, they love to discuss, to advise, to help clients select a perfect little wine for a perfect little meal. Many of the shops listed here are small and specialized, reflecting the personal tastes of their owners. They are not wine supermarkets, so don't expect to find an infinite selection. Rather, think of each visit as a step toward a greater understanding, and appreciation, of wines and spirits.

PALAIS-ROYAL, LES HALLES, OPERA, BOURSE
1st, 2nd, and 4th arrondissements

JEAN DANFLOU
36 Rue du Mont-Thabor
(at the back of the
courtyard, second floor),
Paris 1.
(42.61.51.09).
Métro: Concorde.
Open 8 A.M. to 1 P.M. and
2 P.M. to 6 P.M. Closed
Saturday, Sunday, and the
first two weeks of August.
Credit cards: AE, DC, V.
English spoken.

Set aside a long and languid afternoon for sampling the wide assortment of Jean Danflou's fine fruit-based liqueurs, Calvados, Armagnac, and Cognac. This is a wine and spirits shop, yes, but also an elegant, friendly tasting salon set in a tiny apartment just off the Rue de Rivoli. Jean Danflou, nephew of the man who founded the Paris-based company in 1925, is warm and welcoming, offering sample after sample of his exquisite, clear *eaux-de-vie*, including a fine Poire William, made only from the freshest Rhône Valley pears. (More than 16 pounds of fruit go into preparing each bottle of Danflou's Poire William.) Sample, too, the raspberry *(framboise)*, cherry *(kirsch)*, yellow plum *(mirabelle)*, and purple plum *(quetsch)* liqueurs, all distilled east of Paris, in the Vosges. Along with the tasting, you will learn some history and take a lesson in *eau-de-vie* etiquette (drink it at room temperature, not chilled, but from a chilled glass). Call or stop by for an appointment.

LA GALERIE DES VINS
201 Rue Saint-Honoré,
Paris 1.
(42.61.81.20).
Métro: Palais-Royal.
Open 10 A.M. to 12:45 P.M.
and 2 P.M. to 7 P.M. Closed
Monday and Sunday.
Credit cards: AE, DC, EC, V.
English spoken.

An eclectic assortment of new and old vintages, particularly red Bordeaux, in everything from half-bottles to magnums and double magnums. Worth a stop if you're in the neighborhood.

GAMBRINUS
13-15 Rue des Blancs-
Manteaux, Paris 4.
(48.87.81.92).
Métro: Rambuteau.
Open 11 A.M. to 1:30 P.M. and
3 P.M. to 8 P.M. (until
10 P.M. on Wednesday).
Opens at 9 A.M. on
Saturday. Closed Sunday,
and Monday morning.
Credit card: V.

More than 400 brands of beer from thirty-four different countries, for collectors, connoisseurs, or those just interested in a frothy bottle of beer.

LUCIEN LEGRAND
1 Rue de la Banque, Paris 2.
(42.60.07.12).
Métro: Bourse.
Open 10 A.M. to 7 P.M.
   Monday; 8:30 A.M. to
   7:30 P.M. Tuesday through
   Saturday. Closed Sunday
   and two weeks in August.
Credit card: V.
English spoken.

There are at least two reasons to go out of your way to visit this lovely, well-stocked wine shop. One reason, of course, is the carefully chosen selection of French wines (many from small, independent growers) and alcohols. The other is to examine the perfectly retained decor of this 19th-century *épicerie fine,* packed to the ceiling with candies, coffees, teas, and chocolates. Monsieur Legrand's selection of Laberdolive brand Armagnac is remarkable. (See also Spécialités Gastronomiques.)

THE QUINTESSENTIAL
WINE GLASS

Getting the most out of a good wine involves more than just uncorking the bottle and pouring it into a glass. If the wine is good enough to merit attention, it merits a special wine glass for tasting. The Institut National des Appellations d'Origine (I.N.A.O.) in Paris responded to this need by designing what it considers the perfect tasting glass, as complementary to the wine as it is agreeable to the taster.

The glass has a wide base, a short stem, and an elongated egg-shaped cup that embraces the wine, carefully guarding its bouquet. Made of lead crystal, it is simple and undecorated, holding 1 cup (25 cl).

What are the qualities of a good wine glass? It should allow the wine to breathe without losing its strength; to develop without becoming faint; and it must permit the wine to show its deep, rich colors with no cuttings or etchings to interfere. The stem should be long enough to allow the wine to be swirled without being warmed by one's hand, and the bowl itself should be longer than it is wide, so the bouquet is gently contained.

The I.N.A.O. glass is available in Paris at L'Esprit et Le Vin, 65 Boulevard Malesherbes, Paris 8 (45.22.60.40), and at Simon, 36 Rue Etienne-Marcel, Paris 2 (42.33.71.65).

**LUCIEN LEGRAND FILLES
ET FILS**
12 Galerie Vivienne, Paris 2.
(42.60.07.12).
Métro: Bourse.
Open 9 A.M. to 12:30 P.M. and
2 P.M. to 7 P.M. Tuesday
through Friday; 9 A.M. to
1 P.M. and 3 P.M. to 7 P.M.
Saturday. Closed Sunday
and Monday. Dates for
closing in August not
fixed.
Credit card: V.
English spoken.

While family members tend to the front of the shop, the outgoing, chatty Lucien Legrand still manages to spend some time in the "back shop," offering a select assortment of French wines by the case: The choice is small, but prices are fair. Many wines can be tasted on the spot.

Latin Quarter, Bac, Sevres-Babylone, Ecole Militaire

5th, 6th, and 7th arrondissements

**CAVE JEAN-BAPTISTE
BESSE**
48 Rue de la Montagne
Sainte-Geneviève,
Paris 5.
(43.25.35.80).
Métro: Maubert-Mutualité.
Open 10 A.M. to 1:30 P.M. and
4:30 P.M. to 8:30 P.M.
Tuesday through
Saturday, 11 A.M. to
1:30 P.M. Sunday. Closed
Monday and August.

Jean-Baptiste Besse, who has been at this tumble-down corner grocery since 1932, is a charming, modest little man with a permanent smile and most humble manner. If he has time, he'll talk your head off about Cognac and Armagnac, perhaps even about Bordeaux. Come here when you've plenty of time to chat or wait in line, or look on as he stumbles about the store in search of your request. (Treasures here are not always obvious.) Monsieur Besse can be trusted. You won't be sorry when you buy the Château de Bréat Bas Armagnac. (He advises bottles from the 1960s, saying "anything older is more symbolic than good.")

KING HENRY
44 Rue des Boulangers,
Paris 5.
(43.54.54.37).
Métro: Jussieu.
Open 6 P.M. to 2 A.M. Closed
Sunday and August.

The king of beer in Paris, this combination boutique-restaurant, offers more than 500 different brands of beer, 200 kinds of whiskey, and an assortment of other alcohols and liqueurs. Now open evenings only; a daily *plat du jour* can be enjoyed with the beer and liquor assortment.

PARISIAN VINEYARDS

Vineyards in Paris? Their history dates back to the Middle Ages, when abbey vineyards dotted the city and the wines they produced found their way to the noblest tables. (It was, in fact, the white claret from the suburb of Suresnes that François I said was "as light as a tear in the eye.")

Today the heritage continues as each year a little more than 1,000 bottles of authentic Parisian wines are carefully, ceremoniously bottled.

Tucked away in the hills of Montmartre, hidden among the narrow houses and car-filled sidewalks, there is a minuscule vineyard that annually produces just 500 bottles of a red wine simply labeled "Clos Montmartre." The harvest *fête,* a traditional celebration full of pageantry, takes place the first Saturday of October. For the harvest itself, the basement of the 18th *arrondissement mairie* (town hall) is turned into a wine cellar, and later some 300 bottles are sold there for about 300 francs each. The remainder is sold at auction. The wine does not lay claims to greatness: It is more of an historical amusement than a gustatory treasure.

A second vineyard lies in the suburban community of Suresnes, west of Paris. Once considered the best in the Ile-de-France, the Suresnes vineyard was replanted in 1965. Now the local rugby team turns out to harvest the grapes, and the community celebrates the event on the first Sunday in October. Most of the 2,000 or so bottles of Clos du Pas-Saint-Maurice are sold (for about 35 francs) on the last Saturday of September and the first Sunday of October at the Suresnes *cave municipale.* (It is also sold at Lucien Legrand and Au Verger de la Madeleine wine shops in Paris.)

In 1983, in an apparent effort to revive its illustrious wine heritage, the city of Paris planted another 700 vines of Pinot Noir grapes on the south side of Georges-Brassens Square, in the 15th *arrondissement* park built on the site of the former stockyards. In 1985, neighborhood children, members of the Lions Club, and the elderly helped pick the first Clos des Morillons harvest, which produced a total of 300 bottles of red wine, carefully aged in oak casks. The wine is sold at auction each December 15th, at the 15th *arrondissement mairie.*

For more information about the harvests and wine sales, contact:

Montmartre, Mairie of the 18th *arrondissement,* 1 Rue Jules-Joffrin, Paris 18. (42.52.42.00). Métro: Jules-Joffrin.

Suresnes, Cave Municipale, 28 Rue Merlin-de-Thionville, 92150 Suresnes. (45.06.32.10). Accessible via the No. 244 bus from Porte-Maillot, the No. 144 bus from Pont de Neuilly, or the suburban train from Gare Saint-Lazare. The stop is Suresnes Mont Valérin.

Clos de Morillons, Mairie of the 15th *arrondissement,* 31 Rue Péclet, Paris 15. (48.28.40.12). Métro: Vaugirard.

LA MAISON DU WHISKY
48 Avenue de Saxe, Paris 7.
(47.83.66.21).
Métro: Ségur.
Open 9 A.M. to 12:30 P.M. and
 2 P.M. to 6:30 P.M. Monday
 through Friday; 10 A.M. to
 noon Saturday. Closed
 Sunday and August.
Credit cards: DC, V.

It's hard to imagine a larger selection, even in Scotland or Ireland. The little shop offers dozens of brands and vintages of unblended single malt Scotch whisky (including the superb Macallan and earthy Lagavulin), some prestige vintages (single malts from the 1930s and 1940s), as well as blended Scotch, Irish whisky, bourbon, and Canadian whisky, and rye.

LE PETIT BACCHUS
13 Rue du Cherche-Midi,
 Paris 6.
(45.44.01.07).
Métro: Sèvres-Babylone.
Open 9:30 A.M. to 7:30 P.M.
 Closed Sunday, Monday,
 and August.
English spoken.

This former bistro-wine shop is now part of Steven Spurrier's fine Parisian wine empire. Here you'll find the same carefully chosen assortment of regional French wines. A good place for browsing for a special bottle for a picnic, for an *apéritif,* or to pack in your suitcase for the trip home.

RYST-DUPEYRON
79 Rue du Bac, Paris 7.
(45.48.80.93).
Métro: Bac.
Open 10 A.M. to 12:30 P.M.
 and 1:30 P.M. to 7 P.M.
 Closed Sunday and
 August.
Credit card: V.
English spoken.
Will ship internationally.

A fine, classic old wine shop, a good Left Bank spot for searching out vintage Armagnac, whisky, and port, as well as fine Bordeaux. They will even personalize bottles for special occasions—to celebrate a birthday, anniversary, wedding, or birth. Gift certificates are also available.

CHAMPS-ELYSEES, MADELEINE, GRANDS BOULEVARDS

8th arrondissement

AUGE
116 Boulevard Haussmann,
   Paris 8.
(45.22.16.97).
Métro: Miromesnil.
Open 8:30 A.M. to 12:30 P.M.
   and 2:30 P.M. to 7:30 P.M.
   Monday through Friday;
   8:30 A.M. to 12:30 P.M.
   and 3 P.M. to 7:30 P.M.
   Saturday. Closed Sunday,
   Monday morning, and
   the last three weeks of
   August.
   Credit card: AE, V.
   Some English spoken.

An elegant, classic *épicerie fine,* offering not just fruits and wines but a fine assortment of vintage and nonvintage port, Cognac, Armagnac, and Champagne.

**LA CAVE DE GEORGES
   DUBOEUF**
9 Rue Marbeuf, Paris 8.
(47.20.71.23).
Métro: Alma-Marceau.
Open 9 A.M. to 1 P.M. and
   3:30 P.M. to 7:30 P.M.
   Closed Sunday, Monday,
   and August.

Georges Duboeuf is perhaps the most respected name in Beaujolais, and his small shop off the Champs-Elysées offers Beaujolais as well as a fine selection of Burgundies.

FAUCHON
26 Place de la Madeleine,
   Paris 8.
(47.42.60.11).
Métro: Madeleine.
Open 9:40 A.M. to 7 P.M.
   Closed Sunday.
Credit cards: AE, DC, EC, V.
English spoken.

A well-stocked *cave,* particularly if you're shopping for a fine Armagnac or Cognac. Prices are on the high side. (See also Spécialités Gastronomiques.)

LA CAVE D'HEDIARD
21 Place de la Madeleine,
   Paris 8.
(42.66.44.38).
Métro: Madeleine.
Open 9:15 A.M. to 7 P.M.
   Closed Sunday.
Credit card: AE, DC, EC, V.
English spoken.

An expansive *cave* offering perhaps the largest selection of Bordeaux wines in Paris. Also a large selection of Armagnac, Calvados, and Cognac. Prices are on the high side. (See also Spécialités Gastronomiques.)

LA MAISON DU WHISKY
20 Rue d'Anjou, Paris 8.
(42.65.03.16).
Métro: Madeleine.
Open 9 A.M. to 6 P.M. Monday
   through Friday; 9 A.M. to
   12:30 P.M. Saturday.
   Closed Sunday and
   August.
Credit card: V.
See La Maison du Whisky,
   7th *arrondissement,*
   page 287.

CURNONSKY

Curnonsky, the 20th-century French food critic named "prince of gastronomes" by his peers, classed the five best white wines in France, perhaps the world:

Château d'Yquem: "The matchless sweet wine: true liquid gold."

Château-Chalon: "The prince of the Jura yellow wines, full-bodied, with the penetrating bouquet of walnuts."

Château-Grillet: "The legendary wine of the Côtes-du-Rhône, with a stunning aroma of violets and wild flowers; as changing as a pretty woman."

Montrachet: "The splendid lord of Burgundy, which Alexander Dumas counseled to drink, bare-headed, while kneeling."

Savennières Coulées de Serrant: "The dazzling dry wine from the vineyards of the Loire."

STEVEN SPURRIER/CAVES
   DE LA MADELEINE
25 Rue Royale (Cité Berryer;
   enter between 23 and 25
   Rue Royale), Paris 8.
(42.65.92.40).
Métro: Madeleine.
Open 9 A.M. to 7 P.M. Monday
   through Friday; 10 A.M. to
   2 P.M. Saturday. Closed
   Sunday.
Credit card: AE, V.
English spoken.

The Englishman Steven Spurrier has made his mark on Paris, offering one of the largest selections of both little-known and well-known Burgundies and Bordeaux, along with a fine assortment of wines from France's southwest. Provence, Languedoc, the Loire and Rhône valleys, the Jura, and Corsica—even Spain and Italy. There's also a fine selection of Cognac, Armagnac, and Calvados.

LES CAVES TAILLEVENT
199 Rue du Faubourg Saint-
   Honoré, Paris 8.
(45.61.14.09).
Métro: Ternes.
Open 10 A.M. to 8 P.M. Closed
   Sunday and August.
Credit card: V.
English spoken.

Without batting an eye, I would stand behind anything that Jean-Claude Vrinat supported. He's a remarkable man, and everything he touches has the mark of perfection and authenticity. Since the wine list at his family restaurant, Taillevent, is one of the finest and most fairly priced in town, it comes as no surprise to find that his wine shop offers some 350 different wines, priced from 18 to 300 francs a bottle; as well as 150 different *eaux-de-vie,* liqueurs, port, and sherry, dating back to 1848.

Note that all of his wines are stored in a *cave* kept at—what else—perfect temperature and humidity. I hated to see Monsieur Vrinat give up his passion for gardening—which he did while creating this wine shop—but in the end, all wine lovers will profit from his dedication.

AU VERGER DE LA MADELEINE
4 Boulevard Malesherbes, Paris 8.
(42.65.51.99).
Métro: Madeleine.
Open 10 A.M. to 1 P.M. and 3 P.M. to 8 P.M. Closed Sunday and two weeks in August.
English spoken.

Need an 1820 Cognac, an 1893 Sauternes, or a 1922 Lafite-Rothschild? Maurice and Jean-Pierre Legras will be happy to oblige. Since 1937, the Legras family has operated one of Paris's grand *épiceries fines,* and today they specialize in old bottles, odd bottles, new bottles, little bottles. Just give them a special date—birthday, anniversary, wedding—from within the last 150 years and they should come up with an appropriate bottle to help you celebrate. Effervescent Jean-Pierre is crazy about wine, and loves digging up dust-covered relics from the spacious underground *caves.* He's proud of their collection of Sauternes old and new (especially the 1934 Château d'Yquem), of the fine and rare white Nuits-Saint-Georges from Henri Gouges, the straw-colored *vin de paille* of the Jura, and the Rhône's famous white Château-Grillet, not to mention his exclusive right to sell wine from Liechtenstein, or his stock of the famous Paris red from the vineyards at Montmartre and Suresnes.

NATION

11th and 12th arrondissements

L'ARBRE A VIN, CAVES RETROU
4 Rue du Rendez-Vous, Paris 12.
(43.46.81.10).
Métro: Nation.
Open 8:30 A.M. to 12:30 P.M. and 4 P.M. to 7:30 P.M. Tuesday through Saturday; 8:30 A.M. to 12:30 P.M. Sunday. Closed Monday.
Credit card: V.
English spoken.

A funky sort of wine depot-supermarket, offering a wide variety of seldom-found, inexpensive, often regional wines. Included are some fine Côtes-du-Rhône and Madiran, and lesser-known wines such as the Basque Irouléguy. Be sure to take a stroll around the Place de la Nation, with dozens of chic and lovely shops.

L'OENOPHILE
30 Boulevard Voltaire,
   Paris 11.
(47.00.69.45).
Métro: Nation.
Open 9 A.M. to 1 P.M. and
   3 P.M. to 8 P.M. Tuesday
   through Saturday; 9:30
   A.M. to 1 P.M. Sunday.
   Closed Monday.
Credit card: V.

L'Oenophile is Michel Renaud's second shop, run by his wife, Dominique, offering the same products as the main listing below.

La Maison du Chocolat for fine Champagne as well as chocolate (see Chocolateries, page 259).

CAVE MICHEL RENAUD
12 Place de la Nation,
   Paris 12.
(43.07.98.93).
Métro: Nation.
Open 9 A.M. to 1 P.M. and
   3 P.M. to 8:30 P.M. Tuesday
   through Saturday. Closed
   Sunday afternoon and
   Monday morning.
Credit card: V.

This picturesque, elegant wine shop is neat as a pin, and so is its genteel owner, Michel Renaud. His carefully and personally stocked shop reflects a passion for wine: He even has an interest in a Portuguese cork-producing firm. Monsieur Renaud spends a good deal of time searching out the good little wines of France, but offers as well some better-known Bordeaux, the fine Hermitage of Géraud Chave, and a wonderful, well-priced Bas Armagnac.

ARC DE TRIOMPHE

16th and 17th arrondissements

LA BOUTIQUE LES
   TOQUES
   GOURMANDES
1 Rue d'Armaillé, Paris 17.
(47.66.19.04).
Métro: Ternes.
Open 11 A.M. to 1 P.M. and
   2 P.M. to 9 P.M. Tuesday
   through Saturday. Closed
   Sunday and Monday.
Credit cards: AE, V.
Some English spoken.

For several years Alain Dutournier and fellow Parisian chefs have had a cooperative wine-buying business, and now the wines are available by the bottle at this little Right Bank boutique near the Arc de Triomphe. Their wines and spirits are carefully chosen, and the selection includes many personal favorites, including Etienne Brana's *eaux-de-vie* from the Basque country and a fine selection of Armagnacs.

PETRISSANS
30 bis Avenue Niel, Paris 17.
(42.27.83.84).
Métro: Ternes.
Open 9:30 A.M. to 8 P.M.
  Tuesday through Friday;
  9:30 A.M. to 1:30 P.M.
  Monday and Saturday.
  Closed Sunday and
  August.
Credit cards: AE, V.
English spoken.

A small, old-fashioned family operation, offering fine selections of Burgundy and Bordeaux. A small wine bar adjoins the shop, if you should decide to sample on the spot. (See also Bistros à Vin.)

LE VINOEPHILE
33 Rue Boissière, Paris 16.
(45.53.78.52).
Métro: Boissière.
Open 11 A.M. to 7:30 P.M.
  Closed Sunday.
Credit card: V.
English spoken.

A 1789 Cognac, an 1871 port, or how about a 1930 *prune paysanne,* or prune *eau-de-vie* made right on the farm? These are just a few of the wonders you'll find as you browse through this tidy all-wood shop in the classy 16th. Le Vinoephile is a treasure trove of rare and historic wines, including selections of more recent vintage Bordeaux and Champagnes. There are even wines that you might want to pick up for dinner that night: The current catalog lists wines from 25 francs for a half bottle of white Bordeaux up to 19,500 francs for a bottle of 1860 Cognac.

VINS RARES ET DE COLLECTION
(Peter Thustrup)
3 Rue Laugier, Paris 17.
(47.66.58.15 and
  46.22.54.95).
Métro: Ternes.
Open 10 A.M. to 7 P.M. Closed
  Sunday.
Credit cards: AE, DC, V.
English spoken.

A wine merchant who deals in antiques? That's it. Peter Thustrup's passion for rare vintage wines has grown into a business, and now, in his tidy shop just off the lively Rue Poncelet market, he offers more than 5,000 bottles—what he calls *les introuvables,* or wines that are virtually impossible to find. If you're searching for special bottles of Romanée Conti, Mouton Rothschild, Yquem, or vintage Champagnes, this is the place to look.

Librairies Spécialisées:
Gastronomie
FOOD AND WINE
BOOK SHOPS

Almost every bookstore and department store in Paris has a selection devoted to *cuisine*. The following are just a few suggestions for finding old and new cookbooks, guidebooks, and historical food-related volumes.

LES HALLES, BOURSE, OPERA

1st, 2nd, and 4th arrondissements

BAZAR DE L'HOTEL DE VILLE (B.H.V.)
52 Rue de Rivoli,
Paris 4.
(42.74.90.00).
Métro: Hotel-de-Ville.
Open 9 A.M. to 6:30 P.M.
(Wednesday until 10 P.M.,
Saturday until 7 P.M.)
Closed Sunday.
Credit card: V.

This giant and often confusing department store offers an extensive cookbook selection, particularly good if you're looking for books the French housewife might use. Sales tables can offer some terrific bargains. (See also Pour la Maison.)

BRENTANO'S
37 Avenue de l'Opéra,
Paris 2.
(42.61.52.50).
Métro: Opéra.
Open 10 A.M. to 7 P.M. Closed
Sunday.
Credit card: V.
English spoken.

This English-language bookshop offers a rather extensive selection of cookbooks, most of them British. A good place to go for food- and wine-related guidebooks.

COOKING AND WINE SCHOOLS

The following are the most popular cooking and wine schools in Paris. If you plan to visit any of the schools, write or call for a brochure first, so you know what to expect. In many cases, custom-tailored courses can be arranged for groups of ten or more.

L'Académie du Vin, 25 Rue Royale (Cité Berryer; enter between 23 and 25 Rue Royale), Paris 8. (42.65.09.82). Métro: Madeleine.

A popular wine school, with classes in English or French, founded and directed by an Englishman, Steven Spurrier. L'Académie du Vin offers beginning, intermediate, and advanced wine classes, including theory, history, and tastings of at least six wines during each class.

Le Cordon Bleu, 24 Rue du Champ-de-Mars, Paris 7. (45.55.02.77). Métro: Ecole Militaire.

This famous classic French school has been instructing students in French cooking and pastry since 1895. Visitors may reserve a few days ahead for a single afternoon demonstration, and menus are available in advance for each month's program. Courses are ongoing, in French, and the number of students varies according to the program. Translators will be provided by special request.

Découverte du Vin/Alain Ségelle, 45 Rue Liancourt, Paris 14. (43.27.67.21). Métro: Gaité.

Alain Ségelle is an outgoing young Frenchman with a passion for wine. His classes are serious affairs, in which he discusses in depth a variety of wine subjects. Many different courses are offered, ranging from a beginner's on the principles of wine tasting, to more specific classes on wines from the most important wine regions in France. Courses are in French (though classes in English are available on request). Students sample and discuss three or four wines during each session.

Ecole de Cuisine la Varenne, 34 Rue Saint-Dominique, Paris 7. (47.05.10.16). Métro: Invalides.

This popular American-oriented cooking school was founded by Anne Willan, the English cookbook

Ecole de Cuisine La Varenne.

writer, journalist, and food historian. Situated in small but well-equipped quarters near the Invalides, the school offers both participation and demonstration courses in French cuisine. Students can stop in for a single afternoon demonstration, or stay on for as long as six months working toward a *grand diplôme*. Week-long courses are also offered in regional cooking, summer cooking, *nouvelle cuisine*, and classic French cuisine. Classes, taught by a staff of French chefs and local visiting chefs, are offered year round, although the school is generally closed during Christmas week and on French holidays. For daily demonstrations, limited to about fifty students, reserve a few days in advance. For longer courses, register several months in advance. Classes are in French, and though English translations are provided, an understanding of French is most helpful. Note that special one-week courses are also offered at La Varenne's Château du Fëy in Burgundy in spring and fall.

Ecole de Gastronomie Française Ritz-Escoffier, 15 Place Vendôme, Paris 1. (42.60.38.30). Métro: Opéra.

The famed Ritz Hotel and Restaurant now opens its kitchens and shares its chefs' expertise with students interested in French cuisine. Gregory Usher, former director of two well-known cooking schools—La Varenne and Le Cordon Bleu—has organized a multi-faceted cooking course, offering everything from weekday afternoon demonstration classes to 12-week diploma courses. For many of its classes, the school draws upon the talents of the Ritz executive chef Guy Legay, *sommelier* Georges Lepré, and the hotel's master baker, Bernard Bruban.

The new, spotless kitchens are outfitted with the best in professional cookware and equipment. For groups, courses can be custom-tailored to fit student requests.

Ecole Lenôtre, 40 Rue Pierre-Curie, 78370 Plaisir. (30.55.81.12). Accessible by car or train from the Montparnasse station.

This is where the best pastry chefs of France go for "refresher" courses. Gaston Lenôtre is one of the most respected and successful pastry chefs in France, and his school in the suburbs of Paris is open to professionals only. Ongoing full-participation courses are offered in pastry, chocolate, breadbaking, ice cream, *charcuterie,* and catering. A knowledge of French is essential.

Marie-Blanche de Broglie Cooking School, 18 Avenue de la Motte-Picquet, Paris 7. (45.51.36.34). Métro: Ecole Militaire.

Marie-Blanche de Broglie is an outgoing, enthusiastic woman offering a number of courses in her well-appointed Paris apartment as well as in her Normandy château. In Paris, she offers demonstration courses in the harmony of wine and foods, pastry, and French regional cooking. In her Normandy château, she offers weekend and week-long demonstration and participation classes for groups of five to fifteen. These include regional tours, wine tastings, and a visit to a Calvados distillery. Courses may be arranged in English, French, or Spanish, with translations where necessary.

Paris en Cuisine, 49 Rue de Richelieu, Paris 1. (42.61.35.23). Métro: Palais-Royal.

Robert Noah, a friendly, well-informed American in Paris, offers a variety of food-related tours of Paris. He arranges private or group visits to the Rungis wholesale market; tours of top restaurant kitchens; wine or cheese tastings; visits to Paris *charcuteries,* pastry, or bread shops; and even longer excursions into the countryside of France. The tours are particularly useful for those who do not speak French, for groups are kept to a maximum of ten, and Mr. Noah is a clear and careful translator. Paris en Cuisine also sponsors a professional cooking program, in English, which qualifies students to take an exam for the French *Certificat d'Aptitude Professionel* (CAP), at the Centre de Formations Technologiques Ferrandi.

DELAMAIN
155 Rue Saint-Honoré,
    Paris 1.
(42.61.48.78).
Métro: Palais-Royal.
Open 10 A.M. to 7 P.M. Closed
    Sunday.
Credit cards: AE, DC, V.
Some English spoken.

A serious but friendly old bookstore, with a good selection of French cookbooks devoted to regional cuisine.

FNAC
Forum Les Halles Shopping
    Mall, 1 Rue Pierre Lescot,
    Paris 1.
(40.26.81.18).
Métro: Les Halles.
Open 1 P.M. to 7:30 P.M.
    Monday; 10 A.M. to
    7:30 P.M. Tuesday through
    Saturday. Closed Sunday.
Credit card: V.
Some English spoken.

This mammoth stereo/record/camera/bookshop includes a large book section, with one of the city's best and most up-to-date selections of French books on food and wine. Usually the lowest price in town.

M.O.R.A.
13 Rue Montmartre, Paris 1.
(45.08.19.24).
Métro: Les Halles.
Open 8:30 A.M. to 5:45 P.M.
    Monday through Friday;
    8:30 A.M. to noon
    Saturday. Closed Sunday.
Credit cards: EC, V.
English spoken.

A cookware shop, featuring a small but complete assortment of professional books devoted to breads, pastry, general cooking, and hotel and restaurant cooking. (See also Pour la Maison.)

W. H. SMITH
248 Rue de Rivoli, Paris 1.
(42.60.37.97).
Métro: Concorde.
Open 9:30 A.M. to 7 P.M.
    Monday through
    Thursday; 9 A.M. to
    6:30 P.M. Friday and
    Saturday. Closed Sunday.

W H. Smith offers the city's most extensive selection of English-language books on food and wine, most of them British. Also a good selection of food- and wine-related guidebooks.

SAINT-MICHEL, LUXEMBOURG

5th arrondissement

M. G. BAUDON
Bookseller at Box 11, Quai
   de Montebello, Paris 5.
(42.60.27.50).
Métro: Saint-Michel.
Flexible hours, generally
   open 11 A.M. to 7:30 P.M.,
   depending upon the
   weather. Closed Sunday
   and Monday.

The friendly, outgoing Madame Baudon is herself a passionate collector of old French cookbooks, and many of them find their way into her little wooden stall along the *quai*. A fine place for book browsing in the shadow of Notre-Dame.

GIBERT JEUNE
5 Place Saint-Michel,
   Paris 5.
(43.25.70.07).
Métro: Saint-Michel.
Open 9:30 A.M. to 7:30 P.M.
   Closed Sunday.
Credit card: V.
English spoken.

This is one of Paris's largest bookstores, offering an extensive assortment of food-related books (most in French, a few in English) scattered about the second and third floors.

LIBRAIRIE GOURMANDE
4 Rue Dante, Paris 5.
(43.54.37.27).
Métro: Saint-Michel
Open 10 A.M. to 7 P.M. in
   winter; 10 A.M. to 8 P.M. in
   summer; 2:30 P.M. to
   7 P.M. Sunday year round.

This is the new "branch" of the Quai de Montebello bookselling family, Baudon. Here, in a pleasant shop on a charming Left Bank street, you'll be sure to spend hours browsing amid the collection of cookbooks, tomes recounting the history of the table, assorted food-related antiques, as well as posters, lithographs, and drawings.

LE VERRE ET L'ASSIETTE
1 Rue du Val-de-Grâce,
   Paris 5.
(46.33.45.96).
Métro: Port-Royal.
Open 10 A.M. to 12:30 P.M.
   and 2:30 P.M. to 7 P.M.
   Closed Sunday, Monday
   morning, and two weeks
   in August.
Credit cards: AE, DC, V.
English spoken.

If you've time to visit only one cookbook shop, this is it. You'll find a vast and esoteric collection of some 3,000 French (and English) books devoted to food and wine, along with an assortment of wine-related paraphernalia: corkscrews, wine glasses, vineyard maps, and thermometers. To keep up-to-date on wine and food happenings in Paris, subscribe to their chatty monthly newsletter.

BOULEVARD SAINT-GERMAIN, MONTPARNASSE
6th and 7th arrondissements

LIBRARIE ANCIENNE ELBE
213 bis Boulevard Saint-
 Germain, Paris 7.
(45.48.77.97).
Métro: Rue du Bac.
Open 10 A.M. to 1 P.M. and
 2 P.M. to 6:30 P.M. Closed
 Monday and August.
English spoken.

FNAC
136 Rue de Rennes, Paris 6.
(45.44.39.12).
Métro: Montparnasse-
 Bienvenue.
Open 1 P.M. to 7:30 P.M.
 Monday; 10 A.M. to 7:30 P.M.
 Tuesday through
 Saturday. Closed Sunday.
See FNAC, 1st
 arrondissement, page 297.

EDGAR SOETE
5 Quai Voltaire, Paris 7.
(42.60.72.41).
Métro: Rue du Bac.
Open 10 A.M. to noon and
 2 P.M. to 6:30 P.M. Closed
 Saturday, Sunday, and
 August.

Librairie Ancienne Elbe offers maps, charts, posters, and old books, including a small, eclectic collection that is food-related. Some fine offbeat finds from time to time.

A sober serious shop which devotes itself to cookbooks, some new, some old, some rare. Until they decide you're a serious shopper, the welcome can be stiff and cool.

CONCORDE
8th arrondissement

AU BAIN MARIE
10 Rue Boissy d'Anglas,
 Paris 8.
(42.66.59.74).
Métro: Concorde.
Open 10 A.M. to 7 P.M. Closed
 Sunday.
Credit card: AE, DC, V.
English spoken.

This is, without doubt, my favorite spot in the world to browse for cookbooks and food books, old and new. Aude Clément's new location offers immense space and light, as well as tables for sitting down to leaf through her enormous collection of books. Over the years I've picked up some gems here, including a hilarious 1958 restaurant guide written by the gossip columnist for the Parisian daily *France-Soir.* But Madame Clément offers much more than books. For additional comments, see Pour la Maison, page 312.

ARC DE TRIOMPHE, PLACE VICTOR-HUGO
16th and 17th arrondissments

FNAC
26 Avenue de Wagram,
   Paris 17.
(47.66.52.50).
Métro: Charles-de-Gaulle-
   Etoile.
Open 1 P.M. to 7 P.M. Monday;
   10 A.M. to 7:30 P.M.
   Tuesday through
   Saturday. Closed Sunday.
Credit card: V.
English spoken.
See FNAC, 1st
   arrondissement, page 297.

LIBRAIRIE FONTAINE
   VICTOR HUGO
95 Avenue Victor-Hugo,
   Paris 16.
(45.53.76.72).
Métro: Victor-Hugo.
Open 8:45 A.M. to 7:30 P.M.
   Closed Sunday.
Credit card: V.
English spoken.

This shop has an extensive *cuisine* section, but largely of new releases.

Pour la Maison
KITCHEN AND
TABLEWARE SHOPS

Papeterie Moderne for any sign you desire (see entry, page 303).

If you have been searching for long-wearing cotton chefs' uniforms, odd-size baking tins, antique Champagne glasses, or functional white laboratory pitchers for storing wooden utensils, you need look no more. These, plus lovely pastel-toned turn-of-the-century oyster or asparagus plates, sparkling contemporary glassware, and sturdy copper pots are just a few of the hundreds of particularly French kitchen and table items found in the following shops. Note that some are small and sometimes casually run, so that opening and closing hours may not always be followed to the letter.

LES HALLES, PALAIS-ROYAL, PLACE DES VICTOIRES

1st and 2nd arrondissements

LA BOVIDA
36 Rue Montmartre, Paris 1.
(42.36.09.99).
Métro: Les Halles.
Open 7 A.M. to 5:45 P.M.
  Closed Saturday
  afternoon and Sunday.

A kitchen equipment shop for professionals, La Bovida has an impressive inventory of stainless steel, copper, porcelain, and earthenware, as well as serving platters, a variety of spices in bulk, and paper doilies in more than a dozen shapes and sizes. Service can be cool indeed.

LE CEDRE ROUGE
22 Avenue Victoria, Paris 1.
(42.33.71.05).
Métro: Châtelet.
Open 9 A.M. to 7 P.M. Closed
    Sunday and two weeks in
    August.
Credit cards: AE, DC, V.
English spoken.
Will ship internationally.

A fabulous fantasy shop for home and garden. Most of the items here—garden furniture and umbrellas, gigantic bowls and pots—will be too big to fit into your suitcase, but this is a lovely shop for dreamers. And you're certain to go home with an idea or two.

CENTRAL UNION
28 Rue de la Grande
    Truanderie, Paris 1.
(40.26.35.22).
Métro: Les Halles.
Open 11 A.M. to 1 P.M. and
    2 P.M. to 7:30 P.M. Closed
    Sunday.
Credit cards: AE, EC, V.
English spoken.
Will ship internationally.

This shop specializes in "punk" art objects and whimsical items such as 1950s teapots, some winged, some shaped like houses, and others sporting the Rolls-Royce insignia and hood ornament, certain to have you pouring tea with a smile. They have geometric-design coffee cups and reproductions of old canisters.

CHRISTOFLE
24 Rue de la Paix, Paris 2.
(42.65.62.43).
Métro: Opéra.
Open 9:30 A.M. to 6:30 P.M.
    Closed Sunday and
    Monday (open Monday in
    December).
Credit cards: AE, DC, EC, V.
English spoken.

Gleaming with opulence, this popular boutique is one of Paris's better-known addresses for silver, china, crystal, and giftware.

E. DEHILLERIN
18 Rue Coquillière, Paris 1.
(42.36.53.13).
Métro: Les Halles.
Open 8 A.M. to 12:30 P.M.
    and 2 P.M. to 6 P.M. Closed
    Sunday.
Credit card: V.
English spoken.
Will ship internationally.

A fascinating, though often overwhelming, clutter of professional cookware covering every inch of available wall, floor, and ceiling space. The selection of copper cookware, baking pans, and unusual kitchen tools is remarkable. Professional-size kitchenware is found in the basement. Some English is spoken by the helpful, if gruff, salespeople, and merchandise catalogs are available. They're experts at retinning copper, but plan on waiting two to three weeks. The store will mail purchases.

**DUTHILLEUL
ET MINART**
14 Rue de Turbigo, Paris 1.
(42.33.44.36).
Métro: Les Halles.
Open 9:30 A.M. to 6:30 P.M.
  Closed Sunday.
English spoken.
Will ship internationally.

Artisans' uniforms designed around 1850, natural fiber work clothes, café waiters' vests, shirts, and ties, along with jewelers' smocks, meat deliverers' hooded robes, animal purveyors' *blouses* in red, black, and tan, and professional chef outfits, tailored to fit. They also have an extensive selection of professional-quality cotton and linen dish towels.

**LE LOUVRE DES
  ANTIQUAIRES**
2 Place du Palais-Royal,
  Paris 1.
(42.97.27.00).
Métro: Palais-Royal.
Open 11 A.M. to 7 P.M. Closed
  Monday.
Some merchants accept
  credit cards.
Will ship internationally.

More than 250 antique dealers, right across from the Louvre. There are few bargains, but one can easily spend several hours here wandering through the sparkling shops in search of antique china and silver, folkloric wooden objects for the kitchen and table, as well as crystal, artwork, and furniture. There is a service department for mailing and shipping purchases.

M.O.R.A.
13 Rue Montmartre, Paris 1.
(45.08.19.24).
Métro: Les Halles.
Open 8:30 A.M. to noon and
  1:30 P.M. to 5:45 P.M.
  Closed Saturday
  afternoon and Sunday.
English spoken.
Will ship internationally.

Another in the group of cookware shops near Les Halles, still frequented by professionals. M.O.R.A. has a large assortment of tools, baking tins (including several sizes of *pain de mie* molds), large *baguette* pans, cake molds, and linen-lined wicker bread-rising baskets. (Be sure to come with dimensions of your oven: Many objects are oversize, made to fit large professional ovens.) They also have a good professional cookbook selection. (See Librairies Spécialisées: Gastronomie.)

PAPETERIE MODERNE
12 Rue de la Ferronnerie,
  Paris 1.
(42.36.21.72).
Métro: Châtelet/Les Halles.
Open 8 A.M. to noon and
  1 P.M. to 7 P.M. Monday
  through Thursday and
  Saturday; 11 A.M. to 7 P.M.
  Friday. Closed Sunday
  and two weeks in June.
Will ship in France.

When you see this simple shop, unchanged for decades, you'll know the source of all the city's myriad signs. They're everywhere—all the signs you have ever dreamed of—stashed into corners, piled on counters, hanging from the wall and the ceiling, on nails and thumbtacks. There are signs for cheese, butter, sausages, beef tongue, or headcheese, along with café menus, bakery price lists, requests for people to stop smoking or spitting, even French "beware of dog" and "post no bills" warnings. Signs can be made to order and take about ten days.

**LA PORCELAINE
BLANCHE**
108 Rue Saint-Honoré,
    Paris 1.
(42.36.90.73).
Métro: Louvre.
Open 10 A.M. to 7 P.M. Closed
    Sunday.
Credit card: V.
Some English spoken.

This is one of a chain of shops specializing in simple solid-white porcelain, including bistro plates, *café au lait* bowls, terrines, coffee and tea pots, vases, and vinegar jars. Also some basketry, cutlery, and glassware, all at prices 15 to 30 percent lower than most other shops.

A. SIMON
36 Rue Etienne Marcel and
    48 Rue Montmartre,
    Paris 2.
(42.33.71.65).
Métro: Les Halles.
Open 8:30 A.M. to 6 P.M.
    Closed Sunday and
    holidays.
Credit card: V.
English spoken.
Will ship internationally.

This sedate establishment has professional serving dishes, porcelain, crystal, and china, salt and pepper grinders, mustard jars, lovely white terrines, a wide variety of paper doilies, wicker cheese trays, and bread baskets. At their annex across the street (go through the courtyard at 48 Rue Montmartre), there's professional cookware from copper pots to baking molds, and scales to cookie cutters, along with the attractive marble-base Roquefort cheese cutters used in the best restaurants. Very helpful salespeople.

MARAIS, BASTILLE, ILE SAINT-LOUIS

4th and 11th arrondissements

L'ARLEQUIN
13 Rue des Francs-
    Bourgeois, Paris 4.
(42.78.77.00).
Métro: Saint-Paul.
Open noon to 7 P.M. Closed
    Sunday, Monday, and the
    last week in July through
    the first week in
    September.

Ancient and beautiful glassware on dusty shelves that reach from floor to ceiling. Liqueur glasses, Champagne *coupes*, wine glasses, water glasses, juice glasses. The perfect place to compose your own mixed or matched set. A few vases as well.

Beautiful tableware beautifully displayed is always tempting.

BAZAR DE L'HOTEL DE
   VILLE (B.H.V.)
52 Rue de la Verrerie,
   Paris 4.
(42.74.90.00).
Métro: Hôtel-de-Ville.
Open 9 A.M. to 6:30 P.M.
   (Wednesday until 10 P.M.)
   Closed Sunday.
Credit cards: AE, V.
English spoken.
Will ship internationally.

Almost every contemporary kitchen tool or piece of equipment ever invented is available on the third floor of this enormous catch-all department store, as well as china and crystal, baskets, table linens, and everyday kitchen products. (See also Librairies Spécialisées: Gastronomie.)

JEAN-PIERRE DE CASTRO
17 Rue des Francs-
   Bourgeois, Paris 4.
(42.72.04.00).
Métro: Saint-Paul.
Open 10:30 A.M. to 7 P.M.
   Closed Monday morning.
Credit card: V.
English spoken.
Will ship internationally.

A great shop for silver-lovers, where antique silver knives, forks, spoons—you name it—are sold by weight. Selecting from a stack of wicker baskets, you can put together your own place settings. There's an abundant selection, and prices are generally reasonable. Also silver candlesticks, teapots, and so on.

COEURS D'ALSACE
33 Quai de Bourbon,
   Paris 4.
(46.33.14.03).
Métro: Pont-Marie.
Open 10:30 A.M. to 7 P.M.
   Closed Sunday, Monday,
   and August.
Credit card: V.
English spoken.
Will ship their hand-painted
   furniture internationally.

Like a trip to the old world, this colorful shop has *anis* cookie stamps, pottery, heart-shaped earthenware cake molds, painted furniture, and cookbooks, all direct from the Alsace region in eastern France.

ERIC DUBOIS
9 Rue Saint-Paul, Paris 4.
(42.74.05.29).
Métro: Saint-Paul.
Open 11 A.M. to 7 P.M.
Credit cards: AE, DC.
Will ship internationally.

A charming antique shop filled with a lovely collection of folkloric antiques and curiosities: You'll find old pottery jugs from the southwest, antique cheese draining cups from the Loire, old hand-held metal scales, and copper cooking utensils.

LESCENE-DURA
63 Rue de la Verrerie,
    Paris 4.
(42.72.08.74).
Métro: Hôtel-de-Ville.
Open 9:30 A.M. to 1 P.M. and
    2 P.M. to 6:30 P.M. Tuesday
    through Saturday; 11 A.M.
    to 6:30 P.M. Monday.
    Closed Sunday, the week
    of August 15, and the
    second week of January.
Credit card: V.
Some English spoken.
Will ship internationally.

If it is winter, warm your hands at the old wood stove that may well have been in this shop since it was founded in 1875, then peruse the supply of absolutely everything for the winemaker and wine drinker—bottles and corks, small grape presses, beautiful preprinted wine labels along with those to inscribe yourself for your own house vintage. There are brass-bound wooden measuring containers; casks for aging wine (or making vinegar) along with a variety of corkscrews, tasting cups, and other table accessories.

The shop offers a large selection of glassware, from a special French wine tasting glass (ask for the one approved by I.N.A.O.) to small Riesling glasses with deep green stems. You can also find *express* coffee machines and pocketknives of every price and description. The staff is not terribly eager to serve.

QUIMPER FAIENCE
84 Rue Saint-Martin,
    Paris 4.
(42.71.93.03).
Métro: Châtelet.
Open 11 A.M. to 7 P.M. Closed
    Sunday.
Credit cards: EC, V.
English spoken.
Will ship internationally.

This pretty folkloric shop features the popular, brilliantly colored pottery from Brittany known as Quimper Faïence. There's a good selection, and whether you're picking up a teacup or an entire place setting, they'll be happy to ship the pottery home for you. It's the next best thing to a trip to Brittany!

LAURENCE ROQUE—LE
    COMPTOIR DES
    ETOFFES
69 Rue Saint-Martin,
    Paris 4.
(42.72.22.12).
Métro: Hôtel-de-Ville.
Open 11 A.M. to 7 P.M. Closed
    Monday morning and the
    week of August 15.
Credit card: V
Will ship internationally.

A charming shop for do-it-yourself decorators: beautiful embroidery and needlepoint patterns, lace, jaunty-patterned fabrics for edging kitchen shelves, upholstery patterns and fabrics, and a small but select collection of antique teapots.

The makings of a dream kitchen.

LATIN QUARTER, SEVRES-BABYLONE

5th, 6th, and 7th arrondissements

ATELIER DE SEGRIES
31 Rue de Tournon, Paris 6.
(46.34.62.56).
Métro: Odéon.
Open 11 A.M. to 7 P.M. Closed
Sunday and Monday.
Credit cards: AE, V.
English spoken.
Will ship internationally.

The Provençal village of Moustiers—population 602—is rightly famed for its milky-white-glazed hand-painted *faïence*, or pottery, made there since 1679. The best (and most expensive) comes from the Atelier de Ségriès, which offers a wide choice of patterns, including those embellished with delicate Provençal wildflowers. This shop is their home in Paris.

TIANY CHAMBARD
32 Rue Jacob, Paris 6.
(43.29.73.15).
Métro: Saint-Germain-des-
Prés.
Open 2 P.M. to 7 P.M. Closed
Sunday, Monday, and
mid-July through the
third week in August.
English spoken.

A tiny shop with tiny things like old, colorful, beautifully designed fruit and liqueur labels from obsolete canneries and distilleries, perfect for framing and hanging in the kitchen or in the bar.

CULINARION
99 Rue de Rennes, Paris 6.
(45.48.94.76).
Métro: Saint-Germain-des-
Prés.
Open 10 A.M. to 7 P.M. Closed
Monday morning and
Sunday.
Credit card: V.
Will ship internationally.

O ffering the usual and the unusual for the kitchen and the table. *Madeleine* tins, *financier* molds, a small roaster for home-roasted coffee beans, egg-shaped timers, and colorful cast iron cookware at reasonable prices.

DINERS EN VILLE
27 Rue de Varenne, Paris 7.
(42.22.78.33).
Métro: Rue du Bac.
Open 11 A.M. to 7 P.M. Closed
Monday morning and
Sunday.
Credit card: V.
Will ship internationally.

A n elegant shop that specializes in both useful and frivolous accessories and objects for home and table, stocking a wide variety of 19th- and 20th-century silver, sets of dishes, coffee pots, tea-pots and cups, serving dishes, and some fabrics.

FENETRE SUR COUR
27 Rue Saint-Sulpice,
Paris 6.
(43.26.45.85).
Métro: Odéon.
Open 10 A.M. to 7 P.M. Closed
Sunday and August.
Credit card: V.
English spoken.
Will ship internationally.

W hen I'm in the neighborhood, I pop into this store just to fantasize about a big open dining room filled with the sturdy bistro-style wicker objects displayed in this beautiful shop. As the name suggests, the shop is hidden in a charming courtyard: Within you'll find a smattering of antiques from the 1930s as well as new editions of those marvelous '30s wicker café tables and chairs, available now in bright blues and white, or in traditional reds, greens, and beige.

HELENE FOURNIER-GUERIN
25 Rue des Saints-Pères, Paris 6.
(42.60.21.81).
Métro: Saint-Germain-des-Prés.
Open 11 A.M. to 1 P.M. and 2:30 P.M. to 7:30 P.M.
Closed Monday morning, Sunday, and August.
Credit card: AE.
English spoken.

E ighteenth-century *faïence* (earthenware china) and porcelain from Strasbourg, Rouen, Sceaux, and Moustiers; lovely serving dishes and 18th-century Delft tiles, all displayed like crown jewels.

GALLERY LA CORNUE
11 Rue Princesse, Paris 6.
(46.33.84.74).
Métro: Mabillon.
Open 10 A.M. to 6:30 P.M.
Closed Sunday.
Credit card: V.
English spoken.
Will ship internationally.

A nother shop for dreaming, not for filling your suitcase. But if you love beautiful, sturdy, last-a-lifetime stoves, then take a look at the restaurant-style collection displayed here. Each and every one is individually made to order, using thick metal, quality enamels, bronze, copper, and cast iron. They're available in both gas and electric. So dream on!

JARDINS IMAGINAIRES
9 Rue d'Assas, Paris 6.
(42.22.90.03).
Métro: Rennes.
Open 10:30 A.M. to 7:30 P.M.
Closed Monday morning, Sunday, and August.
Credit cards: AE, V.
English spoken.
Will ship internationally.

I think that if someone locked me inside this shop, I could easily while away hours studying all the objects within. As the name suggests, it is a bit like an imaginary garden, filled with wicker baskets and planters, but also featuring old floral paintings, dried flowers, flowered plates, and all sorts of wonderful things for the home, inside and out. I dare you to leave without buying at least a trinket.

LEFEBVRE ET FILS
24 Rue du Bac, Paris 7.
(42.61.18.40).
Métro: Rue du Bac.
Open 10:30 A.M. to noon and 2:30 P.M. to 6:30 P.M.
Monday through Friday; 10:30 A.M. to noon and 3:30 P.M. to 6:30 P.M.
Saturday. Closed Sunday and mid-July through mid-September.
English spoken.
Will ship in Europe.

G eorges Lefèbvre offers an exclusive collection of *faïence* (earthenware china), with a penchant for 18th-century *trompe-l'oeil* serving dishes shaped like boar's heads, cabbages, a plate of olives. Hours are variable, so call before a visit, to be certain the shop is open.

LA PORCELAINE
   BLANCHE
119 Rue Monge, Paris 5.
(43.31.93.95).
Métro: Censier-Daubenton.
Open 10:30 A.M. to 7:30 P.M.
   Closed Monday morning
   and Sunday.
Credit card: V.
See La Porcelaine Blanche,
   1st *arrondissement*, page
   304.

LA PORCELAINE
   BLANCHE
25 Avenue de la Motte-
   Picquet, Paris 7.
(47.05.94.28).
Métro: Latour-Maubourg.
Open 10 A.M. to 7:15 P.M.
   Closed Monday morning
   and Sunday.
Credit cards: EC, V.
English spoken.
See La Porcelaine Blanche,
   1st *arrondissement*, page
   304.

PROSCIENCES
44 Rue des Ecoles, Paris 5.
(46.33.33.00).
Métro: Maubert-Mutualité.
Open 8:30 A.M.to 6:30 P.M.
   Closed Sunday and
   August.

This store looks as if it is stocked strictly for equipping classrooms or science laboratories, but their functional white porcelain measuring pitchers are great for the kitchen, handy for measuring or storing wooden utensils. Also kitchen scales, mortars and pestles, porcelain spoons, and clear glass jugs with handy spouts.

FLORENCE ROUSSEAU
9 Rue de Luynes, Paris 7.
(45.48.04.71).
Métro: Rue du Bac.
Open 2 P.M. to 6:30 P.M.
  Closed Sunday, Monday,
  and August.

A limited but very high quality selection of table-top furnishings, including *barbotines*—artichoke, oyster, and asparagus plates and serving dishes—turn-of-the-century vases with grandiose patterns, unusual serving platters, silver sugar tongs and spoons. The door of this small shop is locked, so be sure to knock to be let in.

**GALERIE MICHEL
  SONKIN**
10 Rue de Beaune, Paris 7.
(42.61.27.87).
Métro: Rue du Bac.
Open 2:30 P.M. to 7 P.M.
  Closed Sunday and
  August.
Credit cards: AE, DC, V.
Will ship internationally.

As much cozy museum as antique shop, Galerie Michel Sonkin is filled with lovingly restored folk objects, most of them in golden, gleaming wood. Monsieur and Madame Sonkin have searched throughout Europe to find their treasures and are particularly proud of their intricately carved, initialed bread stamps, dating from the days when villagers depended on communal ovens for baking. Each loaf was stamped with the family seal or initials, so the baker could tell loaves apart. Also wooden butter molds, milk filters and carved spoons, porcelain cheese molds, some solid antique chests, and pieces of furniture.

THAT SPECIAL DISH

You can take them with you—the dishes, at least. Two of Paris's most famous landmarks, the restaurant Tour d'Argent and the brasserie La Coupole, sell place settings from their well-known tables. The classic blue and white Tour d'Argent dinner plates are sold at the restaurant's boutique, 19 Quai de la Tournelle, Paris 5 (46.33.45.58), from noon to midnight every day but Monday. La Coupole, 102 Boulevard du Montparnasse, Paris 14 (43.20.14.20), sells its signature Limoges porcelain plates and demitasse cups in the afternoon after 3 P.M.

SURFACE
16 Rue Saint-Simon, Paris 7.
(42.22.30.08).
Métro: Rue du Bac.
Open 9 A.M. to 6 P.M. Monday
  through Friday; 10 A.M.
  to 1 P.M. and 2 P.M. to
  5 P.M. Saturday. Closed
  Sunday.

A vast selection of Italian decorator tiles in a multitude of contemporary designs and colors for mixed, matched, and creative personalized decors. Many are hand-painted. The shop will ship individual orders.

TORVINOKA
4 Rue Cardinale, Paris 6.
(43.25.09.13).
Métro: Saint-Germain-des-
    Prés.
Open 10 A.M. to 7 P.M. Closed
    Sunday and the week of
    August 15.
Credit card: V.
English spoken.
Will ship in France.

A contemporary shop featuring all sorts of fanta-sies from Finland, including sturdy, bright-colored plates, stainless steel and wooden objects, as well as lovely baskets of woven heather or lavender. A nice place to browse, for gifts or for yourself!

LA TUILE A LOUP
35 Rue Daubenton, Paris 5.
(47.07.28.90).
Métro: Censier-Daubenton.
Open 10:30 A.M. to 1 P.M.
    and 3 P.M. to 7:30 P.M.
    Closed Sunday afternoon
    and Monday.
Credit cards: AE, V.
English spoken.
Will ship internationally.

A rustic little shop specializing in French re-gional arts and crafts, pottery dishes in rich green and blue glazes, beautiful handmade wooden bowls, baskets, and candles, and a wide selection of books on the folklore and customs of regional France.

MADELEINE, ARC DE TRIOMPHE

8th arrondissement

AU BAIN MARIE
10 Rue Boissy-d'Anglas,
    Paris 8.
(42.66.59.74).
Métro: Concorde.
Open 10 A.M. to 7 P.M. Closed
    Sunday.
Credit cards: AE, V.
English spoken.
Will ship internationally.

Thanks to the good taste and energy of Aude Clément, Au Bain Marie is the city's most beautiful, most eclectic shop for the kitchen and table. A mouthwatering selection of antique and modern silver, porcelain, and china, including a large and lovely collection of antique *barbotines* (asparagus, artichoke, and oyster plates). There's a fine assortment of silver, porcelain, exquisite crystal carafes, expensive but incredibly outfitted wicker picnic baskets, plus amusing knife rests, asparagus tongs, occasional posters, and odd and enviable food-related collector's items. Also a fine selection of elegant handmade table and bed linens in silk, cotton, and pure linen, and sturdy, handsome wicker furniture.

LA BOUTIQUE DANOISE
42 Avenue de Friedland,
    Paris 8.
(42.27.02.92).
Métro: Charles-de-Gaulle-
    Etoile.
Open 9:45 A.M. to 7 P.M.
    Closed Sunday.
Credit cards: AE, DC, V.

All the sleek modern lines of Danish design are here in wood, glass, and stainless steel furniture and lamps, heavy crystal table accessories and vases, and some porcelain and cutlery. There are wall hangings, rugs, and clothes in rich, subdued colors and natural fibers.

LA CARPE
14 Rue Tronchet, Paris 8.
(47.42.73.25).
Métro: Havre-Caumartin.
Open 9:30 A.M. to 6:45 P.M.
    Closed Sunday, Monday
    morning, and August.
Credit cards: EC, V.
English spoken.
Will ship internationally.

Located just off the Place de la Madeleine, this is the place to find items you didn't know you needed: several different kinds of oyster knives, cherry and peach pitters, an espresso machine that works off a car battery, and many more. The staff is very friendly and helpful.

CHRISTOFLE
12 Rue Royale, Paris 8.
(42.60.19.66).
Métro: Madeleine.
Open 9:30 A.M. to 7 P.M.
    Closed Sunday.
Credit cards: AE, DC, EC, V.
See Christofle, 2nd
    arrondissement, page 302.

PETER CREATIONS
191 Rue du Faubourg Saint-
    Honoré, Paris 8.
(45.63.88.00).
Métro: Saint-Philippe-du-
    Roule.
Open 10 A.M. to 1 P.M. and
    1:30 P.M. to 7 P.M. Closed
    Monday morning,
    Sunday, and the first
    three weeks in August.
Credit card: V.
English spoken.
Will ship internationally.

Elegant, modern, refined: a shop featuring silverware, crystal, china, and giftware along with professional cutlery and cutting boards.

PUIFORCAT
131 Boulevard Haussmann,
   Paris 8.
(45.63.10.10).
Métro: Miromesnil.
Open 9:30 A.M. to 6:30 P.M.
Credit cards: AE, DC, V.
English spoken.
Will ship internationally.

PUIFORCAT
22 Rue François 1er, Paris 8.
(47.20.74.27).
Métro: Franklin-D.-
   Roosevelt.
Open 10 A.M. to 7 P.M.
   Tuesday through Friday
   and Sunday; 10 A.M. to
   1 P.M. and 2:15 P.M. to
   7 P.M. Saturday. Closed
   Monday.
Credit cards: AE, DC, V.
English spoken.
Will ship internationally.
See above listing.

TERRITOIRE
30 Rue Boissy-d'Anglas,
   Paris 8.
(42.66.22.13).
Métro: Concorde.
Open 10:30 A.M. to 7 P.M.
   Closed Sunday.
Credit cards: AE, V.
English spoken.

My favorite Paris shop for superbly designed silver cups—*timbales* (monogrammed, they make perfect baby gifts, ready for use much later in life as brandy or Cognac snifters); elegant silver wine and Champagne buckets; fine reproductions of antique china; and exquisite Puiforcat silver patterns from the 1920s and 1930s. The salesladies are always accommodating.

BURNED AT THE STEAK!

In the Middle Ages, there was a fixed price on all market items, particularly perishables such as meat pies. If the pies were sold for less, it was assumed that they contained contaminated or tainted meat. The cheap pies were bought by the poor or by children, who often became ill. To discourage such practices, merchants caught selling such discount-priced perishables were forced to burn the offending meat pies in front of their shops.

A really wonderful idea for a shop: celebrating *les fêtes et les vacances*! Would that we could spend our lives making use of all the goodies found within. There are objects for picnics (great Thermos-style jugs, picnic hampers, you name it) as well as all sorts of paraphernalia for parties, including menu cards, invitations, fireworks, and a great assortment of fantasy birthday candles.

RUE DE PARADIS, GARE DE L'EST

10th arrondissement

ARTS CERAMIQUES
15 Rue de Paradis, Paris 10.
(47.70.64.93).
Métro: Château-d'Eau.
Open 10 A.M. to 7 P.M.
   Tuesday through
   Saturday. Closed Monday
   morning and Sunday.
Credit cards: AE, DC, EC, V.
English spoken.
Will ship internationally.

This shop has a large selection of reproduction Rouen, Quimper, and Marseilles *faïence* (earthenware china), all hand-painted in true, vivid colors. There is also a selection of pewter tea and coffee pots, plates, and accessories.

EDITIONS PARADIS
29 Rue de Paradis, Paris 10.
(45.23.05.34).
Métro: Château-d'Eau.
Open 9:45 A.M. to 6:30 P.M.
Closed Sunday.
Credit cards: AE, DC, EC, V.
English spoken.
Will ship internationally.

A shop filled with hundreds of pieces of glittering crystal and fragile china. Their most unique item: a silverplate milk pot and tiny gas burner, a replica of one used by the French poet the Countess of Noailles in her travels, perfect for heating milk in a hotel room! Also available here are the silverplate *clochettes* (bell-shaped domes) like those used to present exquisite dishes in grand restaurants throughout the world.

LIMOGES UNIC
12 Rue de Paradis, Paris 10.
(47.70.54.49).
Métro: Château-d'Eau.
Open 10 A.M. to 6:30 P.M.
Closed Sunday and
holidays.
Credit cards: AE, EC, V.
English spoken.
Will ship internationally.

Limoges porcelain everywhere: teapots and chocolate services, and simple, classic sets of dishes in every color. Also Meissen teapots, Baccarat, Saint-Louis, Daum, and Lalique crystal, and Christofle and Têtard silver.

**LA TISANERIE
PORCELAINE**
35 Rue de Paradis, Paris 10.
(47.70.40.49).
Métro: Château-d'Eau.
Open 9:45 A.M. to 6:45 P.M.
Closed Sunday.
Credit card: V.
English spoken.
Will ship internationally.

Almost all white porcelain, including simple Pillivuyt bowls, plates, cups, coffee and tea pots, all of which can be personalized with your initials or a design of your choice, applied and baked on in the stone oven right in the shop. Personalization might take a few days, depending on how many pieces you request. Also available here are tart pans, serving plates, and platters, all at reasonable prices.

MONTPARNASSE

14th and 15th arrondissements

**ATELIER FRANCOISE
CATRY**
16 Rue Ernest-Cresson,
Paris 14.
(45.45.91.39).
Métro: Denfert-Rochereau.
Open 9 A.M. to 12:30 P.M.
and 1:30 P.M. to 7 P.M.
Closed Sunday, Saturday
mid-March through
October, and the first two
weeks in August.
English spoken.
Will ship internationally.

The objects in this bright-white shop window are so beautiful that people can't help but stop and look. The artist and proprietor, Mademoiselle Catry, specializes in painting exact replicas of 17th-century and 18th-century patterns on porcelain and earthenware. Her work is rare and beautiful, from the intricate, vividly colored border designs to the gold leaf she applies with painstaking care, producing pieces that seem to belong in a museum. She also loves to do contemporary designs, in subtle but cheerful color. Specializing in fruit and flower motifs, she paints on porcelain that is hand-thrown to her own specifications. Working right in her shop, Mademoiselle Catry will personalize dishes with names, dates, or initials, or produce a faithful copy of a china pattern.

KITCHEN BAZAAR
11 Avenue du Maine, Paris 15.
(42.22.91.17).
Métro: Montparnasse-Bienvenue.
Open 10 A.M. to 7 P.M. Closed Monday morning and Sunday.
Credit card: V.
Will ship internationally.

LA PORCELAINE BLANCHE
135 Rue d'Alésia, Paris 14.
(45.43.78.95).
Métro: Alésia.
Open 10 A.M. to 7 P.M. Closed Sunday and August.
Credit card: V.
See La Porcelaine Blanche, 1st *arrondissement*, page 304.

Everything for the kitchen, from timers on strings to Italian-designed balancing scales, tiny chocolate molds, and citrus fruit peelers, zesters, curlers, all of good quality. Some baking dishes and a small collection of cookbooks.

E. Dehillerin, filled to overflowing with professional cookware (see entry, page 302).

QUATRE SAISONS
88 Avenue du Maine,
   Paris 14.
(43.21.28.99).
Métro: Gaîté.
Open 10:30 A.M. to 7 P.M.
   Closed Monday morning
   and Sunday.
Credit card: V.
Some English spoken.

QUATRE SAISONS
20 Boulevard de Grenelle,
   Paris 15.
(45.77.46.39).
Open 10:30 A.M. to 7 P.M.
   Closed Monday morning,
   Sunday, and August.
Métro: Bir-Hakeim.
Credit card: V.
See above listing.

A cheery shop, with a huge selection of hand-made baskets, bright striped cotton and cotton/linen blend fabric for making tea towels, Alsatian cookie stamps, wooden furniture, and some bathroom accessories.

BUTTES-CHAUMONT
19th arrondissement

**COMPTOIR DE LA
   MOSAIQUE ET DU
   CARRELAGE**
53 Rue de Général-Brunet,
   Paris 19.
(42.08.90.80).
Métro: Danube.
Open 8 A.M. to 12:30 P.M.
   and 1:30 P.M. to 6 P.M.
   Closed Saturday
   afternoon and Sunday.
Will ship internationally.

It's a long way out to this builder and home decorator's warehouse, filled with tiles for every room in the house. They specialize in unique folk-loric painted tiles, including a series of French Revolution tiles with crowing cock and guillotine, busy bakers and pastry chefs baking in wood-fired ovens, and *montgolfière* hot-air balloon tiles that are miniature works of art. There are miniature Toulouse-Lautrec posters on tiles; individual scenes with Paris's old-time street criers; tiles that, when put together, make a pretty ocean scene; along with tiles of the seasons, of herbs, flowers, and vegeta-bles. The staff is most helpful, and will sell tiles by the piece or by the meter. Orders can be shipped, but because of fragility and time delays, they advise against it.

French/English
FOOD GLOSSARY

Fresh produce, always perfectly ripe.

Even for the French, the local restaurant menu can be confusing. For instance, the average Frenchman would be very hard pressed to tell you exactly what goes into a sauce Albuféra (it's a béchamel with sweet peppers) or how a *canard de Barbarie* differs from a *canard de Nantes* (the latter duck is smaller and more delicate).

The following is a brief glossary of common menu terms—words, phrases, and preparations that you are likely to find on a French menu. In all cases, I have tried to offer brief explanations, limiting entries to those that diners are most likely to need when dining in Paris.

A

A.A.A.A.A.: the Association Amicale des Authentiques Amateurs d'Andouillettes gives this label only to the best *andouillettes,* or chitterling sausages.
A point: medium rare.
Abats: organ meats.

Abricot: apricot.
Acidulé: acidic.
Addition: bill.
Affiné(e): aged or refined.
Agneau (de lait): lamb (young, milk fed).
Agrumes: citrus fruits.
Aiglefin, églefin: haddock.
Aigre: sour.
Aigre-doux: sweet and sour.
Aigrelette (sauce): a sour or

tart sauce.
Aiguillettes: thin slivers, usually of duck breast.
Ail: garlic.
Aile: wing of poultry or game bird.
Aile et cuisse: used to describe white breast meat (aile) and dark thigh meat (cuisse), usually of chicken.
Aileron: wing tip.

Aïoli: garlicky blend of eggs and olive oil.

Airelles: wild cranberries.

Albuféra: béchamel sauce with sweet peppers.

Algues: edible seaweed.

Aligot: mashed potatoes with fresh Cantal cheese and garlic.

Allumettes: puff pastry strips; also fried matchstick potatoes.

Alose: shad.

Alouette: lark.

Aloyau: loin area of beef.

Alsacienne (à l'): Alsace style; often including sauerkraut, sausage, or foie gras.

Amande: almond.

Amande de mer: smooth-shelled shellfish, like a small clam, with a sweet, almost hazelnut flavor.

Amer(ère): bitter, as in unsweetened chocolate.

Amertume: bitterness.

Amourettes: spinal bone marrow of calf or ox.

Amuse-bouche (-gueule): literally, amuse the mouth; appetizer.

Ananas: pineapple.

Anchoïade: purée of anchovies, olive oil, and vinegar.

Anchois: anchovy.

Ancienne (à l'): in the old style.

Andouille: cold smoked chitterling (tripe) sausage.

Andouillette: smaller chitterling (tripe) sausage, usually served grilled.

Aneth: dill.

Anis: aniseed.

Apéritif: a before-dinner drink that stimulates the appetite; usually sweet or mildly bitter.

Arachide (huile d'): peanut (oil).

Araignée de mer: spider crab.

Ardennaise (à l'): Ardennes style; often with juniper berries.

Ardoise: literally, slate; usually refers to the day's specialties.

Arêtes: fish bones.

Argenteuil: usually asparagus-flavored soup, named for the Paris suburb that once was the asparagus capital.

Aromates: spices and herbs.

Artichaut (violet): artichoke (small purple).

Asperge: asparagus.

Assiette: plate.

Assiette du pêcheur: assorted fish platter.

Assorti(e): assorted.

Aubergine: eggplant.

Aumônière: literally, beggar's purse; thin *crêpe,* filled, and wrapped like a bundle.

Aurore: béchamel or cream sauce with tomatoes.

Automne: autumn.

Auvergnat(e): Auvergne style; often with cabbage, sausage, and bacon.

Avocat: avocado.

B

Baba au rhum: sponge cake with rum-flavored syrup.

Baguette: classic long, thin loaf of bread.

Baies: berries.

Baies roses: pink peppercorns.

Baigné: bathed.

Ballottine: usually poultry, boned, stuffed, and rolled.

Banane: banana.

Bar: Mediterranean fish,

also known as *loup,* similar to striped bass.

Barbarie (canard de): Barbary breed of duck (see *Canard de Barbarie*).

Barbue: brill, a Mediterranean flatfish related to turbot.

Baron: hindquarters and legs of lamb.

Baron de lapereau: baron (hindquarters and legs) of young rabbit.

Barquette: small pastry shaped like a boat.

Basilic: basil.

Basquaise: Basque style; usually with ham or tomatoes or red peppers.

Bavaroise: cold dessert; a rich custard made with cream and gelatin.

Bavette: skirt steak.

Béarnaise: tarragon-flavored sauce of egg yolks, butter, shallots, white wine, vinegar, and other herbs.

Béatilles: dish combining various organ meats.

Bécasse: woodchuck.

Béchamel: white sauce made with butter, flour, and milk, usually flavored with onion, bay leaf, pepper, and nutmeg.

Beignet: fritter or doughnut.

Belon: prized flat-shelled *plate* oyster.

Bercy: fish-stock-based sauce thickened with flour and butter and flavored with white wine and shallots.

Berrichonne: garnish of braised cabbage, glazed baby onions, chestnuts, and lean bacon.

Betterave: beet.

Beurre: butter.

Beurre blanc: reduced sauce of vinegar, white

wine, shallots, and butter.

Beurre noir: sauce of browned butter, lemon juice or vinegar, parsley, and sometimes capers.

Beurre noisette: lightly browned butter.

Biche: female deer.

Bien cuit(e): well done.

Bifteck: steak.

Bigarade: orange sauce.

Bigarreau: red, firm-fleshed variety of cherry.

Bigorneaux: periwinkles, tiny sea snails.

Billy Bi, Billy By: cream of mussel soup.

Biscuits à la cuillère: ladyfingers.

Bisque: substantial soup, usually shellfish.

Blanc (de poireau): white portion (of leek).

Blanc (de volaille): usually breast of chicken.

Blanquette: veal, lamb, chicken, or seafood stew with egg and cream–enriched white sauce.

Blette: Swiss chard.

Bleu: blood rare, usually for steak.

Blinis: small, thick pancakes.

Boeuf à la mode: beef marinated and braised in red wine, served with carrots, mushrooms, onions, and turnips.

Boeuf au gros sel: boiled beef, served with vegetables and coarse salt.

Boissons (non) comprises: drinks (not) included.

Bombe: molded, layered ice cream dessert.

Bonne femme (cuisine): home-style (cooking); also a meat garnish of bacon, potatoes, mushrooms, and onions; a fish garnish of shallots, parsley, mushrooms,

and potatoes; or a white wine sauce with shallots, mushrooms, and lemon juice.

Bordelaise: Bordeaux style; also refers to a brown sauce of shallots, red wine, and bone marrow.

Bouchée: a tiny mouthful; may refer to a bite-size pastry or to a *vol-au-vent.*

Boudin: technically a meat sausage, but generically any sausage-shaped mixture.

Boudin blanc: white sausage, of veal, chicken, or pork.

Boudin noir: pork blood sausage.

Bouillabaisse: Mediterranean fish soup.

Bouillon: a light soup or broth.

Boulette: meatball or fishball.

Bouquet: large reddish shrimp (see also *Crevette rose).*

Bourdaloue: hot poached fruit, sometimes wrapped in pastry.

Bourguignonne: Burgundy style; often with red wine, onions, mushrooms, and bacon.

Bouribut: spicy, red wine duck stew.

Bourride: egg-based Mediterranean fish and shellfish soup served with *aïoli.*

Braise: live coals.

Braiser: to braise; to cook meat by browning in fat, then simmering in covered dish with small amount of liquid.

Brandade (de morue): warm garlicky purée of salt cod, milk or cream or oil, and sometimes mashed potatoes.

Brebis (fromage de): sheep (sheep's-milk cheese).

Bretonne: in the style of Brittany; a dish served with white beans; or may refer to a white wine sauce with carrots, leeks, and celery.

Brioche: buttery, egg-enriched yeast bread.

Broche (à la): spit-roasted.

Brochet: pike.

Brochette: cubes of meat or fish and vegetables on a skewer.

Brouillé(es): scrambled, usually eggs.

Brûlé: literally, burned; usually refers to dark caramelization.

Brunoise: tiny diced vegetables.

Buccin: (see *Bulot).*

Buffet froid: variety of dishes, served cold, sometimes from a buffet.

Bugnes: sweet fried doughnuts or fritters, originally from Lyons.

Buisson: literally, a bush; generally a dish including vegetables arranged like a bush; classically, a crayfish presentation.

Bulot: large sea snail, also called *buccin.*

C

Cabécou: small round goat cheese.

Cabillaud: fresh cod.

Cacahuètes: peanuts.

Caen (à la mode de): named after the Normandy town; usually a dish cooked in Calvados and white wine and/or cider.

Café: coffee, as well as a type of eating place where coffee is served.

Café au lait: coffee with milk.

Café crème: coffee with milk.

Café déca: decaffeinated coffee.

Café liégeois: iced coffee served with ice cream (optional) and whipped cream.

Café noir: black coffee.

Cagouille: small *petit-gris* land snail, found in the Saintonge province of western France.

Caille: quail.

Calmar: small squid, similar to *encornet,* with interior cartilage instead of a bone.

Campagne (à la): country-style.

Canapé: triangular pieces of toasted bread, usually served with game; also, an appetizer with a bread base, garnished with a variety of savory mixtures.

Canard: duck.

Canard à la presse: roast duck served with sauce of juices obtained from pressing the carcass, combined with red wine and Cognac.

Canard de Barbarie: Barbary breed of duck raised in southwest France, with strong-flavored flesh; generally used for braising.

Canard de Nantes: also called *canard de Challans;* very delicate-flavored small duck.

Canard de Rouen: cross between domestic and wild duck; classically, Rouen ducks are smothered and not bled, giving a special taste to the meat.

Canard sauvage: wild duck.

Caneton: young male duck.

Canette: young female duck.

Cannelle: cinnamon.

Caprice: literally, a whim; usually a dessert.

Carafe d'eau: pitcher of tap water.

Carbonnade: a braised beef stew prepared with beer and onions; also refers to a cut of beef.

Cardon: cardoon; large celerylike vegetable in the artichoke family.

Carré d'agneau: rack (ribs) or loin of lamb.

Carré de porc: rack (ribs) or loin of pork.

Carré de veau: rack (ribs) or loin of veal.

Carrelet: summer flounder or plaice.

Carte: menu.

Carvi: caraway seeds.

Casse-croûte: literally, breaking bread; slang for snack.

Casse-pierre: edible seaweed.

Cassis: black currant; also black currant liqueur.

Cassolette: usually a dish presented in a small casserole.

Cassoulet: a casserole of white beans, including various combinations of sausages, duck, pork, lamb, mutton, and goose.

Caviar d'aubergine: cold eggplant purée.

Céleri: celery.

Céleri-rave: celeriac.

Cèpe: large, meaty wild boletus mushroom.

Cerfeuil: chervil.

Cerise: cherry.

Cerise noire: black cherry.

Cerneau: walnut meat; also refers to unripe walnut.

Cervelas: garlicky pork sausage; also refers to fish and seafood sausage.

Cervelles: brains, of calf or lamb.

Chair: the fleshy portion of either poultry or meat.

Champêtre: rustic; describes a simple presentation of a variety of ingredients.

Champignon: mushroom.
de bois: wild mushroom, from the woods.
de Paris: cultivated mushroom.
sauvage: wild mushroom.

Champignons à la grecque: tiny cultivated mushrooms cooked in water, lemon juice, olive oil, and spices, served as a cold appetizer.

Chanterelle: pale, curly-capped wild mushroom.

Chantilly: sweetened whipped cream.

Chapon: capon, or castrated chicken.

Chapon de mer: Mediterranean fish, in the *rascasse,* or scorpion fish, family.

Charcuterie: cold cuts, sausages, terrines, pâtés; also, shop selling such products.

Chariot (de desserts): rolling cart, usually carrying varied desserts.

Charlotte: molded dessert with lady-fingers and custard filling, served cold; or fruit compote baked with buttered white bread, served hot.

Charolais: light-colored cow that produces high-quality beef.

Chartreuse: a dish of braised partridge and cabbage; also herb-and-spice-based liqueur made by the Chartreux monks.

Chasse: the hunt.

Chasseur: hunter; also sauce with white wine, mushrooms, shallots, tomatoes, and herbs.

Châtaigne: chestnut, smaller than *marron,* with multiple nut meats.

Chateaubriand: thick filet steak, traditionally served with sautéed potatoes and a sauce of white wine, dark beef stock, butter, shallots, and herbs, or with a *béarnaise* sauce.

Chaud(e): hot or warm.

Chaud-froid: cooked poultry dish served cold, usually covered with a sauce, then with aspic.

Chaudrée: fish stew, sometimes with potatoes.

Chausson: a filled pastry turnover, sweet or savory.

Chemise (en): wrapped; with pastry.

Chèvre (fromage de): goat cheese.

Chevreau: young goat.

Chevreuil: young roe deer.

Chicorée: curly endive.

Chiffonnade: shredded herbs and vegetables, usually green.

Chinchard: saurel; ocean fish with bonelike cartilaginous plates along its backbone, generally used for soups.

Chipiron: Basque name for small squid or *encornet.*

Chocolat: chocolate.

Chocolat amer: bittersweet chocolate, with very little sugar.

Chocolat au lait: milk chocolate.

Chocolat mi-amer: bittersweet chocolate, with more sugar than *chocolat amer.*

Chocolat noir: used interchangeably with *chocolat amer.*

Choix (au): a choice; usually meaning one may choose freely from several offerings.

Choron (sauce): *béarnaise* sauce with tomatoes.

Chou: cabbage.

Chou-fleur: cauliflower.

Chou frisé: kale.

Chou rouge: red cabbage.

Chou vert: curly green Savoy cabbage.

Choucroute: sauerkraut; also main dish of sauerkraut, various sausages, bacon, and pork, served with potatoes.

Choux (pâte à): cream puff (pastry).

Choux de Bruxelles: brussels sprouts.

Ciboulette: chive.

Cidre: cider, either apple or pear.

Citron: lemon.

Citron vert: lime.

Citronelle: lemon grass, an oriental herb.

Citrouille: pumpkin, gourd.

Civelles: spaghettilike baby eels, also called *pibales.*

Civet: a stew of game thickened with blood.

Civet de lièvre: jugged hare.

Clafoutis: traditional tart from the Limousin, made with a kind of *crêpe* batter and fruit, usually black cherries.

Claires: oysters; also a designation given to certain oysters to indicate that they have been put in *claires,* or oyster beds in salt marshes, where they are fattened up for several months before going to market.

Clamart: Paris suburb once famous for its green peas; today a garnish of peas.

Clémentine: small tangerine, from Morocco or Spain.

Clouté: studded with.

Cochon (de lait): pig (suckling).

Cochonnailles: pork products; usually an assortment of sausages and/or pâtés served as a first course.

Cocotte: casserole or cooking pot.

Coeur: heart.

Coeur de filet: thickest (and best) part of beef filet, usually cut into chateaubriand steaks.

Coffret: literally, small box; usually presentation in a small rectangular pastry case.

Coing: quince.

Colin: hake.

Colvert: wild ("green collared") duck.

Compote: stewed fresh or dried fruit.

Concassé: coarsely chopped.

Concombre: cucumber.

Confit: duck, goose, or pork cooked and preserved in its own fat; also fruit or vegetables preserved in sugar, alcohol, or vinegar.

Confiture: jam.

Confiture de vieux garçon: varied fresh fruits macerated in alcohol.

Congeler: to freeze.

Congre: conger eel; a large ocean fish resembling an eel, often used in fish stews.

Consommé: clear soup.

Contre-filet: cut of sirloin taken above the loin on either side of the backbone, tied for roasting or braising (can also be cut for grilling).

Convives (la totalité des): (all) those gathered at a single table.

Copeaux: literally, shavings, such as from chocolate or vegetables.

Coq (au vin): mature rooster (stewed in wine sauce).

Coque: tiny, mild-flavored, clamlike shellfish.

Coque (à la): soft-cooked egg, or anything served in a shell.

Coquelet: young male chicken.

Coquillages: shellfish.

Coquille: shell.

Coquille Saint-Jacques: sea scallop.

Corail: coral-colored egg sac, found in scallops, spiny lobster, or crayfish.

Corbeille (de fruits): basket (of fruit).

Coriandre: coriander, either the fresh herb or dried seeds.

Cornichon: tiny tart pickle.

Côte d'agneau: lamb chop.

Côte de boeuf: beef blade or rib steak.

Côte de veau: veal chop.

Côtelette: thin chop or cutlet.

Cotriade: fish stew from Brittany, which can include sardines, mackerel, and porgy, cooked with butter, potatoes, onions, and herbs.

Cou d'oie (de canard) farci: neck skin of goose (sometimes also duck), stuffed with meat and spices, much like a sausage.

Coulibiac: a hot Russian pâté, usually filled with salmon and covered with *brioche.*

Coulis: purée of raw or cooked vegetables or fruit.

Coupe: cup; refers to dessert served in a goblet.

Courge: squash or gourd.

Courgette: zucchini.

Couronne: ring or circle, usually of bread.

Court-bouillon: broth, or aromatic poaching liquid.

Couscous: granules of semolina, or hard wheat flour; also refers to a complete Moroccan dish that includes the steamed grain, broth, vegetables, meats, hot sauce, and sometimes chick-peas and raisins.

Couteau: knife.

Couvert: a place setting, including dishes, silver, glassware, and linen.

Crabe: crab.

Crapaudine: preparation of grilled poultry or game bird with backbone removed.

Crécy: a carrot garnish or carrot-based dish.

Crème: cream.

Crème anglaise: custard sauce.

Crème brûlée: rich custard dessert with a top of caramelized sugar.

Crème chantilly: sweetened whipped cream.

Crème fouettée: whipped cream.

Crème fraîche: thick, sour, heavy cream.

Crème pâtissière: custard filling for pastries and cakes.

Crème plombières: custard filled with fresh fruits and egg whites.

Crêpe: thin pancake.

Crêpes Suzette: hot *crêpe* dessert flavored with orange butter.

Crépine: caul fat.

Crépinette: small sausage patty wrapped in caul fat.

Cresson(ade): watercress (watercress sauce).

Crête (de coq): cock's comb.

Creuse: elongated, crinkle-shelled oyster.

Crevette grise: tiny soft-fleshed shrimp that remains gray when cooked.

Crevette rose: small firm-fleshed shrimp that turns red when cooked; when large, called *bouquet.*

Criste-marine: edible algae.

Croquant(e): crispy.

Croque-madame: toasted ham and cheese sandwich topped with an egg.

Croque-monsieur: toasted ham and cheese sandwich.

Croquette: ground meat, fish, fowl, or vegetables bound with eggs or sauce, shaped into various forms, usually coated in bread crumbs and deep fried.

Crottin (de Chavignol): firm goat cheese (from Chavignol).

Croustade: usually small, pastry-wrapped dish; also regional southwestern pastry filled with prunes and/or apples.

Croûte (en): in pastry.

Croûte de sel (en): in a salt crust.

Croûtons: small cubes, rounds, or slices of toasted or fried bread.

Cru: raw.

Crudités: raw vegetables.

Crustacés: crustaceans.

Cuillère (à la): to be eaten with a spoon.

Cuisse de poulet: chicken drumstick.
Cuisson: cooking.
Cuissot: haunch, of veal, venison, or wild boar.
Cuit(e): cooked.
Cul: haunch or rear, usually of red meat.
Culotte: rump (usually of beef).
Cure-dent: toothpick.

D

Dariole: usually a garnish in a cylindrical mold.
Darne: a slice or steak from fish, often salmon.
Dattes: dates.
Daube: stew, usually meat.
Daurade: dorade or sea bream, similar to porgy.
Décaféiné: decaffeinated.
Décortiqué(e): shelled or peeled.
Dégustation: tasting or sampling.
Déjeuner: lunch.
Délice: delight, usually used to describe a dessert.
Demi: half; also refers to a 1-cup (25-cl) glass of beer.
Demi-deuil: literally, in half mourning; poached (usually chicken) with truffles inserted under the skin; also, sweetbreads with a truffled white sauce.
Demi-glace: concentrated beef-base sauce lightened with consommé, or a lighter brown sauce.
Désossé: boned.
Diable: method of preparing poultry, served with a peppery sauce, often mustard-based.
Dieppoise: Dieppe style; usually white wine, mussels, shrimp, mush-

rooms, and cream.
Dijonnaise: Dijon style; usually with mustard.
Dinde: turkey ham.
Dindon(neau): turkey, in general (young turkey).
Dîner: dinner; to dine.
Discrétion (à la): on menu usually refers to wine, which may be consumed—without limit—at the customer's discretion.
Dodine: cold, boned stuffed duck.
Dos: back; also refers to the meatiest portion of fish.
Dos et ventre: literally, back and front; both sides (usually fish).
Douceurs: sweets or desserts.
Doux, douce: sweet.
Dugléré: white flour-based sauce with shallots, white wine, tomatoes, and parsley.
Duxelles: chopped mushrooms and shallots sautéed in butter, then mixed with cream.

E

Eau du robinet: tap water.
Ecailler: to scale fish; also refers to an oyster opener, or seller.
Echalotes: shallots.
Echine: spare ribs.
Echiquier: checkered.
Ecrevisse: freshwater crayfish.
Effiloché: frayed, thinly sliced.
Eglefin, aiglefin: haddock.
Emincé: thin slice; usually of meat.
Encornet: small squid; in Basque region called *chipiron.*
Endive: chicory or Belgian endive.

Entrecôte: beef rib steak.
Entrecôte maître d'hôtel: beef rib steak with herb butter.
Entrecôte marchand de vin: beef rib steak with sauce of red wine and shallots.
Entrée: first course.
Entremets: sweets.
Epaule: shoulder, of veal, lamb, mutton, or pork.
Eperlan: smelt or whitebait, usually fried
Epi de maïs: ear of sweet corn.
Epices: spices.
Epinard: spinach.
Escabèche: a Provençal preparation of sardines or *rouget,* in which the fish are browned in oil, then marinated in vinegar and herbs and served very cold; also raw fish marinated in lemon or lime juice and herbs.
Escalope: thinly sliced meat or fish, usually cut at an angle.
Escargot: land snail.
Escargot de Bourgogne: land snail prepared with butter, garlic, and parsley.
Escargot petit-gris: small land snail.
Espadon: swordfish.
Estofinado: fish stew from Auvergne, made with dried Atlantic cod, and cooked in walnut oil with eggs, garlic, and cream.
Estouffade: stew of beef, pork, onions, mushrooms, orange zest, and red wine.
Estragon: tarragon.
Eté: summer.
Etrille: small crab.
Etuvé(e): cooked in ingredient's own juice; braised.

Eventail (en): fan-shaped; usually refers to shape in which vegetables or fish are cut.

F

Façon (à ma): (my) way of preparing a dish.
Faisan(e): pheasant.
Farandole: rolling cart, usually of desserts or ·cheese.
Farci(e): stuffed.
Farine: flour.
Faux-filet: sirloin steak.
Fenouil: fennel.
Féra: salmonlike lake fish.
Ferme (fermier): farm-fresh (farmer).
Fermé: closed.
Feu de bois (au): cooked over a wood fire.
Feuille de chêne: oak-leaf lettuce.
Feuille de vigne: vine leaf.
Feuilletage (en): (in) puff pastry.
Fèves: broad beans.
Ficelle (à la): tied with a string; also small, thin *baguette.*
Figue: fig.
Financière: Madeira sauce with truffle juice.
Fines de claire: elongated, crinkle-shelled oysters that stay in fattening beds (*claires*) up to two months.
Fines herbes: mixture of herbs; usually parsley, chives, and tarragon.
Flageolets: small, pale green kidney-shaped beans.
Flagnarde, flaugnarde: hot fruit-filled batter cake made with eggs, flour, milk, and butter, and sprinkled with sugar before serving.
Flamande (à la): Flemish

style; usually with stuffed cabbage leaves, carrots, turnips, potatoes, and bacon.
Flambé: flamed.
Flamiche: savory tart with rich bread-dough crust.
Flan: sweet or savory tart; sometimes refers to a crustless custard pie.
Flanchet (de veau): flank (of veal).
Flétan: halibut.
Fleur: flower.
Fleurons: puff pastry crescents.
Florentine: with spinach.
Foie: liver.
Foie de veau: calf's liver.
Foie gras d'oie (de canard): liver of fattened goose (duck).
Foies blonds de volaille: chicken livers; also sometimes a chicken liver mousse.
Foin (dans le): cooked in hay.
Fond: cooking juices from meat, used to make sauces; also, bottom.
Fond d'artichaut: heart and base of an artichoke.
Fondant: literally, melting; refers to cooked, worked sugar that is flavored, then used for icing cakes.
Fondu(e): melted.
Forestière: garnish of wild mushrooms, bacon, and potatoes.
Four (au): baked in oven.
Fourchette: fork.
Fourré: stuffed or filled.
Frais, fraîche: fresh or chilled.
Fraise: strawberry.
Fraise des bois: wild strawberry.
Framboise: raspberry.
Frangipane: almond custard filling.

Frappé: usually refers to a drink served very cold or with ice.
Frémis: quivering; often refers to barely cooked oysters.
Friandises: sweets, *petits fours.*
Fricadelles: fried minced meat patties.
Fricandeau: thinly sliced veal or a rump roast, braised with vegetables and white wine.
Fricassée: classically, ingredients braised in wine sauce or butter with cream added; currently denotes any mixture of ingredients—fish or meat—stewed or sautéed.
Frisé(e): curly; usually curly endive.
Frit(es): French fries.
Fritons: coarse pork *rillettes,* or a minced spread that includes organ meats.
Fritot: small organ meat fritter, where meat is partially cooked, then marinated in oil, lemon juice, and herbs, dipped in batter, and fried just before serving; also can refer to any small fried piece of meat or fish.
Friture: frying; also refers to preparation of small fried fish, usually whitebait or smelt.
Froid(e): cold.
Fromage: cheese.
Fromage blanc: a smooth low-fat cheese similar to cottage cheese.
Fromage de tête: headcheese, usually pork.
Fromage maigre: low-fat cheese.
Fruit de la passion: passion fruit.
Fruits confits: preserved

fruits; generally refers to candied fruits.

Fruits de mer: seafood.

Fumé: smoked.

Fumet: fish stock.

G

Galantine: boned poultry or meat that is stuffed, rolled, cooked, glazed with gelatin, and served cold.

Galette: round, flat pastry, pancake, or cake; can also refer to pancake-like savory preparations.

Gambas: large prawns.

Garbure: generally, a hearty soup of cabbage, beans, and preserved pork, goose, duck, or turkey..

Garni(e): garnished.

Garniture: garnish.

Gâteau: cake.

Gaufre: waffle.

Gayettes: small sausage patties made with pork liver and bacon and wrapped in caul fat and bacon.

Gelée: aspic.

Genièvre: juniper berry.

Génoise: sponge cake.

Germiny: garnish of sorrel; sorrel and cream soup.

Gésier: gizzard.

Gibelotte: fricassee of rabbit in red or white wine.

Gibier: game.

Gigot: usually leg of lamb.

Gigot de mer: a preparation, usually of large pieces of monkfish *(lotte),* oven-roasted like a leg of lamb.

Gigue (de): haunch (of) certain game meats.

Gingembre: ginger.

Girofle: cloves.

Girolle: delicate, pale

orange wild mushroom.

Glace: ice cream.

Glacé: iced, crystallized, or glazed.

Gougère: cheese-flavored *chou* pastry.

Goujonnettes: generally used to describe small slices of fish, such as sole, usually fried.

Goujons: small catfish; also often applied to any small fish; also a preparation in which the central part of a larger fish is coated with bread crumbs, then deep fried.

Gourmandises: sweetmeats.

Gousse (d'ail): clove (of garlic).

Graine de moutarde: mustard seed.

Graisse: fat.

Graisserons: crisply fried pieces of duck or goose skin; cracklings.

Grand veneur: usually a brown sauce for game, with red currant jelly.

Granité: water ice.

Gras: fatty.

Gras-double: tripe baked with onions and white wine.

Gratin: crusty-topped dish; also refers to a casserole.

Gratin dauphinois: baked casserole of sliced potatoes, usually with cream, milk, and sometimes cheese.

Gratin savoyard: baked casserole of sliced potatoes, usually with bouillon, cheese, and butter.

Gratiné(e): having a crusty, browned top; also onion soup.

Grattons: crisply fried pieces of pork, goose, or duck skin; cracklings.

Gratuit: free.

Grecque (à la): cold vegetables, usually mushrooms, cooked in seasoned mixture with oil, lemon juice, and water.

Grelot: small white bulb onion.

Grenade: pomegranate.

Grenadin: small veal scallop.

Grenouille (cuisses de): frog legs.

Gribiche (sauce): mayonnaise with capers, *cornichons,* and herbs.

Grillade: grilled meat.

Grillé(e): grilled.

Griotte: shiny, slightly acidic, reddish black cherry.

Grive: thrush.

Grondin: gurnard or gurnet—spiked-head, bony ocean fish, used in fish stews such as *bouillabaisse.*

Gros sel: coarse salt.

Groseille: red currant.

Gruyère: hard, mild cheese.

H

Hachis: minced or chopped meat or fish preparation.

Hareng: herring.

Haricot: bean.

Haricot blanc: white bean, usually dried.

Haricot de mouton: stew of mutton and white beans.

Haricot rouge: red kidney bean; also, preparation of red beans in red wine.

Haricot vert: green bean, usually fresh.

Hiver: winter.

Hochepot: thick stew, usually of oxtail.

Hollandaise: sauce of butter, eggs yolks, and

lemon juice.
Homard: lobster.
Hongroise (à la): Hungarian style; usually with paprika and cream.
Hors-d'oeuvre: appetizer; can also refer to a first course.
Huile: oil.
Huile d'arachide: peanut oil.
Huile de pépins de raisins: grapeseed oil.
Huître: oyster.
Hure de porc: head of pig or boar; usually refers to headcheese preparation.
Hure de saumon: a salmon "headcheese," or pâté, prepared with salmon meat, not actually the head.

I

Ile flottante: literally, floating island; most commonly used interchangeably with *oeufs à la neige,* poached meringue floating in *crème anglaise;* classically, a layered cake covered with whipped cream and served with custard sauce.
Impératrice (à l'): usually rice pudding dessert with candied fruit.
Indienne (à l'): East Indian style, usually with curry powder.
Infusion: herb tea.

J

Jambon: ham; also refers to thigh or shoulder of meat, usually pork.
Jambon cru: usually salt-cured or smoked ham that has been aged but not cooked.

Jambon de Bayonne: raw, dried, salt-cured ham.
Jambon de Paris: lightly salted, cooked ham, very pale in color.
Jambon de York: smoked English-style ham, usually poached.
Jambon d'oie (or de canard): breast of fattened goose (or duck), smoked, or salted, or sugar-cured, and resembling ham in flavor.
Jambonneau: pork knuckle.
Jambonnette: boned and stuffed knuckle of ham or poultry.
Jardinière: garnish of fresh cooked vegetables.
Jarret de veau: stew of veal shin.
Jerez: refers to sherry.
Jésus de Morteau: smoked pork sausage from the Franche-Comté.
Jeune: young.
Joue: cheek.
Julienne: slivered vegetables (sometimes meat).
Jus: juice.

K

Kir: an apéritif made with *crème de Cassis* and most commonly white wine, but sometimes red wine.
Kir royal: a *kir* made with Champagne.
Kougelhopf, kougelhof, kouglof, kugelhopf: sweet, crown-shaped, Alsatian breadlike yeast cake, with almonds and raisins.

L

Lait: milk.

Laitance: soft roe (often of herring), or eggs.
Laitue: lettuce.
Lamelle: very thin slice.
Lamproie: lamprey, eel-shaped fish, either fresh- or saltwater.
Langouste: clawless spiny lobster; sometimes called crawfish or crayfish.
Langoustine: clawed crustacean, smaller than either *homard* or spiny lobster, with very delicate meat.
Languedocienne: garnish, usually of tomatoes, eggplant, and wild *cèpe* mushrooms.
Lapereau: young rabbit.
Lapin: rabbit.
Lapin de garenne: wild rabbit.
Lard: bacon.
Lardon: cube of bacon.
Larme: literally, a teardrop; a very small portion of liquid.
Lèche: thin slice of bread or meat.
Léger(légère): light.
Légume: vegetable.
Lieu (jaune): pollack, a prized small (yellow) saltwater fish.
Lièvre: hare.
Limande: solelike ocean fish, not as firm as sole.
Limande sole: lemon sole.
Lisette: small mackerel.
Lit: bed.
Lotte: monkfish or angler fish, a large, firm-fleshed ocean fish.
Lou magret: breast of fattened duck.
Loup (de mer): Mediterranean fish, also known as *bar,* similar to striped bass.
Lyonnaise (à la): in the style of Lyons, often garnished with onions.

M

Macédoine: diced mixed fruit or vegetables.

Macérer: to steep, pickle, or soak.

Mâche: lamb's lettuce, a tiny, dark green lettuce.

Madeleines: small tea cakes.

Madère: Madeira.

Magret de canard (d'oie): breast of fattened duck (goose).

Maigre: thin, non-fatty.

Maïs: corn.

Maison (de la): of the house, or restaurant.

Maître d'hôtel: head waiter; also compound butter, a mixture of butter, parsley, and lemon juice.

Maltaise: orange-flavored hollandaise sauce.

Mandarine: tangerine.

Mange-tout: literally, eat it all; a podless green runner bean; a snow pea; a type of apple.

Mangue: mango.

Manière (de): in the style of.

Maquereau: mackerel.

Maraîchère (à la): market-garden style, usually referring to a dish, or salad, that includes various greens.

Marbré(e): marbled.

Marc: distilled residue of grape skins or other fruits after they have been pressed.

Marcassin: young wild boar.

Marchand de vin: wine merchant; also a sauce made with red wine, meat stock, and chopped shallots.

Marché: market.

Marée (la): literally, the tide; usually used to indicate that the seafood is fresh.

Marennes: flat-shelled, green-tinged *plate* oysters; also French coastal village where flat-shelled oysters are raised.

Mareyeur: wholesale fish merchant.

Mariné: marinated.

Marinière (moules): method of cooking mussels in white wine with onions, shallots, butter, and herbs.

Marjolaine: marjoram; also, multilayered chocolate and nut cake.

Marmite: small covered pot; also a dish cooked in a small casserole.

Marquise (au chocolat): mousselike (chocolate) cake.

Marron: large chestnut.

Matelote (d'anguilles): freshwater fish stew (or of eels).

Mauviette: wild meadowlark or skylark.

Médaillon: round piece or slice.

Mélange: mixture or blend.

Méli-mélo: an assortment of fish and/or seafood, usually served in a salad.

Melon de Cavaillon: small canteloupelike melon from Cavaillon, a town in Provence known for its wholesale produce market.

Ménagère (à la): literally, in the style of a housewife; usually a simple preparation including onions, potatoes, and carrots.

Menthe: mint.

Menthe poivrée: peppermint.

Mer: sea.

Merguez: small spicy sausage.

Merlan: whiting.

Merle: blackbird.

Merveille: hot sugared doughnuts.

Mesclun, mesclum: mixture of at least seven varieties of multi-shaded salad greens.

Mets: dish or preparation.

Mets selon la saison: seasonal preparation; according to the season.

Meunière (à la): literally, in the style of a miller's wife; refers to a fish that is seasoned, rolled in flour, fried in butter, and served with lemon, parsley, and hot melted butter.

Meurette: in, or with, a red wine sauce; also a Burgundian fish stew.

Miel: honey.

Mignardises: synonym for *petits fours.*

Mignonette: small cubes, usually of beef; also refers to coarsely ground black or white peppercorns.

Mijoté(e) (plat): simmered (dish or preparation).

Mille-feuille: refers to puff pastry with many thin layers; usually a cream-filled rectangle of puff pastry, or a Napolean.

Mimosa: garnish of chopped hard-cooked egg yolks.

Minute (à la): prepared at the last minute.

Mirabeau: garnish of anchovies, pitted olives, tarragon, and anchovy butter.

Mirabelle: yellow plum.

Mirepoix: cubes of carrots and onions or mixed vegetables, usually used in braising to boost the flavor of a meat dish.

Miroton (de): slices (of); also stew of meats flavored with onions.

Mitonnée: a simmered souplike dish.

Mode (à la): in the style of.

Moelle: beef bone marrow.

Moka: refers to coffee, or coffee-flavored dish.

Montagne (de): from the mountains.

Montmorency: garnished with cherries.

Morceau: piece or small portion.

Morille: wild morel mushroom, dark brown and conical-shaped.

Mornay: thickened, milk-based sauce including flour, butter, and egg yolks, with cheese added.

Morue: salted or dried and salted codfish.

Mouclade: creamy mussel stew, sometimes flavored with curry.

Moule: mussel.

Moule de bouchot: small, highly prized cultivated mussel, raised on stakes driven into the sediment of shallow coastal beds.

Moule de Parques: Dutch cultivated mussel, usually raised in fattening beds, or diverted ponds.

Moule d'Espagne: large, sharp-shelled mussel, often served raw as part of a seafood platter.

Moules marinière: mussels cooked in white wine with onions, shallots, butter, and herbs.

Mousse: light, airy mixture usually containing eggs and cream, either sweet or savory.

Mousseline: refers to ingredients that are usually lightened with whipped cream or egg whites, as in sauces, or with butter, as in *brioche mousseline.*

Mousseron: tiny, delicate, wild mushroom.

Moutarde (à l'ancienne en graines): mustard (coarse-grained).

Mouton: mutton.

Mulet: mullet, a rustic-flavored ocean fish.

Mûre: blackberry.

Muscade: nutmeg.

Museau de porc (de boeuf): vinegared pork (beef) muzzle.

Myrtille: bilberry (bluish black European blueberry).

Mystère: cone-shaped ice cream dessert; also dessert of cooked meringue with ice cream and chocolate sauce.

N

Nage (à la): aromatic poaching liquid (served in).

Nantua: sauce of crayfish, butter, cream, and truffles; also garnish of crayfish.

Nappé: covered, as with a sauce.

Nature: refers to simple, unadorned preparations.

Navarin: lamb or mutton.

Navet: turnip.

Newburg: lobster preparation with Madeira, egg yolks, and cream.

Nid: nest.

Nivernaise: in the style of Nevers; with carrots and onions.

Noisette: hazelnut; also refers to a small round piece (such as from a potato), generally the size of a hazelnut, lightly browned in butter; also, center cut of lamb chop; also, hazelnut flavor.

Noix: walnut; nut; nut-size.

Normande: in the style of Normandy; sauce of seafood, cream, and mushrooms; also refers to fish or meat cooked with apple cider or Calvados; or dessert with apples, usually served with cream.

Nouilles: noodles.

Nouveau (nouvelle): new or young.

Nouveauté: a new offering.

Noyau: stone or pit.

O

Oeuf à la coque: soft-cooked egg.

Oeuf brouillé: scrambled egg.

Oeuf dur: hard-cooked egg.

Oeuf en meurette: poached egg in red wine sauce.

Oeuf mollet: egg simmered in water for 6 minutes.

Oeuf poché: poached egg.

Oeuf sauté à la poêle, oeuf sur le plat: fried egg.

Oeufs à la neige: literally, eggs in the snow; sweetened whipped egg whites poached in milk and served with vanilla custard sauce.

Offert: offered, free or given.

Oie: goose.

Oignon: onion.

Omble chevalier: freshwater char, a member of the trout family, with firm, flaky flesh varying from white to deep red.

Onglet: cut similar to beef flank steak; also cut of

beef sold as *biftek* and *entrecôte;* technically a tough cut, but better than flank steak.

Oreilles (de porc): ears (of pig).

Orties: nettles.

Ortolan: tiny wild bird from southern France, Italy, Greece, and Spain, formerly very popular in French cuisine, now forbidden due to diminished supply.

Os: bone.

Oseille: sorrel.

Oursin: sea urchin.

Ouvert: open.

P

Paillard (de veau): thick slice (of veal).

Pailles (pommes): fried straw potatoes (finely shredded).

Paillettes: cheese straws, usually made with puff pastry and Parmesan cheese.

Pain: bread.

Paleron: shoulder of beef.

Paletot: literally, coat; the skin, bone, and meat portion of a fattened duck or goose once the liver is removed.

Palmier: palm-leaf-shaped cookie made of sugared puff pastry.

Palmier (coeurs de): palm hearts.

Palombe: wood or wild pigeon.

Palourde: prized medium-size clam.

Pamplemousse: grapefruit.

Panaché: mixed; now liberally used menu term to denote any mixture.

Panade: panada, a thick mixture used to bind forcemeats and *quenelles,*

usually flour and butter based, but can also contain fresh or toasted bread crumbs, rice, or potatoes; also refers to soup of bread, milk, and sometimes cheese.

Panais: parsnip.

Pané(e): breaded.

Panier: basket.

Pannequet: rolled crêpe filled with either sweet or savory mixture.

Papillote (en): cooked in parchment paper or foil wrapping.

Paquets (en): (in) packages or parcels.

Parfait: a dessert mousse; also mousselike mixture of chicken, duck, or goose liver.

Parfum: flavor.

Parisienne (à la): varied vegetable garnish that always includes potato balls that have been fried and tossed in a meat glaze.

Parmentier: dish with potatoes.

Partager: to share.

Passe-pierre: edible seaweed.

Pastèque: watermelon.

Pastis: anise liqueur.

Pâte: pastry dough.

Pâte à choux: cream puff pastry.

Pâte brisée: pie pastry.

Pâte sablée: sweeter, richer dough than *pâte sucrée,* sometimes leavened.

Pâte sucrée: sweet pie pastry.

Pâté: molded, spiced, minced meat, baked and served hot or cold.

Pâté en croûte: pâté baked in a pastry crust.

Pâtes (fraîches): pasta (fresh).

Pâtisserie: pastry.

Pâtissier: pastry chef.

Patte: paw, foot, or leg of bird or animal.

Patte blanche: small crayfish no larger than 2 to 2½ ounces (60 to 75g).

Patte rouge: large crayfish.

Paupiette: thin slice of meat, usually beef or fish, filled, rolled, then wrapped.

Pavé: literally, paving stone; usually a thick slice of boned beef or of calf's liver; also, a kind of pastry.

Paysan(ne) (à la): country style; also, garnish of carrots, turnips, onions, celery, and bacon.

Peau: skin.

Pêche: peach.

Pêche Melba: poached peach with vanilla ice cream and raspberry sauce.

Pêcheur: literally, fisherman; usually refers to fish preparations.

Pelure: peelings, such as from truffles, often used for flavoring.

Perce-pierre: samphire, edible seaweed.

Perche: perch.

Perdreau: young partridge.

Perdrix: partridge.

Périgourdine (à la): sauce, usually with truffles and foie gras.

Persil: parsley.

Persillade: chopped parsley and garlic.

Petit déjeuner: breakfast.

Petit-gris: small land snail.

Petit-pois: small green peas.

Petits fours: tiny cakes and pastries.

Pétoncle: tiny scallop, similar to American bay scallop.

Pets de nonne: small, dainty fried pastry.

Pibale: small eel, also called *civelle.*

Pièce: portion or piece.

Pied de mouton: meaty, cream-colored wild mushroom; also, sheep's foot.

Pied de porc: pig's foot.

Pigeonneau: young pigeon or squab.

Pignons: pine nuts, or pignoli.

Pilau, pilaf: rice cooked with onions and broth.

Piment (poivre) de Jamaïque: allspice.

Piment doux: sweet pepper.

Pince: claw; also, tongs used when eating snails or seafood.

Pintade: guinea fowl.

Pintadeau: young guinea fowl.

Pipérade: Basque dish of pepper, onions, tomatoes, and often scrambled eggs and ham.

Piquant(e): sharp or spicy tasting.

Piqué: larded; studded.

Pissaladière: a flat openface tart like a pizza, garnished with onions, olives, and anchovies.

Pissenlit: dandelion (leaves).

Pistache: pistachio nuts.

Pistil de safran: thread of saffron.

Pistou: sauce of basil, garlic, and olive oil; also a rich vegetable soup.

Pithiviers: classic puff pastry dessert filled with almond cream.

Plat: a dish.

Plat principal: main dish.

Plate: flat-shelled oyster.

Plates côtes: part of beef ribs usually used in *pot-au-feu.*

Plateau: platter.

Plateau de fruits de mer: seafood platter combin-

ing raw and cooked shellfish; usually includes oysters, clams, mussels, *langoustines,* periwinkles, crabs.

Pleurote: oyster mushroom, very soft-fleshed, feather-edged wild mushroom.

Plie franche: flounder; flat ocean fish; also known as *carrelet* (plaice).

Plombières: dessert of vanilla ice cream, candied fruit, kirsch, and sweetened whipped cream.

Pluches: leaves of herbs or plants, generally used for garnish.

Poché: poached.

Pochouse: freshwater fish stew prepared with white or red wine.

Poêlé: pan-fried.

Pointe (d'asperge): tip (of asparagus).

Poire: pear.

Poireau: leek.

Poires Belle Hélène: poached pears served on vanilla ice cream with hot chocolate sauce.

Pois: pea.

Poisson: fish.

Poitrine: breast (of meat or poultry).

Poitrine demi-sel: unsmoked slab bacon.

Poitrine fumée: smoked slab bacon.

Poivrade: a peppery brown sauce made with wine, vinegar, and cooked vegetables that is strained before serving.

Poivre: pepper.

Poivre frais de Madagascar: green peppercorns.

Poivre noir: black peppercorns.

Poivre rose: pink peppercorns.

Poivre vert: green peppercorns.

Poivron (doux): sweet bell pepper.

Polenta: cooked dish of cornmeal and water, usually with added butter and cheese; also refers to cornmeal.

Pommade (en): usually refers to a thick, smooth paste.

Pomme: apple.

en l'air: caramelized apple slices, usually served with *boudin noir* (blood sausage).

Pommes (de terre): potatoes.

à l'anglaise: boiled.

allumettes: very thin fries, cut in ¼ x 2½-inch (½ x 6½-cm) slices.

boulangère: potatoes cooked with the meat they accompany; also, a potato gratin of sliced potatoes with onions and sometimes bacon and tomatoes.

dauphine: mashed potatoes mixed with *chou* pastry, shaped into small balls and fried.

dauphinoise: baked dish of sliced potatoes, milk, garlic, and cheese.

duchesse: mashed potatoes with butter, egg yolks, and nutmeg, used for garnish.

en robe des champs: potatoes cooked with skins on.

frites: French fries.

gratinées: baked dish of potatoes, browned often with cheese.

lyonnaise: sautéed potatoes, with onions.

paille: potatoes cut into julienne strips, then fried.

Pont-Neuf: classic fries, cut into ½ x 2½-inch

(1 x 6½-cm) slices.

soufflées: small, thin slices of potato fried twice, causing them to inflate, so they look like little pillows.

vapeur: steamed or boiled potatoes.

Porc (carré de): pork (loin).

Porc (côte de): pork (chop).

Porcelet: young suckling pig.

Porto (au): (with) port.

Portugaises: elongated, crinkle-shell oysters.

Potage: soup.

Pot-au-feu: boiled beef prepared with vegetables, often served in two or more courses.

Pot-de-crème: individual custard or mousselike dessert, often chocolate.

Potée: hearty soup of pork and vegetables, generally cabbage and potatoes.

Poularde: fatted hen.

Poule d'Inde: turkey hen.

Poule faisane: female pheasant.

Poulet (rôti): chicken (roast).

Poulet basquaise: Basque-style chicken, with tomatoes and sweet peppers.

Poulet de Bresse: high-quality, free-running, corn-fed chicken.

Poulet de grain: corn-fed chicken.

Poulet fermier: free-range chicken.

Poulpe: octopus.

Pousse-pierre: edible seaweed.

Poussin: baby chicken.

Praire: small clam.

Pralin: ground caramelized almonds.

Praline: caramelized almonds.

Primeur: refers to early fresh fruits and vegetables.

Printanière: garnish of a variety of spring vegetables; or vegetables cut into dice or balls.

Prix fixe: fixed-price menu.

Prix net: service included.

Profiterole: chou pastry dessert, usually filled with ice cream and topped with chocolate sauce.

Provençal(e): in the style of Provence; usually includes garlic, tomatoes, and/or olive oil.

Prune: fresh plum.

Pruneau: prune.

Q

Quenelle: dumpling; usually of veal, fish, or poultry.

Quetsch: small purple Damson plum.

Queue (de boeuf): tail (oxtail).

R

Râble de lièvre (lapin): saddle of hare (rabbit).

Raclette: rustic Swiss dish of melted cheese served with boiled potatoes, *cornichons,* and pickled onions; also the cheese used in this dish.

Radis: small red radish.

Radis noir: large black radish, often served with cream, as a salad.

Ragoût: stew, usually of meat.

Raie: skate (fish) or sting ray.

Raifort: horseradish.

Raisin: grape.

Ramequin: small individual casserole; also a small tart.

Râpé: grated or shredded.

Rascasse: scorpion fish.

Ratatouille: cooked dish of eggplant, zucchini, onions, tomatoes, peppers, garlic, and olive oil.

Rave: category of root vegetables, including celery, turnip, radish.

Ravigote: thick vinaigrette sauce with vinegar, white wine, shallots, herbs; also cold mayonnaise with capers, onions, and herbs.

Réchauffer: to reheat.

Reine-claude: greengage plum.

Reinette (reine de): fall and winter variety of apple.

Rémoulade: sauce of mayonnaise, capers, mushrooms, herbs, anchovies, and gherkins.

Rillettes (d'oie): minced spread of pork (goose); also can be made with duck, fish, or rabbit.

Rillons: usually pork belly, cut up and cooked until crisp, then drained of fat; can also be made of duck, goose, or rabbit.

Rince doigt: finger bowl.

Ris d'agneau: lamb sweetbreads.

Ris de veau: veal sweetbreads.

Rivière: river.

Riz: rice.

Riz à l'impératrice: cold rice pudding with candied fruit.

Riz complet: brown rice.

Riz sauvage: wild rice.

Rognonnade: veal loin with kidneys attached.

Rognons: kidneys.

Romarin: rosemary.

Rondelle: round slice.

Rosé: rare (meat).

Rosette (de porc): dried sausage (of pork), usually

ally from Beaujolais.

Rôti: roast.

Rouelle (de): slice of meat or vegetable cut at an angle.

Rouget (rouget barbet): sweet, red-skinned fish commonly called red mullet; the smallest are most prized.

Rouille: thick, spicy, rust-colored sauce, with olive oil, peppers, tomatoes, and garlic; usually served with fish soups.

Roulade: roll, often stuffed.

Roulé(e): rolled.

Roux: sauce base or thickening made from flour and butter.

S

Sabayon: light sweet sauce of egg yolks, sugar, wine, and flavoring, which is whipped while being cooked in a water bath.

Sablé: shortbreadlike cookie; also, sweet pastry dough.

Safran: saffron.

Saignant(e): very rare (for cooking meat).

Saint-Germain: with peas.

Saint-Hubert: sauce *poivrade* with chestnuts and bacon added.

Saint-Jacques (coquille): sea scallop.

Saint-Pierre: mild, flat, white ocean fish; John Dory.

Saison (suivant la): according to the season.

Salade folle: mixed salad, usually including green beans and foie gras.

Salade panachée: mixed salad.

Salade verte: green salad.

Salé: salted.

Salicorne: edible algae, often pickled and eaten as a condiment.

Salmis: stewlike preparation of game birds or poultry, with sauce made from the pressed carcass.

Salpicon: diced vegetables, meat, and/or fish in a sauce.

Salsifis: salsify, or oyster plant.

Sandre: perchlike freshwater fish.

Sang: blood.

Sanglier: wild boar.

Sarriette: summer savory; also called *poivre d'âne.*

Saucisse: small fresh sausage.

Saucisson: large dried sausage.

Saucisson de Lyon: air-dried pork sausage, seasoned with garlic and pepper, and studded with chunks of pork fat; also sometimes seasoned with truffles or with pistachio nuts.

Sauge: sage.

Saumon (sauvage): salmon (literally, wild; a non-cultivated salmon).

Saumon d'Ecosse: Scottish salmon.

Saumon fumé: smoked salmon.

Saupiquet: classic aromatic wine sauce thickened with bread crumbs.

Sauté: browned in fat.

Sauvage: wild.

Savarin: yeast-leavened cake shaped like a ring, soaked in sweet syrup.

Savoyarde: usually, flavored with Gruyère cheese.

Scarole: escarole.

Seiche: large squid or cuttlefish.

Sel: salt.

Selle: saddle (of meat).

Serpolet: wild thyme.

Service (non) compris: service (not) included.

Serviette: napkin.

Smitane: sauce of cream, onions, white wine, and lemon juice.

Soissons: dried or fresh white beans.

Sorbet: sherbet.

Soubise: onion sauce.

Soufflé: light sweet or savory mixture served either hot or cold, the bulk of whose volume is egg whites.

Steack: beef steak.

Stockfish: salted and air-dried codfish.

Succès au pralin: meringue cake flavored with caramelized almonds and layered with butter cream.

Sucre: sugar.

Suprême: a veal- or chicken-based white sauce thickened with flour and cream; a boneless breast of poultry or a fillet of fish.

T

Tablier de sapeur: tripe that is marinated, breaded, and grilled.

Tagine: spicy North African stew of veal, lamb, chicken, or pigeon with vegetables.

Tanche: tench, a freshwater fish with mild, delicate flavor; often an ingredient in *matelote,* freshwater fish stew.

Tapenade: blend of black olives, anchovies, capers, olive oil, and lemon juice.

Tarama: mullet roe, often made into a spread of the same name.

HARICOT DE MOUTON CHEZ RENE
MUTTON WITH WHITE BEANS

This is a regular plat du jour—*daily special—at the popular left bank bistro, Chez René (see entry, page 56).* Haricot de mouton *is a classic bistro dish, and one that French women prepare often at home, usually with either lamb or mutton shoulder. I prefer it with big, hearty chunks of lamb and lots and lots of white beans. If you have fresh herbs around, all the better.*

Lamb or mutton:
3 tablespoons (1½ oz; 45 g) unsalted butter
3 tablespoons olive oil
3½ pounds (approximately 1.75 kg) lamb or mutton shoulder, cut into 2-inch (5-cm) chunks (a butcher can do this for you)
⅓ cup (45 g) unbleached all-purpose flour
1 cup (250 ml) dry white wine
3 cups (750 ml) water
2 fresh tomatoes, cubed
4 carrots, peeled and cut into 1-inch (2.5 cm) rounds
2 medium onions, halved
2 teaspoons fresh thyme, or 1 teaspoon dried
3 bay leaves
3 tablespoons chopped fresh parsley
4 whole cloves
Salt and freshly ground black pepper to taste
Beans:
1 pound (500 g) dried white beans
2 bay leaves
6 whole cloves
2 teaspoons dried thyme
Salt

1. In a deep 12-inch skillet, heat the butter and oil over medium-high heat. When hot, begin browning the lamb. You may want to do this in batches. Do not crowd the pan, and be sure that each piece is thoroughly browned before turning.

2. When all the lamb is browned, sprinkle with the flour and mix well. Leaving the lamb in the skillet, add the white wine, then the 3 cups of water, and deglaze the pan, scraping up any browned bits. Add the tomatoes, vegetables, herbs, and spices, and cook, covered, over medium heat for about 1 hour and 15 minutes. Season to taste with salt and pepper.

3. While the lamb is cooking, prepare the beans. Rinse them well, put them in a large saucepan, and cover with cold water. Over high heat, bring to a boil. Once boiling, remove the pan from the heat, leave covered, and let rest for 40 minutes.

4. Drain the beans, discarding the cooking liquid (to help make the beans more digestible). Rinse the beans and cover again with cold water. Add the bay leaves, cloves, and thyme, and bring to a boil over medium heat. Cook, covered, over medium heat for about 40 minutes. The beans should be cooked through but still firm. Add salt to taste.

5. To serve, check the lamb and beans for seasoning, then arrange meat on a platter, surrounded by the white beans.
Yield: 6 servings.

Tartare: chopped raw beef, seasoned and garnished with raw egg, capers, chopped onion, and parsley.

Tarte: tart; open-face pie or *flan,* usually sweet.

Tarte Tatin: caramelized upside-down apple pie.

Tartine: open-face sandwich; buttered bread.

Tendre: tender.

Tendrons: cartilaginous meat cut from beef or veal ribs.

Terrine: earthenware container used for cooking meat, game, fish, or vegetable mixtures; also the mixture cooked in such a container.

Tête de veau (porc): head of veal (pork), usually used in headcheese.

Thé: tea.

Thon: tuna fish.

Thym: thyme.

Tian: earthenware gratin dish; also vegetable mixture cooked in such a dish.

Tiède: lukewarm.

Tilleul: lime or linden blossom herb tea.

Timbale: round mold with straight or sloping sides; also, a mixture prepared in such a mold.

Topinambour: Jerusalem artichoke.

Tortue: turtle.

Toulousaine: Toulouse style; usually with truffles, or sweetbreads, cock's combs, mushrooms, or *quenelles.*

Tournedos: center portion of beef filet, usually grilled or sautéed.

Tournedos Rossini: sautéed *tournedos* garnished with foie gras and truffles.

Tourteau: large crab.

Tourtière: shallow cooking vessel; also southwestern pastry dish filled with apples and/or prunes and sprinkled with Armagnac.

Tranche: slice.

Travers de porc: spare ribs.

Tripes à la mode de Caen: beef tripe, carrots, onions, leeks, and spices cooked in water, cider, and Calvados (apple brandy).

Tripoux: mutton tripe.

Trompettes des mort: dark brown "horn of plenty" wild mushrooms.

Tronçon: cut of meat or fish resulting in a piece that is wide; generally refers to slices from the largest part of a fish.

Truffe (truffé): truffle (with truffles).

Truite: trout.

Truite saumonée: salmon trout.

Tuile: literally, tile; delicate almond-flavored cookie.

Turban: usually mixture or combination of ingredients cooked in a ring mold.

Turbot(in): turbot (small turbot).

V, X, Y, Z

Vacherin: dessert of baked meringue, with ice cream and cream; also, strong supple winter cheese; the best is Mont-d'Or.

Vallée d'Auge: region of Normandy; also, garnish of cooked apples and cream.

Vanille: vanilla.

Vapeur (à la): steamed.

Veau: veal.

Velouté: veal- or chicken-based sauce thickened with flour.

Venaison: venison.

Ventre: belly or stomach.

Vénus: American clam.

Verjus: juice from unripe grapes, once used in sauces instead of vinegar.

Vernis: large, fleshy clam with varnishlike shell.

Vert-pré: a watercress garnish, sometimes includes potatoes.

Verveine: lemon verbena (herb tea).

Vessie (en): cooked in a pig's bladder (usually a chicken).

Viande: meat.

Vichy: with glazed carrots; also a brand of mineral water.

Vichyssoise: cold, creamy leek and potato soup.

Vierge (beurre): whipped butter sauce with salt, pepper, and lemon juice.

Vierge (huile d'olive): virgin olive oil.

Vieux (vieille): old.

Vigneron: wine grower.

Vinaigre (vieux): vinegar (aged).

Vinaigre de xérès: sherry vinegar.

Vinaigrette: oil and vinegar dressing.

Vivant(e): living.

Vivier: fish tank.

Volaille: poultry.

Vol-au-vent: puff pastry shell.

Xérès (vinaigre de): sherry (vinegar).

Yaourt: yogurt

Zeste: citrus peel, with white pith removed.

Food Lover's Ready Reference

RESTAURANTS: AN ALPHABETICAL LISTING

(WITH ARRONDISSEMENTS)

Chez Albert, Paris 14

Allard, Paris 6

Ambassade d'Auvergne, Paris 3

L'Ambroisie, Paris 4

L'Ami Louis, Paris 3

Chez André, Paris 8

Androuët, Paris 8

Chez Les Anges, Paris 7

Apicius, Paris 17

L'Aquitaine, Paris 15

Artois, Paris 8

L'Assiette, Paris 14

Astier, Paris 11

Brasserie Balzar, Paris 5

Benoit, Paris 4

Le Boeuf sur le Toit, Paris 8

Bofinger, Paris 4

La Bonne Table de Fés, Paris 6

La Boule d'Or, Versailles

La Boutarde, Neuilly-sur-Seine

Bristol, Paris 8

La Cagouille, Paris 14

Le Caméléon, Paris 6

Carré des Feuillants, Paris 1

Cartet, Paris 11

Caviar Kaspia, Paris 8

Chardenoux, Paris 11

Charlot, Le Roi des Coquillages, Paris 9

Aux Charpentiers, Paris 6

Chiberta, Paris 8

Au Cochon d'Or, Paris 19

Au Cochon d'Or des Halles, Paris 1

Le Coq de la Maison Blanche, Saint-Ouen

La Coquille, Paris 17

Le Bistrot d'à Côté, Paris 17

La Coupole, Paris 14

Le Divellec, Paris 7

Dodin Bouffant, Paris 5

Le Duc, Paris 14

L'Epi d'Or, Paris 1

Jacqueline Fénix, Neuilly-sur-Seine

La Fermette du Sud-Ouest, Paris 1

Brasserie Flo, Paris 10

La Fontaine de Mars, Paris 7

Chez Fred, Paris 17

La Galoche d'Aurillac, Paris 11

Chez Georges, Paris 2

Chez Georges, Paris 17

Gérard et Nicole, Paris 14

Le Globe d'Or, Paris 1

Le Gourmet des Ternes, Paris 17

Le Grand Véfour, Paris 1

La Gueuze, Paris 5

Brasserie de l'Ile Saint-Louis, Paris 4

Restaurant Jamin, Paris 16

Chez Jenny, Paris 3

Julien, Paris 10

Lescure, Paris 1

Louis XIV, Paris 1

Chez Louisette, Saint-Ouen

La Lozère, Paris 6

Lucas-Carton, Paris 8

Aux Lyonnais, Paris 2

La Maison Blanche, Paris 15

La Maison du Valais, Paris 8

Chez Maître Paul, Paris 6

Mère-Grand, Paris 20

Moissonnier, Paris 5

Le Restaurant d'Olympe, Paris 15

Chez Pauline, Paris 1

Perraudin, Paris 5

Le Petit Marguery, Paris 13

Le Petit Zinc, Paris 6

Pharamond, Paris 1

Chez Philippe, Paris 11

Au Pied de Cochon, Paris 1

Pierre Traiteur, Paris 1

Pile ou Face, Paris 2

Polidor, Paris 6

Le Potager du Roy, Versailles

Chez René, Paris 5

Ritz-Espadon, Paris 1

Le Roi du Pot-au-Feu, Paris 9

Michel Rostang, Paris 17

Le Ruban Bleu, Paris 1

Guy Savoy, Paris 17

La Sologne, Paris 7

A Sousceyrac, Paris 11

Brasserie Stella, Paris 16

La Table de Jeannette, Paris 1

Taillevent, Paris 8

Tan Dinh, Paris 7

La Tchaïka, Paris 6

La Tchaïka, Paris 11

Brasserie du Théâtre, Versailles

Thoumieux, Paris 7

Timgad, Paris 17

La Tour d'Argent, Paris 5

La Tour de Montlhéry, Paris 1

Chez Toutoune, Paris 5

Terminus Nord, Paris 10

Le Train Bleu, Paris 12

Au Trou Gascon, Paris 12

Le Trumilou, Paris 4

Vaudeville, Paris 2

Jules Verne, Paris 7

Chez la Vieille, Paris 1

RESTAURANTS LISTED BY ARRONDISSEMENTS

Palais-Royal, Les Halles, Opéra, Bourse
1st and 2nd arrondissements

Carré des Feuillants

Au Cochon d'Or des Halles

L'Epi d'Or

La Fermette du Sud-Ouest

Chez Georges

Le Globe d'Or

Le Grand Véfour

Lescure

Louis XIV

Aux Lyonnais

Chez Pauline

Pharamond

Au Pied de Cochon

Pierre Traiteur

Pile ou Face

Ritz-Espadon

Le Ruban Bleu

La Table de Jeannette

La Tour de Montlhéry

Vaudeville

Chez la Vieille

République, Bastille, Les Halles, Ile Saint-Louis
3rd, 4th, and 11th arrondissements

Ambassade d'Auvergne

L'Ambroisie

L'Ami Louis

Astier

Benoit

Bofinger

Cartet

Chardenoux

La Galoche d'Aurillac

Brasserie de l'Ile Saint-Louis

Chez Jenny

Chez Philippe

A Sousceyrac

La Tchaïka

Le Trumilou

Latin Quarter, Luxembourg, Sèvres-Babylone
5th and 6th arrondissements

Allard

Brasserie Balzar

La Bonne Table de Fés

Le Caméléon

Aux Charpentiers

Dodin Bouffant

La Gueuze

La Lozère

Chez Maître Paul

Moissonnier

Perraudin

Le Petit Zinc

Polidor

Chez René

La Tchaïka

La Tour d'Argent

Chez Toutoune

Faubourg Saint-Germain, Invalides, Ecole Militaire
7th arrondissement

Chez Les Anges

Le Divellec

La Fontaine de Mars

La Sologne

Tan Dinh

Thoumieux

Jules Verne

Madeleine, Saint-Lazare, Champs-Elysées
8th arrondissement

Chez André

Androuet

Artois

Le Boeuf sur le Toit

Bristol

Caviar Kaspia

Chiberta

Lucas-Carton

La Maison du Valais

Taillevent

Grands Boulevards, Place de Clichy, Gare du Nord
9th and 10th arrondissements

Charlot, Le Roi Des Coquillages

Brasserie Flo

Julien

Le Roi du Pot-au-Feu

Terminus Nord

Gare de Lyon, Vaugirard, Montparnasse, Denfert-Rochereau
12th, 13th, 14th, and 15th arrondissements

Chez Albert

L'Aquitaine

L'Assiette

La Cagouille

La Coupole

Le Duc

Gérard et Nicole

La Maison Blanche

Le Restaurant d'Olympe

Le Petit Marguery

Le Train Bleu

Au Trou Gascon

Arc de Triomphe, Trocadéro, Bois de Boulogne, Neuilly-sur-Seine
16th arrondissement,
Neuilly-sur-Seine

La Boutarde

Jacqueline Fénix

Restaurant Jamin

Brasserie Stella

Arc de Triomphe, Place des Ternes, Porte Maillot
17th arrondissement

Apicius

La Coquille

Le Bistro d'a Côté

Chez Fred

Chez Georges

Le Gourmet des Ternes

Michel Rostang

Guy Savoy

Timgad

Saint-Ouen, La Villette, Belleville, Père-Lachaise
19th and 20th arrondissements and Saint-Ouen

Au Cochon d'Or

Le Coq de la Maison Blanche

Chez Louisette

Mère-Grand

Paris Envrions: Versailles

La Boule d'Or

Le Potager du Roy

Brasserie du Théâtre

RESTAURANTS: BISTROS

Allard, Paris 6

L'Ami Louis, Paris 3

Chez André, Paris 8

Artois, Paris 8

Astier, Paris 11

Benoit, Paris 4

La Boutarde,
Neuilly-sur-Seine

Le Caméléon, Paris 6

Cartet, Paris 11

Chardenoux, Paris 11

Aux Charpentiers, Paris 6

Au Cochon d'Or, Paris 19

Au Cochon d'Or des Halles,
Paris 1

La Coquille, Paris 17

Le Bistrot d'à Côté, Paris 17

L'Epi d'Or, Paris 1

La Fermette du Sud-Ouest,
Paris 1

La Fontaine de Mars, Paris 7

Chez Fred, Paris 17

La Galoche d'Aurillac,
Paris 11

Chez Georges, Paris 2

Chez Georges, Paris 17

Le Gourmet des Ternes,
Paris 17

Lescure, Paris 1

Louis XIV, Paris 1

Chez Louisette, Saint-Ouen

Aux Lyonnais, Paris 2

Chez Maître Paul, Paris 6

Mère-Grand, Paris 20

Moissonnier, Paris 5

Chez Pauline, Paris 1

Perraudin, Paris 5

Le Petit Marguery, Paris 13

Le Petit Zinc, Paris 6

Chez Philippe, Paris 11

Pierre Traiteur, Paris 1

Polidor, Paris 6

Chez René, Paris 5

Le Roi du Pot-au-Feu, Paris 9

Le Ruban Bleu, Paris 1

A Sousceyrac, Paris 11

Thoumieux, Paris 7

La Tour de Montlhéry,
Paris 1

Chez Toutoune, Paris 5

Le Trumilou, Paris 4

Chez la Vieille, Paris 1

RESTAURANTS: BRASSERIES

Brasserie Balzar, Paris 5

Le Boeuf sur le Toit, Paris 8

Bofinger, Paris 4

La Coupole, Paris 14

Brasserie Flo, Paris 10

Brasserie de l'Ile Saint-Louis,
Paris 4

Chez Jenny, Paris 3

Julien, Paris 10

Au Pied de Cochon, Paris 1

Brasserie Stella, Paris 16

Terminus Nord, Paris 10

Le Train Bleu, Paris 12

Vaudeville, Paris 2

RESTAURANTS FEATURING REGIONAL SPECIALTIES

ALSACE

Bofinger, Paris 4

Brasserie Flo, Paris 10

Brasserie de l'Ile Saint-Louis,
Paris 4

Chez Jenny, Paris 3

AUVERGNE

Ambassade d'Auvergne,
Paris 3

La Galoche d'Aurillac,
Paris 11

La Lozère, Paris 6

BURGUNDY/LYONS

Allard, Paris 6

Chez Les Anges, Paris 7

Cartet, Paris 11

Le Bistrot d'à Côté, Paris 17

Aux Lyonnais, Paris 2

Chez Pauline, Paris 1

Le Train Bleu, Paris 12

JURA

La Boule d'Or, Versailles

Chez Maître Paul, Paris 6

Moissonnier, Paris 5

NORMANDY

Pharamond, Paris 1

SOLOGNE

La Sologne, Paris 7

SOUTHWEST/BORDEAUX

L'Aquitaine, Paris 15

Carré des Feuillants, Paris 1

La Fermette du Sud-Ouest,
Paris 1

Le Globe d'Or, Paris 1

Chez Philippe, Paris 11

Au Trou Gascon, Paris 12

LESS EXPENSIVE RESTAURANTS (100 to 150 francs)

Astier (95-franc menu),
Paris 11

La Coupole (95-franc menu),
Paris 14

L'Epi d'Or (90-franc menu),
Paris 1

La Fontaine de Mars
(60-franc lunch menu),
Paris 7

La Gueuze, Paris 5

Brasserie de l'Ile Saint-Louis,
Paris 4

Chez Jenny (84-franc menu),
Paris 3

Lescure (75-franc menu),
Paris 1

La Lozère (70- to 104-franc
menus), Paris 6

Chez Louisette, Saint-Ouen

Aux Lyonnais, Paris 2

La Maison du Valais, Paris 8

Mère-Grand (44- to 129-franc
menus), Paris 20

Perraudin, Paris 5

Polidor, Paris 6

Thoumieux, Paris 7

Chez Toutoune, Paris 5

Le Trumilou (65- and
120-franc menus), Paris 4

RESTAURANTS OPEN AFTER 11 P.M.

The following restaurants keep later than normal hours. The approximate time at which final orders will be taken is noted in parentheses. In all cases, reservations are advised.

Chez André, Paris 8 (11:45)

Brasserie Balzar, Paris 5
(12:30 A.M.)

Bofinger, Paris 4 (1 A.M.)

La Bonne Table de Fés,
Paris 6 (12:15 A.M.)

La Cagouille, Paris 14
(midnight)

Caviar Kaspia, Paris 8
(11:30)

Charlot, Le Roi des
Coquillages, Paris 9 (1A.M.)

Aux Charpentiers, Paris 6
(11:30)

La Coupole, Paris 14 (1:30
A.M.)

Dodin Bouffant, Paris 5
(1 A.M.)

L'Epi d'Or, Paris 1 (1:30 A.M.)

Brasserie Flo, Paris 10
(1:30 A.M.)

Chez Georges, Paris 17
(11:30)

La Gueuze, Paris 5 (2 A.M.)

Brasserie de l'Ile Saint-Louis,
Paris 4 (1 A.M.)

Chez Jenny, Paris 3 (1 A.M.)

Julien, Paris 10 (1:30 A.M.)

Le Restaurant d'Olympe, Paris 15 (midnight)

Au Pied de Cochon, Paris 1 (open 24 hours)

Ritz-Espadon, Paris 1 (11:30)

Brasserie Stella, Paris 16 (1 A.M.)

Terminus Nord, Paris 10 (12:30 A.M.)

Thoumieux, Paris 7 (11:30)

La Tour de Montlhéry, Paris 1 (open 24 hours)

Vaudeville, Paris 2 (1:30 A.M.)

RESTAURANTS OPEN ON SATURDAY

Chez Albert, Paris 14

Ambassade d'Auvergne, Paris 3

L'Ambroisie, Paris 4

L'Ami Louis, Paris 3

Chez André, Paris 8

Androuët, Paris 8

Chez Les Anges, Paris 7

L'Aquitaine, Paris 15

L'Assiette, Paris 14

Brasserie Balzar, Paris 5

Le Boeuf sur le Toit, Paris 8

Bofinger, Paris 4

La Bonne Table de Fés, Paris 6

La Boule d'Or, Versailles

La Boutarde, Neuilly-sur-Seine

Bristol, Paris 8

La Cagouille, Paris 14

Caviar Kaspia, Paris 8

Chardenoux, Paris 11

Charlot, Le Roi des Coquillages, Paris 9

Aux Charpentiers, Paris 6

Chiberta, Paris 8

Au Cochon d'Or, Paris 19

Au Cochon d'Or des Halles, Paris 1

Le Coq de la Maison Blanche, Saint-Ouen

La Coquille, Paris 17

Le Bistrot d'à Côté, Paris 17

La Coupole, Paris 14

Le Divellec, Paris 7

Dodin Bouffant, Paris 5

L'Epi d'Or, Paris 1

La Fermette du Sud-Ouest, Paris 1

Brasserie Flo, Paris 10

La Fontaine de Mars, Paris 7 (lunch)

Chez Fred, Paris 17

La Galoche d'Aurillac, Paris 11

Chez Georges, Paris 2

Chez Georges, Paris 17

Le Grand Véfour, Paris 1 (dinner)

La Gueuze, Paris 5

Brasserie de l'Ile Saint-Louis, Paris 4

Chez Jenny, Paris 3

Julien, Paris 10

Lescure, Paris 1 (lunch)

Chez Louisette, Saint-Ouen

La Lozère, Paris 6

La Maison Blanche, Paris 15

La Maison du Valais, Paris 8

Chez Maître Paul, Paris 6

Moissonnier, Paris 5

Chez Pauline, Paris 1

Le Petit Marguery, Paris 13

Le Petit Zinc, Paris 6

Pharamond, Paris 1

Au Pied de Cochon, Paris 1

Polidor, Paris 6

Le Potager du Roy, Versailles

Ritz-Espadon, Paris 1

Le Roi du Pot-au-Feu, Paris 9

Michel Rostang, Paris 17 (dinner)

Guy Savoy, Paris 17 (dinner)

La Sologne, Paris 7

Brasserie Stella, Paris 16

Tan Dinh, Paris 7

La Tchaïka, Paris 6

La Tchaïka, Paris 11

Terminus Nord, Paris 10

Brasserie du Théâtre, Versailles

Thoumieux, Paris 7

Timgad, Paris 17

La Tour d'Argent, Paris 5

Chez Toutoune, Paris 5

Le Train Bleu, Paris 12

Le Trumilou, Paris 4

Vaudeville, Paris 2

Jules Verne, Paris 7

RESTAURANTS OPEN ON SUNDAY

Chez Albert, Paris 14

Ambassade d'Auvergne, Paris 3

L'Ami Louis, Paris 3

Chez André, Paris 8

Chez Les Anges, Paris 7

L'Assiette, Paris 14

Brasserie Balzar, Paris 5

Le Boeuf sur le Toit, Paris 8

Bofinger, Paris 4

La Boule d'Or, Versailles (lunch)

Bristol, Paris 8

Charlot, Le Roi des Coquillages, Paris 8

Au Cochon d'Or, Paris 19

La Coupole, Paris 14

Brasserie Flo, Paris 10

Chez Georges, Paris 17

Brasserie de l'Ile Saint-Louis, Paris 4

Chez Jenny, Paris 3

Julien, Paris 10

Chez Louisette, Saint-Ouen

Moissonier, Paris 5

Le Restaurant d'Olympe, Paris 15 (dinner)

Café Parisien, Paris 6 (brunch)

Le Petit Zinc, Paris 6

Au Pied de Cochon, Paris 1

Ritz-Espadon, Paris 1

La Sologne, Paris 7

Brasserie Stella, Paris 16

Terminus Nord, Paris 10

Brasserie du Théâtre, Versailles

Thoumieux, Paris 7

Timgad, Paris 17

La Tour d'Argent, Paris 5

Le Train Bleu, Paris 12

Le Trumilou, Paris 4

Vaudeville, Paris 2

Jules Verne, Paris 7

RESTAURANTS OPEN ON MONDAY

Chez Albert, Paris 14

Allard, Paris 6

Ambassade d'Auvergne, Paris 3

L'Ambroisie, Paris 4

Chez André, Paris 8

Androuët, Paris 8

Chez Les Anges, Paris 7

Apicius, Paris 17

Artois, Paris 8

Astier, Paris 11

Brasserie Balzar, Paris 5

Benoit, Paris 4

Le Boeuf sur le Toit, Paris 8

Bofinger, Paris 4

La Boutarde, Neuilly-sur-Seine

Bristol, Paris 8

Carré des Feuillants, Paris 1

Cartet, Paris 11

Caviar Kaspia, Paris 8

Chardenoux, Paris 11

Charlot, Le Roi des Coquillages, Paris 9

Aux Charpentiers, Paris 6

Au Cochon d'Or, Paris 19

Au Cochon d'Or des Halles, Paris 1

Le Coq de la Maison Blanche, Saint-Ouen

Le Bistrot d'à Côté, Paris 17

La Coupole, Paris 14

Dodin Bouffant, Paris 5

L'Epi d'Or, Paris 1

Jacqueline Fénix, Neuilly-sur-Seine

La Fermette du Sud-Ouest, Paris 1

Brasserie Flo, Paris 10

La Fontaine de Mars, Paris 7

Chez Fred, Paris 17

Chez Georges, Paris 2

Chez Georges, Paris 17

Gérard et Nicole, Paris 14

Le Globe d'Or, Paris 1

Le Gourmet des Ternes, Paris 17

Le Grand Véfour, Paris 1

La Gueuze, Paris 5

Brasserie de l'Ile Saint-Louis, Paris 4

Restaurant Jamin, Paris 16

Chez Jenny, Paris 3

Julien, Paris 10

Lescure, Paris 1

Louis XIV, Paris 1

Chez Louisette, Saint-Ouen

Lucas-Carton, Paris 8

Aux Lyonnais, Paris 2

La Maison du Valais, Paris 8

Mère-Grand, Paris 20

Chez Pauline, Paris 1

Perraudin, Paris 5

Le Petit Zinc, Paris 6

Pharamond, Paris 1

Chez Philippe, Paris 11

Au Pied de Cochon, Paris 1

Pierre Traiteur, Paris 1

Pile ou Face, Paris 2

Chez René, Paris 5

Ritz-Espadon, Paris 1

Le Roi du Pot-au-Feu, Paris 9

Michel Rostang, Paris 17

Le Ruban Bleu, Paris 1 (lunch)

Guy Savoy, Paris 17

A Sousceyrac, Paris 11

Brasserie Stella, Paris 16

La Table de Jeannette, Paris 1

Taillevent, Paris 8

Tan Dinh, Paris 7

Terminus Nord, Paris 10

Brasserie du Théâtre, Versailles

Timgad, Paris 17

La Tour de Montlhéry, Paris 1

Le Train Bleu, Paris 12

Au Trou Gascon, Paris 12

Vaudeville, Paris 2

Jules Verne, Paris 7

Chez la Vieille, Paris 1 (lunch)

RESTAURANTS OPEN IN AUGUST

Chez Albert, Paris 14

Ambassade d'Auvergne, Paris 3

Androuët, Paris 8

Chez Les Anges, Paris 7

L'Aquitaine, Paris 15

Le Boeuf sur le Toit, Paris 8

Bofinger, Paris 4

La Boutarde, Neuilly-sur-Seine

Bristol, Paris 8

La Cagouille, Paris 14

Carré des Feuillants, Paris 1

Caviar Kaspia, Paris 8

Charlot, Le Roi des Coquillages, Paris 9

Au Cochon d'Or, Paris 19

Au Cochon d'Or des Halles, Paris 1

Le Coq de la Maison Blanche, Saint-Ouen

Le Duc, Paris 14

La Fermette du Sud-Ouest, Paris 1

Brasserie Flo, Paris 10

Chez Georges, Paris 2

Gérard et Nicole, Paris 14 (from mid-August)

Restaurant Jamin, Paris 16

Chez Jenny, Paris 3

Julien, Paris 10

Chez Louisette, Saint-Ouen

Lucas-Carton, Paris 8

Aux Lyonnais, Paris 2

La Maison Blanche, Paris 15

La Maison du Valais, Paris 8

Mère-Grand, Paris 20

Chez Pauline, Paris 1

Le Petit Zinc, Paris 6

Au Pied de Cochon, Paris 1

Le Potager du Roy, Versailles

Ritz-Espadon, Paris 1

Michel Rostang, Paris 17 (from mid-August)

La Sologne, Paris 7

La Table de Jeannette, Paris 1

Tan Dinh, Paris 7 (from mid-August)

La Tchaïka, Paris 6 (from mid-August)

La Tchaïka, Paris 11 (from mid-August)

Terminus Nord, Paris 10

Brasserie du Théâtre, Versailles

Thoumieux, Paris 7

Timgad, Paris 17

La Tour d'Argent, Paris 5

La Tour de Montlhéry, Paris 1 (from mid-August)

Chez Toutoune, Paris 5 (to
  mid-August)

Le Train Bleu, Paris 12

Le Trumilou, Paris 4

Vaudeville, Paris 2

Jules Verne, Paris 7

RESTAURANTS WITH SIDEWALK TABLES OR OUTDOOR TERRACE

Chez André, Paris 8

L'Aquitaine, Paris 15

Benoit, Paris 4

Bofinger, Paris 4

La Boutarde,
  Neuilly-sur-Seine

La Cagouille, Paris 14

Chardenoux, Paris 11

Aux Charpentiers, Paris 6

Le Coq de la Maison Blanche,
  Saint-Ouen

Le Bistrot d'à Côté, Paris 17

Dodin Bouffant, Paris 5

La Fontaine de Mars, Paris 7

Chez Fred, Paris 17

La Galoche d'Aurillac,
  Paris 11

Chez Georges, Paris 17

Le Gourmet des Ternes,
  Paris 17

Chez Jenny, Paris 3

Lescure, Paris 1

Louis XIV, Paris 1

Le Petit Marguery, Paris 13

Le Petit Zinc, Paris 6

Pharamond, Paris 1

Au Pied de Cochon, Paris 1

Pile ou Face, Paris 2

Le Roi du Pot-au-Feu, Paris 9

La Table de Jeannette, Paris 1

Terminus Nord, Paris 10

Vaudeville, Paris 2

AIR-CONDITIONED RESTAURANTS

Chez Albert, Paris 14

Allard, Paris 6

Ambassade d'Auvergne,
  Paris 3

L'Ambroisie, Paris 4

Chez André, Paris 8

Chez Les Anges, Paris 7

Apicius, Paris 17

L'Aquitaine, Paris 15

Benoit, Paris 4

Le Boeuf sur le Toit, Paris 8

Bofinger, Paris 4

Bristol, Paris 8

Carré des Feuillants, Paris 1

Charlot, Le Roi des
  Coquillages, Paris 9

Chiberta, Paris 8

Au Cochon d'Or, Paris 19

Au Cochon d'Or des Halles,
  Paris 1

La Coquille, Paris 17

La Coupole, Paris 14

Le Divellec, Paris 7

Dodin Bouffant, Paris 5

Jacqueline Fénix,
  Neuilly-sur-Seine

Brasserie Flo, Paris 10

Chez Georges, Paris 2

Le Grand Véfour, Paris 1

Restaurant Jamin, Paris 16

Julien, Paris 10

La Maison Blanche, Paris 15

La Maison du Valais, Paris 8

Le Restaurant d'Olympe,
  Paris 15

Chez Pauline, Paris 1

Au Pied de Cochon, Paris 1

Pile ou Face, Paris 2

Le Potager du Roy, Versailles

Ritz-Espadon, Paris 1

Michel Rostang, Paris 17

Guy Savoy, Paris 17

A Sousceyrac, Paris 11

La Table de Jeannette, Paris 1

Taillevent, Paris 8

Timgad, Paris 17

Vaudeville, Paris 2

Jules Verne, Paris 7

RESTAURANTS WITH PRIVATE DINING ROOMS OR AREAS

The following restaurants provide private dining rooms or areas for groups. The maximum number of diners each can serve is noted in parentheses. In all cases, you must reserve in advance. In most cases, special menus can be arranged.

L'Ambroisie (14), Paris 4

Androuët (26), Paris 8

Chez Les Anges (75), Paris 7

Apicius (25), Paris 17

Artois (12), Paris 8

Benoit (18), Paris 4

Bofinger (25), Paris 4

Bristol (100), Paris 8

La Cagouille (12), Paris 14

Carré des Feuillants (12), Paris 1

Caviar Kaspia (20), Paris 8

Chardenoux (20), Paris 11

Au Cochon d'Or (40), Paris 19

Au Cochon d'Or des Halles (18), Paris 1

Le Coq de la Maison Blanche (120), Saint-Ouen

La Fermette du Sud-Ouest (20), Paris 1

La Fontaine de Mars (25), Paris 7

Chez Georges (35), Paris 17

Gérard et Nicole (16), Paris 14

Restaurant Jamin (18), Paris 16

Chez Jenny (120), Paris 3

Lescure (12), Paris 1

Louis XIV (10), Paris 1

Lucas-Carton (14), Paris 8

La Maison du Valais (30), Paris 8

Chez Maître Paul (25), Paris 6

Chez Pauline (16), Paris 1

Le Petit Marguery (14), Paris 13

Pharamond (18), Paris 1

Au Pied de Cochon (50), Paris 1

Pile ou Face (12), Paris 2

Polidor (35), Paris 6

Ritz-Espadon (150), Paris 1

Michel Rostang (10), Paris 17

Guy Savoy (20), Paris 17

La Sologne (24), Paris 7

La Table de Jeannette (60), Paris 1

Taillevent (36), Paris 8

Tan Dinh (35), Paris 7

Terminus Nord (10), Paris 10

Thoumieux (120), Paris 7

La Tour d'Argent (60), Paris 5

Le Train Bleu (30), Paris 12

Chez la Vieille (15), Paris 1

Index

Mouffetard, Rue, 172
Moule à Gâteau, Le (10 Rue Poncelet), 193
Moule à Gâteau, Le (111 Rue Mouffetard), 186
Moulin de la Vierge, Le (105 Rue Vercingétorix), 212
Moulin de la Vierge, Le (166 Boulevard de Suffren), 213
Mulot, Gérard, 206
Muscade, 137
Musée Français du Pain, 217
Nouvelle Mairie (Café de la Nouvelle Mairie), 158

O

Oenophile, L', 290
Olivier (A l'Olivier), 270
Onfroy, 202
Ordering, in restaurants, 6–7
Organic markets, 173
Oysters, 42–43

P

Pain et le Vin, Le, 164
Paix (Café de la Paix), 130
Palette, La, 128
Panetier, Au, 208
Panetons, Les (47 Rue Saint-Louis-en-l'Ile), 204
Panetons, Les (113 Rue Mouffetard), 205
Papeterie Moderne, 303
Paris en Cuisine, 296
Paris-Vierzon, 146
Passage Reine de Hongrie, 176
Passy (Marché de Passy), 175
Pastry shops, 181–98
Pâtisserie Alsacienne (C. Brocard), 192
Pâtisserie Alsacienne Boulangerie (André Lerch), 184
Pâtisserie Clichy, 257

Pâtisserie de Montmartre, 195
Pâtisserie Millet, 19
Pâtisserie Pottier, 183
Pâtisseries, 181–98
Pâtisserie Viennoise, La, 148, 195
Paul Corcellet, 267
Pauline, Chez, 18
Paying bills, 5
  with credit cards, 5–6
Peltier, 189
Peny, 146
Pepper, in restaurants, 8
Père Tranquille, Le, 163
Perraudin, 52
Perrier, 8
Peter Creations, 313
Petit Bacchus, Le, 159, 287
Petit Boulé, Le, 144–45
Petit Café Cluny, Au, 128
Petit Château d'Eau, Le, 122
Petit Châtelet, Le, 194
Petite Fabrique, La, 257
Petite Marquise, La, 217
Petit Fer à Cheval, Au, 123
Petit Marguery, Le, 94
Petit Quenault (Vieux Vins de France), 268
Petit Zinc, Le, 53
Petrissans, 165, 292
Petrossian, 273
Pharamond, 19
Philippe, Chez (Auberge Pyrénées-Cévennes), 40
Pied de Cochon, Au, 20
Pierre Traiteur, 22
Pile ou Face, 24
Place Monge Market, 205
Plats du jour, 7
Poilâne, Lionel (8 Rue du Cherche-Midi), 206–207, 219
Poilâne, Lionel (49 Boulevard de Grenelle), 213
Poilâne, Max, 213–14, 219
Polidor, 55
Poncelet, Rue, 166, 167, 169, 172–73
Pont Royal, Au, 189
Popincourt, 179

Porcelaine Blanche, La (25 Avenue de la Motte-Picquet), 310
Porcelaine Blanche, La (108 Rue Saint-Honoré), 304
Porcelaine Blanche, La (119 Rue Monge), 310
Porcelaine Blanche, La (135 Rue d'Alésia), 316
Potager du Roy, Le, 110
Poteau (Rue du Poteau), 174
Pottier, Pâtisserie, 183
Poujauran, 191, 210
Poultry, in restaurants, 8
Pré aux Clercs, Le, 129
Prepared foods to go, 242–54
  See also Charcuteries
Prices, 4–5
Priori Thé, A, 136
Private dining rooms, 6
Procope, Le, 115–16
Produits Hongrois, 248
Prosciences, 310
Puiforcat (22 Rue François 1er), 314
Puiforcat (131 Boulevard Haussmann), 314
Puyricard, 258

Q

Quatre Saisons (20 Boulevard de Grenelle), 317
Quatre Saisons (88 Avenue du Maine), 317
Queen of Hungary Passage, 176
Quentin, Boulangerie, 219
Quimper Faîence, 306
Quinet, Edgar, 180

R

Rallye, Le, 164
Raspail, 178
R. Clément, 204
Ready Reference (Food Lover's Ready Reference), 336

Recipe Index

A

Almond Cakes, 190
Alsatian Coffee Cake, 187
Ambassade d'Auvergne's
    Stuffed Cabbage, 30
André Lerch's Alsatian Cof-
    fee Cake, 187
Appetizers, See First courses
Apple(s)
    Cider, Mackerel in, 21
    Warm, Shortbread Cook-
        ies with Seasonal
        Fruit Jam and, 97
Apricot Tart, 140

B

Bacon
    and Cabbage Salad, Hot,
        29
    Endive, and Cheese
        Salad, Warm, 50
    Sauerkraut, Sausages
        and, 39
Basil Sauce, Salmon with,
    89
Beans, White, Mutton with,
    335
Beef Simmered with Vegeta-
    bles, 80–81
Beet and Cabbage Soup, 57
Bernard Ganachaud's Bos-
    tock, 220
Bistro fare
    Fricassee of Chicken
        with Morels, 111
    Mackerel in Cider, 21
    Mutton with White
        Beans, 335
    Rabbit with Mustard, 45
    Salad of Tuna and Curly
        Endive, 86
Borscht La Tchaïka, 57

Bostock Bernard Gana-
    chaud, 220
Breads
    Bostock, 220
    Brioche, 198
    Crusty Oval-Shaped
        Rolls, 222
    Natural Sourdough,
        208–9
    Sandwich Loaf, 216
Brioche Mousseline Denis
    Ruffel, 198
Bristol's Grilled Fish on Bed
    of Creamy Lentils,
    72–73

C

Cabbage
    and Bacon Salad, Hot,
        29
    and Beet Soup, 57
    Stuffed, 30
Cagouille's Salad of Tuna
    and Curly Endive, 86
Cakes
    Almond, 190
    Alsatian Coffee, 198
    Chocolate, 76–77
    Chocolate, 90
    Lemon Tea, 185
Cheese
    Comte, and Morels on
        Grilled Toast, 35
    Endive, and Bacon
        Salad, Warm, 50
    Fontainebleau, 239
    Goat, Marinated in Oil
        with Herbs, 233
    and Ham Sandwich,
        Grilled, 125
Chez Jenny's Sauerkraut,
    Sausages, and Bacon,
    39
Chez René's Mutton with
    White Beans, 334

Chicken Fricassee with
    Morels, 111
Chiffonnade de Saumon, 85
Chocolate
    Bitter-, Cream, Mint
        Soufflé with, 61
    Cake, 76–77
    Cake, 90
    Macaroons, 265
Choucroute Chez Jenny, 39
Chou Farci Ambassade
    d'Auvergne, 30
Cider, Mackerel in, 21
Cod, Salt, Fricassee of To-
    matoes, Potatoes, On-
    ions and, 49
Coffee Cake, Alsatian, 198
Comte Cheese and Morels
    on Grilled Toast, 35
Cookies
    Almond Cakes, 190
    Chocolate Macaroons,
        265
    Lemon Tea Cakes, 185
    Shortbread, with Warm
        Apples and Seasonal
        Fruit Jam, 97
Coquille's Fricassee of
    Chicken with Morels,
    La, 111
Coquille's Hazelnut Soufflé,
    La, 104–5
Cornichons, 280
Crème Fraîche, 237
Croque-Monsieur, 125
Croûtes aux Morilles Ma-
    dame Cartet, 35
Crust, Salt, Roasted Lamb
    with Herbs Cooked
    in, 100

D

Denis Ruffel's Brioche, 198
Denis Ruffel's Sandwich
    Loaf, 216

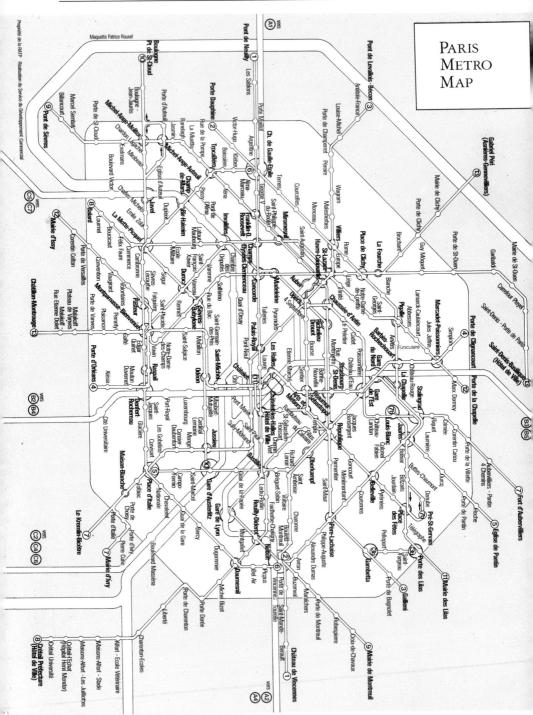

PARIS
METRO
MAP